HONOURING
A NATION

A HISTORY OF AUSTRALIA'S
HONOURS SYSTEM

HONOURING A NATION

A HISTORY OF AUSTRALIA'S HONOURS SYSTEM

KAREN FOX

Australian
National
University

ANU PRESS

For Jamie.
My beloved, my friend.

Australian
National
University

ANU PRESS

Published by ANU Press
The Australian National University
Canberra ACT 2600, Australia
Email: anupress@anu.edu.au

Available to download for free at press.anu.edu.au

ISBN (print): 9781760465001
ISBN (online): 9781760465018

WorldCat (print): 1289458137
WorldCat (online): 1289458189

DOI: 10.22459/HN.2022

Cover design and layout by ANU Press

This book is published under the aegis of the Social Sciences Editorial Committee of ANU Press.

Contents

Acknowledgements

This book has been a long time in the making. Its beginnings lie in my Master of Arts thesis, completed at the University of Canterbury under the supervision of Katie Pickles and John Cookson in 2005. Through that project my interest in the history of honours systems was fired, and I thank Katie for providing the spark.

I have been fortunate to complete this book at The Australian National University (ANU), where I have the privilege of working as a research editor on the *Australian Dictionary of Biography*. Heartfelt thanks go to my colleagues and friends at the National Centre of Biography (NCB) and the School of History. I have benefited tremendously from their knowledge and encouragement, and I greatly appreciate being part of such a warm and collegial scholarly community. I am especially grateful to Melanie Nolan, the director of the NCB, for her friendship and support, including through providing a period of internal release in 2017 that allowed me to focus on the writing of this book. Special thanks are due to the members of the School of History's book writing group, and the NCB's Feedback Merchants, who generously provided feedback on drafts of various chapters. I also extend warm thanks to the following, who variously read drafts, offered comments, shared their research and expertise, and gave encouragement: Gemma Betros, Sir David Cannadine, Peter Galloway, Peter Hamburger, Tobias Harper, Hilary Howes, Christopher McCreery, Keri Mills, John Nethercote, Heather Roberts, Marian Sawer, Stuart Ward, and Richard White.

I have also benefited from presenting my research at a number of conferences and workshops, and I thank the organisers and participants of those forums. I extend my appreciation also to the reviewers of the manuscript, whose thoughtful comments helped to improve it. I wish to gratefully acknowledge the help of staff at the National Archives of Australia and the National Library of Australia, and to thank the

Honours and Awards Secretariat of the Ontario Ministry of Citizenship and Immigration, who provided a copy of the proceedings of the first conference on Commonwealth honours and awards, held in Canada in 2006. Thanks are also due to the staff of ANU Press, especially Emily Tinker; to Frank Bongiorno, the chair of the Social Sciences Editorial Board, whose encouragement and support as this book was in preparation has been deeply valued; and to Beth Battrick for her expert copyediting. Financially, the production of this book was assisted by an ANU Press Publication Subsidy, for which I am most thankful.

It is not possible over such a lengthy project to tally all the many debts of gratitude I have incurred, and to anyone I have omitted to mention I offer apologies and sincere thanks.

Finally, as ever, thank you to my friends and family, whose love and laughter make my world go round. Most of all, I thank Jamie, my dear husband and the companion of my heart.

Karen Fox
December 2021

Author's note

Throughout this book I provide brief statistical data and commentary on awards conferred, to whom, and for what kinds of achievements and services. In compiling this analysis I have drawn on the Australian Government's invaluable searchable online database, available on the 'It's an Honour' website, particularly as it stood in 2011, when the majority of the statistical detail was produced.[1] It should be acknowledged that the figures given are not necessarily comprehensive and may not include all Australians who have been honoured over the period considered. For example, some Australian-born individuals may have received titles through British honours lists, and may therefore not appear in the data analysed. For the details of individual awards, I have relied on this database, as well as the announcements of awards in official gazettes and local newspapers. Quotations are given as they appear in the original sources. While this book employs Australian spelling throughout, I have retained the spelling of 'honors' rather than 'honours' when it appears thus in source material. As well, although the Australian Labor Party initially used the spelling 'Labour', I have adopted the modern spelling of 'Labor' throughout the book for consistency.

---

1   See Australian Government, Department of the Prime Minister and Cabinet, 'Australian Honours Search Facility', *It's an Honour*, Department of the Prime Minister and Cabinet, accessed 29 May 2021, honours.pmc.gov.au/honours/search.

List of honours

AC	Companion of the Order of Australia
AD	Dame of the Order of Australia
AK	Knight of the Order of Australia
AM	Member of the Order of Australia
AO	Officer of the Order of Australia
BEM	British Empire Medal
CB	Companion of the Order of the Bath
CBE	Commander of the Order of the British Empire
CMG	Companion of the Order of St Michael and St George
CVO	Commander of the Royal Victorian Order
DBE	Dame Commander of the Order of the British Empire
DCB	Dame Commander of the Order of the Bath
DCMG	Dame Commander of the Order of St Michael and St George
DCVO	Dame Commander of the Royal Victorian Order
GBE	Knight or Dame Grand Cross of the Order of the British Empire
GCB	Knight or Dame Grand Cross of the Order of the Bath
GCMG	Knight or Dame Grand Cross of the Order of St Michael and St George
GCVO	Knight or Dame Grand Cross of the Royal Victorian Order
ISO	Companion of the Imperial Service Order
KBE	Knight Commander of the Order of the British Empire
KCB	Knight Commander of the Order of the Bath

KCMG	Knight Commander of the Order of St Michael and St George
KCVO	Knight Commander of the Royal Victorian Order
KG	Knight of the Garter
KT	Knight of the Thistle
LG	Lady of the Garter
LT	Lady of the Thistle
LVO	Lieutenant of the Royal Victorian Order (until 1984 known as Member, fourth class)
MBE	Member of the Order of the British Empire
MVO	Member of the Royal Victorian Order
OAM	Medal of the Order of Australia
OBE	Officer of the Order of the British Empire
OM	Order of Merit

Introduction

Late one afternoon in March 2014, Prime Minister Tony Abbott made an announcement as unexpected as it was controversial: knighthoods and damehoods would return to the Order of Australia. Described by the prime minister as 'an important grace note in our national life', the titles had last been conferred in the 1980s.[1] Their reinstatement generated a storm of public debate, with many observers mocking the idea of titular distinctions in an egalitarian democracy and depicting the decision as a nostalgic attempt to revive an imperial past long since outgrown. Christine Milne, the leader of the Green Party, was quoted suggesting that Abbott was attempting to establish a 'bunyip aristocracy' in Australia, while the national director of the Australian Republican Movement, David Morris, reportedly said the move was 'turning the clock back to a colonial frame of mind that we have outgrown as a nation'.[2] Abbott's initiative took on new political significance in January 2015, when he selected Prince Philip for one of the titles. As Aaron Patrick observed, if the decision to revive knighthoods had been unpopular, the awards 'were only a minor blip on the political landscape', eccentric but harmless. The choice of Prince Philip as a recipient, on the other hand, brought national ridicule.[3] Journalists and political commentators portrayed it as a sign that Abbott was out of touch with public opinion, and many have since considered it a crucial element in his downfall.

---

1   Tony Abbott, 'Press Conference, Parliament House, Canberra', transcript, 25 March 2014, *PM Transcripts: Transcripts from the Prime Ministers of Australia*, Australian Government, Department of the Prime Minister and Cabinet, accessed 3 June 2019, pmtranscripts.pmc.gov.au/release/transcript-23367.
2   Jared Owens, 'Tony Abbott Living in the Past by Restoring Knights and Dames, Say Critics', *Australian*, 26 March 2014 [online]; Matthew Knott, 'Tony Abbott Reintroduces Knight and Dame Honours for Australians', *Sydney Morning Herald*, 25 March 2014 [online].
3   Aaron Patrick, *Credlin & Co.: How the Abbott Government Destroyed Itself* (Melbourne: Black Inc., 2016), 105–16, quote on 107.

As these events recede into the past, it may be tempting to consider the brief revival of Australian knighthoods, and the controversy over Prince Philip's award, as merely sound and fury, signifying very little—nothing more than an individual act by an out-of-touch prime minister that was quickly reversed by his successor. But these events were significant for more than just their impact upon the Abbott Government: they also reinvigorated an important and ongoing debate in Australia's national life. How should the honours system express the nation? Do Australians look back to a British heritage for models of honour and people to recognise and revere, or embrace that which has developed as distinctively Australian? What values and achievements does the community most want to celebrate, and whom does it most highly esteem? How can the honours system be made inclusive and meaningful for all Australians? Although the controversies erupting around the reintroduction of knighthoods and damehoods in 2014, and the award to Prince Philip the following year, sometimes seemed to have come from nowhere, they were in fact only the latest in a string of occasions when Australia's honours system became a focus of public debate. Canvassing ideas about the nation and its relationship with Britain, issues of inclusivity and diversity, and contested concepts of merit and recognition, these earlier debates were rarely remembered in the avalanche of commentary about Abbott's honours decisions, but they display a remarkable continuity over more than a century. In each case, the honours system became an arena for much bigger arguments, a receptacle for all kinds of symbolic meanings, and a proxy for debating crucial issues of place, identity, values, and citizenship. A history of this national institution, and of the battles it has generated, is long overdue. In this book I aim to tell this story.

Honours systems in Australia and the world

Most countries in the world have an honours system. Often complex, sometimes elaborate, these constellations of awards are almost as indispensable a part of statehood as flags, anthems, and coats of arms. In the English-speaking world in the twenty-first century, they are usually conceived as a way to recognise and celebrate the achievements and meritorious services of a country's citizens in a wide variety of fields.

The Department of the Prime Minister and Cabinet has described honours as 'help[ing to] define, encourage and reinforce national aspirations, ideals and standards by identifying role models', and explained their purpose as being 'to recognise, celebrate and say thank you to those who make a difference, those who achieve their best and those who serve others'.[4] Across the Tasman, New Zealand's honours system has been similarly portrayed as a means for the country 'to say thanks and well done to those who have served and those who have achieved'.[5] In effect, modern honours systems provide a means for the state to sanction and approve particular kinds of achievements and service, thereby helping to shape the way that ideas of merit, valuable service, and recognition are understood within a particular society.

Right across Britain's former empire, honours systems are generally derived at least in part from that of the United Kingdom, as are most of these countries' legal, constitutional, and parliamentary institutions and traditions. As the British empire expanded across the globe, so did the British honours system. It would eventually come to be used in many parts of the world, including the white settler dominions, such as Australia, New Zealand, and Canada; India, the 'jewel in the crown' of the empire; and the many British colonies and crown colonies, such as Jamaica, Barbados, the Bahamas, and Belize. A variety of awards, some now obsolete and others still in use, and the rituals and regulations associated with them, formed a complex system that changed over time, as different strands were discarded or created. While many of these countries—including Australia, New Zealand, and Canada—have now established their own national systems of awards, the British heritage of those systems can still be seen in their forms, and in the ways they have been conceived, created, and administered.

---

4   Australian Government, Department of the Prime Minister and Cabinet, *It's an Honour*, Department of the Prime Minister and Cabinet, accessed 17 August 2017, www.pmc.gov.au/government/its-honour.
5   Department of the Prime Minister and Cabinet/Te Tari o te Pirimia me te Komiti Matua, 'Overview of the New Zealand Royal Honours System', Department of the Prime Minister and Cabinet/Te Tari o te Pirimia me te Komiti Matua, accessed 17 August 2017, www.dpmc.govt.nz/our-programmes/new-zealand-royal-honours/new-zealand-royal-honours-system/overview-new-zealand-royal.

When the decision was made to establish a penal colony on the Australian continent, the British honours system was one of the most exclusive in Europe. Yet small and highly restricted though it was, it nevertheless consisted of several parts. At its apex was the peerage, the group of people holding titles directly inherited from one generation by the next: duke, marquess, earl, viscount, and baron, in descending order of rank. Positioned between the peerage above and the knightage below was the baronetage, created by King James I in 1611 to raise funds for the royal coffers. In exchange for this hereditary dignity, the 200 gentlemen to whom it was offered were required to pay an amount equalling three years of wages for 30 soldiers paid eight pence each per day. Peers were addressed as 'Lord'; baronets took the title 'Sir'. Next came the knightage. Knights were either created as simple knights—knights bachelor, for example—or within an order of knighthood. In common with baronets, they were granted the title of 'Sir', but unlike baronets, theirs was not a hereditary honour, but held for life only.[6] Finally, decorations such as medals, chains, or armorial augmentations, which did not confer titles, were bestowed by the sovereign as marks of favour or rewards for gallantry, bravery, or devotion to duty. Honours within the peerage, baronetage, and knightage granted the holder a defined place in the order of precedence, which dictated the seating at official and social events, as well as the sequence in which people arrived, left, and were greeted or announced on official occasions. All honours were also ranked in an order of wearing, and regulations prescribed how insignia and medals should be worn.

Until the 1970s, honours in Australia consisted almost entirely of the knightage, and the lower-level awards incorporated into orders of knighthood—the member, officer, and companion awards, which do not confer titles but do bestow postnominals (letters after the name). Hereditary honours were rarely granted in Australia, but proposals for their use, opposition to them, and the infrequent grants that did take place are significant to the discussion. I exclude decorations, which are both extensive and of a different character to the orders of knighthood,

---

6   In this category were also knights banneret and Knights of the Bath, although both honours had dropped out of use by the late eighteenth century and are therefore not discussed in this book. Knight banneret was a medieval title, briefly revived as a military honour in 1743 when George II created 16 such knights. Antti Matikkala, *The Orders of Knighthood and the Formation of the British Honours System, 1660–1760* (Woodbridge: Boydell, 2008), 1. Knight of the Bath was likewise a medieval honour, and had last been used in 1661, at the coronation of Charles II. Peter Galloway, *The Order of the Bath* (Chichester: Phillimore, 2006), 1.

generally being used to reward gallantry rather than as marks of favour or patronage. Many are military, or are given to members of other uniformed services (such as police, firefighters, and ambulance personnel), although several civilian bravery decorations also exist. A history of the use of decorations in Australia would address different themes to those that are the focus of this book. While awards in the orders of knighthood could sometimes reward gallantry, the orders were part of a medieval and early modern patronage system that slowly altered in character and use as patronage became less acceptable, transforming into general honours for marking and celebrating service to humanity or the nation, or great achievement. It is the use of these honours in Australia that is the focus of this history.[7]

Most prestigious of the orders of chivalry was the Most Noble Order of the Garter. Officially recognised as having been founded in 1348 by Edward III, it came to be considered one of the most valued orders in Europe, and in the world.[8] Membership was restricted to 25 (later 24) knights and the sovereign, although from the late eighteenth century descendants of the king, and later also foreigners, could be appointed as extra members.[9] Next in precedence was the Most Ancient and Most Noble Order of the Thistle, the highest honour in Scotland. Although held by legend to have been founded during the ninth century, and claimed in some sources to have been first established by James III, King of Scots (1460–1488), there is no reliable evidence that a Scottish order of knighthood existed before 1687, when James II of England (James VII of Scotland) instituted the Thistle 'to reward Scottish peers who supported

---

7   Two other honours are also little mentioned in these pages. Privy councillorships, though considered a mark of great honour in the Australasian colonies, are a somewhat unusual distinction. Granting the right to use the prefix 'Right Honourable' and the postnominals 'PC', membership of the Privy Council was an honour generally confined in the former dominions to senior politicians and judges; it continued to be conferred in Australia for much of the twentieth century. The Hanoverian Royal Guelphic Order is also excluded. This order was only briefly part of the British honours system, between its creation in 1815 and the separation of the United Kingdom from Hanover in 1837; it is therefore of little significance to the history of honours in Australia.

8   Ivan de la Bere, *The Queen's Orders of Chivalry* (London: Spring Books, 1964), 52–62; D'Arcy Jonathan Dacre Boulton, *The Knights of the Crown: The Monarchical Orders of Knighthood in Later Medieval Europe 1325–1520* (Woodbridge: Boydell, 1987), 113, 153–59; Hugh E. L. Collins, *The Order of the Garter 1348–1461: Chivalry and Politics in Late Medieval England* (Oxford: Oxford University Press, 2000), 12; Stephanie Trigg, *Shame and Honor: A Vulgar History of the Order of the Garter* (Philadelphia: University of Pennsylvania Press, 2012), 57–71. doi.org/10.9783/9780812206630; The Royal Household, 'Order of the Garter', *Official Website of the British Monarchy*, accessed 17 October 2014, www.royal.gov.uk/monarchUK/honours/Orderofthegarter/orderofthegarter.aspx (site discontinued).

9   Matikkala, *Orders of Knighthood*, 113.

the king's political and religious aims'.[10] On James's deposition in 1688 the order fell into abeyance, until it was revived by Queen Anne in 1703–1704. Initially consisting of the sovereign and 12 knights, its membership would in 1827 increase to 16. The Most Illustrious Order of St Patrick, which was to be Ireland's national order, followed the Thistle in precedence. It had been founded in 1783, as a distinction for 'those in high office in Ireland and Irish peers who supported the government of the day'.[11] Membership was limited to 15 knights as well as the sovereign; this would later be increased to 22. None of these three orders, focused on British peers and foreign royals as they were, would ever play a large role in Australian life, neither in the colonial era nor after Federation. Three Australians would be appointed to the Order of the Garter (Richard Casey in 1969; Paul Hasluck in 1979; and Ninian Stephen in 1994); only one to the Order of the Thistle (Robert Menzies in 1963); and none to the Order of St Patrick, which was to fall into abeyance on the creation of the Irish Free State in 1922, its last member dying in 1974.

More relevant in the Australian colonies would be the Most Honourable Order of the Bath. A military order, it had been constituted by George I in 1725, its name deliberately echoing an older tradition of creating Knights of the Bath, which can be traced at least to the fourteenth century.[12] The custom from which the name derived, a ritual whereby new knights bathed and kept vigil before being dubbed, symbolically cleansing themselves of any impurity, has been claimed to have existed as early as the twelfth century.[13] Such a ceremony was certainly being used in the fourteenth century, and those knighted this way were known as Knights of the Bath, and were considered to hold a superior type of knighthood.[14] As with the Thistle, the establishment of this order was part of an elite movement during the eighteenth century to revive—albeit with much

---

10 Matikkala, *Orders of Knighthood*, 77, 81; The Royal Household, 'Order of the Thistle', *Official Website of the British Monarchy*, accessed 15 October 2014, www.royal.gov.uk/MonarchUK/Honours/OrderoftheThistle.aspx (site discontinued); Katie Stevenson, 'The Unicorn, St Andrew and the Thistle: Was There an Order of Chivalry in Late Medieval Scotland?' *Scottish Historical Review* 83, issue 1 (2004): 3–22. doi.org/10.3366/shr.2004.83.1.3.
11 Peter Galloway, *The Most Illustrious Order: The Order of St Patrick and its Knights* (London: Unicorn, 1999), 1; The Royal Household, 'Order of St Patrick', *Official Website of the British Monarchy*, accessed 6 October 2014, www.royal.gov.uk/MonarchUK/Honours/OrderofStPatrick.aspx (site discontinued).
12 Galloway, *Order of the Bath*, 1; James C. Risk, *The History of the Order of the Bath and its Insignia* (London: Spink and Son, 1972), 5–6.
13 The Royal Household, 'Order of the Bath', *Official Website of the British Monarchy*, accessed 6 October 2014, www.royal.gov.uk/MonarchUK/Honours/OrderoftheBath.aspx (site discontinued).
14 Galloway, *Order of the Bath*, 1.

transformation—selected chivalric rituals.[15] The instigators of the order presented it as a revival of the medieval honour, including the bathing ritual in its statutes, although new knights were never actually required to undertake it. Instead, the name and rituals gave 'an aura of antiquity' to the new honour, its founders spinning older traditions into 'a protective web ... to conceal its newness'.[16] Its formation may be thus understood as an example of the 'invention of tradition', according to which constructed traditions 'attempt to establish continuity with a suitable historic past'; such an exercise is especially evident in relation to the emergence of nations and the creation of national identities.[17] At the time of the First Fleet, the Bath was a single-class order, consisting of the sovereign, a great master, and 36 knights companion, and it was increasingly becoming an honour for military men. Although it had begun life as an order given largely to parliamentarians and politicians, over the last three decades of the eighteenth century, it came to be 'firmly established principally as an honour for the armed forces'.[18] How these honours, and those that would be created in the following century and a half, operated in Australia, along with the eventual transition to an Australian system of honours in the latter half of the twentieth century, are the subject of this book.

A neglected history

Relatively little research has been undertaken on honours systems in Australia or in other English-speaking countries. The majority of studies have focused on the British system, particularly knighthood in medieval and early modern times, patronage and political corruption, the histories of individual orders, and the expansion and transformation of the

---

15   Jonathon Satherley-Peacocke, 'Victoria's Gentlemen of Honour: Symbols, Rituals, and Conventions of Colonial Honours' (Master's thesis, Victoria University of Wellington, 1997), 376; Matikkala, *Orders of Knighthood*, 48.
16   Galloway, *Order of the Bath*, 4; Matikkala, *Orders of Knighthood*, 360.
17   Eric Hobsbawm, 'Introduction: Inventing Traditions', in *The Invention of Tradition*, eds Eric Hobsbawm and Terence Ranger (Cambridge: Cambridge University Press, 1983), 1–14, quote on 1. doi.org/10.1017/cbo9781107295636.001.
18   Galloway, *Order of the Bath*, 56, 85.

system in the twentieth century.[19] A number of popular books published in the United Kingdom have taken a critical approach, highlighting scandals and inequalities.[20] Honours in the wider British empire and Commonwealth have attracted only limited scholarly attention, focusing

---

19   On medieval and early modern knighthood see, for example, Boulton, *Knights of the Crown*; Matikkala, *Orders of Knighthood*. On political corruption, see, for example, H. J. Hanham, 'The Sale of Honours in Late Victorian England', *Victorian Studies* 3, no. 3 (1960): 277–89; T. A. Jenkins, 'The Funding of the Liberal Unionist Party and the Honours System', *English Historical Review* 105, no. 417 (1990): 920–38. doi.org/10.1093/ehr/CV.CCCCXVII.920. Examples of work on specific orders include Collins, *Order of the Garter*; Peter Galloway, *The Order of the British Empire* ([London]: Central Chancery of the Orders of Knighthood, 1996); Galloway, *Most Illustrious Order*; Peter Galloway, *The Order of St Michael and St George* ([London]: Third Millennium for the Central Chancery of the Orders of Knighthood, 2000); Peter Galloway, *Companions of Honour* (Hinckley: Chancery Publications, 2002); Galloway, *Order of the Bath*; Peter Galloway, *The Order of the Thistle* (London: Spink, 2009); Peter Galloway, *Exalted, Eminent and Imperial: Honours of the British Raj* (London: Spink, 2014); Stanley Martin, *The Order of Merit: One Hundred Years of Matchless Honour* (London and New York: I. B. Tauris, 2007); Risk, *Order of the Bath*; Trigg, *Shame and Honor*. On the twentieth-century history of British honours, see Christian Bailey, 'Honor Among Peers: A Comparative History of Honor Practices in Postwar Britain and West Germany', *Journal of Modern History* 87, no. 4 (2015): 809–51. doi.org/10.1086/683600; Tobias Harper, 'Voluntary Service and State Honours in Twentieth-Century Britain', *Historical Journal* 58, no. 2 (2017): 641–61. doi.org/10.1017/S0018246X1400048X; Tobias Harper, 'The Order of the British Empire after the British Empire', *Canadian Journal of History* 52, no 3 (2017): 509–32. doi.org/10.3138/cjh.ach.52.3.05; Tobias Harper, 'Philanthropy and Honours in the British Empire', *New Global Studies* 12, no. 2 (2018): 257–76. doi.org/10.1515/ngs-2018-0028; Tobias Harper, 'Harold Wilson's "Lavender List" Scandal and the Shifting Moral Economy of Honour', *Twentieth Century British History* 31, no. 1 (2020): 79–100. doi.org/10.1093/tcbh/hwy048; Tobias Harper, *From Servants of the Empire to Everyday Heroes: The British Honours System in the Twentieth Century* (Oxford: Oxford University Press, 2020). doi.org/10.1093/oso/9780198841180.001.0001; Ian Inglis, 'The Politics of Stardust or the Politics of Cool: Popular Music and the British Honours System', *International Review of the Aesthetics and Sociology of Music* 41, no. 1 (2010): 51–71. Samuel Clark's *Distributing Status: The Evolution of State Honours in Western Europe* deploys a wider lens, seeking to explain the development of official honours not only in Britain, but more broadly in Western Europe over several centuries, as do Robert Aldrich and Cindy McCreery in their chapter considering honours as an element 'of colonial and postcolonial rule'. Samuel Clark, *Distributing Status: The Evolution of State Honours in Western Europe* (Montreal and Kingston: McGill-Queen's University Press, 2016); Robert Aldrich and Cindy McCreery, 'European Royals and Their Colonial Realms: Honors and Decorations', in *Realms of Royalty: New Directions in Researching Contemporary European Monarchies*, eds Christina Jordan and Imke Polland (Bielefeld: transcript Verlag, 2020), 63–88, quote at 64. doi.org/10.14361/9783839445839-005.
20   See, for example, Michael De-la-Noy, *The Honours System* (London: Allison and Busby, 1985); John Walker, *The Queen Has Been Pleased: The British Honours System at Work* (London: Martin Secker and Warburg, 1986).

on India, Canada, Australia, and New Zealand.[21] Not nearly enough attention has been paid to the particular history and functioning of the honours system in Australia. The most extensive treatment is to be found in the official report of the committee tasked with reviewing the Australian system in 1995.[22] Reference works rarely extend beyond basic description, while dictionaries and databases provide lists of recipients, but little to no analysis.[23] What little scholarly work there has been has tended to focus on the use of imperial honours in the Australasian colonies in the nineteenth century, and on William Charles Wentworth's attempt to introduce a hereditary aristocracy in New South Wales in 1853.[24] No comprehensive history of the Order of Australia has been written since

---

21   Examples include Aldrich and McCreery, 'European Royals', 63–88; Karen Fox, 'Grand Dames and Gentle Helpmeets: Women and the Royal Honours System in New Zealand, 1917–2000', *Women's History Review* 19, no. 3 (2010): 375–93. doi.org/10.1080/09612025.2010.489346; Karen Fox, '"Housewives' Leader Awarded MBE": Women, Leadership and Honours in Australia', in *Seizing the Initiative: Australian Women Leaders in Politics, Workplaces and Communities*, eds Rosemary Francis, Patricia Grimshaw, and Ann Standish (Melbourne: eScholarship Research Centre, University of Melbourne, 2012), 171–84; Karen Fox, '"A Pernicious System of Caste and Privilege": Egalitarianism and Official Honours in Australia, New Zealand and Canada', *History Australia* 10, no. 2 (2013): 202–26. doi.org/10.1080/14490854.2013.11668468; Karen Fox, 'An "Imperial Hangover"? Royal Honours in Australia, Canada and New Zealand 1917–2009', *Britain and the World* 7, no. 1 (2014): 6–27. doi.org/10.3366/brw.2014.0118; Karen Fox, 'Ornamentalism, Empire and Race: Indigenous Leaders and Honours in Australia and New Zealand', *Journal of Imperial and Commonwealth History* 42, no. 3 (2014): 486–502. doi.org/10.1080/03086534.2014.89548; Karen Fox and Samuel Furphy, 'The Politics of National Recognition: Honouring Australians in a Post-Imperial World', *Australian Journal of Politics and History* 63, no. 1 (2017): 93–111. doi.org/10.1111/ajph.12317; Galloway, *Exalted, Eminent and Imperial*; Christopher McCreery, *The Order of Canada: Its Origins, History, and Development* (Toronto: University of Toronto Press, 2005). doi.org/10.3138/9781442627963; John McLeod, 'The English Honours System in Princely India, 1925–1947', *Journal of the Royal Asiatic Society*, 3rd ser., 4, no. 2 (1994): 237–49. doi.org/10.1017/S1356186300005460; Satherley-Peacocke, 'Victoria's Gentlemen of Honour'.
22   Review of Australian Honours and Awards, *A Matter of Honour: The Report of the Review of Australian Honours and Awards* (Canberra: Australian Government Publishing Service, 1995).
23   Examples of reference works include: Anthony N. Pamm, *Honours and Rewards in the British Empire and Commonwealth*, 2 vols. (Aldershot: Scolar, 1995). Listings of recipients may be found in the following sources, among others: Australian Government, Department of the Prime Minister and Cabinet, 'Australian Honours Search Facility', *It's an Honour*, Department of the Prime Minister and Cabinet, accessed 13 June 2021, honours.pmc.gov.au/honours/search; Michael Maton, *Australian Recipients of Imperial Honours and Awards: 1901–1989* (Sydney: M. Maton, 2002); National Foundation for Australian Women, *Faith, Hope, Charity: Australian Women and Imperial Honours: 1901–1989*, 2003, accessed 27 November 2014, www.womenaustralia.info/exhib/honours/honours.html; Alistair Taylor, ed., *The Australian Roll of Honour: National Honours and Awards 1975–1996* (Sydney: Roll of Honour, 1997).
24   C. N. Connolly, 'The Origins of the Nominated Upper House in New South Wales', *Historical Studies* 20, no. 78 (1982): 53–72. doi.org/10.1080/10314618208595671; Bruce Knox, 'Democracy, Aristocracy and Empire: The Provision of Colonial Honours, 1818–1870', *Australian Historical Studies* 25, no. 99 (1992): 244–64. doi.org/10.1080/10314619208595909; Ged Martin, *Bunyip Aristocracy: The New South Wales Constitution Debate of 1853 and Hereditary Institutions in the British Colonies* (Sydney: Croom Helm, 1986).

its establishment in 1975, nor any full account of the operation of the British system in Australia. My own previous work has begun to outline the themes of such a history; this book brings that research together, along with new research into other aspects of Australia's experience of honours, to produce the first full-length history of honours in this country.

Two of the most important exceptions to this general pattern of scholarly indifference focus on the British system. In his *Ornamentalism: How the British Saw Their Empire* (2001), David Cannadine examined honours within a broader analysis of hierarchy and status in the British imperial system. His conceptualisation of honours as mechanisms by which the empire was structured and unified has been fundamental to my own understanding of the way honours operated in the Australasian colonies and in Australia in the first decades of the twentieth century. Understanding the empire as a 'vehicle for the extension of British social structures' and 'the setting for the projection of British social perceptions' around the world, Cannadine argued that the empire was as much concerned with 'the "construction of affinities"' as with 'the creation of "otherness"', and that it was 'in large part about the domestication of the exotic'.[25] Honours, in this conceptualisation of empire, were a tool in the process of domestication. Cannadine's account, however, focuses on particular parts of the British empire—particularly India, Asia, and Africa—and does not pay as much attention to the settler colonies, where indigenous peoples tended to be excluded from honours while white settlers received them. Moreover, he focuses on the nineteenth and early twentieth centuries, giving little space to the dramatic changes taking place in the imperial honours system in the twentieth century, as women were gradually incorporated into the various orders, the system itself was democratised by the inclusion of a much wider range of social classes and occupations, and the former colonies and dominions discarded British honours in favour of their own.

This democratisation and expansion of honours 'to include more and different people and groups' in the twentieth century is a theme of the second major scholarly work on the modern British honours system, Tobias Harper's *From Servants of the Empire to Everyday Heroes: The British Honours System in the Twentieth Century*.[26] In this book,

---

25 David Cannadine, *Ornamentalism: How the British Saw Their Empire* (Oxford: Oxford University Press, 2001), xix.
26 Harper, *Servants of the Empire*, 10.

Harper deploys the honours system as a means 'to examine how British attitudes towards service and hierarchy changed in the twentieth century', focusing particularly on 'imperial expansion and decolonization' and 'democratization and other forms of social and political change within Britain'. In a similar vein to Cannadine, he understands honours 'as an imperial as well as a domestic project for the creation of a loyal trans-imperial elite', considering how the abandonment of British honours across the former empire influenced the system, and the 'legacy' of this imperial past in the contemporary institution. Harper argues that the British honours system was a vehicle by which 'the expansion of the state and the validation of state work was … inextricably tied … to a defense of hierarchy, at home and abroad'.[27] Not only were new sections of society co-opted into hierarchy through the award of honours—provided they met particular 'cultural expectations'—but elites were 'reconciled' to democratisation; 'honours', he writes, 'democratized hierarchy'.[28] Harper also emphasises the role of the British honours system in encouraging and acknowledging charitable and philanthropic service, and thus in 'the "moral economy" of humanitarian action'.[29] He is as much interested—if not more—in the 'lower-rank honours', which he considers more significant 'in terms of the practical reach and meaning of the honours system' than the more exalted awards.[30]

In this book, I focus on the honours system in Australia, both initially the British system and then from 1975 the Order of Australia. This study is a history of an imperial institution transposed to the colonies, into a democratic and egalitarian world perceived to be less receptive to hierarchy and, by extension, to honours. The book investigates the history of the award of honours in Australia from the nineteenth century up to the present day, critically analysing how the Australian honours system has negotiated the tensions between the gendered, racialised, and classed dimensions of Australia's evolving national identity and its imperial and post-imperial inheritances. It seeks to ask and answer questions such as: what is encompassed by the honours system in Australia? How has it changed over time? What has been its place within concepts of the nation and imperial affinities? How and why have Australian practices,

---

27 Harper, *Servants of the Empire*, 3.
28 Harper, *Servants of the Empire*, 3–4, quotes on 4.
29 Harper, *Servants of the Empire*, 17. See also Harper, 'Voluntary Service', 641–61; Harper, 'Philanthropy and Honours', 257–76.
30 Harper, *Servants of the Empire*, 9.

outcomes, or opinions diverged from those in comparable countries, especially Canada, New Zealand, or the United Kingdom? Who has received honours and for what, and how have these patterns changed over time? In what ways have gender, race, class, and other dimensions of identity become implicated in the system over time? And how do concepts of merit relate to ideas of citizenship and egalitarianism?

Merit, citizenship, and the nation

In examining the social, cultural, and political history of honours over more than a century, I seek to do three things. First, to produce the first full-length history of the official honours system in Australia. Second, to understand how the honours system has negotiated the transition from an imperial to a post-imperial context, and the role it has played in the evolution of ideas of the nation. Third, to investigate the assumptions about gender, race, and class inherent in the system, and to analyse how it complements or conflicts with cherished cultural ideals of egalitarianism. The central proposition of this book is that concepts of merit and recognition are not fixed, but historically contingent, and they do not operate in a vacuum, but are embedded in wider social, cultural, and political contexts and debates. Understandings of merit, achievement, service, and recognition are contested, and they change over time. Inevitably, ideas about all these things are inflected by the cultural, social, and political assumptions of the day. Moreover, because honours systems are national institutions, their meanings are always produced in negotiation with shifting ideas of what, or who, constitutes the nation, what its values are, and where it is heading. Telling the story of Australia's experiences with honours, this book explores these ideas by focusing on three major themes: the country's altering relationship with Britain, and the related shifts in understandings of what it means for a person, or an institution, to be Australian; the changing face of Australian society and citizenship, and the extent to which those transformations have been reflected in the nation's honours system; and evolving ideas about what it means to be meritorious, and about what, or whom, is deserving of recognition.

The first of those themes—the shifts in Australia's relationship with Britain and the question of independence as a nation—is one that has been explored many times in relation to many different subjects, by historians, cultural commentators, political scientists, lawyers, and others. It is also one with particular relevance in the second decade of the twenty-first century, when the issue of identity, through the lens of citizenship, became a focus of controversy and debate in the nation's parliament, and an official inquiry was launched into 'nationhood, national identity and democracy'.[31] As for many former British colonies and dominions, the trajectory of Australia's honours system, and the meanings that system has been assigned in public debate, government policy, and private experience, have been complicated by the country's history as part of the British empire, and by the gradual nature of its transition to becoming an independent nation. Ideas of national identity and independence, and issues surrounding the country's relationship with Britain, have been central to contests over the honours system since well before Federation, and it has repeatedly become a vehicle for contests over those issues. Throughout this book, I explore how honours have been a key symbol for these debates, from the fierce arguments over whether or not titles of merit could be transplanted from an aristocratic and monarchical Old World into democratic and egalitarian (although still monarchical) colonies in the nineteenth century, through to the political split between the Labor and Liberal parties over whether imperial honours belonged in an independent Australia, and all the way to the 'barbeque stopper' that was the conferral of an Australian title upon a British royal on Australia's national day in 2015.[32]

Identity and citizenship are also central to the second theme of this book: inclusivity and diversity. The demographic make-up of Australia has changed dramatically over the century or more since Federation, and throughout that time the ability of the honours system to reflect who Australians are, in all their diversity, has been questioned. Early suggestions that women deserved honours equally with men did not end with the inclusion of women into the honours system on equal terms with men during World War I, but have survived in questions of whether women were receiving honours in sufficient numbers or at

31 An inquiry into this subject was referred by the Australian Senate to the Legal and Constitutional Affairs References Committee in July 2019. It delivered its report in February 2021. Legal and Constitutional Affairs References Committee, Australian Senate, *Nationhood, National Identity and Democracy* (Canberra: Senate Printing Unit, 2021).
32 The phrase was former Liberal treasurer Peter Costello's description of the news that one of the newly revived Australian knighthoods had been bestowed on Prince Philip on Australia Day in 2015. Peter Costello, 'Knighthood of Prince Philip the BBQ Stopper of the Century', *Daily Telegraph*, 2 February 2015 [online].

sufficient levels. Despite decades of feminist activity and many advances in Australian women's status, this remains a key criticism of the country's honours system. Other aspects of equity and diversity have also been raised in criticisms of honours, although less often. In each of its chapters this book addresses in some way the question of whether and how the Australian honours system has reflected the diversity of Australian life, be it through the inclusion of Indigenous Australians, the recognition of migrants in the wake of the dismantling of the White Australia policy, or the ongoing question of whether women's contributions to society are appropriately recognised.

The book's third theme tackles the honours system's relationship with community identity in a rather different way. Perennial as have been arguments about the inclusion of women in the honours system, or its adherence to British models of honour, equally persistent have been criticisms and comments regarding who is honoured, and for what, in other respects. Questions such as whether or not people should receive honours for doing well jobs that they are paid to do, or which already confer a level of status, and whether or not honours may be used as rewards for doing work that might not be as well paid as other options in a person's field, are equally persistent. As Harper has noted in relation to the British honours system as a whole, '[w]hether or not British subjects should be honoured for doing their jobs (and what jobs qualified) has ... always been central to debates about public honour', and criticisms of the system 'often centered on a sense that they were automatic civil service and military awards rather than a wider reflection of heroism and distinction in British society'.[33] Although he suggests that the latter was less an issue in the empire than in Britain itself, as will be seen, it was certainly also a key strand of critiques in Australia.[34]

This book considers the changing qualifications for honours, and the community's changing—but also surprisingly fixed—ideas about who and what are most deserving of recognition by the state. From concerns about a potential recipient's loyalty to the empire, financial stability, and respectability, through to anxiety that a particular occupation was being overlooked and thus devalued, to today's emphasis on the pre-eminent value and worthiness of voluntary and unseen contributions to the community, the potential of the honours system to grant the imprimatur of the state

---

33   Harper, *Servants of the Empire*, 2, 6–7.
34   Harper, *Servants of the Empire*, 7.

or the nation to particular kinds of service and achievement—to mark out particular things as especially worthy—has always been recognised. More than either national identity or community diversity, this theme goes to the very heart of what it is to live a good life, and what is success. As Harper has put it, '[t]he British honours system produced a persistent but inconsistent model of social worth: of who is exalted and who is good', which has been both 'embraced' and critiqued.[35] He points out, too, that those 'on the margins of or outside established elites', including feminists, Labour figures, and colonial nationalists, 'were all conscious of honours as a symbol of inclusion and exclusion'.[36] Each of these themes, in some way, considers the role of the honours system in defining the nation and its values, and asks whether the honours system has been a vehicle for cultural inclusion or exclusion. It is my firm belief that it both can and should be a vehicle for good, a way to elevate those things that are best about both a specific community and broader humanity, and that only by exploring these contests can we really think well about what the honours system should look like, and what role it should play in the national life.

Structure of the book

The controversies over the reinstatement of titles in the Order of Australia and the award of a knighthood within it to Prince Philip seemed to erupt on to the national political stage out of nowhere. In fact, as I have suggested, they were part of a long history of controversy over honours in this country. At certain moments the honours system became a focus for conflicting ideas about the nation: its values and identity, its place in the world, and how citizenship and inclusion are understood. In this book I trace these controversies in order to cast new light on these longstanding issues in Australian history. Chapter 1 begins with the arrival of the British honours system along with the First Fleet in 1788. It charts the growth and development of that system in the century leading up to Federation, and examines the debates that took place over the appropriateness of honours in the New World as awards began to proliferate. Beginning with the national celebrations that took place at Federation in 1901, Chapter 2 investigates how the creation of a new nation and the establishment of new federal government machinery influenced the honours system, in a

35   Harper, *Servants of the Empire*, 247.
36   Harper, *Servants of the Empire*, 81.

context where the States retained the right to make use of this potentially valuable patronage tool. Chapter 3 considers the transformation of the system wrought by World War I. Although the Order of the British Empire, created in 1917, was not the democratic award initially envisaged, it was a dramatic new departure within the British honours system, perhaps most significantly because it opened the institution to women.

No sooner had a new order been established for the empire, however, than its imperial reach was threatened. Chapter 4 turns to the scandals over honours selling that rocked Britain in the 1920s, and their reverberations around the empire, as both Canada and South Africa abolished imperial awards, and attempts were made to abandon them in Australia. This chapter also considers the hardening of the Australian Labor Party's objection to imperial honours and titles—a policy that would remain a point of difference between the major parties for decades—and asks why the interwar period was nevertheless a high point of women's participation in the system, which would not be reached again until the century's end.

With the outbreak of World War II in September 1939, the honours system returned to a war footing, and in a sense to its traditional roots as a military institution. Chapter 5 considers the use of British honours in Australia both during the war and in the years of reconstruction and prosperity that followed, focusing especially on the controversies caused by the major parties' disagreement on honours policy. At the same time, I explore the dark side of honours—the question of political patronage—and the meanings of honours both for recipients and for those who chose to decline awards. Chapter 6 explores the changing environment of the late 1960s and early 1970s, as rising new nationalism and a shifting world environment led to changes in Australia's relationship with Britain. It outlines the creation of the Order of Australia, and considers its reception in a context of political division over honours and an increasingly virulent argument over States' rights. Australia's own order was almost brand new when the dismissal of Whitlam and the election of Malcolm Fraser as prime minister put its existence in doubt. Chapter 7 discusses this history, surveying the bizarre situation that unfolded over the next two decades, as Australia ran two honours systems in parallel. In this chapter I also revisit issues of patronage and corruption through a focus on the controversies surrounding the government of Joh Bjelke-Petersen in Queensland.

By the early 1990s, disputes over honours might have seemed a thing of the past, as imperial honours were finally abandoned and the Order of Australia approached two decades of existence. As Chapter 8 shows, however, this was not the case. I consider three moments that reveal continuing debate about the purpose and meaning of an honours system in a modern democracy: the 1995 review of Australia's system, the increase in criticisms over the lack of representation of women, and Abbott's decisions to revive Australian titles and to confer an Australian knighthood on Prince Philip. Throughout, I focus on moments, issues, and episodes that reveal the deep tensions over questions of national identity and values, Australia's place in the world, and inclusion and citizenship that have long been part of Australian history, and which remain live issues in the twenty-first century. I end with an epilogue reflecting upon how many of these fundamental questions about honours and the nation, and about ideas of merit and recognition, remain unanswered.

Tracing the history of controversies in the honours system is not to suggest that it is in a hopeless situation, an endlessly contested and hence unsatisfactory institution. Rather it is to show the system's centrality to the national life, and its potential for embodying what is seen to be of value to the Australian community. If it were not important—if it did not represent an opportunity for Australians to express who they are, how they fit in the world, and what they hold dear—it would not be fought over, or attract such passionate argument. Moreover, there is considerable public support for an honours system, as a way to acknowledge and celebrate the great things that members of the community do, and the amazing and selfless ways they serve each other. It is a hope of this book that knowing the history of this important national institution—with all its ups and downs, possibilities and problems—can help to inform its future. Only by knowing our past can we engage in informed, intelligent, and hopeful conversations about what we value, and who we want to be.

1

Spirit of democracy, 1788–1900

When the First Fleet sailed into Botany Bay in January 1788, the British honours system was small in size and restricted in reach. Closely linked to military service, honours were rare, and determinedly aristocratic. The concept of merit was not entirely lacking in their bestowal, but it was understood quite differently to twenty-first-century definitions, and the idea that birth was an element was just beginning to fade. In continental Europe, ideas of merit had become more important within honours systems during the early 1700s, and this shift was likely also occurring in the British system, albeit slowly.[1] Unlike in the rest of Europe, where honours were increasingly a diplomatic instrument given to foreign dignitaries, and where orders could include thousands of members, the British orders remained strictly limited—the largest being the Bath, at 36 knights—and were rarely given to foreigners.[2] British honours were also almost entirely male, except in times of queens regnant, when a woman became the sovereign of the various orders.[3] While a small number of women held peerages in their own right, European innovations such as Russia's Order of St Catherine, an order for ladies created in 1713, had not been copied.[4]

---

1   Antti Matikkala, *The Orders of Knighthood and the Formation of the British Honours System, 1660–1760* (Woodbridge: Boydell, 2008), 185.
2   Matikkala, *Orders of Knighthood*, 253.
3   The limited role that a few noble women had once had, as associates (though not formal members) of the Order of the Garter, had disappeared during the reign of Henry VIII (1509–1547). Raymond B. Waddington, 'Elizabeth I and the Order of the Garter', *Sixteenth Century Journal* 24, no. 1 (1993): 97–113. doi.org/10.2307/2541800.
4   Matikkala, *Orders of Knighthood*, 243, 253.

Neither had imperial expansion led to significant innovation. Although ideas for an American peerage were occasionally floated, none had eventuated.[5] Honours were not in principle unavailable in the colonies, but the small size of the orders of knighthood made it unlikely that membership would be bestowed on their residents. There was also considerable resistance to the idea of creating hereditary titles in new and sometimes unruly societies, where the social order was not as firmly established as in the old country, and where it was by no means clear that a leading family would continue to hold its position down the generations. Knights bachelor and baronets were likewise rarely conferred. Honours came to the colonies most frequently only in the persons of British-born aristocratic governors or military men who had already been honoured, or who received honours for their administrative efforts or military service in the colonies. As were such men themselves, honours were mere sojourners in the outposts of empire.

Even if that had not been so, a penal colony was not an auspicious location to expect a lavish distribution of honours. New South Wales and Van Diemen's Land had been chosen as locations for the transportation of convicts after the loss of the North American colonies meant Britain could no longer exile prisoners there. While free settlers soon began to join the colonists, and emancipated convicts to build productive lives in their new home, the stain of being born in a penal settlement was not easily left behind. As honours were only likely to be granted to elite men of British descent, many other groups of people—including non-English-speaking immigrants, Indigenous Australians, women, and those of the lower classes—were unlikely to receive them. At least to begin with, then, the residents of these first Australasian colonies were unlikely to see honours conferred among their number. By the end of the nineteenth century and the coming of Federation, however, this situation had changed dramatically. Although women and those not of Anglo-Celtic descent remained almost entirely excluded from the system, the number of honours bestowed on Australians had increased sharply, sparking debates over the acceptability and role of imperial honours and titles in these New World colonies, where there had developed a powerful spirit of democracy and egalitarianism.

---

5   Ged Martin, *Bunyip Aristocracy: The New South Wales Constitution Debate of 1853 and Hereditary Institutions in the British Colonies* (Sydney: Croom Helm, 1986), 16–17.

Making colonial honours, 1815–1868

Over the course of the nineteenth century, the British honours system would be transformed and expanded, eventually coming to encompass the entire empire. This slow process of expansion began in 1815 with the Order of the Bath, which was enlarged to three grades, and granted a much increased total membership, in order to meet the demand for recognition of military services created by the Peninsular War.[6] Efforts to further reform it during the next 30 years, however, met with scant success, while several proposals to extend honours to the colonies were equally unsuccessful. In the 1820s Lord Bathurst thought to establish an order specifically for Canada, but the idea was not supported by King George IV. Creation of a colonial order was twice proposed in the 1830s, derailed on those occasions by the expense that would be incurred in producing regalia.[7] But the idea of colonial honours would not go away. With the empire expanding, there was an increasing hunger for honours in the colonial service, which could not be satisfied within the limits of the existing highly restricted orders. Many colonies were advancing in wealth and importance, and beginning to look for more responsibility for their own governance, and greater recognition of their significance to the mother country. Moreover, to some British politicians and statesmen, honours seemed a bulwark against runaway democracy in these unruly New World settlements, for they might bring aspects of the established order and hierarchy of home to the far reaches of empire. As the secretary of state for war and the colonies Lord Glenelg expressed it, distributing honours would 'draw more closely the bonds connecting the British colonies with the mother country, and … keep alive in settlements so remote from the seat of government, the spirit of the institutions of Great Britain'.[8]

The matter of further reforming the Bath, and with it the question of colonial honours, began to receive more serious attention in the 1840s. Action was spurred by the growing need to be able to reward civil service,

---

6   Peter Galloway, *The Order of the Bath* (Chichester: Phillimore, 2006), 83–85, 116–118.

7   Bruce Knox, 'Democracy, Aristocracy and Empire: The Provision of Colonial Honours, 1818–1870', *Australian Historical Studies* 25, no. 99 (1992): 248. doi.org/10.1080/10314619208595909.

8   Public Record Office (hereafter PRO): CO/447/1, draft letter, approved by Lord Glenelg, to A. J. Spearman, 30 November 1839, cited by Peter Galloway, *The Order of St Michael and St George* ([London]: Third Millennium for the Central Chancery of the Orders of Knighthood, 2000), 61. Note that Glenelg had left office in February 1839; this letter may be incorrectly dated.

not only in the United Kingdom but across the empire. Continuing imperial expansion, along with moves toward self-government in the more established settler colonies, had made it clear that some way of rewarding civilian service throughout the empire was necessary.[9] For their part, the Australasian colonies of New South Wales and Van Diemen's Land were growing in population, prosperity, and pride, and beginning to seek greater autonomy from the home authorities. Free settlers were arriving in increasing numbers, and beginning to outnumber those who had arrived as convicts; in New South Wales transportation had been suspended in 1840, while by the middle of the decade it had become the focus of sustained opposition in Van Diemen's Land.[10] Meanwhile, European settlement was also growing at Moreton Bay in the north, and on the Swan River in the west, and new colonies without a convict past were being established in South Australia and New Zealand. As the Canadian and Australasian colonies developed, the contributions of their governors and officials gained in visibility at home, but it was no easy task to find room for them in the small and overloaded honours system.[11]

Extending the Bath enough to allow it to fulfil the function of supplying colonial honours was not the answer. Such a large expansion, it was feared, might decrease the esteem in which the order was held.[12] Instead Lord Stanley, the secretary of state for war and the colonies from 1841 to 1845, proposed the creation of separate colonial honours. In early 1844 he raised the possibility of a new order of knighthood for the empire, which would not be as prestigious as the Bath, but would allow many more people to be honoured. In order to prevent an impression that colonial service was not equal to service at home, he advocated multiple new orders—for the West Indies, British North America, and Australasia—as well as the reservation of a number of places in the Bath for the colonies.[13] A circular despatch to the colonial governors sought their opinions on the idea. Mixed responses were received. Sir George Gipps, in New South Wales, supported the idea of an order of knighthood for the whole empire as a means to 'strengthen the bonds' between the colonies and the 'Mother Country', suggesting it should have three classes to which colonists could be appointed according

---

9   Galloway, *Order of the Bath*, 169.
10   Transportation to New South Wales was briefly and controversially revived later in the decade, with the last convicts reaching the colony in 1850.
11   Martin, *Bunyip Aristocracy*, 12.
12   Galloway, *Order of the Bath*, 170.
13   Martin, *Bunyip Aristocracy*, 33; Galloway, *Order of the Bath*, 170; Knox, 'Democracy, Aristocracy and Empire', 248–249.

to their standing.[14] But while the South Australian governor, Sir George Grey, also backed the idea, Sir John Eardley Wilmot in Van Diemen's Land thought there would be few men in his colony who could merit appointment to such an order.[15]

In any case, Stanley left office in late 1845, and the idea was not pursued. Modest reforms were made to the Order of the Bath, opening it to civil appointments in the second and third classes and tidying up anomalies and anachronisms in the statutes, but pressure on it continued to build.[16] The idea of colonial honours was ripe for revival. In 1851 the governor-general of all the Australian possessions, Sir Charles FitzRoy, proposed the creation of a colonial order to an unreceptive Colonial Office.[17] Not long after, with the Colonial Office having agreed that New South Wales should have responsible government, a scheme of hereditary honours was championed by William Charles Wentworth, a key figure in the campaign seeking responsible government.[18] Embodying an assumption that 'social hierarchy was essential to social stability', Wentworth's plan— which would eventually have seen the creation of an upper legislative house composed of local peers—promised to embed the existing social elite as a constitutionally enshrined aristocracy, both ensuring against loss of position stemming from decline in individual fortunes and encouraging among the populace 'habits of deference which would prevent the triumph of democracy'.[19] Even with moderate conservatives, however, the scheme was unpopular, and it was lampooned by radicals. Famously, Daniel Deniehy ridiculed the idea of an Australian nobility

---

14   Knox, 'Democracy, Aristocracy and Empire', 250; Martin, *Bunyip Aristocracy*, 34–35; Jonathon Satherley-Peacocke, 'Victoria's Gentlemen of Honour: Symbols, Rituals, and Conventions of Colonial Honours' (Master's thesis, Victoria University of Wellington, 1997), 105–6. See also Paul de Serville, *Pounds and Pedigrees: The Upper Class in Victoria 1850–1880* (Melbourne: Oxford University Press, 1991), 207.

15   Martin, *Bunyip Aristocracy*, 35.

16   Galloway, *Order of the Bath*, 176. Previously, while civilians could be appointed to the top level of the Bath (knight grand cross, GCB), they could not be appointed knight commander (KCB) or companion (CB). Galloway, *Order of the Bath*, 118.

17   Satherley-Peacocke, 'Victoria's Gentlemen of Honour', 84–85.

18   This was not the first time a colonial peerage had been considered. Creation of a local aristocracy that would supply such an upper house was debated for Quebec in 1791, and the idea was raised again in Canada in 1794–1795 and 1818–1819. In Australia, an upper house of hereditary title-holders had been suggested in South Australia in 1849, and Wentworth's scheme was very like a proposal for an hereditary upper house put forward by Supreme Court Justice John Dickinson in 1852. Martin, *Bunyip Aristocracy*, 21–30, 45–46, 76–80; Andrew Tink, *William Charles Wentworth: Australia's Greatest Native Son* (Sydney: Allen and Unwin, 2009), 235.

19   C. N. Connolly, 'The Origins of the Nominated Upper House in New South Wales', *Historical Studies* 20, no. 78 (1982): 53. doi.org/10.1080/10314618208595671.

as a 'bunyip aristocracy', a phrase that would echo down the years in critiques of honours.[20] (A bunyip is a water-dwelling creature from Indigenous Australian mythology; the word came to mean 'humbug' or 'pretender'.[21]) Before long, the hereditary element of the Constitution Bill was dropped, leaving an upper house that was nominated, rather than elected, but not aristocratic.[22]

While the creation of local colonial aristocracies appeared a faint possibility by the 1850s, the prospects for a systematic extension of some form of honours to the colonies soon began to seem brighter. With the advent of responsible government, Queen Victoria had warmed to the possibility, as a means to assert the unity of the colonies and the mother country. As well as appointing Canadians and Australians companions (CB) and knights commander (KCB) in the Order of the Bath, she supported the conferral of baronetcies on native-born colonists, albeit in small numbers.[23] Sir Edward Bulwer Lytton, who became colonial secretary in June 1858, also supported the bestowal of honours in the colonies, seeing in them a way of promoting a form of aristocracy in these overseas territories, which might both join the colonies more closely to Britain and preserve them from the dangers of democracy.[24] In a confidential circular in January 1859, Lytton sought names of colonists who might receive CBs or baronetcies. Before replies had been received from all colonies, however, his party had left office. Lytton's successors did not pursue the plan, leaving honours to continue to be conferred idiosyncratically, as each colonial secretary considered most appropriate.[25]

Thus by the middle of the century, despite numerous proposals, separate colonial honours remained merely an idea, and those resident or serving in the colonies rarely received appointment to either the orders of

---

20   John Hirst, *The Strange Birth of Colonial Democracy: New South Wales 1848–1884* (Sydney: Allen and Unwin, 1988), 37; Martin, *Bunyip Aristocracy*, 114; Tink, *Wentworth*, 237–38.

21   Ann Curthoys and Jessie Mitchell, *Taking Liberty: Indigenous Rights and Settler Self-Government in Colonial Australia, 1830–1890* (Cambridge: Cambridge University Press, 2018), 227–28, quotes on 228. doi.org/10.1017/9781316027035. As Curthoys and Mitchell have shown, John Dunmore Lang had also used the term 'bunyip' to ridicule the idea of a local nobility, in response to Dickenson's 1852 proposal. Curthoys and Mitchell, *Taking Liberty*, 228.

22   Connolly, 'Origins of the Nominated Upper House', 53; Hirst, *Strange Birth*, 35; Martin, *Bunyip Aristocracy*, 118–42.

23   Knox, 'Democracy, Aristocracy and Empire', 252–54. The prime minister, Lord Derby, preferred the idea of creating separate orders for the colonies, but Victoria considered that this might be divisive rather than unifying. Knox, 'Democracy, Aristocracy and Empire', 254.

24   Knox, 'Democracy, Aristocracy and Empire', 251–58.

25   Martin, *Bunyip Aristocracy*, 165; Knox, 'Democracy, Aristocracy and Empire', 258–60.

knighthood or the peerage. Hereditary honours, in particular, were never viewed favourably by officials in the Colonial Office, who tended to be sceptical that they could be supported in the colonies, where individuals might not maintain their wealth and status, or remain long in the colony in which the honour was bestowed. Appointments to the orders of knighthood, meanwhile, were bound to be rare because the numbers allowed by statute were tightly restricted, and because colonial service was seldom as highly regarded as that in the metropole. Moreover, the nature of colonial society itself seemed to imperial officials to be opposed to the extension of honours to the colonies in any systematic way. To those considering the possibility, there appeared considerable difficulties in introducing honours into the disordered world of the colonies, where assumptions about the natural order of society appeared not to apply, and where an egalitarian ideology frequently seemed to be in evidence. Such concerns continually influenced the decisions of imperial authorities to reject proposals for formal systems of colonial honours.[26]

The colonial order: St Michael and St George

Nevertheless, after decades of relative inertia, Britain's honours system was about to enter a period of rapid transformation. Over the next 60 years it would be vastly increased in size, and remodelled into a truly imperial institution. The first sign of this metamorphosis was the creation in 1861 of a new order, to be called the Order of the Star of India, to provide a vehicle for recognition in the 'jewel in the crown' of the empire. The turn of the rest of the empire came in 1868, when the Order of St Michael and St George was revamped to become a general colonial honour. Created in 1818 to be given to the residents of Malta and the Ionian islands after they came under British jurisdiction, its rationale had disappeared in 1864, when the Ionian protectorate was abandoned.[27] The Duke of Newcastle, colonial secretary as the cession of the islands approached, sought advice on the feasibility of extending the order to the rest of the empire, but the idea was rejected by his successor, Edward Cardwell. After the Duke of Buckingham and Chandos became colonial secretary in 1867, the question of the order's future was revisited, and the Queen and the prime minister,

---

26   Satherley-Peacocke, 'Victoria's Gentlemen of Honour', 93, 120–21.
27   Galloway, *Order of St Michael and St George*, 59.

Benjamin Disraeli, accepted Buckingham's proposal to use it to satisfy the need for recognition across the empire.[28] Reorganised, the order was restricted to 25 knights grand cross (GCMG), 60 knights commander (KCMG), and 100 commanders (CMG), the quotas chosen to avoid the charge that it was too freely given and therefore of little value.[29]

The order's new role, according to the circular despatch that announced the changes, was an acknowledgement of the empire's importance to Victoria, and to Britain. Observing the 'constant progress' of the empire, which had provided 'increased opportunities' for service to Queen and country, Victoria had decided that 'a special form of distinction' was required for the colonies, as it had been for India. She believed, so the despatch said, that the move would supply

> evidence of the importance which her Majesty attaches to her colonial dominions, as integral parts of the British Empire, of her constant interest in their progress, and of her desire that services of which they are the scene or the occasion, may not pass without adequate and appropriate recognition.[30]

Others, however, would consider the whole idea of a colonial order flawed. William Gisborne, a civil servant and Cabinet minister in New Zealand, was one. Not only did the colonies differ greatly from each other, he was to observe in 1886, 'presenting no common ground of earning distinction', but '[t]he effect ... of creating such an order is to make many think that colonists are not treated on equal terms ... with their fellow-subjects in the United Kingdom', thus tending against rather than towards 'the closer union of all portions of the empire'.[31]

Among the first to be appointed to the newly enlarged order was Colonel Thomas Gore Browne, who was retiring as governor of Tasmania, and who had previously held the same post in St Helena and New Zealand. He became a KCMG, while a former premier of New South Wales, Charles Cowper, was made a CMG, as was the Victorian government botanist, Baron Ferdinand von Mueller. Over the following years, appointments were generally men who had given long and loyal service around the empire, either as residents of the colonies or during tours of

---

28 Galloway, *Order of St Michael and St George*, 62–70.
29 Knox, 'Democracy, Aristocracy and Empire', 262.
30 'Order of Knighthood in the Colonies', *Sydney Morning Herald*, 24 February 1869, 5.
31 William Gisborne, *New Zealand Rulers and Statesmen: 1840 to 1885* (London: Sampson Low, Marston, Searle, & Rivington, 1886), 145.

duty.[32] Enlarged in 1877, the order also began to be given to members of the diplomatic service and others whose service was carried out abroad, as well as to eminent foreign nationals, with the Foreign Office receiving an allocation of awards in 1879.[33]

So far as the Australasian colonies were concerned, the honours system had now reached essentially the shape it would retain for the rest of the century, and into the next. Regular enlargements of the statutory limits of the various orders, along with the creation of new ones designed to meet specific needs, continued to expand its size and reach incrementally. Two more Indian orders—the Order of the Indian Empire and the Order of the Crown of India—were created in 1877, when Victoria took the title of empress. The Distinguished Service Order was instituted in 1886 as a companion to the Order of the Bath, to provide for junior ranks. A decade later, in 1896, the Royal Victorian Order was created to be an honour given by the Queen personally, rather than on ministerial advice. Intended to reward personal service to the sovereign, it had five levels, and there was no restriction on the number of awards that could be made. None of this growth, however, extended or transformed the colonial experience of honours as greatly as had the reorganisation of the Order of St Michael and St George.

Conferring honours in Australasia, 1870–1900

Developing a system of colonial honours greatly increased the number of colonists and colonial officials who received honours, as contemporaries recognised. 'Only a generation ago', ran an article in the Perth *Daily News* in 1890, 'no colonist would ever dream of receiving some titular distinction from his Queen'.[34] From the 1870s, however, this had begun to change, and before long it was a common refrain in the press that honours were being given too liberally, and were losing their value. But who were these multiplying recipients? Some patterns can be easily discerned. In a study of colonial honours during the nineteenth century, Jonathon Satherley-Peacocke identified the general trends: the GCMG 'became

---

32 Galloway, *Order of St Michael and St George*, 72, 77.
33 Galloway, *Order of St Michael and St George*, 78–97.
34 'By Favour', *Daily News* (Perth), 20 May 1890, 3; 'By Favour', *Inquirer and Commercial News* (Perth), 21 May 1890, 6.

the preserve of secretaries of state for the colonies, governors, and retired colonial politicians of considerable distinction and achievement'; the KCMG 'became associated with colonial ministerial office (particularly premierships) and scientific achievement'; and the CMG went to 'relatively minor colonial politicians, and a few leading civil servants'.[35] At times awards became almost automatic. By the end of the century, new colonial governors received KCMGs on appointment, while the chief justice of each colony could expect a knight bachelorship.[36] There is no doubt that many more colonists received honours after 1868, although to the eyes of a twenty-first-century viewer, accustomed to biannual lists containing several hundred names, the numbers remained relatively small. In June 1885, for instance, nine men with connections to the Australian colonies appeared in the Queen's Birthday list of appointments to, and promotions in, the Order of St Michael and St George; 10 years later, the six Australian colonies received a total of four KCMGs and one CMG.[37]

Naturally, as time went on, increasing numbers of recipients were Australasian-born. The colonial honours system also displayed much greater social mobility than existed in its counterpart at home in Britain. Individuals in the colonies could more easily rise to positions where honours were likely—such as that of premier or parliamentary speaker— despite a background likely to have debarred them from such high office in Britain.[38] Perhaps the most famous example is Sir Henry Parkes. His 'erratic colonial career', observed Penny Russell, has 'often serve[d] as an emblem for social mobility in nineteenth-century Australia'. Enjoying a 'rapid rise from unemployed to labourer to toyshop owner, newspaper editor and at last successful politician', he became premier of New South Wales five times, and received both a KCMG (1877) and a GCMG (1888), even though he also went bankrupt three times.[39] Such social permeability caused some concern among British, and occasionally also colonial, commentators, who perceived a lack of dignity and order in the unruly colonial parliaments full of men of varied, and sometimes rough,

---

35 Satherley-Peacocke, 'Victoria's Gentlemen of Honour', 131.
36 Galloway, *Order of St Michael and St George*, 124; Satherley-Peacocke, 'Victoria's Gentlemen of Honour', 164.
37 *Supplement to the London Gazette*, no. 25477, 6 June 1885, 2631–32; *Supplement to the London Gazette*, no. 26628, 25 May 1895, 3080.
38 See Hirst, *Strange Birth*, 176–78.
39 Penny Russell, 'The Brash Colonial: Class and Comportment in Nineteenth-Century Australia', *Transactions of the Royal Historical Society*, 6th ser., 12 (2002): 439. doi.org/10.1017/S008044010200018X.

backgrounds.[40] It must have seemed a topsy-turvy world indeed where such persons could receive royal honours and social precedence, perhaps even being placed above individuals of more genteel birth and upbringing on official occasions.

Nevertheless, there were limits to this social mobility, and one of them was gender. As Parkes's own wives experienced, it was much more difficult for women to rise in colonial society than for men. Men who had been knighted and received the title of 'Sir', stated Beverley Kingston, 'were treated with circumspection according to their place in the political system', but 'their ladies could be snubbed or ridiculed if their behaviour was unacceptable to the select inner circle of the governor's wife and her friends'.[41] Two of Parkes's three wives, Clarinda and Eleanor, faced just this kind of social exclusion.[42] According to Russell, 'the sort of economic or political power that could force social recognition' for men 'remained virtually unattainable' for women 'throughout the nineteenth century'.[43] Though women might gain a title along with their husbands, their opportunities for social mobility were powerfully limited by their gender and judgements about their respectability.

Selecting individuals for honours was not simply a matter of positions held, however, and over the last decades of the nineteenth century the process by which distinctions were conferred evolved as much as did the rest of the system. For many years, the practice had been somewhat haphazard. Rather than regular lists of awards at predetermined times, individuals negotiated honours through patronage relationships, and there was no 'uniformity, consistency, or clarity of procedure'.[44] Nor were there clear selection criteria. As Satherley-Peacocke noted, '[t]he individual views of successive secretaries of state on criteria of economic, political, and social standing [were] highly personalised and lack[ed] institutional permanence'.[45] Among the criteria he identified prior to the reinvention of the Order of St Michael and St George were 'a degree of dignified

40   See Hirst, *Strange Birth*, 174–78.

41   Beverley Kingston, 'The Lady and the Australian Girl: Some Thoughts on Nationalism and Class', in *Australian Women: New Feminist Perspectives*, eds Norma Grieve and Ailsa Burns (Melbourne: Oxford University Press, 1986), 31.

42   Russell, 'Brash Colonial', 440–42.

43   Russell, 'Brash Colonial', 443.

44   Satherley-Peacocke, 'Victoria's Gentlemen of Honour', 77.

45   Satherley-Peacocke, 'Victoria's Gentlemen of Honour', 103.

wealth' sufficient to maintain the distinction, some form of Crown service or other services that had advanced the colony, and 'the vague criterion of social pre-eminence', as well as suitable conduct and character.[46]

After 1868 more systematic policies and processes began gradually to take shape. Some indication of selection criteria for the new colonial order was provided by the statutes, which stipulated that those appointed would hold (or have held) 'High and Confidential Offices', or 'render Extraordinary and Important Services to Us as Sovereign … in relation to any of Our Colonial Possessions', or 'become eminently Distinguished therein by their Talents, Merits, Virtues, Loyalty, or Services'.[47] Discussing the selection and appointment process in this period, Satherley-Peacocke observed both 'formal and informal criteria'. The formal related to 'exhibited qualities of eminence, loyalty, achievement, and performance in their service to the Crown'; the informal encompassed attributes such as

> the high dignity of current office within the colony; some degree of individual political power or scientific knowledge; some degree of personal wealth to sustain the dignity of the honour; and the perception that the honour would prove 'gratifying' to the colony in general.[48]

There were also obstacles to distinction, including lack of sufficient wealth to maintain one's new dignity, having previously declined an offered honour, or a wife deemed unfit to bear the title of 'Lady' and to gain precedence at Government House.[49]

A key part of decisions was precedent. The Colonial Office was increasingly aware of, and careful about, the example that awards might set.[50] In part, this was out of necessity, for if honours were given without due regard to the precedent they might suggest, sticky situations could follow, especially in colonial settings believed to be marked by intense jealousies. Colonial hopefuls were quite willing to attempt to use precedent to their advantage. In 1893, for example, the president of the Victorian Legislative Council, William Zeal, declined the offer of a knight bachelorship and requested instead a KCMG, presumably aware that four other heads of colonial

46 Satherley-Peacocke, 'Victoria's Gentlemen of Honour', 100–101.
47 Satherley-Peacocke, 'Victoria's Gentlemen of Honour', 127–28.
48 Satherley-Peacocke, 'Victoria's Gentlemen of Honour', 190.
49 Galloway, *Order of St Michael and St George*, 117, 125–27; Satherley-Peacocke, 'Victoria's Gentlemen of Honour', 239.
50 Satherley-Peacocke, 'Victoria's Gentlemen of Honour', 151.

legislatures had received the higher award.[51] Jealousies were not only individual; entire colonies could be slighted if care was not taken. The Colonial Office was thus also careful to distribute the Order of St Michael and St George as evenly across the empire as possible, bearing in mind not only geography but also population and level of responsibility.[52] Even so, the Australasian colonies provide plenty of examples of injured dignity on behalf of particular locales. Sir Joseph Abbott, the speaker of the New South Wales Legislative Assembly, objected in 1894 to the bestowal of a KCMG upon Jenkin Coles, the South Australian speaker, for he himself was then only a knight bachelor:

> I thought this was most unfair to me and also to the colony which I represent. I have had far greater responsibilities in public life … and I have been now nearly four years Speaker and that over the Assembly of the Mother of the Australian colonies … I do think that New South Wales ought to be at the top of the list, when honours are distributed.[53]

Whether or not his protests were taken seriously in London, he must have thought them efficacious when, the very next year, he too received his KCMG.[54]

Attempts to deal with these issues were part of a growing rationalisation and codification of process in relation to honours. Constitutional conventions developed as to who was to recommend whom, and what were the respective roles of colonial and imperial ministers, governors, and the Colonial Office. For honours in the Order of St Michael and St George, recommendations were made to the Queen by the secretary of state for the colonies, generally after being received from colonial governors and scrutinised by the registrar of the order, an office held by a member of the Colonial Office. Other distinctions, such as that of knight bachelor, were recommended to the sovereign by the British prime minister, who liaised over colonial appointments with the colonial secretary. In neither case did local colonial ministries have any formal role, except in the case of the title of 'Honourable', which premiers could request that retired

---

51 Galloway, *Order of St Michael and St George*, 114.
52 Galloway, *Order of St Michael and St George*, 110; Satherley-Peacocke, 'Victoria's Gentlemen of Honour', 156.
53 PRO: CO/447/57, Sir Joseph Palmer Abbott to Sir Saul Samuel, 13 March 1894, cited in Galloway, *Order of St Michael and St George*, 114–15.
54 Bede Nairn, 'Abbott, Sir Joseph Palmer (1842–1901)', *Australian Dictionary of Biography*, accessed 4 September 2017, adb.anu.edu.au/biography/abbott-sir-joseph-palmer-2858/text4069.

executive members be permitted to hold for life. In practice, however, they were not wholly ignored, and by the end of the century it had become a tacit practice, if not a formal convention, that honours would not be given if a governor supported the nomination but his premier did not.[55] Announcements also became more regularised, with biannual lists at New Year and on the sovereign's official birthday (then in May) a standard feature of the calendar from 1888.[56] Nevertheless, 'a surprising degree of personalised and individualised informality survived', and would continue into the next century.[57]

Elite, white, and male?

If trends may be detected in who received honours in the nineteenth century, it is equally possible to discern patterns regarding those who did not. For the first half of the century honours were overwhelmingly the preserve of men of Anglo-Celtic descent, and while innovations in the second half of the century went some way to transforming this situation, there were some important limits. The creation of the Indian orders was the most significant of these innovations, but there was also an increasing willingness to appoint high-ranking members of indigenous elites in other parts of the empire. British historian David Cannadine has characterised honours as a means by which to 'unify and merge different elites'. Just as the Order of St Patrick had been 'an instrument for the assimilation of the Irish colonial elite into the imperial metropolis', he argued, the various orders distributed across the empire were used 'to structure and unify this greater British world'.[58] A 'common lust for titles' thus 'brought together the British proconsular elite and the indigenous colonial elites into a unified, ranked, honorific body', creating 'one integrated, ordered, titular, transracial hierarchy'.[59] Understanding honours in this way

55   Satherley-Peacocke, 'Victoria's Gentlemen of Honour', 139–57, 334; Galloway, *Order of St Michael and St George*, 126; Brian L. Blakeley, *The Colonial Office 1868–1892* (Durham: Duke University Press, 1972), 131–33.

56   Satherley-Peacocke, 'Victoria's Gentlemen of Honour', 317, 319; David Cannadine, *The Decline and Fall of the British Aristocracy* (New York: Vintage, 1999), 300.

57   Satherley-Peacocke, 'Victoria's Gentlemen of Honour', 369.

58   David Cannadine, *Ornamentalism: How the British Saw Their Empire* (Oxford: Oxford University Press, 2001), 86.

59   Cannadine, *Ornamentalism*, 88, 90. On this coming together of elites, see also Jesse S. Palsetia, '"Honourable Machinations": The Jamsetjee Jejeebhoy Baronetcy and the Indian Response to the Honours System in India', *South Asia Research* 23, no. 1 (2003): 55–75. doi.org/10.1177/0262728 0030231003.

advances a somewhat different view of empire to that which emerges in scholarship about empire focused on ideas of difference. As a 'vehicle for the extension of British social structures' and 'the setting for the projection of British social perceptions' around the world, the empire was in Cannadine's conception as much concerned with 'the "construction of affinities"' as with 'the creation of "otherness"'; 'it was in large part about the domestication of the exotic'.[60]

Cannadine's emphasis on similarities, rather than differences, and his characterisation of empire as being about 'the construction of affinities' is a useful corrective. Clearly, honours did perform this role within the empire, not only in the nineteenth century but well into the twentieth. The Indian orders were central in creating this new role for the honours system. In the settler colonies, however, honours performed this assimilationist role in a somewhat different way. It was not indigenous elites who were appointed to the orders of knighthood in the Australasian colonies or Canada, but white settlers.[61] This is not surprising, since by the time of the widespread extension of honours to the colonies, and especially in the six Australian colonies, indigenous peoples were outnumbered and marginalised, and for many colonists posed no more than a minor nuisance to the project of developing the colony. In such a situation, if the possibility was considered at all, it must have seemed that there was little use in spending any of the small numbers of honours available to assimilate or conciliate such marginalised peoples.

Here it is illuminating to compare the experiences of Aboriginal and Torres Strait Islander peoples in the Australian colonies and Māori in New Zealand. Although both experienced great suffering and loss under colonisation, Māori were not marginalised and oppressed to the extent Aboriginal groups were. As far as can be ascertained, no Māori person was appointed to any of the orders of knighthood during the nineteenth century, but Māori were not entirely excluded from honours, and the possibility of such appointments was at least raised. When a New Zealand Cross was created by the governor, Sir George Bowen, to recognise service during the New Zealand wars of the 1840s–1860s, Māori men were

---

60   Cannadine, *Ornamentalism*, xix.
61   See Cannadine, *Ornamentalism*, 27–28, 87.

among the recipients.[62] It was not impossible to imagine a Māori man being knighted, especially after four designated parliamentary seats were created for Māori in 1867. In 1892 one correspondent to a newspaper asked why a knighthood should not be bestowed on a leading Māori man, given that Indian princes had received baronetcies.[63] The closest Aboriginal Australians came to receiving honours in the nineteenth century, on the other hand, were so-called 'king plates', engraved metal plaques which hung around the neck, similar to the gorgets worn by infantry officers. These were given both to individuals identified as chiefs ('kings' or 'queens'), and for a range of other reasons, such as to reward a service or to acknowledge someone considered to be the 'last' of a people.[64]

If non-Anglo-Celtic men were incorporated into the honours system only in limited ways, women were even more thoroughly excluded. Two distinctions specifically for women were established in the second half of the nineteenth century—the Order of the Crown of India, which was generally given to the wives of governors and other officials, and the Royal Red Cross, a military nursing decoration—and occasionally a woman was appointed in her own right to one of the Indian orders.[65] A few women also held peerages in their own right. For the most part, however, women were ineligible for honours, and no way was open for them to receive titles, besides sharing in a husband's knighthood, baronetcy, or peerage by way of the courtesy title 'Lady'. Despite her own sex, Queen Victoria had refused to allow women to be eligible for the Royal Victorian Order, when it was begun in 1896.[66]

62   Ministry for Culture and Heritage, 'New Zealand Cross Created', updated 12 April 2017, *New Zealand History*, Ministry for Culture and Heritage, accessed 4 September 2017, nzhistory.govt.nz/the-new-zealand-cross-is-instituted-by-order-in-council; Birkenhead Returned Services Association, 'The New Zealand Cross (1869)', Birkenhead Returned Services Association, accessed 6 June 2019, www.birkenheadrsa.com/gallantry-bravery-awards/new-zealand-cross-1869/.

63   *Manawatu Herald* (Foxton), 21 June 1892, 2.

64   Jakelin Troy, *King Plates: A History of Aboriginal Gorgets* (Canberra: Aboriginal Studies Press, 1993). Robert Aldrich and Cindy McCreery also remark on the use of king plates in colonial Australia, noting it as an example of 'British ambivalence about the conferment of honors on "native" subjects'. Robert Aldrich and Cindy McCreery. 'European Royals and Their Colonial Realms: Honors and Decorations', in *Realms of Royalty: New Directions in Researching Contemporary European Monarchies*, eds Christina Jordan and Imke Polland (Bielefeld: transcript Verlag, 2020), 73. doi.org/10.14361/9783839445839-005.

65   Cannadine, *Ornamentalism*, 89–90; Ivan de la Bere, *The Queen's Orders of Chivalry* (London: Spring Books, 1964), 83.

66   Peter Galloway, *The Order of the British Empire* ([London]: Central Chancery of the Orders of Knighthood, 1996), 15.

Yet for all their exclusion from titles of honour, women were frequently assumed to long for them. Popular commentary portrayed women as hungrier for titular distinctions than men, so eager for social elevation that they would push their reluctant husbands to accept knighthoods even where the idea was repugnant to them. Discussing speculation that George Reid might be knighted in the birthday honours for 1895, for example, the *Clarence and Richmond Examiner* remarked that while Reid had said in the past that he would not accept, he was now married, and 'with hardly any exception, women have an insatiable craving for titles'.[67] Rhetorical exaggeration this may be, or an expedient fiction allowing men to affect reluctance while accepting supposedly for the pleasure of their wives. Yet it is not inconceivable that titles did indeed hold more allure for women than for their menfolk. In her exploration of gender and gentility in the colonies, Russell suggested that 'association with titles' through attendance at 'select parties' appealed more to women than to men, who 'had greater access to a diversity of social occasions, and enjoyed social intercourse at many levels', as well as being 'less conscious of the pressing need to establish respectability'.[68] The idea that a longing for titles was feminine underwrote some of the opposition to them found in the colonies. Real manliness, as it was depicted by such critics, was a simple and straightforward thing, which required adornment in the form of decorations or titles no more than it did the fussy fashions of the aristocratic male, himself portrayed as effeminate and weak.[69] A correspondent to the Sydney *Evening News* in 1881 implicitly drew this comparison between the frivolity of both women and aristocrats when he wrote of 'those hollow distinctions, which men of real grit are beginning to despise'.[70]

Whatever the truth of women's attitudes to their husbands' titles, the last years of the nineteenth century saw the first stirrings of agitation for women to be eligible for titles and other honours in their own right. The women's movement had begun to achieve successes, among

---

67   'Political & Social Notes', *Clarence and Richmond Examiner* (Grafton), 25 May 1895, 4.

68   Penny Russell, *A Wish of Distinction: Colonial Gentility and Femininity* (Melbourne: Melbourne University Press, 1994), 76.

69   Such a contrast between unadorned manliness and effete aristocracy would be drawn by Prime Minister Andrew Fisher in the early years of the twentieth century. Bethany Phillips-Peddlesden, '"A Stronger Man and a More Virile Character": Australian Prime Ministers, Embodied Manhood and Political Authority in the Early Twentieth Century', *Australian Historical Studies* 48, no. 4 (2017): 517. doi.org/10.1080/1031461X.2017.1323932.

70   Thomas Courtney, letter to the editor, *Evening News* (Sydney), 20 January 1881, 3.

them reforms to laws regarding divorce and married women's property rights, and the winning of the franchise in New Zealand (1893) and South Australia (1894); Western Australia would follow in 1899. In this climate of campaigning for greater rights and equality for women, it is not surprising that some began to include the honours system in their critiques. In New Zealand in 1894, less than a year after the vote had been won, Napier's liberal *Daily Telegraph* asked why there were not 'titles of honour for women'. '[H]onourable women' had never been lacking, the paper argued, 'but ... the stronger sex, with the selfishness characteristic of them, [had] monopolised all titular honours'. The writer went on to suggest the establishment of an order especially for women, noting the 'peculiar appropriateness' of such an honour being created by Queen Victoria, 'one of the most illustrious of female sovereigns'.[71] A few years later, in early 1899 the Australasian press reported on a paper given by Mrs Alec K. Morrison at the Grosvenor Crescent (Ladies) Club in London, discussing the question 'Should Women Have Titles?' Morrison argued that women 'had raised themselves to prominent positions in the scientific and medical world', but were 'without the honours conferred upon men'. Why should there not be dames, she asked, as well as knights?[72]

A 'passion for distinction'?

Honours were not always a source of desire or envy. A wide range of attitudes toward them was expressed in the Australasian colonies during the nineteenth century, especially as they came to be conferred in increasing numbers. One positive view, found in both the imperial centre and the colonies, was that they could help to bind the colonies to the mother country, by creating a mirror of metropolitan society in these far-flung outposts of empire. Governors of colonies, for example, seem often to have perceived titles of honour in this way, as instruments for rendering colonial society more like that of Britain, with a hierarchically ordered range of social classes, thereby encouraging the political and social development of the colonies, and, perhaps, counteracting any dangerous

---

71 'Odds and Ends', *Daily Telegraph* (Napier), 2 June 1894, 2; 'Bound to Come', *Waikato Times* (Hamilton), 14 July 1894, 5.
72 'Should Women Have Titles?' *West Australian* (Perth), 25 January 1899, 6.

tendencies towards too great an embrace of democracy.[73] Launceston's *Daily Telegraph* too saw titles as a form of imperial glue, with or without the social engineering function, suggesting that:

> to recognise the faithful services of old colonists is a sure way of cementing the bond of union which, it is hoped, will ever exist between the colonies and the mother country.[74]

It was, of course, such views of titles that had lain behind many arguments for the extension of honours to the colonies in the first place, and these stances took for granted that both the retention of the bonds of empire and the recreation of a British social order were ends to be desired.

But another side to these views of honours was that they were nothing more than tawdry bribes, distributed by cunning imperial authorities in an effort to prevent the colonies from forging their own way and to create in them an oppressive aristocratic order of the kind that existed in Britain. In 1882, for example, the bestowal of a KCMG upon the Queensland premier, Thomas McIlwraith, prompted 'Faugh-a-Ballagh' in the *Northern Miner* to denounce honours as an instrument in an imperial attempt to avert separationist ambitions and create feelings of loyalty in Australasia, and as a reward for abandoning democratic goals and pursuing policies that pleased the imperial government.[75] With such 'gewgaws' had the champions of democracy and the people been 'nobbled', the author contended, induced 'to forsake the popular cause' and 'become renegades from democracy and recruits to Conservatism, friends to the Imperial policy to transplant in Australia the class distinctions and social grades of the old world, fortified with a monied, landed, and titled aristocracy' and supported by a system of unfree coloured labour.[76] Making the situation worse, the titles being given to colonists were the least prestigious, part of a newly founded order restricted to the colonies and ranking below those

---

73   See, for example, Satherley-Peacocke, 'Victoria's Gentlemen of Honour', 90–91, 111–12; Cannadine, *Ornamentalism*, 28–32; Knox, 'Democracy, Aristocracy and Empire', 244–47.

74   *Daily Telegraph* (Launceston), 13 May 1884, 2.

75   'Faugh-a-Ballagh', 'Sir Thomas McIlwraith, K.C.M.G.', *Northern Miner* (Charters Towers), 5 December 1882, 2; 'Faugh-a-Ballagh', 'Sir Thomas McIlwraith, K.C.M.G.', *Northern Miner* (Charters Towers), 12 December 1882, 2.

76   'Faugh-a-Ballagh', 'Sir Thomas McIlwraith, K.C.M.G.', *Northern Miner* (Charters Towers), 12 December 1882, 2.

used in the imperial centre. As the *Maryborough Chronicle* disdainfully described them, colonial honours were 'cheap-jack knighthoods invented purposely as a bait for colonials'.[77]

A milder version of this argument worried that honours might be used as a means of controlling colonial politicians, especially as they were conferred not on the advice of colonial ministers, but of imperial advisers. As the Melbourne *Age* put it in 1888:

> There is some risk of a colonial Minister, aspiring to a knighthood, being lukewarm in a local cause when he knows that cause to be frowned upon by his prospective patrons.[78]

Many suggested it was invidious, in colonies with responsible government, for the Colonial Office to recommend the grant of honours to the monarch, rather than the colony's own responsible ministers. In New Zealand, Sir George Grey had protested to the colonial secretary about this while premier, after two knighthoods were conferred upon his political opponents without consulting the colonial government. In a colony with representative government, he had argued, surely it was not constitutional to confer awards for services given in that colony 'in regard to its internal management or its internal political affairs ... without the advice of Ministers, who are responsible to the people of that colony'.[79] Commenting on this incident in a lengthy article about colonial honours in 1881, New Zealand politician (Sir) Robert Stout asserted that it was 'time ... that this phase of Imperial dominion was at an end'.[80]

Another set of attitudes expressed by many commentators was that titles were inappropriate in young and vibrant democracies, nothing but worn-out remnants of an old-world class structure. Scholars have noted an egalitarian and democratic spirit in the New World, and posited that it encouraged opposition to titles of honour in the settler colonies. Peter Galloway, for example, suggested that colonial attitudes to the Order of St Michael and St George were shaped by 'the levelling spirit' of individuals who had emigrated to the colonies in the hope of making 'a new life away from such things as titles and honours', in a 'free and classless society'.[81]

---

77   *Maryborough Chronicle, Wide Bay and Burnett Advertiser*, 6 December 1887, 2.
78   *Age* (Melbourne), 26 March 1888, 4.
79   George Grey, letter to Sir Michael Hicks-Beach, quoted in Robert Stout, 'Titles for Colonists', *Melbourne Review* 6, no. 23 (1881): 228.
80   Stout, 'Titles for Colonists', 230–31; quotes on 231.
81   Galloway, *Order of St Michael and St George*, 113. See also Cannadine, *Ornamentalism*, 144–45.

In his analysis of egalitarianism in the Australian colonies, John Hirst identified several forms of egalitarianism—including those of outcome, opportunity, and manners—and suggested that, paradoxically, the broadening of democracy in the colonies had provoked, in some quarters at least, a hunger for honours, as political office no longer carried with it elite status.[82] It was perhaps in response to this eagerness that 'egalitarian forces' such as J. F. Archibald's *Bulletin* inveighed against imperial honours and those who 'scrambled after' them.[83] At least rhetorically, diatribes against titles on the grounds of egalitarianism and democracy were remarkably common in the newspapers of the nineteenth century, across the seven Australasian colonies.

Referring to the knighting of Henry Parkes and John Robertson in 1877, for instance, the *Clarence and Richmond Examiner and New England Advertiser* remarked that 'we regard the bestowal of a barren title upon the public men of a democratic community as reflecting little honour either on the recipients or the colony'. The paper recalled the 'derision' that had greeted Wentworth's scheme for hereditary titles, arguing that 'the democratic spirit of this country' had only continued to grow, and that while titles were acceptable in Britain they were 'utterly out of place here'. 'The essential spirit of a country like our own,' the writer proclaimed, 'demands the social equality of its citizens, and deprecates any adventitious aids to social distinction.'[84] A letter to the editor of Sydney's *Evening News* in 1881 referred to titles as 'pseudo suckers from the butt of a decaying old aristocratic tree' that were being 'grafted upon the sturdy young democratic plant springing up in Australia'.[85] And in 1895, having criticised a recent award—on the basis that there was no discernible reason for distinguishing the hapless recipient from any of 'the other political mediocrities in the country'—Melbourne's *Age* argued that '[t]itles which confer no powers and impose no duties are not in accordance with the democratic instincts of a colonial population'.[86]

Indeed, a number of men were believed to have declined titles on these grounds, although it is difficult in many cases to determine the precise motives for a refusal. One who was identified as having turned the

---

82   John Hirst, 'Egalitarianism', *Australian Cultural History*, no. 5 (1986): especially 22–23. See also Hirst, *Strange Birth*, 106–17.
83   Hirst, 'Egalitarianism', 24–26.
84   *Clarence and Richmond Examiner and New England Advertiser* (Grafton), 5 June 1877, 2.
85   Thomas Courtney, letter to the editor, *Evening News* (Sydney), 20 January 1881, 3.
86   *Age* (Melbourne), 2 January 1895, 4.

distinction down for ideological reasons was George Higinbotham, the Victorian radical politician and then chief justice, whom the *Otago Daily Times* stated had 'distinctly insisted that it is incompatible with the attitude of a democratic statesman to accept one'.[87] Higinbotham's objection was not necessarily to titles per se, however, but to titles bestowed through the Colonial Office, rather than by the local governor after nomination by the colonial parliament.[88] Victorian government minister and later federal prime minister Alfred Deakin also famously declined titles and honours, including a KCMG in 1887 and several times a privy councillorship. Like Higinbotham, whom he admired, he was opposed to the involvement of British politicians in Australian matters, and despite his desire to retain the British connection, refused to accept any distinction that might place him in a position of obligation to anyone at the Colonial Office.[89] Although such arguments usually spoke of titles, it appears the term was often understood as encompassing any appointment to an order of knighthood, including to its non-titular ranks; for many in the colonies, becoming a CMG and gaining the title of 'Sir' seem to have carried a similar connotation of ascension to the nobility.

Opposition to the conferral of titles in the colonies extended beyond rhetoric and personal publicised refusals. One inveterate opponent of titular honours was David Buchanan, a member of the New South Wales House of Assembly who tried several times to get the House to resolve against titles. First elected in 1860, Buchanan had early in his parliamentary career earned a reputation as 'a demagogue with dangerous republican leanings'.[90] One of his attempts to move against titles took place in April 1884, when he moved that the grant of titles was 'inconsistent with the spirit of our democratic institutions, and ought to be discontinued', and that a resolution to that effect should be sent to the Queen. He argued that 'a society based on the principles of pure democracy' was being formed in the colony, and that the conferral of titles was an insulting attempt by the English Government 'to introduce a spirit

---

87   *Otago Daily Times* (Dunedin), 28 May 1892, 2.
88   J. M. Bennett, *George Higinbotham: Third Chief Justice of Victoria 1886–1892* (Sydney: Federation, 2006), 202–3; Geraldine Moore, *George Higinbotham and Eureka: The Struggle for Democracy in Colonial Victoria* (Melbourne: Australian Scholarly, 2018), 277.
89   J. A. La Nauze, *Alfred Deakin: A Biography* (Melbourne: Melbourne University Press, 1965), vol. 1: 91, 202–3, vol. 2: 635.
90   Martha Rutledge, 'Buchanan, David (1823–1890)', *Australian Dictionary of Biography*, accessed 24 February 2015, adb.anu.edu.au/biography/buchanan-david-3099.

of aristocracy'.[91] Although basing his argument on support for democracy rather than freedom from English oversight, Buchanan also supported the separationist cause, which he saw as linked, stating that he thought the distribution of titles would continue 'until separation from the mother country takes place'.[92] The motion was easily defeated, however, with Buchanan 'alone on the side of the ayes'.[93]

While not all who held such opinions about titles and honours wished to see the colonies separate from the mother country, or were supporters of republicanism, the two viewpoints did at times coincide, since the ideal republic was imagined as egalitarian and democratic, a system of governance by the people that was not only independent and free, but also lacked hierarchies and distinctions, in contrast to monarchical systems that were imagined as pitting the interests of the aristocracy and the monarchy against the people. In 1886, for example, in a letter to the editor of the *Darling Downs Gazette* in Queensland, a writer using the pen name 'Young Australian' expressed surprise that Samuel Griffith, 'the democratic leader of this fair, sunny, and prosperous colony', would 'inthral [sic] himself to "monarchy" and aristocaracy [sic]' by accepting a title. 'Young Australian' wished to see knighthoods abolished, and argued that '[w]e want to be governed by the people, not by a worthless despotic aristocracy'.[94] Such views of titles, opposed to them on republican grounds or considering them as an issue linked to the republican cause, may be located within what Luke Trainor and Antony Taylor have called a 'flowering of republican advocacy in the newspapers [in] the late 1880s and early 1890s'. As they observed, in this period '[a]nti-monarchism was a part of the received opinions of … radical and working-class organs' in the press, the most famous being the *Bulletin*. It was also a useful spectre, even for those who were not generally of a republican bent: even in the more conservative parts of the press, 'the hint of separation, independence and republicanism was a standby of leader writers fulminating against the British Colonial Office or the general failure of the British government to meet Australian demands'.[95]

---

91   New South Wales, Legislative Assembly, *Parliamentary Debates*, 29 April 1884 (David Buchanan).

92   New South Wales, Legislative Assembly, *Parliamentary Debates*, 29 April 1884 (David Buchanan).

93   'Parliament of New South Wales', *Sydney Morning Herald*, 30 April 1884, 4; New South Wales, Legislative Assembly, *Parliamentary Debates*, 29 April 1884.

94   'Young Australian', letter to the editor, *Darling Downs Gazette* (Toowoomba), 2 August 1886, 3.

95   Antony Taylor and Luke Trainor, 'Monarchism and Anti-Monarchism: Anglo–Australian Comparisons c. 1870–1901', *Social History* 24, no. 2 (1999): 168. doi.org/10.1080/03071029908 568060.

For those who did advocate the superiority of the republican form of government, titles were often considered inimical to it. This view perhaps derived from a knowledge of the United States of America's firm opposition to titles of nobility, which was frequently referenced. In section 9 of article I, the constitution of the United States avowed that '[n]o Title of Nobility shall be granted by the United States', and nor should any official accept one 'from any King, Prince, or foreign State', without the approval of Congress. Section 10 extended the prohibition against granting such titles to State governments.[96] Numerous commentators in the Australasian colonies contrasted this stance, assumed to be part of a manly republicanism under which individuals were content to be adorned only with their own innate worth, with a degenerate British system of gaudy decorations, greedily sought by individuals too weak to stand on their own merits. In April 1881, in the regular column 'Our American Letter' in the *Otago Daily Times* and the *Otago Witness*, the author, Jacob Terry, contrasted republicanism, as 'the highest and noblest form of government, because it is really and truly self-government', with monarchy, which was 'government by cajolery, force, and fraud'. Among the characteristics of a republic, according to Terry, was that 'men seek for no higher distinction, know no higher honour, than that of citizen'. 'Titles and honours are the strong points of the monarchical system', he wrote:

> To suit the fastidious tastes of a Monarchist he must derive his patent of nobility from another mortal; the Republican holds his direct from God Almighty, and believes he cannot improve upon his Maker's work.[97]

Others, however, were sceptical of such depictions of the United States. Politician John Burns—who would himself later decline a CMG—took up this point in a rebuttal of Buchanan's 1884 motion in the New South Wales House of Assembly. There 'is no country in the world', he said, 'in which titles are more sought after than in the United States'.[98]

In any case, having made pronouncements against titles, however cautiously, a man could find himself in an awkward position if he later decided to accept one. After Robert Stout accepted a KCMG in 1886,

---

96 'The Constitution of the United States: A Transcription', *America's Founding Documents*, U. S. National Archives and Records Administration, accessed 3 August 2021, www.archives.gov/founding-docs/constitution-transcript.

97 Jacob Terry, 'Our American Letter', *Otago Daily Times* (Dunedin), 16 April 1881, 1 (supplement); [Jacob Terry], 'Our American Letter', *Otago Witness* (Dunedin), 23 April 1881, 8.

98 New South Wales, Legislative Assembly, *Parliamentary Debates*, 29 April 1884 (John Burns).

he was reminded of his former remarks suggesting that perhaps titles were out of place in the democratic, egalitarian arena of the colonies. Although the majority of newspaper commentary seems to have been congratulatory, the apparent contrast with his avowed opinions was noted.[99] Even several years later, the *Tuapeka Times* would report the comments of 'a contemporary' that he had:

> used to rail in the most offensive language against the tinselled glory of knighthood, and yet, when the honor … was proferred to him, he grabbed it as eagerly as a donkey does a bunch of carrots.[100]

On the other side of the Tasman, in 1892 the premier of New South Wales, George Dibbs, was censured not only for his acceptance, but even more for his explanation of the decision. An article in the British *Daily Chronicle*, reported in the colonies, was said to have declared that his decision had 'greatly displeased the people of New South Wales, who consider that his Republican views do not harmonise with his title'.[101] The *Pall Mall Gazette*, likewise covered in the colonies, reportedly remarked on 'the conversion and capture of Mr. Dibbs, an avowed Separatist and supposed Republican'.[102] Dibbs's reasoning was reported to have been that since the Queen would personally invest him with the honour, it would be ungrateful to refuse. This, thought the *Daily Chronicle*, was 'the worst possible kind of apology', and his 'acceptance … a worse humiliation to the Crown than if [he] had refused it with rudeness'.[103] Meanwhile, the *Goulburn Evening Penny Post* doubted Dibbs had ever been a republican, since '[n]o genuine republican would have been afforded an opportunity of either accepting or refusing', and the Hobart *Mercury* exclaimed, 'What

---

99 Satherley-Peacocke, 'Victoria's Gentlemen of Honour', 303–4.

100 'Local and General News', *Tuapeka Times* (Lawrence), 6 June 1891, 2. In the case of Stout, such criticisms were perhaps not entirely fair. The frequently cited diatribe against titles he had authored five years before accepting his own was more measured and nuanced than most critiques recognised. His main objection then had been to the awarding of titles without the advice of the responsible ministers in the colonial government, and he had only suggested that it might be time to reconsider their use in the colonies if a change to that practice could not be made. Stout, 'Titles for Colonists', 221–32. See also Jonathon Satherley-Peacocke's detailed discussion of Stout's shifting opinions regarding titles. Satherley-Peacocke, 'Victoria's Gentlemen of Honour', 297–305.

101 'Sir George Dibbs', *Advertiser* (Adelaide), 27 October 1892, 5; 'General Cable News', *Barrier Miner* (Broken Hill), 27 October 1892, 4; 'Sir George Dibbs's Knighthood', *Age* (Melbourne), 28 October 1892, 5.

102 'Mr. Dibbs in London', *North Queensland Register* (Townsville), 27 July 1892, 9; 'Mr. Dibbs in England', *Brisbane Courier*, 25 July 1892, 5.

103 'Sir George Dibbs's Knighthood', *Age* (Melbourne), 28 October 1892, 5.

a poor, shadowy, personification of republicanism must be that George Richard Dibbs, who has gone down on his knees because fanned by the slightest breeze of Royal favour.'[104]

Not all Australasian sentiment was against titles of honour, however, and another view was that titles and awards were simply merited rewards for worthy service or high achievement, useful as a means to inspire emulation, and in no way inimical to either democracy or republicanism. The Rockhampton *Morning Bulletin*, for example, thought it perfectly reasonable, and even desirable, '[t]o mark out a man who has distinguished himself above his fellows in the public service ... because it provokes emulation'.[105] The Melbourne *Argus* too defended titles, arguing that '[a] democratic country should be the first to encourage the idea that titles should be earned by merit, and not inherited through the accident of birth'. 'Some honour must be conferred upon the man who, in any department, deserves well of the state,' the paper continued, 'and the honour is most easily conveyed through a title, which will mark him as having achieved something.'[106] Responding to Buchanan's motion in the New South Wales House of Assembly in 1884, Henry Copeland thought 'most men desire to have conferred upon them a title of distinction, and while human nature remains as it is that feeling will last'. He saw no harm in 'conferring patents of nobility on men who have done good service to their country'.[107]

Moreover, many considered it human nature to hope for reward or seek renown. In 1874, observing that James Frances, the Victorian chief secretary, had declined knighthood, the *Sydney Morning Herald* remarked that while some 'democratic prints' pontificated on 'the impropriety of introducing titular distinctions among us', evidence seemed to suggest that 'we can never overcome the passion for distinction' that existed in all levels of society.[108] Besides being natural, this desire could be beneficial, if it led to individuals working for the benefit of society or devoting themselves to public service. As the *Argus* saw the case, 'if a man is inspired to achieve distinction in statesmanship, art, letters, science, or war by the hope of such a reward, the ambition is not altogether an ignoble one'; if nothing else, it was better than

---

104 *Goulburn Evening Penny Post*, 26 July 1892, 2; *Mercury* (Hobart), 26 July 1892, 2.
105 'Imperial Honours', *Morning Bulletin* (Rockhampton), 25 June 1887, 4.
106 *Argus* (Melbourne), 11 April 1887, 4.
107 New South Wales, Legislative Assembly, *Parliamentary Debates*, 29 April 1884 (Henry Copeland).
108 'Our Melbourne Letter', *Sydney Morning Herald*, 4 May 1874, 2.

being motivated by the pursuit of money.[109] Or, as the Christchurch *Press* put it rather less flatteringly: 'Public men, like donkeys, work best under the stimulus of expected reward.'[110]

Some corollaries, however, often accompanied these arguments in support of titles of honour. First, those who defended them often confined their support to those that were not hereditary. As South Australian premier Thomas Playford put it in 1890:

> I do not object to any man taking a title if he has worked hard and done good service for the country, and likes to take it; but to take a title to hand down to his children and his children's children, who may be idiots, or drunkards, or fools, or cowards, is something that these colonies ought not to countenance.[111]

Such views of titles allowed the reconciling of titular distinctions with a commitment to egalitarianism and democracy. Understood as being about equality of opportunity or manners rather than outcome, egalitarianism was no barrier to embracing titles of honour.[112] Second, some commentators were willing to accept titles given for non-political service—in the military, for instance, or the arts and sciences—while opposing those given for political service or to reward the friends of a particular government or party. Finally, titles and honours must be bestowed wisely. Such provisos were, perhaps, prompted by what seems to have been a widespread recognition that not all recipients of honours had fully merited them. The *West Australian* in 1885, for example, stated that while honours were given 'for good service ... at times', they were equally often bestowed 'as a matter of policy or as a result of intrigue and favouritism'. As a reward for personal achievement, the paper thought, knighthood 'ought to be ... a sort of guaranty [sic] that its recipient has done something which deserves recognition'.[113]

---

109 *Argus* (Melbourne), 31 May 1877, 4.
110 'Democrats and Titles', *Press* (Christchurch), 14 June 1895, 4.
111 South Australia, House of Assembly, *Parliamentary Debates*, 19 August 1890 (Thomas Playford). In fact, Playford was personally opposed to non-hereditary distinctions as well, asserting that he did not think anyone need wish for such titles, and that he himself would decline knighthood if it were ever offered—which he did, more than once. John Playford, 'Playford, Thomas (1837–1915)', *Australian Dictionary of Biography*, accessed 22 August 2016, adb.anu.edu.au/biography/playford-thomas-8064/text14071; South Australia, House of Assembly, *Parliamentary Debates*, 19 August 1890 (Thomas Playford).
112 On such understandings of egalitarianism in the Australian colonies, and their relation to ideas about titles and honours, see Hirst, 'Egalitarianism', 12–31; Karen Fox, '"A Pernicious System of Caste and Privilege": Egalitarianism and Official Honours in Australia, New Zealand and Canada', *History Australia* 10, no. 2 (2013): 202–26. doi.org/10.1080/14490854.2013.11668468.
113 *West Australian* (Perth), 1 June 1885, 3.

Conclusion

Penny Russell has argued that in nineteenth-century Australia 'English manners' were understood differently by different social groups, seeming 'a last bastion of civilisation in a wilderness of social disintegration' to those among 'the elite', and 'absurd remnants of a class-ridden "Old World"' to 'self-made Australians'.[114] Much the same might be said of titles of honour, and thus, like manners, this system of awards offers an intriguing lens onto wider matters of political and social life, and identity, in the colonies. In the case of manners, Russell goes on to contend that responsibility for maintaining this crucial aspect of colonial society was given to women, and thus 'relegated to the feminine sphere'.[115] Here too one might discern a parallel with colonial views of titles, not only in the snide suggestion that it was women who were most hungry for such distinctions, but also in the subtle equivalence sometimes drawn between aristocracy—in the form of titles—and effeminacy. Right from the earliest extension of honours to the colonies, a significant strand of thought in Australasia despised titles as unmanly, effeminate, associated with Old World class privilege and aristocracy, and tied to the institution of monarchy. At the same time, there existed support for titles as markers of individual merit, mechanisms for deepening the bonds of empire, and expressions of appreciation from an admired sovereign. None of these views were unique to the Australasian colonies, being found both in other colonies and, if perhaps weaker, at home in Britain. But they were to develop in unique ways in the coming nation of Australia, and the history of how honours were used, transformed, and understood in this country can reveal much about the nation's political life, its social and cultural formations, and its shifting identity. To explore this history is the task of the rest of this book. The next chapter begins that story, starting at the moment of Federation, and examining how this creating of 'a nation for a continent' shaped the history of the honours system in Australia for years to come.

---

114 Russell, 'Brash Colonial', 431.

115 Russell, 'Brash Colonial', 448–53, quote on 453. Beverley Kingston has argued something similar—'that it was by relegating some of the essential responsibility for differentiating status and maintaining social distances to women that male-dominated Australia was able to project itself as egalitarian'. Kingston, 'Lady and the Australian Girl', 40.

2
Nation and state, 1901–1914

Ceremonies and celebrations heralded the inauguration of the Commonwealth of Australia on 1 January 1901. In Sydney, the proclamation of the Constitution was read at Centennial Park, and the new governor-general, the Earl of Hopetoun, and the first federal ministry were sworn in, with Edmund Barton as prime minister. Across the country people enjoyed picnics, concerts, parades, banquets, fireworks, and other entertainments, and decorative arches were constructed to commemorate the event. A few months later, in May, the Duke and Duchess of Cornwall and York arrived for the opening of the first Commonwealth Parliament, and another round of parades, concerts, balls, dinners, and reviews began. A number of honours also greeted the birth of the new nation. Hopetoun had wanted to mark the occasion by conferring KCMGs (Knight Commander of the Order of St Michael and St George) on all six premiers, as well as knighting the mayors of the State capitals, but while such an inclusive gesture had drawn some support in the Colonial Office, 12 titles was deemed too generous a measure. With the South African War increasing the pressure on the honours system, and other colonies expecting a shower of honours to accompany the Duke and Duchess on their tour of the empire, it was judged impossible. Nevertheless, a sprinkling fell in January, and this was followed by a second, smaller list in May, which ensured the inclusion of all six States.[1]

---

1   Peter Galloway, *The Order of St Michael and St George* ([London]: Third Millennium for the Central Chancery of the Orders of Knighthood, 2000), 118–19; 'New Year Honours', *Sydney Morning Herald*, 2 January 1901, 8; 'The Honour List', *Sydney Morning Herald*, 11 May 1901, 10.

The Australia that came into being in January 1901 was not an independent nation, but one firmly located within the British empire, a dominion under the British crown. And while national sentiment and a sense of Australianness had been integral to the achievement of Federation, the new century also saw increasing empire loyalty among Australians, and a decrease in republicanism and anti-monarchism. Australians' attachment to the British empire had been evident in their enthusiastic desire to support the British in the South African War when it began in 1899, and while that enthusiasm had begun to wane by the moment of Federation, Australian troops would continue to serve in South Africa until the end of the war in May 1902. Most Australians embraced a national feeling that incorporated pride in being part of Britain's large and powerful empire. In this new era, the honours system took on new significance and meanings. If in many ways a minor matter, not explicitly dealt with by the drafters of the federated nation's constitution, it soon came to have an importance that could hardly have been anticipated during the whirl of celebrations in January 1901. In a context where six strong States were attempting to maintain their power, and freshly minted Australian statesmen were seeking to build the new nation, matters of status and prestige—and thus of honours—mattered in an entirely new way. Honours became a proxy for arguments over States' rights that had not been resolved prior to the moment of Federation. For much of the population, honours were probably little more than a twice-yearly ritual glanced at in the newspapers over breakfast, affording perhaps a moment of pride at the elevation of a local statesman, or maybe feelings of scepticism at an award viewed as undeserved. But for the nation's politicians they held far more significance. In these years, honours were both a site of struggle—between State and federal governments, and with the Colonial Office over the country's status and independence—and a symbol of national prestige and Australia's importance within the empire. Far more than a question of mere personal desire or revulsion, in this era of nation-building honours became the site of intense battles over status—at personal, State, and national levels.

'What on earth did they federate for?'

After the fanfare and festivities of Federation came the complicated business of managing relations between the new federal government and those of the six States, which retained substantial powers. On top of these challenges, there also remained the at times fractious relationship with the imperial authorities. For its part, the Colonial Office had hoped Federation would 'make life easier', since there would be 'one government to deal with rather than six'.[2] They were to be disappointed. The States had no intention of giving up their right to deal directly with the Colonial Office, and they would fight tenaciously against anything they perceived as an attempt to remove it. Federation had been achieved as a matter of sentiment, and by leaving aside difficult issues, such as tariffs and the franchise, for discussion and resolution by the first Commonwealth administration.[3] Part of the appeal of Federation, for supporters such as Sir Samuel Griffith, had been the idea that it would raise the status of Australians to be a nation, and thus to be able to 'meet the rest of the world as equals', rather than colonials.[4] But Federation was also to set off a new series of battles about status: over the relative positions of the federal and State governments, as the latter sought to preserve their status as sovereign States from encroachment by the Commonwealth. One battleground in this war was the honours system. The question of whose responsibility nominations would become seems to have escaped notice at the federal conventions of the 1890s.[5] Surprisingly quickly, however, the issue became a source of considerable friction, and it would remain a niggling irritation for most of the century.

No firm policy controlled recommendations for honours in the Australian colonies before Federation. As discussed in the previous chapter, granting honours was a Crown prerogative, although in practical terms it required the involvement of at least the governors resident in the colonies. Names were sent to the Colonial Office by governors, who were empowered to make recommendations without recourse to their ministerial advisers, although in practice they rarely did. Colonial ministries could nominate individuals, but had no specific constitutional right to do so, and the governors were not bound to accept their advice. The Colonial Office

---

2   John Hirst, *The Sentimental Nation: The Making of the Australian Commonwealth* (Melbourne: Oxford University Press, 2000), 223.

3   For this argument as to the supremacy of sentiment in achieving federation, see Hirst, *Sentimental Nation*.

4   See Hirst, *Sentimental Nation*, 26–44, quote on 28.

5   Keyword searching of online records of the 1890s conventions (using the terms 'titles of hono[u]r'; 'titles' and 'hono[u]r'; 'hono[u]rs'; and 'knighthood') produced no results indicating such discussion took place. A petition presented in 1898 did seek to include a ban on the conferral of titles in the constitution, but appears not to have been further discussed. *Official Record of the Debates of the Australasian Federal Convention (Third Session), Held at Parliament House, Melbourne, Victoria, Thursday, 20th January 1898*, accessed 17 April 2018, available via parlinfo.aph.gov.au/parlInfo/search/search.w3p.

then made its own decisions about which of the names to place before the monarch for approval. In selecting the honours bestowed in May 1901, the new federal ministry had reportedly been consulted; this, the *Argus* observed in December, had been 'the first time another body than the state Ministries was approached by the home authorities'.[6]

For nearly a year of the Commonwealth's existence the issue of responsibility for honours lay dormant. By December, however, it had flared into a controversy, at the heart of which lay the matter of States' rights. Newspapers across the new nation reported that the premiers had discovered 'a disposition on the part of the Federal Government to try and obtain the sole right to nominate distinguished citizens for honours'.[7] Federal ministers denied any such desire, and asserted that the same situation existed regarding honours as before. One was quoted stating that the federal government had 'done nothing to try and deprive the state Ministries of this privilege', and nor did it intend to.[8] The *Argus* was not so sure the premiers' fears were unfounded, observing there was 'excellent authority' to suggest that Sir John Anderson, an undersecretary at the Colonial Office, had suggested to federal authorities that the imperial government would prefer it if only the federal ministry were involved in recommendations.[9] Many reports stated that there would be few awards at the New Year, since Barton would be able to discuss honours with the secretary of state for the colonies, Joseph Chamberlain, while in London for the coronation of Edward VII in June.[10] Barton himself was reported to have said that he thought the States' worries 'entirely groundless', the federal government having 'no desire to exercise any domination in these matters', and that the issue would be solved by the Colonial Office.[11]

The States had not taken the possible loss of their privilege as calmly. More than one governor had expressed their ministers' displeasure in despatches to the Colonial Office, which had indeed suggested that it would be proper, now there was a federal government, for all honours recommendations to be sent to the governor-general, and thence to itself.[12] Frederick Darley, the lieutenant-governor of New South Wales,

---

6   'Titles for Australians', *Argus* (Melbourne), 31 December 1901, 5.
7   'Commonwealth Matters', *Brisbane Courier*, 31 December 1901, 4.
8   'Titles for Australians', *Argus* (Melbourne), 31 December 1901, 5.
9   'Titles for Australians', *Argus* (Melbourne), 31 December 1901, 5.
10   For example, 'Commonwealth Matters', *Brisbane Courier*, 31 December 1901, 4.
11   'Titles for Australians', *Argus* (Melbourne), 31 December 1901, 5.
12   Galloway, *Order of St Michael and St George*, 120.

told Chamberlain the issue was 'exciting much interest'. His government were 'wholly opposed' to the idea, although they allowed that copies of despatches making nominations should be sent to the governor-general. A future incumbent of that position, Darley observed, might lack the knowledge needed to judge who was deserving of honours across the States, leading him to seek advice from the federal prime minister, which would be 'exceedingly distasteful' to the States. Any move to make the governor-general the only channel for recommendations would 'be productive of much disappointment, heart-burning, and possible friction'. Darley advised that:

> the more the Commonwealth and the State are considered as completely separate entities, each with its own separate duties to discharge, the better it will be for the Commonwealth and the State, to say nothing of Imperial interests.[13]

(The response to this argument in the Colonial Office is evident in a marginal note: 'What on earth did they federate for?'[14]) As others would also do, Darley pointed out that Canadian practice—where recommendations did proceed only from the governor-general—formed 'no precedent', as the Canadian constitution was fundamentally different to that of Australia.[15] In Canada, so the argument went, the provinces had been stripped of their powers and made subservient to the federal government, whereas Australia's States remained sovereign, equal to the federal government, having conceded responsibility only for selected matters.[16] This assertion of the States' full equality with the federal government would become a regular refrain in States' rights disputes over honours.

The denials of federal ministers did not defuse the controversy, which was debated in the press around the country. In March 1902 Chamberlain responded to the complaints. He sent Hopetoun copies of the despatches he had addressed to the governors, explaining that he had decided

---

13   National Archives of Australia (hereafter NAA): A2922, NN, Honours 1901, despatch to Joseph Chamberlain from Frederick M. Darley, Lieutenant-Governor [of New South Wales], 23 December 1901.
14   Public Record Office (hereafter PRO): CO/447/67, Lieutenant-Governor of New South Wales to Colonial Secretary, 23 December 1901, cited in Galloway, *Order of St Michael and St George*, 120.
15   NAA: A2922, NN, Honours 1901, despatch to Joseph Chamberlain from Frederick M. Darley, Lieutenant-Governor [of New South Wales], 23 December 1901.
16   See, for example, *Argus* (Melbourne), 6 January 1902, 4; 'State Rights and the Imperial Power', *Advertiser* (Adelaide), 9 January 1902, 4.

nominations for State services would be made to him directly by the governors, who would send copies of them to the governor-general. Hopetoun's role would be more active than simply being kept informed, however. Chamberlain stated that he wished to know the governor-general's observations on the recommendations made, and he intended to 'defer taking action upon them' until he had heard those observations.[17] Writing to the governors of Queensland, Tasmania, and South Australia, from which States he had received communications on the issue, Chamberlain stressed that the proposal had not been intended 'to derogate from the functions of State Governors in making [recommendations]', but rather because he thought it 'very important' that they were 'considered from the point of view of the whole of the Commonwealth'.[18] Chamberlain also sent despatches outlining his decision to the governors of Victoria and Western Australia, who apparently had not written to him on the subject, and to the governor of New South Wales, from whence had come the most antagonistic response.[19] To none of them did he write of his request to the governor-general for his opinions of their nominations.

Still the question did not go away. In May 1902 in the federal parliament one of the Labor members for Tasmania, King O'Malley, asked whether Federation had altered the relationship between the States and the imperial government 'so that the State Premiers can no longer approach the Throne with requests for honours for deserving citizens'. If it had, he asked, would the prime minister take any recommendations State premiers made to him to the King? The reply of the minister representing the prime minister, Alfred Deakin, was more likely to confuse the matter than to clarify it. Titles were bestowed by royal prerogative, he explained, and there was 'no reference in any way to any such prerogative' in the constitution. Recommendations 'of any kind' that State premiers made would 'receive the attention of' the federal government.[20]

---

17   NAA: A11812, Bundle 1/1, despatch to the Earl of Hopetoun, Governor-General, from J. Chamberlain, 14 March 1902.
18   NAA: A11812, Bundle 1/1, despatch to Sir H. C. Chermside, Governor [of Queensland], Sir A. E. Havelock, Governor [of Tasmania], and Lord Tennyson, Governor [of South Australia], from J. Chamberlain, 14 March 1902.
19   NAA: A11812, Bundle 1/1, despatch to Sir George Clarke, Governor [of Victoria] and Sir Arthur Lawley, Governor [of Western Australia], from J. Chamberlain, 14 March 1902; NAA: A11812, Bundle 1/1, despatch to the Officer Administering the Government of New South Wales from J. Chamberlain, 14 March 1902; Galloway, *Order of St Michael and St George*, 120.
20   Commonwealth of Australia, House of Representatives, *Parliamentary Debates*, 27 May 1902 (King O'Malley and Alfred Deakin).

Governors-general offering advice

After this flurry of debate and despatches, the issue subsided for a while. Governors followed Chamberlain's direction, sending their recommendations to the secretary of state for the colonies and copying them to the governor-general. If they were under the impression that this was to be a mere formality keeping the governor-general informed, however, they were mistaken. Files in the National Archives of Australia show governors-general habitually commenting upon the governors' recommendations, weighing the names against each other, and against other previous or potential recipients, and sometimes advising the secretary of state against accepting them. This active role, it appears, was what the Colonial Office desired from the governor-general. In 1904 a Colonial Office memorandum noted the governor-general might be reminded that 'we look to [him] to extract from the recommendations of the state governors those which are most deserving of consideration'— with the caveat that he was to be influenced in his views by the governors, rather than by the federal prime minister.[21] It is not clear from existing Australian records the extent to which the first two governors-general, Hopetoun and Lord Tennyson, had been providing such guidance— given the reminder, perhaps not much—but at first all seems to have gone relatively smoothly. The calm was not to last, however. The spark that rekindled the dispute was the approach to honours adopted by the third governor-general, Henry Stafford Northcote, first Baron Northcote.

During his term, which began in January 1904, Lord Northcote commented carefully and in detail on the recommendations sent to London by the State governors, taking each in turn. In March 1906, for example, he stated that he could not 'endorse' the recommendation by Sir Harry Rawson, governor of New South Wales, for a KCMG for Joseph Carruthers, the State's premier, for he was 'not popular even in his own State', his 'abilities' were 'very moderate', and he was 'largely responsible for much of the friction that exists between the Commonwealth and New South Wales'. As well, Northcote thought, bestowing the relatively high honour of the KCMG upon him might encourage the other premiers to believe they too could claim a similar reward. Victoria's premier, Thomas Bent, fared no better, with Northcote writing firmly that he could not support a KCMG for him either. Nor did he wholeheartedly

---

21   PRO: CO/447/75, memorandum by Sir Montagu Ommanney, 2 June 1904, cited in Galloway, *Order of St Michael and St George*, 147.

support the recommendation of Professor Thomas Anderson Stuart for a knighthood, for while he thought his public services 'sufficient to justify' the nomination, Anderson Stuart had in 1904 declined a CMG (Companion of the Order of St Michael and St George), and had not kept this quiet. On the other hand, he 'quite concur[red]' with Rawson's recommendation that Supreme Court judge William Owen be knighted, and wrote that he could 'thoroughly endorse all that the Governor says in his favour'. Northcote clearly expected that his opinions would carry considerable weight. He finished his despatch with an aggregated list of 'final recommendations', being those from the State governors and the federal prime minister that he supported as well as his own, and a second list in which the names appeared in 'the order in which I should wish to see the Honours conferred'.[22]

In much of their correspondence on honours, Northcote and his fellow governors-general—as well as the colonial secretaries who received the recommendations and advice—had a dampening effect on the States' hopes. In part this was inevitable, for numerical limits on the various honours meant that only a small number of the recommendations made could be put into effect, and some winnowing was always necessary. A range of considerations proved useful in the task of weighing nominees' claims and suggesting which recommendations should succeed. Both the governors-general and the colonial secretaries were each concerned, to varying degrees, to ensure that the threshold for particular honours, especially the senior ones, should be kept high, and that those who received honours were suitable people to hold them.

Northcote was always on the watch for dubious moral characters or persons of limited abilities. In 1906 he observed that he could not recommend New South Wales parliamentarian Bernhard Wise, suggested for a KCMG by Deakin, because although he was 'a gentleman of undoubted ability', he was 'not a man who inspires public confidence here'. Wise's 'management of his private affairs [was] notorious', he wrote, 'and his private character leaves much to be desired from a moral point of view'.[23] Likewise, in his determined opposition to Carruthers and Bent receiving

---

22   NAA: A2922, NN, Honours 1906, despatch to [the Secretary of State for the Colonies] from the Governor-General of the Commonwealth of Australia, 31 March 1906 and addition dated 2 April 1906.
23   NAA: A2922, NN, Honours 1906, despatch to [the Secretary of State for the Colonies] from the Governor-General of the Commonwealth of Australia, addition to letter of 31 March 1906 dated 2 April 1906. Northcote gave no further details of Wise's mismanagement of his 'private affairs', but he may have been adverting to Wise's personal finances, for Wise was '[n]ever financially secure'. J. A. Ryan, 'Wise, Bernhard Ringrose (1858–1916)', *Australian Dictionary of Biography*, accessed 23 March 2021, adb.anu.edu.au/biography/wise-bernhard-ringrose-9161/text16175.

KCMGs—honours he successfully held off for several lists—Northcote was motivated at least partly by a belief that they were not proper persons to receive the distinction, although for different reasons. In August 1904 he made it clear he did not think Bent, who had not long been premier, deserved any honour, stating that 'his language on public occasions is often grossly offensive; and, though I am told he is endeavouring to atone for a discreditable past, he certainly, at present, merits no reward'.[24] The following year he reiterated that he could not support a recommendation for Bent, made again by the Victorian governor, Sir Reginald Talbot, and nor could he approve of one for Carruthers, who had not then been premier for a year and 'is not, in my judgement, fit for that post at all'.[25]

Again in 1907 he rejected both of them. Carruthers was 'ordinary', and potentially tarnished in public opinion by his party's involvement in land scandals in New South Wales, and Bent, while 'abler' than Carruthers, was an inappropriate person to be honoured.[26] Summed up in the witticism 'bent by name, bent by nature', Bent's reputation was that of an unscrupulous and manipulative intriguer, a fact of which Northcote must surely have been aware.[27] 'I fear,' he wrote, 'were [Bent] to receive the K.C.M.G, the better class of the Australian public would feel that the Order had been degraded.' Bent was 'popular with the mob; sings comic songs at public meetings; and is a smart electioneer', but he was 'no statesman', and Northcote could not 'understand how he has acquired so much influence over Sir Reginald Talbot'.[28] Talbot himself was by this stage becoming more than a little irritated at Bent's failure to appear on the honours list, judging by the tone of his 1907 recommendation. 'This is the fifth occasion upon which I have suggested Mr Bent's name for favourable consideration,' he stated, 'and in my mature opinion there is no one in the State whose services more deserve recognition.'[29] Northcote's

---

24 NAA: A2922, NN, Honours 1904, despatch to [the Secretary of State for the Colonies] from [Lord Northcote], 7 August 1904.

25 NAA: A2922, NN, Honours 1905, despatch to the Secretary of State, Colonial Office, from [Lord Northcote], 20 March 1905.

26 NAA: A2922, NN, Honours 1907, despatch to the Secretary of State for the Colonies from [Lord Northcote], 6 April 1907.

27 See Margaret Glass, *Tommy Bent: Bent by Name, Bent by Nature* (Melbourne: Melbourne University Press, 1993).

28 NAA: A2922, NN, Honours 1907, despatch to the Secretary of State for the Colonies from [Lord Northcote], 6 April 1907.

29 NAA: A2922, NN, Honours 1907, despatch to the Earl of Elgin, Secretary of State for the Colonies, from R. Talbot, Governor of Victoria, 18 March 1907. On Northcote's opposition to Bent's knighthood, see also Christopher Cunneen, *King's Men: Australia's Governors-General from Hopetoun to Isaacs* (Sydney: George Allen and Unwin, 1983), 60.

judgements in relation to honours are not merely the quaint echoes of past moral opinions. Rather, they provide an insight into what—in the view of an elite Englishman at the beginning of the twentieth century—made an honourable man. Ability was certainly required, but equally important was appropriate, decorous behaviour, and uprightness in one's dealings.

Another factor that could improve—or scuttle—a recommendation's chance was the nominee's previous behaviour regarding honours. In 1905 the secretary of state for the colonies, Alfred Lyttelton, observed that Charles Harper, a member of the Legislative Assembly in Western Australia, had excluded himself from consideration for other honours by declining the CMG.[30] A suitably grateful disposition, on the other hand, could aid a recommendation. Northcote's successor, Lord Dudley, gave strong support to one recommendation for the CMG because the intended recipient, Frank Wilson, the new premier of Western Australia, was willing to accept it rather than expecting the higher KCMG. He observed:

> I think it is well to encourage a Premier who is willing to accept a Companionship so as to minimise as much as possible the exceptions to the rule about admission to an order.[31]

The rule to which he referred, which had been laid down by Chamberlain in 1902, was that, in general, people should be appointed to the Order of St Michael and St George first as companions, being promoted later if they gave further service; it caused continual problems in the colonies, where many public men felt a CMG was too lowly for their positions, especially when their predecessors had not been held to the same rule.[32]

Northcote also advised against honours on the grounds they could appear political, or might rouse ire in the particular political situation of the moment. Commenting on a recommendation that the Queensland premier, Robert Philp, receive a KCMG, he remarked that he thought 'it would not be wise to select him, at present, for special recognition', as '[t]wo years ago his Government was swept out of Office in Queensland

---

30 NAA: A2922, NN, Honours 1905, despatch to Sir F. G. D. Bedford, Governor [of Western Australia] from Alfred Lyttelton, 15 September 1905.

31 NAA: A2922, NN, Honours 1911, despatch to the Secretary of State [for the Colonies] from [Lord Dudley], 27 March 1911.

32 NAA: A2922, NN, Honours 1902, despatch from J. Chamberlain, 17 February 1902; Galloway, *Order of St Michael and St George*, 120.

by an overwhelming majority'.[33] In 1907, in relation to the Queensland governor's nominations for the knighthood of Arthur Morgan, the president of the Legislative Council, and Joshua ('Joey') Bell, the secretary for railways and public lands, he advised that he thought Morgan might have the honour, but that one such award was enough 'and Mr Bell can wait', particularly 'as he is an active party politician; and an Election is imminent'.[34] Similarly, Dudley was alert to the potential for honours to allay annoyance or shore up loyalty. In March 1911, drafting his honours despatch to the colonial secretary, he supported recommendations for Major-General John Hoad and Rear Admiral William Cresswell to receive KCMGs, observing it would be 'sound policy' to confer distinctions on the heads of the Australian military and naval forces 'at the present juncture', for it would help to 'allay … the irritation which has been aroused in certain quarters by the introduction of Imperial Officers', and perhaps 'do good as an expression of the recognition by the Home Authorities of the potential value of the armed Forces of the Dominions'.[35]

In the context of a new and fractious Federation, and with the States ever anxious to defend their status, another consideration was the balance between the States. In 1904 Northcote included among his recommendations for the CMG—albeit last—John Henry of Tasmania, with the note 'I put him in as Tasmania gets little'.[36] Likewise, recommending a GCMG (Knight Grand Cross of the Order of St Michael and St George) for Sir John Madden, the chief justice and lieutenant-governor of Victoria, in March 1906, he observed that:

> as New South Wales has two G.C.M.G's; and Queensland, and Western Australia each one , the State of Victoria would be gratified by such a recognition of one of her most distinguished citizens.

In the same despatch, regarding a suggestion made to him 'privately' by Bedford that a KCMG be bestowed upon Sir George Shenton, the retiring president of the Western Australian Legislative Council, he commented,

---

33 NAA: A2922, NN, Honours 1906, despatch to [the Secretary of State for the Colonies] from the Governor-General of the Commonwealth of Australia, addition to letter of 31 March 1906 dated 2 April 1906.
34 NAA: A2922, NN, Honours 1907, despatch to the Secretary of State for the Colonies from [Lord Northcote], 6 April 1907.
35 NAA: A2922, NN, Honours 1911, despatch to the Secretary of State [for the Colonies] from [Lord Dudley], 27 March 1911.
36 NAA: A2922, NN, Honours 1904, despatch to Secretary of State for the Colonies from [Lord Northcote], 18 April 1904.

'I am always glad to see the distant States get a share of Honours', adding that there were 'few men in a State like Western Australia on whom they could be conferred'.[37] Some years later, Lord Denman, Dudley's successor, appears to have taken the question of balance between the States a little too far as a guiding principle. In his October 1911 honours despatch he observed he had found difficulty in weighing up the various State recommendations for knighthood, and had therefore used as a guide an effort to ensure each State received an honour of some kind, recommending that the one available knight bachelor go to South Australia because he was preferring candidates from the other States for the CMGs and KCMGs.[38] By 1913, however, he had apparently been instructed not to use the goal of a balanced distribution across the States as a way of choosing: 'I have borne in mind your instruction that I should take into consideration the merits of individuals without reference to the proportion of honours awarded to the States.'[39] In all of this correspondence, it seems evident the governors-general took their role in the award of honours seriously, attempting to balance questions of worthiness or desert with other, more practical, considerations, from the broader political context of a recommendation to the geographical distribution of distinctions, and always constrained by the small numbers allocated. It was, perhaps, an impossible task to do so without provoking annoyance from colonial politicians eager to assert both their own position and the significance of their constituency.

Defending States' rights

If the States initially accepted the governor-general's role in advising upon honours—possibly because it had not been made entirely clear to them in the first place—they did not accept it for long. Northcote's heavy hand perhaps alerted them to what they had missed under the lighter touches of his predecessors. In 1905 the issue of who should have the privilege of recommending, and what part the governor-general should play, erupted

---

37   NAA: A2922, NN, Honours 1906, despatch to [the Secretary of State for the Colonies] from the Governor-General of the Commonwealth of Australia, 31 March 1906. Nevertheless, Northcote did not think Shenton's case involved sufficient 'exceptional circumstances ... as to warrant' an exception to the general rule that admission to the order should be via the companionship. NAA: A2922, NN, Honours 1906, despatch to [the Secretary of State for the Colonies] from Governor-General of the Commonwealth of Australia, 31 March 1906.
38   NAA: A2922, NN, Honours 1912, despatch to [the Secretary of State for the Colonies] from [the Governor-General of the Commonwealth of Australia], 25 October 1911.
39   NAA: A2922, NN, Honours 1913, despatch to Lewis Harcourt, Secretary of State for the Colonies, from [Lord Denman], 2 April 1913.

into an angry dispute. Having learned that Talbot planned to write to the colonial secretary about State governors having a right to know whether or not the governor-general supported their recommendations, Northcote had asked him to wait until the two had had a chance to speak about the subject, and written to London himself in case Talbot did not. Northcote wrote that Talbot was the only governor to have claimed such a right, and argued that to grant it would put governors-general 'in a position of considerable difficulty'. The cause of the trouble appears to have been Thomas Bent. Northcote had received information about Bent from a 'confidential' source, and he expressed concern that if informants knew that their information might become known to another party—such as a State governor who supported the recommendation under discussion— they would be reluctant to tell him anything. While he felt '[i]t would hardly be courteous' simply to tell a governor that he had not endorsed a recommendation, he foresaw the possibility of 'an endless, & possibly acrimonious' correspondence if he did offer reasons. Another concern was confidentiality. As it stood, he argued, neither potential recipients nor governors knew whether the reason a person was not honoured was the governor-general, or the secretary of state, or simply that there were too many names on the list: 'This uncertainty, in my judgement, on the whole averts more friction than it creates.'[40]

Talbot did eventually write to the secretary of state, after receiving from him a despatch on Canadian honours practices, sent to provide information on certain other aspects of procedure. His contention was that the current arrangement 'virtually deprives the Governor of the privilege of recommendation', because the governor-general could 'practically cancel his recommendation', without giving reasons or even informing him, as had happened, he said, 'in a recent and ... very important case in which I claim to be the best Judge'. 'I am still ignorant of the grounds upon which the Governor-General disagreed with me,' he complained, 'and after my submission of the name for the second time His Excellency will not inform me whether he has again vetoed my recommendation'; he believed Northcote had done just that, as the honour had not been given. Adverting to the old argument that it was contrary to the principles of the Federation agreement for the States to lose the right to nominate for honours, he argued that it was not 'in the spirit of the Constitution' to

---

40 NAA: A2922, NN, Honours 1905, despatch to the Secretary of State, Colonial Office, from [Lord Northcote], 29 March 1905.

appear to leave the responsibility with the governor 'while the actual power to refuse a recommendation is with the Governor-General'. '[T]here can be no doubt,' he said, 'that it does detract from the independent position and power of the Governor.' The situation was made more objectionable because the governor-general did not have to discuss his views with the governors or let them know that he disagreed, meaning 'a Governor might continue for years to recommend an individual's name without the smallest chance of success', rather than making another nomination that might be successful.[41]

Again in 1907 the issue arose. Sir John Madden, the lieutenant-governor of Victoria, protested to the colonial secretary about the governor-general's role in the process, which he described as 'the subject of much objection & dissatisfaction'. If the governor-general chose to consult his ministers, Madden stated:

> the claims of the State Ministers or of people of distinction in the State will be subjected to the criticism of, & possibly ruled by, those who may very well be their adversaries in Public life; while the recommendations based on the opinions of their friends will be Disregarded.

Should the governor-general not consult his advisers, on the other hand, his views would 'be those of one who must ... be less qualified to judge of the claims of the person recommended than is the Governor of his own State', who was, in any case, supposed to be his 'co-equal' in the matter of honours. Madden requested—as he had been asked to do, presumably by his ministers—that the practice be changed, so that the governor could submit nominations to the King through the colonial secretary 'independently' of the governor-general.[42] Northcote appeared unconcerned, dismissing Madden's complaints in his own despatch to the colonial secretary. He had told Madden he did not consult his ministers about State recommendations, he said, adding that '[t]he other points in his Despatch, having been fully considered, and disposed of, by His Majesty's Government, it seems unnecessary to revive the controversy'.[43]

---

41   NAA: A2922, NN, Honours 1905, despatch to the Secretary of State for the Colonies from the Governor of Victoria, 27 June 1905.
42   NAA: A2922, NN, Honours 1907, copy of paras 6 and 7 of despatch of 22 June 1907 to [Lord Elgin] from [John Madden], sent to [Lord Northcote] from John Madden, Lieutenant-Governor [of Victoria], 4 July 1907.
43   NAA: A2922, NN, Honours 1907, despatch to the Secretary of State for the Colonies from Northcote, Governor-General, 3 August 1907.

The following year saw further dispute. In June the governor of Queensland, Lord Chelmsford, sent a letter from the State's acting premier, Andrew Barlow, to the colonial secretary, the Earl of Crewe. It contained two resolutions adopted at a recent premiers' conference.[44] The first was that the conference objected to nominations from State governors being sent via the governor-general, and the second that the objection should be forwarded to the secretary of state by the governors.[45] The federal ministers, on the other hand, had no problem with existing arrangements. Instead, they wished the governor-general's role to be strengthened, so that any recommendation he opposed would be suspended, and, if he still did so after discussing it with the relevant governor and the colonial secretary, rejected.[46] A couple of months later, Crewe responded. He had given 'careful consideration' to the resolution, there being 'some divergence of opinion' between the States and the Commonwealth, and need for 'an authoritative pronouncement'. While '[t]he independence of the States in domestic matters cannot be questioned', he stated:

> in such a matter as the grant of an honour by the Crown the views of the Governor General, the principal Representative of the Crown in Australia, cannot be left out of account.

Further, the governor-general's 'personal judgment, unbiassed by local considerations', was a valuable aid in weighing up the claims of the various persons nominated for the few honours available. That being so, he set out a practice that was substantially the same as the previous one. The governors would send recommendations directly to him, and copies to the governor-general; 'acting in his individual capacity', the governor-general would 'make such observations … as he thinks fit' to both the governors and the colonial secretary. Should there be a difference of opinion that could not be resolved, it was up to the secretary of state to make the final decision.[47] Writing to the governor-general, he added that he thought the federal ministers' suggestion went too far. He remarked that:

44 NAA: A11812, Bundle 1/1, despatch to the Secretary of State for the Colonies from Chelmsford, Governor [of Queensland], 3 June 1908.
45 NAA: A11812, Bundle 1/1, despatch to the Governor of Queensland from A. H. Barlow, Acting Chief Secretary, 30 May 1908.
46 NAA: A11812, Bundle 1/1, despatch to Lord Northcote, Governor-General, from Crewe, 18 August 1908.
47 NAA: A11812, Bundle 1/1, despatch to [the governors of Victoria, New South Wales, South Australia, Queensland, Tasmania and Western Australia] from Crewe, 18 August 1908.

to furnish the Governor-General with an absolute and permanent veto on the advancement of any particular candidate for an honour would come perilously near to an infringement, not only of State rights, inherent in the constitution of the Commonwealth, but also of the prerogative of His Majesty as the 'fountain of honour'.[48]

Meanwhile, in July, Talbot had also written to Crewe complaining about a recommendation for knighthood made by Northcote, at the request of the prime minister, Alfred Deakin. The man put forward was Victorian Supreme Court judge Henry Hodges. Talbot argued that as Hodges had not performed any federal services, at least to his knowledge, the recommendation contravened a rule laid down by Crewe's predecessor, the Earl of Elgin, in 1906, stating that nominations for solely State services should come from the State premier or governor. Even if Hodges had given some service beyond his State of which Talbot was unaware, he pointed out that the same rule provided that the State government ought to have been consulted. If a Victorian judge was to be honoured, Talbot wished it to be Thomas a'Beckett, whom he considered both senior to, and better than, Hodges.[49] Despite vehement protest from Deakin, who both asserted that Hodges had given service to the Commonwealth and disputed that the Colonial Office had set down any such rule, the recommendation was withdrawn, and Hodges was not knighted until 1918.[50] In passing Deakin's memorandum on to the Colonial Office, Northcote noted that if Talbot's position were accepted, governors-general would not be able to make any recommendations without first gaining agreement from the relevant governor, whereas the governors would be able to 'recommend whom they pleased' without any such regard for the governor-general.[51] Crewe, who might be pardoned if he were exasperated by the protracted nature of this argument, replied with a clarification: if the Commonwealth government nominated a State official, the State government would be given an opportunity to offer their opinion, but they had no veto over federal recommendations, for the colonial secretary remained free to act as he saw fit.[52]

48   NAA: A11812, Bundle 1/1, despatch to Lord Northcote, Governor-General, from Crewe, 18 August 1908.
49   NAA: A11812, Bundle 3/29, despatch to the Secretary of State for the Colonies from R. Talbot, Governor of Victoria, 4 July 1908.
50   NAA: A11812, Bundle 3/29, Alfred Deakin, memorandum, 9 July 1908.
51   NAA: A11812, Bundle 3/29, despatch to the Secretary of State for the Colonies from the Governor-General, 11 July 1908.
52   NAA: A11812, Bundle 3/29, despatch to the Earl of Dudley, Governor-General, from Crewe, 10 September 1908.

A good many of these complaints and difficulties appear to have stemmed from Northcote's intrusive approach to overseeing nominations, and his essentially 'centralist' position on the relationship between the States and the federal government. In his view, the federal administration must be placed 'as a superior authority' within the Federation.[53] Yet even after Crewe's 'authoritative pronouncement' and Northcote's departure (in September 1908), the issue did not go away. Each new governor-general continued to comment on the recommendations made by the State governors, weighing them against each other and offering his own opinions, and the States continued to grumble. In October 1912 the Victorian premier, William Watt, had written to the governor complaining about the treatment of State personages in honours lists. Pointing out that the Australian States had federated along different lines to those adopted in Canada, Watt declared that 'the autonomy and sovereignty' of the States were 'jealously preserved in theory and practice', and argued that the imperial authorities should place 'a higher value' than they did on 'the working of State functions and institutions'. Since Federation, he thought, the imperial government had tended to give State figures 'an inferior status' in honours lists. The president of the Victorian Legislative Council, John Davies, had refused a knighthood, according to Watt, because prior to Federation holders of that position had received a KCMG, and Watt was aggrieved that a KCMG had been given to a federal civil service official, while a higher honour for Davies had been ruled out. He could see no other reason for this 'invidious discrimination' than that the imperial government considered the federal civil service of greater importance than State parliaments. Like so many before him, he urged reconsideration of the procedures.[54] A year later, in the Senate, Labor's Arthur Rae requested explanation as to whether, if someone were 'deemed a fitting person' for a title, the Commonwealth ministry recommended them to the King through the governor-general, and if the States were also able to make such nominations, or if all must go via the governor-general. What difference, he asked, had Federation made?[55]

---

53   Cunneen, *King's Men*, 61.
54   NAA: A2922, NN, Honours 1913, W. A. Watt, Premier, Memorandum for His Excellency the Governor, 1 October 1912.
55   Commonwealth of Australia, Senate, *Parliamentary Debates*, 2 October 1913 (Arthur Rae); Commonwealth of Australia, Senate, *Parliamentary Debates*, 22 October 1913 (Arthur Rae).

The struggle between vice-regal and executive powers

It was not only the channel through which recommendations were made, and the potential influence of federal prime ministers over State honours lists, that were at issue in disputes over honours during this period. Another process question receiving attention was whether—in the context of responsible government—the governor-general and the governors might make recommendations on their own account, or only as directed by their responsible advisers, the prime minister or premier and his cabinet. Premiers and ministers appear at times to have been reluctant to allow that the governor had an ability to recommend people independent of their advice, a not altogether surprising stance given the potential value of honours as a tool of political patronage. In November 1903, for example, Sir George Le Hunte, the governor of South Australia, wrote to Lord Tennyson, the governor-general, with a request from his ministers to know who was responsible for the recommendation of James George Russell, the commissioner of insolvency, for the ISO (Companion of the Imperial Service Order).[56] Le Hunte had already explained to them that Russell's name had been on Tennyson's list, and that, Tennyson having telegraphed to ask if he agreed with the nomination, he had supported it. He told Tennyson the ministers had 'expressed themselves strongly' that no nomination should be made for an honour to their State 'except on their recommendation'.[57] Tennyson replied that he did not have a record of how Russell's name had come to be placed first on his list of names for the ISO—it may be that the situation had resulted from Russell's name being carried over from a previous list. He stated, however, that Le Hunte was quite able to nominate him 'without any approval of your Ministers'.[58]

Like the matter of the governor-general's role, the position of the premiers and prime ministers as responsible advisers to the vice-regal representatives provoked numerous despatches to and from the Colonial Office. The issue, however, proved almost as intractable as the question of State and federal nomination rights. In 1911, for example, the governor of South

---

56 NAA: A11812, Bundle 2/14, despatch to Lord Tennyson, Governor-General of Australia, from George R. Le Hunte, 21 November 1903.
57 NAA: A11812, Bundle 2/14, despatch to Lord Tennyson, Governor-General of Australia, from George R. Le Hunte, 21 November 1903.
58 NAA: A11812, Bundle 2/14, despatch to Governor of South Australia from the Governor-General, 25 November 1903.

Australia, Sir Day Bosanquet, sought guidance about making his own recommendations. Noticing that no medical men had yet been honoured in South Australia, unlike in other States, he had discussed this situation with the premier. The premier, however, had conferred with his ministers and they had decided they did not wish to make any recommendations to remedy the lack. Bosanquet, explaining this to the colonial secretary, sent details of the services of two of the State's distinguished medical men, Edward Stirling and Joseph Verco. He suggested that, '[i]f it is to be considered that the Governor—apart from his Ministers—can recommend for Scientific Services to the State', he wished to nominate the pair, one for a KCMG and one for a CMG. Perhaps in order to circumvent the ministers' annoyance at his having made these nominations against their wishes, he suggested 'the Secretary of State might see fit to telegraph to me desiring me to ascertain from my Ministers if they see any reason why the names ... should not be submitted in this matter'.[59] The secretary of state, then Lewis Harcourt, responded that a rule laid down in April 1905 permitted a governor to initiate recommendations for

> Imperial or Municipal services or public services of a charitable, literary or scientific character ... provided that he first communicates to the Premier for his remarks the names which it is proposed to submit.[60]

If Bosanquet did go ahead with the recommendations, however, they were not successful, though both men would eventually be knighted, Verco in 1912 and Stirling in 1917.[61]

Over time, it seems clear that prime ministers and premiers were gaining in power and control over nominations, at the expense of the governor-general and the governors. Moreover, as the dominions grew in population, influence, and wealth, their prime ministers—and Australia's State premiers—became increasingly powerful also in their dealings with the Colonial Office. In some cases, this growing influence allowed the leaders of governments in the dominions to circumvent or ignore policies established

---

59   NAA: A2922, NN, Honours 1911, despatch to Lewis Harcourt, Secretary of State for the Colonies, from Day H. Bosanquet, Governor [of South Australia], 27 March 1911.

60   NAA: A2922, NN, Honours 1911, despatch to Admiral Sir Day Bosanquet, Governor [of South Australia], from L. Harcourt, 27 July 1911.

61   R. V. Southcott, 'Verco, Sir Joseph Cooke (1851–1933)', *Australian Dictionary of Biography*, accessed 5 September 2017, adb.anu.edu.au/biography/verco-sir-joseph-cooke-8914/text15663; Hans Mincham, 'Stirling, Sir Edward Charles (Ted) (1848–1919)', *Australian Dictionary of Biography*, accessed 5 September 2017, adb.anu.edu.au/biography/stirling-sir-edward-charles-ted-939/text7675.

by the Colonial Office, such as the much-maligned and often-broken rule that entry to the Order of St Michael and St George should be first as a companion. Peter Galloway, the historian of the order, noted:

> A colonial prime minister who was forcefully persistent in his requests, could often breach accepted practice, and the Colonial Office, for all that they huffed and puffed about rules and standards and criteria, found it difficult to resist a determined colonial prime minister who flexed his increasingly powerful muscles.

The two dominions most guilty of such rule-breaking were Canada and Australia, 'the principal self-governing dominions', whose prime ministers were always 'ready to argue their case and increasingly disinclined to accept a rebuff' from the imperial authorities.[62]

Galloway's main Australian example is Alfred Deakin, who held the office of prime minister three times between 1903 and 1910. Finding Deakin unhappy about honours procedures once more in 1908, and having only recently taken up the post of colonial secretary, Crewe was informed by the senior assistant undersecretary of state for the colonies and registrar of the order, Sir Francis Hopwood, that Deakin was

> never satisfied and never accepts any explanation. He merely goes on repeating the same demands. He treats it that the Secretary of State can confer any honour he pleases, and that he should only be an instrument to give effect to Australian demands.[63]

Clearly Deakin, at least, was becoming increasingly assertive in demanding what he considered to be Australia's due within the imperial honours system. A fear of harming imperial unity, or rousing nationalist feelings in the dominions, hampered the Colonial Office in its efforts to resist their prime ministers, who more and more often seem to have prevailed in these contests. Australians' loyalty to the empire, and to broader notions of Britishness or the British 'race', was no barrier to asserting national interests, and Australian statesmen frequently defended Australia's interests without materially weakening their affection for, and their loyalty to, the mother country.[64] Honours were but one of numerous arenas in which Australian leaders sought the recognition they believed due their new nation.

---

62   Galloway, *Order of St Michael and St George*, 147.
63   PRO: CO/447/80, Sir Francis Hopwood to Earl of Crewe, 6 July 1908, cited in Galloway, *Order of St Michael and St George*, 148–49.
64   See, for example, Neville Meaney, 'Britishness and Australian Identity: The Problem of Nationalism in Australian History and Historiography', *Australian Historical Studies* 32, no. 116 (2001): 76–90. doi.org/10.1080/10314610108596148.

New World nation: Imperial honours in a 'classless' nation?

For many Australian statesmen, it seems, their views of the level of recognition due their new nation through the honours system were distinctly different from the views of the imperial authorities. Australian leaders continually sought greater numbers of honours than the Colonial Office was prepared to allot to them, and Federation only increased the difficulty of insufficient allocations of awards. Recommending several persons to the governor-general, Tennyson, in January 1903, Barton attempted to win support for all of his nominations by arguing that his list was in fact 'shorter than would have been the aggregate' of the six State lists prior to Federation, and, after all, the federal list had to encompass all six of those States.[65] Deakin, that bane of the Colonial Office, tried the same tactic in 1904, receiving in response a set of statistics designed to show that his list was, in fact, greater than the combined efforts of the States before 1901, as well as a rebuke for attempting to evade the rule that entry to the Order of St Michael and St George ought to be as a companion rather than as a knight commander.[66] Deakin regularly complained that Australia did not receive a large enough share of honours: in 1909, for example, he informed the governor-general that 'as compared with the States' the federal government was 'already in arrears & entitled to greater liberality than we have hitherto enjoyed'.[67] A mere two days later, acknowledging the governor-general's reply, he stated that '[t]he proposed allotment to Australia is preposterous seeing that we were omitted altogether from the last list so far as public men were concerned'.[68] While one view in the Colonial Office was that the dominions ought to receive more in the way of distinctions, as evidence that they were considered 'equal partners in the empire', another view was that they—and especially Australia—were simply being demanding.[69]

---

65   NAA: A2922, NN, Honours: Recommendations 1903, letter to Lord Tennyson from Edmund Barton, 1 September 1903.
66   NAA: A11812, Bundle 1/1, despatch to Lord Northcote, Governor-General, from Alfred Lyttelton, 8 July 1904.
67   NAA: A2922, NN, Honours 1909, letter to the Earl of Dudley, Governor-General, from Alfred Deakin, 24 August 1909.
68   NAA: A2922, NN, Honours 1909, letter to Governor-General from Alfred Deakin, 26 August 1909.
69   Galloway, *Order of St Michael and St George*, 166–68, quote on 168.

As the idea of honours acknowledging partnership in empire suggests, honours in this era continued to carry imperial meanings: whatever they were to become, they had not yet transformed into a recognition of national service alone. Melbourne's *Argus*, for instance, supported what it referred to as 'the Imperial recognition of public service, in whatever portion of the British dominions it may be rendered', and seemed to see honours as an aid to securing the rosy future of the new Commonwealth of Australia, within the framework of the wider empire:

> Admission to the empire roll of honour—which is, or ought to be, the meaning of an Imperial title—is an incentive to and a fitting reward of the individual aim and sacrifice and achievement that enrich and strengthen and advance the Commonwealth.[70]

On the other side of the equation too, imperial loyalty appears to have been considered a point in favour of a potential recipient, if not a necessary qualification. Recommending Edward Holroyd, a Victorian Supreme Court justice, for the award of knight bachelor in 1903, Sir George Clarke, the governor of Victoria, noted that he was 'an Imperialist of the best type'.[71] A decade later, in 1913, Sir Gerald Strickland, then governor of Western Australia, extolled the efforts of Bishop Charles Riley in using '[h]is commanding personality and influence' to encourage 'feelings of loyalty to the Crown for which the Australia of today has become conspicuous', in a way it had not previously been, and observed that Riley had been 'conspicuous in this State for the inculcation of sentiments of Imperial Unity as well as for the promotion of many movements for social betterment and intellectual uplifting'.[72] Thus, at least in some quarters, honours were still seen as instruments for encouraging imperial unity, as they had been in the years before Federation.

The strong demand for British honours tends to suggest that they were highly valued, at least by some Australians. Indeed, it is tempting to wonder if imperial awards had increased in popularity in a post-Federation atmosphere of reinvigorated empire loyalty and declining republicanism and anti-monarchism. Several scholars have observed the decreasing strength of radical nationalism and republicanism, and a

---

70   *Argus* (Melbourne), 6 January 1902, 4.

71   NAA: A11812, Bundle 2/14, despatch to the Secretary of State for the Colonies from G. S. Clarke, Governor of Victoria, 11 August 1903.

72   NAA: A2922, NN, Honours 1913, despatch to Lewis Harcourt from G. Strickland, Governor [of Western Australia], 21 February 1913.

corresponding rise in imperial sentiment, in the first years of the federated nation's life. In 1958 Charles Grimshaw suggested that '[o]nce it became almost universally accepted, as it was by 1900, that Australian nationalism was compatible with continued Empire membership, a form of Empire imperialism became a component of the nationalism of possibly the majority of Australians', although Australia's differing national interests would lead to a gradual shift 'towards national independence within the framework prescribed by its dual loyalties'.[73] Although there remained 'a residue of republicanism in 1900', he suggested that 'the separation movements [of the 1880s] were a spent force'.[74] More recently, Mark McKenna has observed that Federation 'effectively quashed' any possibility of an Australian republic, at least for the time being, and Neville Kirk has noted that even '[b]y the mid-1890s republican movements had largely "disintegrated" and anti-British republican sentiment was on the wane'.[75] Russell McGregor, meanwhile, has argued that while Australians enthusiastically sought nationhood, they were also 'deeply committed' to the 'ethno-cultural principle' of Britishness, 'not as an alternative or impediment to Australian nationalism but as a vital component of that nationalism'.[76] One example of the renewed enthusiasm for the empire was the keen support of many Australians for the South African War from 1899 to 1902, during which Australian contingents of troops headed for South Africa accompanied by jingoistic expressions of loyalty for the empire.[77] The Boer War, as it was known at the time, also brought a smattering of war honours to Australia, and a renewed presence for

---

73   Charles Grimshaw, 'Australian Nationalism and the Imperial Connection 1900–1914', *Australian Journal of Politics and History* 3, no. 2 (1958): 161. doi.org/10.1111/j.1467-8497.1958.tb00380.x.

74   Grimshaw, 'Australian Nationalism', 162.

75   Mark McKenna, *The Captive Republic: A History of Republicanism in Australia 1788–1996* (Cambridge: Cambridge University Press, 1996), 10; Neville Kirk, 'The Conditions of Royal Rule: Australian and British Socialist and Labour Attitudes to the Monarchy, 1901–11', *Social History* 30, no. 1 (2005): 71. doi.org/10.1080/0307102042000337297.

76   Russell McGregor, 'The Necessity of Britishness: Ethno-Cultural Roots of Australian Nationalism', *Nations and Nationalism* 12, no. 3 (2006): 493–511, quote on 507. doi.org/10.1111/j.1469-8129.2006.00250.x.

77   See C. N. Connolly, 'Class, Birthplace, Loyalty: Australian Attitudes to the Boer War', *Historical Studies* 18, no. 71 (1978): 210–32. doi.org/10.1080/10314617808595588; Grimshaw, 'Australian Nationalism', 163–164. On objections to Australia's participation in the war, see Bobbie Oliver, '"A Wanton Deed of Blood and Rapine": Opposition to Australian Participation in the Boer War', in *The Boer War: Army, Nation and Empire*, eds Peter Dennis and Jeffrey Grey (Canberra: Army History Unit, 2000), 191–99.

the Order of the Bath, which as an almost entirely military honour had been little used in recent times in the Australian colonies: at least 22 CBs (Companion of the Order of the Bath) were conferred in 1901 and 1902.[78]

Republicanism and anti-monarchism had not disappeared, however, and neither had opposition to titles and honours on the grounds of support for egalitarianism, democratic values, or separation.[79] These oppositional views continued to be expressed, particularly in the radical and labour press. In 1908, for example, an article appeared in the *Barrier Miner* in the mining town of Broken Hill, arguing that Australia was 'a new country which ought to be free from class prejudices and absurdities', and that titles such as knighthood were antithetical to democracy and must be abolished.[80] It is too difficult a task to attempt to determine whether or not such hostility to honours and titles had declined along with republican and anti-monarchical opinion, but it is possible to discern the first evidence that opposition to the system was becoming enshrined in Labor politics. As early as 1904 the governor-general, Northcote, was writing to London that the federal Labor government of Chris Watson had decided not to make any nominations for honours, leading Northcote to choose not to send any either.[81] In 1909 a telegram explained that no recommendations were forthcoming from Prime Minister Andrew Fisher because making such nominations would be 'contrary to [the] principles of [the] Labour Party'; Fisher, however, had 'no objection' to the governor-general—by then Dudley—putting forward names of his own.[82] Here was the beginning of a longstanding divide in Australian politics, discussed in later chapters, whereby Labor administrations generally refused to make use of the British honours system, while conservative and non-Labor governments were usually supportive of it.

---

78   The return of the Order of the Bath to Australasia was welcomed by the *Australasian*, which noted that the award of these and other distinctions in recognition of services in South Africa was 'the highest possible official confirmation of the estimate in which the troops from this part of the empire are held by the Imperial Government's military advisers'. 'The Shower of Honours', *Australasian* (Melbourne), 27 April 1901, 929.
79   On the continuance of anti-monarchical and anti-imperialist views in labour and socialist publications in particular, see Kirk, 'Conditions of Royal Rule', 73.
80   'Outlander', 'Titles and Democracy', *Barrier Miner* (Broken Hill), 14 December 1908, 2.
81   NAA: A2922, NN, Honours 1904, despatch to [the Secretary of State for the Colonies] from [Lord Northcote], 7 August 1904.
82   NAA: A2922, NN, Honours 1909, telegram to the Secretary of State for the Colonies from Dudley, 28 March [1909].

Meanwhile, in Britain itself, a new order had been created that offered another possibility for honouring an individual reluctant to accept the title of 'Sir', and which at the same time brought the concept of merit—rather than state or public service or military prowess—into the heart of the honours system. Shortly before the coronation of Edward VII, in June 1902, it was announced that an Order of Merit had been established to honour those who had given 'exceptionally meritorious service' advancing art, literature, learning, or science, or in the army or navy.[83] In the personal gift of the sovereign, the order carried no title, permitting recipients simply to use the postnominal letters 'OM', and it was highly exclusive, being restricted to 24 living recipients at any time. Another innovation of the new order was that women were eligible for it. Although this openness was apparently not envisaged at its inception, with the King (an opponent of female suffrage) asserting a year later that women were ineligible, the order's statutes in fact referred to 'persons', and by the end of 1907 His Majesty's approval had been won for the appointment of Florence Nightingale.[84] Yet women's membership of the order was not secure. After Nightingale's death in 1910, a committee considered the possible creation of an order of merit for women only, to prevent 'a second "embarrassment"'.[85] The plan did not proceed, but it was not until 1935 that an amendment of the statutes would formally recognise that women might be members.[86] A second new order created in 1902 was the Imperial Service Order, which along with an associated medal was to recognise long and meritorious service in the civil services of Britain and the empire, and which became effectively a fourth class of the Order of St Michael and St George.[87]

Although the Order of Merit was in some ways a step towards greater inclusivity in the system, the tight numerical control and ambivalence about women's participation limited its impact on the demographic profile

---

83 Stanley Martin, *The Order of Merit: One Hundred Years of Matchless Honour* (London and New York: I. B. Tauris, 2007), 1.

84 Martin, *Order of Merit*, 447–49; Jane Ridley, *Bertie: A Life of Edward VII* (London: Chatto and Windus, 2012), 372. Oddly, given the King's view about Nightingale's appointment, he also revived the tradition of appointing women as Ladies of the Garter. Almost immediately after his accession to the throne, he appointed his wife, Queen Alexandra, a Lady of the Garter, and had her banner hung in St George's Chapel over the objections of the Herald, who asserted that women 'were not admitted to the order'. Ridley, *Bertie*, 354.

85 Martin, *Order of Merit*, 450.

86 Martin, *Order of Merit*, 449.

87 Galloway, *Order of St Michael and St George*, 138, 146. At the same time, a Royal Victorian Chain was created as another honour in the sovereign's personal gift, intended as a mark of royal esteem.

of recipients. It would have a relatively small presence in Australia over the coming decades, with few Australian-born recipients, not all of whom resided in the country.[88] In the first decade after Federation, the ranks of honoured Australians remained male and white, and heavily clustered in a small number of occupational groupings. Between 1901 and 1913, some 85 knighthoods of various kinds conferred in Australia. Of these, around 57 may be classified as public or political services, including eight governors-general and governors, 10 premiers and prime ministers, 21 other politicians, seven high commissioners or agents-general in London, and three mayors. Another 15 were chief justices and judges, and the remainder were medical men, military leaders, and others, including three philanthropists and one university chancellor. Of 64 CMGs awarded from 1901 to 1913, meanwhile, nearly three-quarters (47) can be classified as rewarding political or public service, going to mayors, public servants, politicians, agents-general, or others holding government posts of some kind. The rest may be classified as for military service (13) or education (four, including a professor of geology and the headmaster of Sydney Grammar School). Besides the 22 CBs mentioned earlier, three CVOs (Commander of the Royal Victorian Order) were also conferred in the period, all upon governors.

Conclusion

Over and above personal views of honours as something to be desired or reviled, honours in the Federation era were a site of struggle, between State and federal politicians and governors, and between the leaders of the new nation and the Colonial Office. A vehicle for personal elevation, they were also a means by which to assert the prestige of the united— and increasingly powerful—dominion. And while Australia remained a dominion, and thus was not in the position of nations that would emerge later through the processes of decolonisation, for whom the creation of national symbols was an urgent task, there was at least one serious

---

88   The Australian Government's database of honours recipients lists seven appointees to the Order of Merit: philosopher Samuel Alexander (1930), classicist Gilbert Murray (1941), medical researchers Macfarlane Burnet and Howard Florey (1958 and 1965 respectively), judge and diplomat Owen Dixon (1963), artist Sidney Nolan (1983), and opera singer Joan Sutherland (1991). Australian Government, Department of the Prime Minister and Cabinet, 'Australian Honours Search Facility', *It's an Honour*, Department of the Prime Minister and Cabinet, accessed 13 June 2021, honours.pmc. gov.au/honours/search. Two others were scientist Robert May (2002) and former prime minister John Howard (2012).

proposal for a new honour that was uniquely Australian in the years after Federation. In 1911 William Sowden, the editor of the South Australian *Register* and a member of the Australian Natives' Association—a friendly society for white men who had been born in Australia—suggested that Australia establish its own 'Order of the Wattle Blossom'. Himself to be knighted in 1918, Sowden was politically a Liberal, and he was a keen advocate for the Australianisation of the instruments and symbols of government, supporting also Australian-born governors and the substitution of 'three cheers' with 'three cooees'.[89] Although considering imperial titles 'a real bond of Empire', he suggested that Australia ought to have an order of its own to recognise non-political services, because it 'need[ed] more demonstrations of sentiment'.[90] This perception of a need for 'more demonstrations of sentiment' may be viewed as part of a wider impetus of nationalism and a drive to create in truth the new nation that had formally come into being in 1901. Indeed, both those who were demanding a greater share of honours and those who rejected them as unsuited to Australia may be understood as seeking to ensure that the new country's national identity and prestige were clear and firmly established in the way the matter of honours was approached. These moves towards nation-building in the matter of honours, however, remained always within the framework of empire. Recognition of the nation through the bestowal of awards, and the development of national distinctiveness and pride, both sat comfortably within a broader imperial identity, as Sowden's own view of titles as ties of empire demonstrates.

---

89 'Travellers' Dinner', *Daily Herald* (Adelaide), 21 August 1911, 3; Carl Bridge, 'Sowden, Sir William John (1858–1943)', *Australian Dictionary of Biography*, accessed 6 September 2017, adb.anu. edu.au/biography/sowden-sir-william-john-8593/text15005; Will. J. Sowden, *An Australian Native's Standpoint: Addresses* (London: Macmillan, 1912), 121–22.
90 Sowden, *Australian Native's Standpoint*, 115–16.

3
New empire order, 1914–1918

The years leading up to the outbreak of war in August 1914 have been described as a 'belle epoque', a pleasant time of optimism and enjoyment that was abruptly shattered when Britain, France, and their allies went to war against Germany and its allies in what became known as the 'Great War', known to us today as World War I. Australia, like New Zealand and the other British dominions, rushed to support the mother country, and became embroiled in the cataclysm and carnage of this destructive conflict. '[T]o our last man and our last shilling', Australia would stand with Britain 'to help and defend her', famously declared Labor leader Andrew Fisher, then in opposition.[1] No formal declaration of war was needed, however: Australia was automatically at war with Germany from the time Britain declared war on 4 August 1914. Initially, the conflict made little difference to the operation of the honours system, but over time, the exigencies of war placed increasing pressure on it. By the time peace returned in 1918, the British honours system looked very different than it had in 1914, being vastly expanded by the creation of a large new order, and at last permitting women to be honoured in their own right in significant numbers.

In Australia, these developments would reignite the tussle over State and federal responsibilities for honours recommendations, as the nation's involvement in war introduced a new element to the uneasy

---

1   National Archives of Australia, 'Andrew Fisher: During Office', *Australia's Prime Ministers*, National Archives of Australia, accessed 3 September 2020, www.naa.gov.au/explore-collection/australias-prime-ministers/andrew-fisher/during-office#last-shilling.

truce that had been achieved on this question. Before the war's end, controversy would also erupt over the conferral of a barony on Sir John Forrest—a somewhat surprising award given the tradition of passionate opposition to hereditary titles among some sections of the population, and the wary cognisance at the Colonial Office of such feelings. Yet while Forrest's elevation to the peerage aroused the ire of some democrats, and although the new distinctions were not the class-free innovations initially envisaged, the overwhelming impact of the war upon the honours system would be to bring an element of democratisation to it. Most significant of all, perhaps, was the choice to include women in the new order on equal terms, a decision that was to permanently alter the institution of honours. The terrible conflict of the Great War would bring a new democratisation, and a fresh set of values, to this ancient institution, changing the face of honours in Australia for years to come.

Snakes in Iceland

Initially, the outbreak of war changed relatively little in the operation of the honours system. Twice-yearly lists published the latest awards; premiers and prime ministers rubbed against each other, the vice-regal representatives, and the Colonial Office; and the press scrutinised each announcement, dispensing paeans of praise for some choices and firing off salvoes of outrage at others. Jealousies and complaints among the States were unabated. In January 1914 Adelaide's *Register* had grumbled that '[i]n accordance with curiously numerous precedents, the claims of South Australia have been entirely ignored'. Such a situation, the writer thought, must be because no one had made a recommendation, or because the Colonial Office had refused it, since '[i]t would be an absurd confession of poverty in distinguished citizenship to suggest ... South Australia possesses no men of eminence beyond those whose accomplishments have already been titularly marked'.[2] The next list, in June, was greeted with hardly more warmth. South Australia had been neglected for several years, the author asserted, and although it had not been completely overlooked this time, 'one can hardly say that its claims to notice have been acknowledged with a hopelessly rash liberality'.[3] Indeed the *Register* had something of a bee in its bonnet about South Australia's experience

2   'New Year Titles', *Register* (Adelaide), 2 January 1914, 6.
3   'The Honours List', *Register* (Adelaide), 23 June 1914, 8.

of honours. In January 1915 it was complaining that 'as usual, South Australia is almost entirely ignored', and in June the following year that its position in relation to honours 'suggests that of Iceland in relation to snakes—there aren't any!'[4] The complaint was not entirely unfounded. In October 1914 the governor-general, Sir Ronald Munro Ferguson, had written to the secretary of state for the colonies, Lewis Harcourt, that honours were too much concentrated in New South Wales, with the result that the other States were beginning to show signs of jealousy.[5]

Others bemoaned the treatment of Australia as a whole, protesting that the nation was not being recognised in a manner commensurate with its importance in the empire. Alongside its remonstrations about the lack of awards for South Australia in January 1914, the *Register* critiqued the imperial authorities' approach to honours more generally. Services performed in the colonies, the writer argued, were 'wholly passed over, or recognised in some relatively inadequate way', while being 'appraised at an immeasurably higher rate if performed in the mother country'. Rather sarcastically, the paper suggested that recent lists tended to weaken the theories of 'Republican scoffers' who thought honours 'bribes intended to ensure an otherwise somewhat unstable loyalty to the Throne', because '[i]f fealty to the Sovereign depended upon the number of royal distinctions vouchsafed to Australians … the prospect of Imperial cohesion on this side of the ocean would be decidedly murky'.[6] The following year the paper made the same point, this time in the context of Australia's willing help in a time of crisis.[7] How Australia fared in the honours lists may have been a particular bugbear of the *Register*, but it was not alone in its opinion that the new nation was not receiving its due share. In his October 1914 despatch, Munro Ferguson had informed Harcourt that he thought the number of awards allotted to Australia 'insufficient', particularly when some went 'by precedent' to certain office-holders.[8]

---

4   'New Year Honours', *Register* (Adelaide), 2 January 1915, 8; 'Birthday Honours', *Register* (Adelaide), 5 June 1916, 4.
5   National Archives of Australia (hereafter NAA): A2922, NN, Honours 1915, despatch to the Secretary of State for the Colonies from R. M. Ferguson, 9 October 1914.
6   'New Year Titles', *Register* (Adelaide), 2 January 1914, 6.
7   'New Year Honours', *Register* (Adelaide), 2 January 1915, 8.
8   NAA: A2922, NN, Honours 1915, despatch to the Secretary of State for the Colonies from R. M. Ferguson, 9 October 1914.

Alongside these grievances there were wider critiques of the system, its structure, and its operation. Together with other Australian newspapers, the *Sydney Morning Herald* reported on a particularly interesting example in early July 1914, just before war broke out. In England, the paper stated, the Women's Freedom League, a breakaway group from the Women's Social and Political Union, had written to the prime minister and the King

> complaining of the absence of women from the Birthday and New Year's honours lists, and enclosing a list of names of prominent women who they claim should have honours bestowed upon them.[9]

A month or so later, more details were available. Suffragette Nina Boyle had penned the letter, which insisted—'[i]n tones of some acerbity and with an exquisitely autocratic touch'—that in the future no list of honours should appear that failed to recognise women. Suggesting more than 50 women who deserved honours, Boyle had included names in social services, science, the arts, education, health, and imperial and national services, or with the armed forces.[10] Criticisms of the conferral of titles in a new nation conceiving of itself as egalitarian and democratic likewise continued to appear in the Australian press. From Britain, too, had come reports that a bill for the abolition of hereditary titles had been put before the British House of Commons. Introduced by a Scottish Liberal, Arthur Ponsonby, it would have seen noble heirs succeed only to properties, not to titles.[11]

Closer to home, the Australian Labor Party, sympathetic to both democratic and nationalistic arguments against the imperial honours system, had become reluctant to continue its use. In October 1914 Labor prime minister Andrew Fisher informed Munro Ferguson that he thought his government would advise him not to make recommendations.[12] Munro Ferguson found this 'self-denying' dictate problematic, writing to Harcourt that since most of the States (including those with Labor governments) would continue to use the system, the result would simply be that Commonwealth servants missed out, while those at the State level received recognition. Moreover, he argued, there was no other avenue by

---

9   'Women and Honours', *Sydney Morning Herald*, 6 July 1914, 11.
10   'Concerning People', *Register* (Adelaide), 11 August 1914, 11.
11   'Inherited Titles', *Argus* (Melbourne), 22 May 1914, 9.
12   NAA: A2922, NN, Honours 1915, despatch to L. V. Harcourt from R. M. Ferguson, 7 October 1914.

which deserving individuals in the military, academia, or other professions might be given distinctions, while it would mean the loss of 'an Imperial tie of real value' to be unable to appoint Australians as privy councillors.[13] At first, Munro Ferguson hoped that he might still put forward some nominations on his own account, but by March the following year he was writing to Harcourt that he had 'no names to submit' for honours, 'owing to the position taken up by the Federal Government' and 'in view of the official regulations', which did not permit him to recommend 'without the assent of Ministers'.[14]

The 'official regulations' were likely 'Australian No. 224', a Colonial Office despatch setting out the 'rules to be observed with regard to recommendations for honours', dated December 1914. According to this document, recommendations (with reasons spelled out) were to be made by each State premier to his respective governor, with the governor then sending that list, along with his own comments and 'an indication as to the order in which he thinks each case should be considered', to both the governor-general and the colonial secretary. Nominations for 'Imperial or municipal services', or for 'public services of a charitable, literary, or scientific character', might be initiated by either the governor or the premier, but the governor was to seek the opinion of the premier on any such recommendation, and forward his views to the colonial secretary.[15] While this appeared to leave open the question of whether or not an honour of this kind would be granted if the premier did not approve, in practice his agreement seems to have been required. In April 1915 Munro Ferguson cabled the governor of Queensland with the information that it could be 'tacitly assumed' that the colonial secretary 'does not accept recommendations for honours save those made with concurrence of Ministers'.[16] Since premiers and ministers were often jealous of their role, and did not wish any of their choices to miss out in

13   NAA: A2922, NN, Honours 1915, despatch to L. V. Harcourt from R. M. Ferguson, 7 October 1914.

14   NAA: A2922, NN, Honours 1915, despatch to the Secretary of State for the Colonies from [R. M. Ferguson], 26 March 1915.

15   NAA: A2922, NN, Honours 1915, Colonial Office, 'Australian No. 224: Australia. Rules to be Observed with Regard to Recommendations for Honours', 24 December 1914. Note that in relation to 'political services', the change had already been made. In such cases, the colonial secretary told Munro Ferguson in June 1915, it was 'a recognised rule that the initiative … rests solely with the Prime Minister', and not the governor-general. NAA: A2922, NN, Honours 1915, despatch to the Governor-General, Sir R. Munro-Ferguson, from A. Bonar Law, 23 June 1915.

16   NAA: A2922, NN, Honours 1915, telegram to Governor of Queensland from [R. M. Ferguson], 26 April 1915.

order for one of the governor's to succeed, such agreement was not easy to secure. In March 1915, for example, the governor of South Australia, Sir Henry Galway, noted that his ministers' opposition to his submitting the names of two medical men was 'prompted by the fear that their repeated nomination' for another person, the newspaper editor William Sowden, 'might be passed over in favour of one of the gentlemen recommended by me'.[17] The effective ending of the right of governors and governors-general to make nominations on their own account thus made it possible for a government politically opposed to imperial honours to block their use, at least within its specific purview. This would create considerable tension and controversy in years to come.

'Australian No. 224' also attempted to ease tensions over honours between the States and the federal government. Nominations 'for recognition of services rendered solely to any one State', it said, 'should emanate from the Governor or Premier of that State', and if the Commonwealth Government were to put forward 'a State official, or other person unconnected with the Commonwealth, for services which have not been confined to any one State', the opinion of the relevant State government was to be sought, and conveyed to the colonial secretary. This left room for ambiguity, however, especially in the definition of the phrase 'unconnected with the Commonwealth', and although regularly referenced, 'Australian No. 224' would not be the oil upon troubled waters the Colonial Office might have hoped. Moreover, the document did nothing to remove State objections to the role of the governor-general. After receiving his copies of the State lists, it specified, the governor-general 'acting in his individual capacity'—as opposed to on the advice of his ministers—would 'make such observations on them as he thinks fit', to the State governor and to the secretary of state. If faced with 'a difference of opinion', the colonial secretary would 'naturally attach due weight' to any objection by the governor-general, given 'his position and the advantages which he enjoys in forming a judgement'. In a case where agreement could not be reached in Australia through 'consultation and correspondence', it was up to the colonial secretary to decide the ultimate fate of the recommendation. The governor-general's opinion was vital, the document asserted, 'to assist [the secretary of state] in deciding fairly between the relative claims of

---

17   NAA: A2922, NN, Honours 1915, despatch to the Secretary of State for the Colonies from H. L. Galway, Governor [of South Australia], 9 March 1915.

various States', given the limited numbers of awards available.[18] As this was essentially a restatement of the practice already being followed, it was unlikely to soothe State frustrations. Nor did it. In July 1916 it was reported that the Victorian premier, Sir Alexander Peacock, had said 'that Victoria would continue to assert its rights as a sovereign State' in making nominations directly to British authorities, 'and he believed that the other States would do likewise'. '[T]he Federal Government had not the right to revise recommendations to the King for honours,' he declared.[19]

Catering for war service

As the war dragged on, it began to have a greater impact on the honours system. Regular appointments to the Order of St Michael and St George for colonial service were quickly eclipsed by those made for military service.[20] Wars had long created difficulties for those administering honours. At the turn of the century the South African War had caused considerable strain on the system, and the Colonial Office had found itself under pressure from the War Office to use the Order of St Michael and St George to relieve that strain by conferring the order on individuals not deemed worthy of the Order of the Bath, or otherwise unable to be accommodated within the military orders.[21] In the years of peace after 1902 the issue had faded away, but with the outbreak of World War I it soon reappeared, and with even greater intensity.[22] More than any previous conflict, this war involved the mobilisation of large swathes of the populations of Britain and its empire, and it touched the lives of entire communities. Vast numbers of people were contributing to the war effort, but as the honours system was so restricted, especially for those of lower ranks or social classes, there was no way of rewarding most of them. Before long it was evident that the existing system—even with the War Office poaching from the colonial order—could not meet the demands of this war.[23]

---

18   NAA: A2922, NN, Honours 1915, Colonial Office, 'Australian No. 224: Australia. Rules to be Observed with Regard to Recommendations for Honours', 24 December 1914.
19   'Granting of Honours', *Argus* (Melbourne), 26 July 1916, 11; 'Imperial Honours', *Sydney Morning Herald*, 27 July 1916, 10.
20   Peter Galloway, *The Order of St Michael and St George* ([London]: Third Millennium for the Central Chancery of the Orders of Knighthood, 2000), 196.
21   Galloway, *Order of St Michael and St George*, 183–86.
22   Galloway, *Order of St Michael and St George*, 186–87.
23   Galloway, *Order of St Michael and St George*, 188–204; James C. Risk, *The History of the Order of the Bath and Its Insignia* (London: Spink and Son, 1972), 93.

These problems were to lead directly to a major change in the British honours system that would shape Australians' experiences of honours for many years: the founding of the Order of the British Empire, and alongside it the Order of the Companions of Honour. By late 1915, informal discussion was taking place in London over the possibility of creating a new honour that would permit recognition of the war work of a wide swathe of the British population.[24] From the beginning it was envisaged that women would be eligible as well as men, although whether this would be through inclusion in the planned new order or via the institution of another decoration specifically for women—perhaps an Order of St Margaret, identified as the only female British saint—was not initially certain.[25] Considerable debate was to take place between these early suggestions and the final announcement of the new orders. At various moments, there were proposals for one or two new orders; for a single-class or a multi-class order; for knighthood to be included, absent, or optional; and—rather than creating any new decoration—for the addition of extra classes to transform the Orders of the Bath and St Michael and St George into five-class honours.[26]

Many of these questions arose because the proposed new distinction was intended to be democratic, capable of use to reward people at all levels of society for their contributions to the war effort. The argument over whether the order should contain one or multiple classes was just such an issue. Sir Edward Troup, the permanent undersecretary of state at the Home Office, considered that a single-class order, given regardless of social rank or the nature of the service being rewarded, would avoid the challenge of having to assign recipients to different classes.[27] Sir Frederick Ponsonby, the keeper of the privy purse and a driving force behind the new honour, articulated a different view of democracy. In his view, it was easy enough to place recipients in grades:

> If an Admiral of the Fleet jumps overboard and saves the King's life, he gets the Grand Cross; if a Midshipman rescues the Monarch from the deep, he receives the lowest class.[28]

---

24   Peter Galloway, *The Order of the British Empire* ([London]: Central Chancery of the Orders of Knighthood, 1996), 1–2.
25   Galloway, *Order of the British Empire*, 3.
26   See Galloway, *Order of the British Empire*, chapter 1.
27   Galloway, *Order of the British Empire*, 5.
28   Sir Frederick Ponsonby to Sir Edward Troup, 20 May 1916, in OBE Letters, Box 1, Central Chancery of the Orders of Knighthood, cited by Galloway, *Order of the British Empire*, 5.

For Ponsonby, the way to create a democratic honour was to ensure that everyone could receive something, not that everyone received the same thing. Another suggestion, if the order were to be multi-class, was that all recipients would nevertheless use the same postnominal letters: OBE. Neither King George V nor the Cabinet approved of this proposal, and it was dropped.[29] Yet another formulation of the new order as democratic was—as is discussed further below—that it would have multiple grades, but that it would not be a matter of social class where a person was placed in it, but only of the value of their achievements.

Another attempt to make the new order more acceptable to those of democratic opinions was a suggestion that none of its grades carry knighthood. Since there were a number of people in Britain, not only in the Labour Party but more broadly, who did not wish to receive a title, this arrangement would ensure that they could accept appointment to the upper levels of the new order, if that was the appropriate level at which to recognise them. Objections were raised on the basis of precedence, since the innovation would lead to untitled men and women holding precedence over titled individuals, and on the grounds that the order ought to be designed with an eye to its dignity rather than the desires of potential recipients. Still seeking to ensure that the new honour would be supported as widely as possible, the King and the British prime minister, David Lloyd George, suggested that knighthood be instead made optional for recipients of the two upper grades. That way, those who wished for the title could have it, while those who held ideological objections or simply did not want to be titled, could still accept the honour. Problems of precedence and nomenclature remained, however, and after considerable discussion and debate both ideas would be abandoned in favour of the more familiar configuration of a multi-class order conferring knighthood in its upper two levels, accompanied by a second new order that conferred neither titles nor precedence.[30]

The first whispers of these new distinctions reached Australia early in 1917, and particular interest was taken in the idea that women might be included. The Adelaide *Register* commented favourably in July:

---

29   Galloway, *Order of the British Empire*, 7.
30   Galloway, *Order of the British Empire*, 7–14.

> Even those who most earnestly object ... to women being endowed
> with the vote can have nothing to say against the bestowal of
> honours on women who have done magnificent, unselfish and
> truly patriotic work for the Empire in this time of need.[31]

Any opposition to women's inclusion in the honours system appears to
have melted away in the face of their war services. Indeed, the war had
brought about something of a change in popular attitudes towards female
equality and citizenship. Women's suffrage had been a matter of fierce
contestation in the United Kingdom before 1914, but there had been
a significant shift in opinion as a result of women's work for the war effort,
and the praise their efforts had received.[32] Many speeches in both Houses
of Parliament in 1917 emphasised that 'women had earned the vote by
their work for the war'.[33] In a similar way, women's contributions during
the war had rendered their full inclusion in the honours system—at least in
an order specifically aimed at rewarding war service—not only imaginable
but irresistible. Yet even after the principle was conceded, difficulties
remained. One was the question of what title, if any, women should hold
when appointed to the upper two levels of the proposed order, which
bestowed knighthood and the title of 'Sir' on men. Ponsonby suggested
'Dame', while others thought 'Lady' the best option, but there were also
those who opposed the whole idea of a title for women.[34] Eventually,
however, although the King did not much like the title of 'Dame', in the
absence of a better alternative it was selected.[35]

Official notification of the new honours arrived in Australia shortly after
rumours began appearing in the press. On 3 February 1917, a cablegram
from the colonial secretary announced that the King had decided to create
an Order of the British Empire for recognising war services. It would have
five classes, to 'be assigned strictly according to the public value of the war
work done', and women were to be eligible. This initial cablegram stated
that the order would 'not carry knighthood in any class'. The governor-
general was asked to consult the prime minister, and to submit no more
than six recommendations for the first list; more would be possible

---

31   'Equality of the Sexes', *Register* (Adelaide), 20 July 1917, 6.
32   Andrew Rosen, *Rise Up, Women! The Militant Campaign of the Women's Social and Political Union 1903–1914* (London and Boston: Routledge and Kegan Paul, 1974), 256. doi.org/10.4324/9780203104002.
33   Rosen, *Rise Up, Women!*, 263.
34   Galloway, *Order of the British Empire*, 15–17.
35   Galloway, *Order of the British Empire*, 17.

later.[36] Prime Minister Billy Hughes delayed, seeking more information.[37] A reply from London provided little help. It explained that the order was to cover '[s]ervices primarily those connected with war in widest possible sense other than those in the field', and that it was 'the intention to confer classes strictly according to merit of services rendered', so that 'persons of high social status will often be in lower class than others of no special standing'.[38] A despatch from the colonial secretary, Walter Long, arrived soon after, but it too was unable to provide firm information, as the details of the new honour were still being settled, and Hughes sought a further postponement of the task of submitting names, until his anticipated arrival in London for the first meeting of the Imperial War Cabinet.[39]

The eventual shape of the new order was somewhat different to that foreshadowed in these early communications. In fact, as noted above, two orders were eventually created. The Most Excellent Order of the British Empire was made up of five classes—knights and dames grand cross (GBE), knights and dames commanders (KBE/DBE), commanders (CBE), officers (OBE), and members (MBE)—plus a medal (BEM), which was intended for those whose service did not qualify them for the order, particularly those of a lower class or social standing.[40] Initially designated the National Service Order, the second new order was that of the Companions of Honour. A single-class award, it bore neither title nor precedence, and it was designed to cater for those whose services rendered them eligible for one of the first two grades of the Order of the British Empire, but who were unwilling to accept knighthood.[41] In this innovation, and in the scale and reach of the Order of the British Empire, the aim of a democratic recognition of the war services of the whole population remained alive. It was a particular vision of democracy, however. Despite early intimations that the grade of a person's award would be determined

---

36   NAA: A12378, 1/A/1, cablegram from the Secretary of State for the Colonies to [R. M. Ferguson], 3 February 1917.

37   NAA: A12378, 1/A/1, cable to Secretary of State from R. M. Ferguson, 7 February 1917.

38   NAA: A12378, 1/A/3, cablegram from the Secretary of State for the Colonies to [R. M. Ferguson], 8 February 1917.

39   NAA: A12378, 1/A/2, despatch to Sir R. Munro Ferguson, Governor-General, from Walter H. Long, 8 February 1917; NAA: A12378, 1/A/2, telegram to Secretary of State from R. M. Ferguson, 2 March 1917.

40   The Medal of the Order of the British Empire was established at the same time as the order, and initially recipients were treated as members of it. After 1922, however, it was merely affiliated with the order, and was given for meritorious civilian service or for gallantry.

41   NAA: A12378, 1/A/3, cablegram to [the Governor-General] from the Secretary of State for the Colonies, 25 April 1917.

solely by the value of their services, a scale of eligibility was soon produced that laid out which ranks of the armed services were eligible for which grades of the Order of the British Empire, and similar guidelines would come to direct appointments from the various levels of the diplomatic and civil services.

The first awards

Still not having received names from Australia (Hughes had now become preoccupied with an election) and having little more luck with the other dominions, the imperial authorities decided in May to publish the first batch of awards anyway, with a note that dominion and colony lists would appear at a later date.[42] Unsurprisingly, when the Australians finally did get around to selecting names for the new order, controversy erupted between the States and the federal government as to the process to be followed. In November, a cablegram from the colonial secretary announced that a list including the colonies and dominions was to be issued at the beginning of 1918. Nominations were to be made only for war-related services, 'mainly' to civilians, and up to specified maximum numbers, with further lists to follow that might cater for 'less urgent cases'. More controversially, the list was to be prepared on the advice of the prime minister, and sent by the governor-general. The quotas stipulated (2 GBEs, 5 KBEs or DBEs, 20 CBEs, 70 OBEs, and 90 MBEs) had been allocated for the whole of the country, and the colonial secretary expected that in drawing up the list the governor-general or prime minister would 'make any necessary consultation with [the] States'.[43] Perhaps concerned that Hughes would persist in his lack of interest, Munro Ferguson telegraphed the official secretary at the federal Government House, asking him to '[p]oint out' to Hughes the possibility that if he did not deal with the honours, they would be given through the States. The '[p]restige of [the] Federal Government', he wrote ingeniously, would be 'enhanced' if the recommendations came from that source.[44] The gambit worked. In February, Hughes wrote to

---

42   Galloway, *Order of the British Empire*, 21; NAA: A12378, 1/A/3, telegram to Secretary of State from R. M. Ferguson, 2 May [1917]; NAA: A12378, 1/A/3, cablegram to [the Governor-General] from Secretary of State for the Colonies, 3 May 1917.
43   NAA: A12378, 2/B/1, cablegram from the Secretary of State for the Colonies to [R. M. Ferguson], 1 November 1917.
44   NAA: A12378, 1/A/4, telegram to Official Secretary, Federal Government House, Melbourne, from R. M. Ferguson, 24 November 1917.

each of the premiers, informing them of the establishment of the order, providing details about it, and asking that any nominations include an indication of what each person's services were, and how they should be prioritised.[45] A similar letter from Munro Ferguson went to each of the governors.

The States were predictably unhappy. The governor of Western Australia, Sir William Ellison-Macartney, protested to the colonial secretary. He had received a request for nominations from the governor-general—although, he pointed out, he had not then been officially informed of the new honour—and had treated it in the same manner as any other honours list, simply communicating with Munro Ferguson to let him know the names he planned to submit to the Colonial Office. Having learned that the usual procedures might not be followed, he wished to convey his premier's 'strong opposition to any departure' from past practice. Henry Lefroy, the Nationalist premier, was willing to concede that in wartime his own 'concurrence or initiation' might not be required, since the governor 'was more closely associated with, and had more intimate knowledge of, the working of the special war organisations' than did government ministers, but he was 'absolutely opposed' to anybody other than the governor proposing honours for his State.[46]

Further protests followed. New South Wales premier William Holman told the governor, Sir Walter Davidson, and Hughes that his ministers vigorously objected to the proposed change in the channel of communication for recommendations.[47] The following day, the governor of South Australia, Galway, wrote to Munro Ferguson, and the colonial secretary, to say that his premier, Archibald Peake, was not inclined to submit nominations until he learned the result of Holman's complaint. Galway expressed 'regret' that he could not send any names, but stated that he felt it was 'my duty … to support my Ministers in their defence of a privilege hitherto enjoyed by the States … and which is jealously guarded as a State right'.[48] All three protests also alluded to the possibility that

---

45 NAA: A12378, 1/A/4, 'Copy of letter forwarded by Prime Minister to the Premiers of the several States', 28 February 1918.
46 NAA: A12378, 3/E/1, despatch to Walter Long, Colonial Office, London, from the Governor [of Western Australia], [29?] February 1918.
47 NAA: A12378, 1/A/4, letter to the Prime Minister of the Commonwealth of Australia from W. A. Holman, Premier [of New South Wales], 8 March 1918.
48 NAA: A12378, 3/A/1, despatch to the Governor-General from H. L. Galway, Governor [of South Australia], 9 March 1918.

nominations would be sought from organisations such as the Red Cross Society, and each opposed this innovation as well. Galway had told the colonial secretary, Long, that since the governor-general had already asked State Red Cross branches to nominate for the order, his premier refused to make any recommendations 'as [he] is not prepared to submit any names which might be passed over in favour of such recommendations'.[49] Long's response to all this was unsympathetic. As he told Munro Ferguson, he had replied to Galway that the regulations laid out in 'Australian No. 224' of 1914 did not apply to the new order. '[A]ppointments thereto,' he said, were 'intended as reward for war services and as such can only be dealt with through [the] Commonwealth Government and Governor General.'[50] Hughes agreed, informing Munro Ferguson that he 'fully concur[red]' with Long that, since it was 'a reward for war services', appointments to the order could 'only be dealt with through the Commonwealth Administration'.[51]

Meanwhile, Munro Ferguson had been persisting in the unenviable task of producing a list of recommendations. By the beginning of April, as he informed Long, he had managed to obtain—though only 'unofficially'— names from the South Australian and Victorian governors, but the Tasmanian and Western Australian governors had refused to make any more suggestions, after an official protest from all the State premiers, acting through Holman, had been sent to Long by the New South Wales governor, Davidson.[52] As it transpired, Ellison-Macartney had instead sent a list of recommendations for Western Australia directly to the colonial secretary:

---

49   NAA: A12378, 3/B/1, cablegram from the Secretary of State for the Colonies to [R. M. Ferguson], 2 March 1918. Munro Ferguson rejected this complaint, telling Long in May that he had not approached any Red Cross branch, and that 'communication between [the] President [of the] Australian Red Cross and [the] President [of the] South Australia[n branch] were purely of a personal and informal character'. NAA: A12378, 3/B/1, telegram to Secretary of State from R. M. Ferguson, 16 May 1918. The communications had been between his wife—whom Hughes had asked, as the national president of the Red Cross, to suggest names—the wife of the Western Australian governor, and Galway and his wife, whom she had consulted 'informally and confidentially' in this task. NAA: A12378, 3/B/1, despatch to the Secretary of State for the Colonies from [the Governor-General], 29 May 1918; NAA: A12378, 3/B/1, despatch to the Secretary of State for the Colonies from [the Governor-General], 10 June 1918.
50   NAA: A12378, 3/B/1, cablegram from the Secretary of State for the Colonies to [R. M. Ferguson], 2 March 1918.
51   NAA: A12378, 3/A/3, letter to the Governor-General from W. M. Hughes, 17 April 1918.
52   NAA: A12378, 3/A/2, despatch to the Secretary of State for the Colonies from R. M. Ferguson, 1 April 1918. For the protest by the State premiers, see NAA: A12378, 3/C/2, cablegram to the Secretary of State for the Colonies from Davidson [Governor of New South Wales], 15 March 1918; NAA: A12378, 3/C/2, despatch to Sir Ronald Munro Ferguson, Governor-General and Commander-in-Chief of the Commonwealth of Australia, from W. E. Davidson, 19 March 1918.

'doubtless', Munro Ferguson told Hughes, he would be '"snubbed"'.[53] As for Queensland, its governor, Sir Hamilton Goold-Adams, rarely communicated with Munro Ferguson, 'and, if despatches are being written, the copies are not reaching me'. The governor-general explained that he had 'pointed out' to the governors 'the reasonableness of the course adopted … seeing that the Order is bestowed for War Service and that to attempt to regulate recognition by geographical areas was impossible', and noted that he had 'reminded' Davidson that the New South Wales Government had 'shown a constant disposition to trespass upon the Federal sphere in matters pertaining to Defence and External Affairs', meaning that the federal ministry was 'unlikely to disagree with' the method adopted for nominations for the new order. Hopefully, he stated his view that the States would 'come to accept the position and that already excitement on the question is dying out', although 'much' would 'depend' on the awards eventually given by the Commonwealth Government. In this, his trouble was the mercurial Hughes, whose 'inaccessibility and the impossibility of getting him to devote time and consideration to the lists' was rendering the task 'difficult'. Nevertheless, he hoped that the majority of the honours were 'quite as satisfactory as this kind of thing ever is', and was reassured that 'mistakes' could be set right in future lists.[54]

Far from the matter dying quietly away, however, it was discussed at a premiers' conference in May, and the States stuck to their guns. New South Wales and Tasmania had proposed that 'the States should, by resolution, protest against any departure from the established constitutional usage' for making honours nominations, and the wider issue of Commonwealth encroachment into the domain of the States was also discussed.[55] A unanimous resolution asserted that, while the premiers 'recognis[ed] that the bestowal of honors in recognition of war services is a matter for the decision of the Federal Government', they held that State governments 'should not be asked to accept the responsibility of making nominations'; that if they were asked to do so, those nominations 'should be made in the accepted constitutional manner through the Governors of the States'; and that 'where the State Governments are requested to

---

53   NAA: A12378, 3/A/3, memo to the Prime Minister from the Governor-General, 17 April 1918.
54   NAA: A12378, 3/A/2, despatch to the Secretary of State for the Colonies from R. M. Ferguson, 1 April 1918. In fact, it appeared that Goold-Adams was as dilatory in his communications with London as he was in those with Canberra. Acknowledging Munro Ferguson's letter, Long told him that he had not heard from the Queensland governor about the matter. NAA: A12378, 3/A/2, despatch to the Governor-General, Sir R. Munro Ferguson, from Walter H. Long, 4 June 1918.
55   'Premiers' Conference', *Kalgoorlie Miner*, 10 May 1918, 3.

make nominations, no nominations should be invited from persons or associations who do not share the responsibilities of the Government'. Copies were sent to the acting prime minister and the colonial secretary.[56] But no sympathy was forthcoming from London, or from Hughes, and the selection of recipients continued to be the responsibility of the federal government.[57]

Yet even now the issue was not finally resolved. As late as September 1919 Munro Ferguson was informing Goold-Adams that 'nominations to the British Empire Order must be submitted to the Secretary of State by my Government'.[58] There are none so deaf, however, as those who will not hear. Goold-Adams claimed he had 'neither mental or written records' of Munro Ferguson's request for nominations, with which he would have cooperated had he known of it, and implied the governor-general was preventing deserving Queenslanders from receiving awards by 'blocking' his recommendations in their favour.[59] Clearly losing patience, Munro Ferguson responded that both Goold-Adams and his prime minister had certainly been sent information about the order, and that Goold-Adams's

> failure to provide me with the views of your Government ... and the fact that my Government's communications ... remained unacknowledged were unquestionably responsible for recognition being given only to those Queensland citizens whose services were brought to the notice of the Secretary of State through the Federal Government.

He closed by reiterating that he would draw Hughes's attention to any individuals Goold-Adams wished to suggest 'unofficially', and with a mild rebuke. 'I am sure Your Excellency cannot seriously have meant to suggest that I am "blocking your recommendations"', he wrote, since he had only requested that they be submitted to him according to the instructions laid down by the colonial secretary.[60]

---

56   NAA: A1606, A22/1, letter to the Acting Prime Minister of the Commonwealth of Australia from W. A. Holman, Premier [of New South Wales], 22 May 1918.

57   On this dispute over the new order, see also Christopher Cunneen, *King's Men: Australia's Governors-General from Hopetoun to Isaacs* (Sydney: George Allen and Unwin, 1983), 144.

58   NAA: A12378, 3/D/2, despatch to Sir Hamilton Goold-Adams, Governor of Queensland, from R. M. Ferguson, 26 September 1919.

59   NAA: A12378, 3/D/2, despatch to the Governor-General from Hamilton Goold Adams, 1 October 1919.

60   NAA: A12378, 3/D/2, despatch to Sir Hamilton Goold-Adams, Governor of Queensland, from R. M. Ferguson, 15 October 1919.

Making a list, checking it twice

A series of files in the National Archives of Australia document the selection of recipients. In the letters and telegrams that went to and fro, and the draft lists covered with annotations, additions, and crossings-out, a degree of back-and-forthing is evident. One reason for the indecision was likely an attempt to forestall jealousies between the States, especially given the tensions provoked by the procedure chosen for recommendations. In January 1918, for example, Munro Ferguson suggested Hughes might consider changing the class of award envisaged for several women who were to be recognised for their work for the Australian Comforts Fund, on the grounds that the existing list appeared to treat the Victorian ladies more generously than those from New South Wales.[61] Another was haste and lack of information, which occasionally led to errors. The businessman and member of the newspaper dynasty James Oswald Fairfax appears to have received an award somewhat against his will: in an unusual lapse, it seems he was not sounded beforehand as to his willingness to accept, and would have preferred not to have received anything for his Red Cross work.[62] Another person was nominated, but the telegram adding his name to the list was received in London too late to be acted upon, and before the next list was announced Munro Ferguson had received information that made him 'doubt [his] suitability on [the] score of character'.[63] And 'Miss

---

61   NAA: A12378, 6/A/11, memorandum to the Prime Minister from the Governor-General, 10 January 1918.

62   Fairfax had been appointed OBE on 15 March 1918. In a letter dated 29 March, Munro Ferguson explained that he had just cabled London to 'rectify errors' in the list, one of which was to place Fairfax among the CBEs rather than the OBEs. He had evidently seen Fairfax shortly after sending the cable, and discovered to his consternation that 'your acquiescence had not been obtained'. He hoped, however, that Fairfax would allow the correction 'as one involving the prestige of the Red X and its standing v.a.v other organisations'. NAA: A12378, 6/A/9, letter to J. O. Fairfax, Esq, from R. M. Ferguson, 29 March 1918. Fairfax, for his part, reiterated that he would 'have preferred not to receive any distinction for Red Cross work', but agreed that since it was, as Munro Ferguson had noted, 'a matter affecting the Red Cross Society', he would leave the issue with Munro Ferguson. NAA: A12378, 6/A/9, letter to the Governor-General from J. O. Fairfax, 30 March 1918. He was appointed CBE on 24 May 1918. Australian Government, Department of the Prime Minister and Cabinet, 'Australian Honours Search Facility', *It's an Honour*, Department of the Prime Minister and Cabinet, accessed 13 June 2021, honours.pmc.gov.au/honours/awards/1065399.

63   NAA: A12378, 5/D/2, telegram to the Secretary of State for the Colonies from R. M. Ferguson, 17 December 1918. The individual in question was Hugh Ward, probably Hugh Joseph Ward (1871–1941). See Martha Rutledge, 'Ward, Hugh Joseph (1871–1941)', *Australian Dictionary of Biography*, accessed 13 May 2021, adb.anu.edu.au/biography/ward-hugh-joseph-8983/text15811.

'Scobie' was omitted from one list because the governor-general had 'never heard of the lady', and had been unable to learn any details regarding either her or her war work.[64]

Even without these pressures, it would have been a difficult task. Selecting a relatively small number of people from among a population that had been widely mobilised was a challenge in itself, and the necessity of drawing distinctions between their contributions so as to allot them to the order's various classes could only increase the complexity. 'It is almost impossible,' wrote Munro Ferguson to the colonial secretary in January 1918, 'to differentiate between the merits of workers all engaged on similar tasks.'[65] He summed up the difficulties in a despatch the following month, suggesting the assignment was even more testing in Australia:

> It is probable that in no part of His Majesty's Dominions is the selection of persons ... more difficult than it is in Australia. The fact that there are six States and the Federal Territories, in each of which all the various patriotic organisations are represented by equally energetic Committees with President, Secretary and other officials, all having equal claim to recognition for exactly the same work, makes it difficult to discriminate between them without exciting not merely personal, but what is worse, State jealousies. There is the further difficulty that the Prime Minister and all Politicians are rarely in touch with the persons carrying on patriotic work, and are apt, if they include any such names in the list, to recommend persons who have but inferior claims to recognition because they happen to have come in contact with them. Such persons get precedence which it is difficult to dispute, for, in most instances, they have done good work though of a kind which in a general and impartial survey of the situation would rank them behind many who remain unrecognised ...[66]

---

64 NAA: A12378, 7/A/5, 'Memorandum on Certain Nominations made by Mr. Watt'. The omission appears to have been only temporary. On 4 October 1918 Grace Lockie Scobie was appointed OBE. Australian Government, Department of the Prime Minister and Cabinet, 'Australian Honours Search Facility', *It's an Honour*, Department of the Prime Minister and Cabinet, accessed 13 June 2021, honours.pmc.gov.au/honours/awards/1108100.

65 NAA: A12378, 2/E/1, despatch to the Secretary of State for the Colonies from the Governor-General, 8 January 1918.

66 NAA: A12378, 4/B/1, despatch to the Secretary of State for the Colonies from [Munro Ferguson, the Governor-General], 5 February 1918.

Nevertheless, the lists were drawn up, and a total of 369 men and 54 women received awards in the first lists issued in 1918 and 1919, their services covering a wide range of types of work, as well as being scattered across the continent.[67] Further lists would be issued in the early 1920s, adding many more to the roll of people recognised for their war services.

Among those appointed to the new order were Nellie Melba, Australia's famous operatic soprano, who received a DBE for her labour '[o]rganising patriotic work' and fundraising during the war; Rear Admiral William Clarkson of the Royal Australian Navy, whose KBE recognised both his navy service and his efforts 'in connection with the control and re-organisation of coastal shipping'; Hugh McKay, the man behind the famous Sunshine Harvester, who was granted a CBE for his 'services in connection with war industries', especially through 'the improvisation of machinery required … in connection with the War'; Reginald Edward Weigall, given an OBE for his work as 'President and Organiser of an Honorary Motor Service for the reception of returned and wounded soldiers'; and Millicent (Lily) and Alice Fisken, sisters, for their services to the Australian branch of the British Red Cross Society overseas.[68] After a military division of the order was instituted in December 1918—to date from the order's establishment in June 1917—recipients were allotted either to it or to the newly delineated civil division, and existing recipients eligible for appointment to the military division were transferred into it. Military division awards included men serving in the various branches of the armed forces, individuals working for the War Office or other war-related government departments, those in the nursing services, and women working with any of the women's auxiliaries.[69] The resulting division between civil and military awards would play a part in a controversial chapter of Australia's experience in the next great global conflict.

When the first recipients were announced in the *London Gazette*, the Australian press naturally reported on the list. The awardees were 'drawn from every walk in life', noted the Hobart *Mercury*, and were 'persons

---

67   Australian Government, Department of the Prime Minister and Cabinet, 'Australian Honours Search Facility', *It's an Honour*, Department of the Prime Minister and Cabinet, accessed 4 May 2021, honours.pmc.gov.au/honours/search. These figures do not include two awards conferred in 1917: a KBE to Thomas Bilbe Robinson and a GBE to Florence Reid.

68   NAA: A12378, 6/A/5, 'Short Statement of Services of Nominees to British Empire Order'.

69   NAA: A1606, A22/1, extract from the *London Gazette*, no. 31084, 27 December 1918, Central Chancery of the Orders of Knighthood, 27 December 1918.

whose services during the war have won particular notice'.[70] Many of the reports were positive, appreciating both the services given by the awardees and the desire to reward them represented by the new order. In the British context, Tobias Harper has also noted the pleasure of recipients, for many of whom their honour 'was celebrated as an important sign of inclusion in the war effort and in the nation and empire more broadly'.[71] But not everyone was impressed. The Perth *Sunday Times* observed rather cuttingly that the distinction had been established

> with the object of recognising the services of war workers, but truth to tell it is cutting no ice to speak of. Nobody cares a row of pins whether Mrs. So-and-So or Mr. Such-and-Such is a D.B.E., a K.B.E., a C.B.E., an O.B.C., [sic] or a plain M.B.E.[72]

What precisely lay behind this sneer at the order is not clear, but it may have reflected the belief of a number of observers that it was being distributed far too liberally. In late 1918 it was reported that New Zealand's Greymouth Patriotic Association had passed a motion to inform the government of 'the dissatisfaction' found among New Zealanders at the conferral of the order in that country, and to request that the British authorities be asked to refrain from bestowing it further.[73] Responding to the report, John Peerybingle in the Victorian *Weekly Times* observed that the order was 'now known as the Order Belong to Everybody', and suggested that:

> The trouble in New Zealand as in Australia, appears to be that it looks as if it is only a matter of time before 50 per cent. of the population will have the doubtful privilege of attaching the letters O.B.E. to their names.[74]

Other 'jeering remarks and music-hall jokes' included references to it in Britain as 'the "Order of the Bad Egg" or the "Order for Britain's Everybody"'.[75] Indeed, as the order's historian, Peter Galloway, has acknowledged, it was dispensed in numbers 'unprecedented within the United Kingdom', with membership reaching 25,419 persons by February

---

70 'British Empire Order', *Mercury* (Hobart), 25 August 1917, 7.
71 Tobias Harper, *From Servants of the Empire to Everyday Heroes: The British Honours System in the Twentieth Century* (Oxford: Oxford University Press, 2020), 48. doi.org/10.1093/oso/978019 8841180.001.0001.
72 'Perth Prattle', *Sunday Times* (Perth), 31 March 1918, 17.
73 'Order of British Empire', *Argus* (Melbourne), 14 October 1918, 6.
74 John Peerybingle, 'Peerybingle Papers', *Weekly Times* (Victoria), 2 November 1918, 30.
75 Ivan de la Bere, *The Queen's Orders of Chivalry* (London: Spring Books, 1964), 157.

1921.[76] While noting that new honours are often greeted sceptically or viewed as less illustrious than older, more established distinctions, Galloway and others have tended to agree that the vast scale of the Order of the British Empire as compared to other British orders made it a particular target of such criticisms.[77] One side effect of this disdain for the Order of the British Empire was to raise the status of the Order of St Michael and St George. As Galloway put it:

> If one single event removed the phrase 'inferior colonial Order' from conversations about the Order of St Michael and St George, it was the creation of the Order of the British Empire.[78]

A peerage for Australia: Sir John Forrest

Australian scepticism about honours had—as discussed in previous chapters—long centred particularly upon titles, and still more so upon hereditary titles. In 1911, at the same time as proposing an Australian 'Order of the Wattle Blossom', William Sowden had asserted 'that Australians will never approve of the bestowal of hereditary distinctions'.[79] The whole idea, he thought, was 'essentially wrong and mischievous', for '[a] son has no more right to be titularly distinguished because of his father's eminent deeds than to be hanged because his father had committed murder'.[80] Despite this, Western Australian and then federal politician Sir John Forrest was created Australia's first native-born peer in 1918, when a barony of the United Kingdom was conferred on him 'in recognition of his long and distinguished services to the Empire'.[81] Seeking a title 'as free as possible from anything that might give rise to controversy', he took the name Lord Forrest of Bunbury, in the State of Western Australia, thus retaining his own surname, and choosing Bunbury as it was not only his birthplace and the home of his parents, but also his electorate during his time in State parliament.[82] The idea for the peerage had been floated several years before. Sir Gerald Strickland, the governor of Western

---

76   Galloway, *Order of the British Empire*, 19.
77   de la Bere, *Queen's Orders*, 156–57; Galloway, *Order of the British Empire*, 19, 38.
78   Galloway, *Order of St Michael and St George*, 204.
79   Will. J. Sowden, *An Australian Native's Standpoint: Addresses* (London: Macmillan, 1912), 114.
80   Sowden, *Australian Native's Standpoint*, 115.
81   NAA: A2923, H3, cablegram to [the Governor-General] from the Secretary of State for the Colonies, 6 February 1918.
82   NAA: A2923, H3, letter to Sir Ronald [Munro Ferguson], the Governor-General, from John Forrest, 10 February 1918.

Australia, had put forward the recommendation in 1909, and renewed it in 1913.[83] On the latter occasion it had failed to win the support of the governor-general, Lord Denman, who informed London that he had reached an understanding with Labor prime minister Andrew Fisher that he would not make nominations for hereditary titles, and who foresaw '[g]rave difficulties' in his relations with the federal government should he bring up the idea.[84]

The proposal had been renewed, however, in 1918. Early in January, the governor-general, by then Munro Ferguson, had cabled Long, the colonial secretary, suggesting that Forrest—the 'most outstanding figure in Australia and universally popular'—should receive a peerage. Prime Minister Hughes, he assured Long, supported the idea.[85] In a 'very strong personal recommendation ... accepting full responsibility' for the nomination, Munro Ferguson said, Hughes had stressed Forrest's achievements as an explorer and political leader, his part in the Federation movement, his exemplary private life, and his age and declining health, ending with his belief that the distinction would be well received in Australia.[86] This represented something of a change of heart. Only a few months before, Munro Ferguson had told Long of his desire to recommend Forrest for a peerage, lamenting that Hughes did not support it—a communication that led to confusion at the Colonial Office when the nomination arrived in January.[87] Wisely, Long requested the recommendation from Hughes, taking responsibility for it, before proceeding.[88]

83   NAA: A2922, NN, Honours 1909, despatch to the Earl of Crewe from G. Strickland, Governor [of Western Australia], 25 July 1909; NAA: A2922, NN, Honours 1913, despatch to Lewis Harcourt from G. Strickland, Governor [of Western Australia], 21 February 1913.
84   NAA: A2922, NN, Honours 1913, despatch to the Secretary of State for the Colonies from [Lord Denman], 2 April 1913.
85   NAA: A2923, H3, despatch to Secretary of State for the Colonies from R. M. Ferguson, 9 January 1918.
86   NAA: A2923, H3, despatch to Secretary of State [for the Colonies] from R. M. Ferguson, 15 January 1918.
87   NAA: A2923, H3, memorandum to the Secretary of State for the Colonies from R. M. Ferguson, 8 October 1917; NAA: A2923, H3, telegram to [R. M. Ferguson] from Long, Secretary of State [for the Colonies], 12 January 1918.
88   NAA: A2923, H3, telegram to [R. M. Ferguson] from Long, Secretary of State [for the Colonies], 12 January 1918. Indeed, Hughes must have changed his mind just before making the recommendation, since in a letter to Munro Ferguson on the 6th, he had stated that he thought that recommending Forrest for a peerage could be 'open to misconstruction' and should not go ahead. NAA: A2923, H22, letter to Governor-General from W. M. Hughes, 6 January 1918.

Reports of the honour highlighted its novelty, identifying Forrest as the first Australian elevated to the peerage. Many responses were positive, effusive in their praise for Forrest and surprisingly free of animosity to hereditary distinctions. More than 300 telegrams flooded the new Lord with congratulations. Among them were messages from the Western Australian Chamber of Mines, the editor of the *Bunbury Herald*, the Adelaide Stock Exchange, the United Commercial Travellers' Association of Australia, the mayor of Brisbane, the 88th Perth Infantry regiment, the Bunbury Harbour Board, the staff of the National Bank in Perth, the Royal Military College at Duntroon, and Fairbridge Farm School. Henry Lefroy, the Western Australian premier, sent:

> congratulations … on the distinguished honor of becoming [the] first Australian Peer—a distinction which all will recognise as a fitting tribute to the great and honourable services rendered to your country.

The president and members of the West Australian Chamber of Manufactures telegrammed '[h]earty congratulations', while the former mayor of Perth, Thomas Molloy, wrote that '[a]ll Western Australia will be delighted that your immense services to the Empire and Western Australia have been recognised'.[89]

Nevertheless, the public reaction was far from the 'unanimous approval' predicted by the *Brisbane Courier*, as the paper's own report made clear. While the Melbourne City Council passed a motion 'expressing gratification' at the barony, the New South Wales branch of the Australian Labor Party passed one stating that its executive 'strongly resents the attempt to establish an hereditary aristocracy in Australia' and 'considers it a direct affront to our democratic interests'. Articulating a hope that 'the first Australian lord will be the last', the motion suggested that 'the time has arrived when no title should be bestowed on any Australian citizen'. The Queensland Labor State treasurer, Ted Theodore, was also reported to have spoken 'in a condemnatory tone of privileged castes and old-world aristocracies'.[90] A little later in the year, the Australian Natives' Association would also register its displeasure. A letter from its general

---

89 NAA: A2923, H3, typescript of '… telegrams received by Lord Forrest congratulating him on the bestowal of the Peerage by His Majesty'.
90 'Australia's First Peer', *Brisbane Courier*, 11 February 1918, 6.

secretary informed Hughes that at its annual conference the association had passed a resolution stating that it 'strictly disapproves of the conferring of hereditary titles on Australian Citizens'.[91]

Press reactions were likewise mixed. Some, like the *Bunbury Herald*, were thrilled. No one was more worthy, declared that paper, certain that individuals of all political stripes would concur in that belief.[92] Others, like Melbourne's *Truth*, were not so pleased. Although shying away from criticising Forrest or his honour per se, *Truth* concluded that 'all true Australians' would look with 'distrust' on the conferral of hereditary titles in the antipodes.[93] In the Adelaide *Mail* there appeared a thoughtful piece by journalist and Hansard staffer—and compiler of *Johns's Notable Australians*, later to become *Who's Who in Australia*—Fred Johns, previously published in the *Public Service Review*. Blending approval for Forrest's award with displeasure at the arrival of peerages for Australians, Johns wrote:

> I don't know that a very large number of our people would welcome the planting of an hereditary aristocracy in the Commonwealth, but if they had been invited to nominate or elect an Australian to sit in the gilded Chamber at Westminster the popular vote would have been cast overwhelmingly in favour of [Forrest].[94]

Similarly, the Catholic *Freeman's Journal* deprecated the use of British titles, viewing them as detrimental to Australian independence and nationhood, but nevertheless considered that '[n]o one will begrudge Baron Forrest his new title, if it gives him pleasure'.[95] But not everyone was willing to temper their opposition of hereditary titles in the case of Forrest. Broken Hill's *Barrier Miner* thought Forrest not 'unworthy' of receiving a title, but vigorously critiqued the practice of inheriting distinctions as undemocratic. Forrest was an elderly man with no children for the title to descend to, but this made no difference to the writer, who observed that whether or not he had descendants was 'a matter of detail', for '[t]he principle is the same in either case, and even if Lord Forrest has no heirs

---

91   NAA: A2, 1918/2998, letter to the Prime Minister from the General Secretary of the Australian Natives' Association, [S. W. Griffith?], 17 September 1918.

92   'Lord Bunbury?' *Bunbury Herald*, 9 February 1918, 4.

93   'Oh, Lord!' *Truth* (Melbourne ed.), 16 February 1918, 7.

94   Fred Johns, 'Forrest of Bunbury', *Mail* (Adelaide), 2 March 1918, 3.

95   'In and Out of Parliament: Should Our Public Men Look for English Titles?' *Freeman's Journal* (Sydney), 14 February 1918, 23.

to-day he may have one to-morrow for all anyone can know'.[96] This was an unlikely scenario, given that he was then aged 70, and seriously ill; he would die only a few months later, before the letters patent creating him a peer had arrived from London.[97]

Conclusion

In 1918 the *Kalgoorlie Miner* opined that:

> the old idea—that only military and naval service or high political distinction should be recognised by 'handles' to names, and that only great territorial possessions or diplomatic standing justified a peerage—has been revolutionised since Edward VI. ascended the British throne.

'Titular distinctions', the paper said,

> have been democratised, by conferring them upon men of mark in all professions and walks of life—on poets, novelists, scientists, journalists, captains of commerce and industry, explorers and philanthropists, eminent financiers, and colonial Lord Mayors.

Not only that, but '[t]he war also has both increased and extended the area and scope of personal distinctions, and multiplied the reasons and causes why they should be conferred'.[98] Seen by some as the order of British democracy, the Order of the British Empire had indeed greatly widened the reach of the honours system, and increased the numbers of people who held distinctions, notwithstanding that it 'contained more rather than fewer hierarchical distinctions'.[99] From the beginning of discussions about a new order, it had been anticipated that it might be used after the war to remedy some of the inadequacies of the honours system, such as the lack of a general decoration that could be given for services to the arts and sciences, or to recognise charitable and philanthropic work, or to women.[100]

96   'Lord John Forrest, Baron', *Barrier Miner* (Broken Hill), 9 February 1918, 4.
97   F. K. Crowley, 'Forrest, Sir John (1847–1918)', *Australian Dictionary of Biography*, accessed 3 November 2015, adb.anu.edu.au/biography/forrest-sir-john-6211/text10677.
98   'Imperial Honours and the Dominions', *Kalgoorlie Miner*, 7 June 1918, 4.
99   See Harper, *Servants of the Empire*, 62–67, quote on 65.
100 See Galloway, *Order of the British Empire*, 2–6, 46.

Clarification of the nature the order would take in peacetime came with the gazetting of new statutes in 1922. Awards in the civil division, it was stated, would acknowledge 'prominent local or general services, whether of an official or unofficial character', while military appointments would reward both 'combatant or non-combatant duties', but would be restricted to 'commissioned officers'. The medal of the order would be given to those who were not eligible to be appointed to the order, but who had 'performed acts of gallantry, or have rendered such meritorious service as to deserve recognition'.[101] The Order of the Companions of Honour was also retained, transformed into an honour for recognising 'services of national importance'; it has come to be '[s]ometimes regarded as a junior class of the Order of Merit'.[102] If these measures were not a wholesale democratisation of Britain's honours system—as the graded nature of the Order of the British Empire and the existence of a medal for those deemed ineligible made clear—they nevertheless changed the honorific landscape in both Britain and its empire, making the receipt of such a distinction seem a plausible aspiration for many more people. Arguably the most transformative consequence, however, was that women gained a permanent place within the system. Beyond the mere fact of their presence, the inclusion of women would contribute to a change in the very nature of the system, as activities traditionally gendered feminine became services meriting official approbation. With the shadow of war passed, and a more inclusive future envisaged for it, it might have seemed that the prospects were bright for the honours system. For those with eyes to see, however, a new cloud of coming scandal lay on the horizon.

---

101 NAA: A12378, 21/A/3, memorandum, [1922?].
102 de la Bere, *Queen's Orders*, 170; The Royal Household, 'Companion of Honour', *The Royal Family*, accessed 13 October 2020, www.royal.uk/companion-honour.

4

Repugnant to the people? 1919–1939

'Honours. System of Award. Debate in Commons. Commission to be Appointed.' So ran a series of decreasing-in-size headlines above one article in the *Sydney Morning Herald* in July 1922. Hidden below this sober headline was a startling allegation. Two days before, during a debate on the awarding of honours in the British House of Lords, the Duke of Northumberland had read a letter purporting to 'offer … a knighthood or baronetcy' for the price of £12,000 or £35,000, respectively, and promising 'no nonsense of [the Order of the British Empire] kind', but something more prestigious.[1] Alarming as the claim was, what was yet more perturbing was the assertion that this was not an isolated case. Newspapers across Australia that year would tell the ignoble story of Britain's first cash-for-honours scandal. Such sordid transactions might have been long suspected by the system's most strident critics, but for its supporters, and for much of the Australian public, these revelations must have been shocking. Although the system had attracted its share of scepticism in the past, and although many observers had questioned the suitability of honours and titles to the egalitarian and democratic societies of the New World, the title of 'Sir' still held a solemn cachet to the ears of many. What did it mean to learn just how coldly it had been reduced to an item of commerce, and how undeserving were some of those who held it?

---

1   'Honours', *Sydney Morning Herald*, 19 July 1922, 11.

With the arrival of peace and the decision to maintain the Order of the British Empire on a permanent footing, it might have seemed a new dawn of democracy and inclusivity for Britain's honours system. But the horizon was already dark. Even before the war had ended, there was beginning to emerge an issue with the potential to change dramatically Australian opinions of imperial honours: the sale of titles for political purposes. In the postwar years, disquiet over this practice ballooned into outrage. The resulting scandal fuelled antagonism to the system in Australia and hardened the attitudes of those who already considered it an undemocratic and outdated institution. Tussles between State and federal authorities over the right to nominate took on yet another new dimension, as the Australian Labor Party solidified its opposition to imperial honours, beginning a long contest over the use of British awards that would last almost to the end of the century.

Yet intense though it was, the scandal was soon to fade, leaving the future of the system apparently secure again only a decade later. As the portents of war built up once more in Europe, the honours system entered something of a golden age in Australia: generally accepted and esteemed by nominees, awards were dispensed to a much broader cross-section of the community than ever before. The most dramatic transformation, however, was to the system's gender profile. Having gained admittance at least to some parts of it, women were at last beginning to see their contributions to society recognised alongside those of men. As feminist women in Australia and elsewhere developed the concept of the maternal citizen, the Australian state began officially to acknowledge and reward this newly conceived form of state service. Despite the pitfalls of conceptualising women's services to the nation in terms of their maternal role—which later feminists were quick to highlight—in these years such arguments provided a route for a new appreciation of women's work within the honours system. That ancient institution, it appeared, had begun to move towards a new future as an inclusive means of acknowledging the varied services of the nation's citizens.

Honours for sale

It had not always been considered immoral or corrupt to sell honours; in Britain in the seventeenth century they were openly sold as a way to raise revenue. By the mid-nineteenth century, selling or bartering distinctions had come to be considered inappropriate, but as early as the 1880s and 1890s standards had begun to slip once more, and the exchange of honours for party political services, support, or significant donations slowly became routine.[2] During the prime ministership of David Lloyd George from 1916 to 1922, the sale of honours peaked, as knighthoods and baronetcies were sold by touts in the clubs of London, gathering considerable sums of money for Lloyd George's political fund.[3] Under Lloyd George, the practice was both more open and more flagrant than in the past. As a later British prime minister, Harold Macmillan, was to observe, earlier bargains had been covered by 'a decent veil', and those who received their titles this way were at least individuals who had long served the party and were largely respected. During Lloyd George's administration, on the other hand, 'the system degenerated into something like an open sale', some recipients were distinctly disreputable, and the money raised went into a mysterious private fund controlled by Lloyd George himself.[4]

Such blatant abuses began to cause alarm. In 1917, the government in the House of Lords accepted a resolution urging that when an honour was bestowed a public statement of the reasons should be made, and that before recommending anyone, the prime minister ought to 'satisfy himself that no payment or expectation of payment to any Party or Political Fund is directly or indirectly associated with the grant or promise' of it.[5] The King had also become concerned at the number and character of nominees for honours, by Lloyd George's lack of consultation ahead of making promises of distinctions, and by the selling of what was supposed to be a royal prerogative.[6]

It was impossible that such a level of shady behaviour could continue without check. An investigation was demanded. The last straw was the list of June 1922, which included four questionable peerages, one of whom—Sir Joseph Robinson, whose business dealings had recently been condemned in the courts of South Africa and by the judicial

---

2   H. J. Hanham, 'The Sale of Honours in Late Victorian England', *Victorian Studies* 3, no. 3 (1960): 277, 280–88; T. A. Jenkins, 'The Funding of the Liberal Unionist Party and the Honours System', *English Historical Review* 105, no. 417 (1990): 920–28. doi.org/10.1093/ehr/CV.CCCCXVII.920.
3   Hanham, 'Sale of Honours', 289.
4   Harold Macmillan, *The Past Masters: Politics and Politicians 1906–1939* (London: Macmillan, 1975), 50–52, quotes on 50.
5   National Archives of Australia (hereafter NAA): A11804, 1923/285, Report of the Royal Commission on Honours (1922), 10. The resolution was also accepted in the House of Commons. NAA: A11804, 1923/285, Report of the Royal Commission on Honours (1922), 10.
6   Kenneth Rose, *King George V* (London: Weidenfeld and Nicolson, 1983), 247.

committee of the Privy Council—was effectively forced to decline the distinction.[7] In September a royal commission was appointed, not to investigate what had gone on in the past, but to propose new procedures for recommending honours that might prevent future misuse of the system. Reporting in December, the commissioners noted that their task had necessitated some examination of past practices, despite their instructions, and accordingly they had interviewed past and present prime ministers, patronage secretaries, and people 'responsible for the Party organisations', as well as receiving memoranda from 'the Departments of State charged with the duty of compiling lists' and exploring various other sources.[8] With many aspects of the system—including the process for receiving and finalising nominations from Australia—the commissioners found no fault.[9] Nor had they improvements to suggest in relation to the procedure for honouring individuals distinguished in literature, art, science, philanthropy, or charitable work, noting only an expectation that the prime minister would 'doubtless make enquiries as to what we may call the professional opinion of these cases and as to the general public repute of the persons concerned'.[10]

It was political honours that had brought the system into disrepute, and it was to reforming the processes for bestowing political honours that the commissioners devoted most of their report. Even the existence of such honours could be debated, as they acknowledged, but their proposals focused upon ensuring those that were conferred were not the result of corruption.[11] A fine line had to be walked: while it could not be a 'disqualification' for a person to have contributed to party funds, it was 'repugnant to honest feeling' that someone who was 'otherwise undeserving' should be honoured 'simply because he promised to contribute so much'.[12] In order to prevent such an outcome, the commissioners recommended the establishment of a small committee of privy councillors, who would be provided with information on the services of each proposed recipient and the background to the nomination, and who would then make enquiries, reporting any adverse finding to the prime minister; if the prime minister nevertheless submitted the name to the King, the committee's report

7 Rose, *King George V*, 250–52.
8 NAA: A11804, 1923/285, Report of the Royal Commission on Honours (1922), 4.
9 NAA: A11804, 1923/285, Report of the Royal Commission on Honours (1922), 5–7.
10 NAA: A11804, 1923/285, Report of the Royal Commission on Honours (1922), 7.
11 NAA: A11804, 1923/285, Report of the Royal Commission on Honours (1922), 7.
12 NAA: A11804, 1923/285, Report of the Royal Commission on Honours (1922), 9.

should accompany the recommendation.[13] Finally, the commissioners proposed legislation imposing penalties on any person either seeking an honour, or offering to procure one, in exchange for money or some other 'valuable consideration'.[14] After a change of government, the Political Honours Scrutiny Committee was formed in 1923, and the Honours (Prevention of Abuses) Act passed in 1925. In 1933 the notorious tout, Arthur Maundy Gregory, became the first person convicted under the Act.[15] Yet, as Tobias Harper has argued, this was not dramatic reform, but rather a reversion 'to pre-war mechanisms of patronage that defended against the excesses of Lloyd George's practices rather than creating a new system'.[16]

The unfolding scandal, and the resulting moves toward reform, were closely followed in the Australian press. Like the *West Australian*, most commentators deplored the degeneration of honours from 'the mark of the King's recognition of meritorious service to the nation' to 'a vulgar commodity to be offered in the market place to the highest bidder'.[17] Indeed, the impropriety of such practices appears to have been sufficiently taken for granted that few felt the need to remark on it. Adelaide's *Register* declared that '[t]he democratic conscience strongly revolts against the monstrous idea' of a person receiving a title or entering the House of Lords as a legislator through having donated to a political party.[18] For the *Daily Mail* in Brisbane, suspicion was likely to remain while honours lists continued to include awards given for party political services, and a 'plain citizen' might well consider that the whole institution needed amendment, while the *Northern Star*, in Lismore in New South Wales, proclaimed that 'the British race' would 'never countenance trafficking in honours, or the odious power that patronage confers'.[19] When the commission's report was issued, Perth's *Western Mail* greeted it with the comment that 'tightening up of the system … should meet with general endorsement',

---

13 NAA: A11804, 1923/285, Report of the Royal Commission on Honours (1922), 9–10.

14 NAA: A11804, 1923/285, Report of the Royal Commission on Honours (1922), 11.

15 See Andrew Cook, *Cash for Honours: The Story of Maundy Gregory* (Stroud: History Press, 2008); Tom Cullen, *Maundy Gregory: Purveyor of Honours* (London: Bodley Head, 1974).

16 Tobias Harper, *From Servants of the Empire to Everyday Heroes: The British Honours System in the Twentieth Century* (Oxford: Oxford University Press, 2020), 58. doi.org/10.1093/oso/9780198841180. 001.0001.

17 'Titles of Honour', *West Australian* (Perth), 20 July 1922, 6.

18 'Titular Honours', *Register* (Adelaide), 19 July 1922, 6.

19 'Spurs, Won or Gilded', *Daily Mail* (Brisbane), 1 July 1922, 6; 'Honours and Titles', *Northern Star* (Lismore), 11 September 1922, 4.

except from those who might have wished to take advantage of the previous arrangements, and suggested that people deserved 'to know why a fellow citizen is raised above them in rank'.[20]

Supporters of honours might have advocated reform, but convinced sceptics needed no fuel to add to their fire. As in previous decades, outbursts against the whole idea of titles and honours continued to appear in the pages of newspapers around the country. Describing those who had received titles in Australia as 'a somewhat motley crew', Melbourne's *Herald* believed that '[m]ost sensible folk look upon the system of local knighthoods as ridiculous', thought it heightened 'snobbery and class difference', and wanted it abolished. Knighthood, the writer asserted, was '[u]nlike rabbits, sparrows, and prickly pear'—a rather unfortunate set of examples—in that it could not be 'acclimatised' in Australia.[21] For the Catholic *Freeman's Journal*, British titles were both out of place 'in a country which is endeavouring to combat snobbery and old-world class distinctions', and unpatriotic, in that they were bestowed by another government 'thousands of miles across the seas'. If 'public-spirited citizens' were to be rewarded, the writer suggested a home-grown 'Legion of Hono,r [sic]'.[22] Such views were, as in the past, sometimes strongly expressed in the radical and labour press. The Brisbane *Worker* thought 'hankering after tin-pot "honors" ... a peculiarity of the subservient Tory mind', while militant socialist Percy Brookfield, a member of the New South Wales Legislative Assembly, made sneering reference in the *Australian Worker* to 'knighthoods or some other bauble which denotes ignorance and stupidity'.[23]

The end of imperial honours?

Whether or not opinions were changed by the scandal, it is surely not a coincidence that in its wake serious efforts were made to abolish titles and honours in several of the dominions. The constitution of the Irish

---

20 'Honours and Titles', *Western Mail* (Perth), 4 January 1923, 28.
21 NAA: A6661, 78, 'Aristocracy—Real and Unreal', *Herald* (Melbourne), 12 September 1925; 'Autocracy—Real and Unreal', *Weekly Times* (Melbourne), 19 September 1925, 48.
22 'Titles and Democracy', *Freeman's Journal* (Sydney), 12 May 1927, 24. See also 'English Honors for Australians', *Freeman's Journal* (Sydney), 5 January 1928, 22; 'Australian Honors for Australians', *Catholic Freeman's Journal* (Sydney), 12 May 1938, 24.
23 '"Honors": Have Australians Any Pride?' *Worker* (Brisbane), 12 January 1927, 6; P. Brookfield, 'The Prince's Visit', *Australian Worker* (Sydney), 6 May 1920, 19.

Free State, enacted in 1922, declared in its fifth article that titles of honour could not be bestowed upon its citizens 'except with the approval or upon the advice of the Executive Council of the State'.[24] In South Africa the same year, former Senate president Francis Reitz put a motion in that house that, in light of the revelations in the United Kingdom, the government should not recommend or permit titles 'bestowed from outside the Union on the citizens of this dominion'.[25] Although the motion was defeated, imperial honours were not to survive much longer in South Africa. In December 1924 it was reported in Australia that the South African prime minister, General Barry Hertzog, had refused to put forward nominations for the New Year honours list, as he considered titles—besides academic ones or awards given for civil servants for their services to the state—to be 'in conflict with the spirit of the people in South Africa' and with his party's principles.[26] The following year, the House of Assembly adopted a motion that the King be asked not to confer titles on residents of South Africa.[27]

In Canada too the disclosures may have hastened the end of recommendations for British honours. As early as 1918 the Canadian parliament had begun discussing the possibility of banning hereditary titles, at the least. Poor choices of recipients, along with the honours-selling scandal in Britain, had brought the system into disrepute, and it had become, as Christopher McCreery noted in his history of honours in Canada, 'identified with eastern domination, party corruption, out-of-date habits of deference, and a servile relationship with [Britain]'.[28] William Folger Nickle, a Conservative parliamentarian from Ontario, was the immediate driver of change. In 1918, he introduced into the House of Commons a resolution asking the King to confer no more hereditary titles upon Canadians, and no honours that could be used by someone other than the person receiving them. This latter part of the resolution was intended to prevent women receiving the title of 'Lady' when their husbands were knighted.[29] Following the adoption of an amended

---

24 'Constitution of the Irish Free State (Saorstát Eireann) Act, 1922', *Electronic Irish Statute Book*, Government of Ireland, accessed 30 September 2016, www.irishstatutebook.ie/eli/1922/act/1/enacted/en/print.html.
25 'Titles or Honours', *Sydney Morning Herald*, 17 July 1922, 9.
26 'South African Titles', *Sydney Morning Herald*, 17 December 1924, 15.
27 'Titular Honours', *Sydney Morning Herald*, 26 February 1925, 9; 'Opposition to Titles', *Argus* (Melbourne), 28 February 1925, 33.
28 Peter Galloway, *The Order of the Bath* (Chichester: Phillimore, 2006), 328–29; Christopher McCreery, *The Order of Canada: Its Origins, History, and Development* (Toronto: University of Toronto Press, 2005), 24–48, quote on 24. doi.org/10.3138/9781442627963.
29 Canada, House of Commons, *Debates*, 8 April 1918 (W. F. Nickle).

resolution, a Special Committee on Honours and Titles was established, which recommended the ending of all civilian honours. The House passed a motion of concurrence with the committee's report in 1919, causing the relatively limited Nickle resolution to effectively become a ban on imperial honours.[30]

Australian voices were also raised against British honours, particularly titles. In April 1925 a letter from the Australian Natives Association (ANA) to the governor-general, Henry Forster, advised that at its annual conference the ANA had passed a resolution against titles. The resolution requested that the prime minister would inform the imperial government 'that titles of any description are repugnant to the Australian people', and the letter sought Forster's assistance in ensuring 'that the spirit of the resolution is carried into effect'.[31] The next year, the association's federal council unanimously passed a resolution approving of the ending of titles in New South Wales, and hoping that they would soon be abolished across the country.[32]

Although a little late in coming, the ANA's resolution likely referred to a surprise success enjoyed by the Labor Party in the New South Wales Legislative Assembly in 1923. In September that year, Labor parliamentarian George Cann had sought to have a motion conveyed to the King stating that conferring titles was 'contrary to the sentiment of the citizens' of the State. He noted that Canada had already passed a similar resolution, discussed the report of the British royal commission, and pronounced titles 'a confounded nuisance as far as our parliamentary institutions are concerned'.[33] After an oration that became rather sidetracked into the rights and wrongs of titles and postnominals of all

---

30 McCreery, *Order of Canada*, 24, 34–37. Although no legislation prevented future governments recommending Canadians for imperial honours, no such recommendations were made until 1933. This change in practice followed the election in 1930 of a Conservative government led by Richard Bedford Bennett, who made recommendations for British honours to be conferred on a variety of people, including for charitable and philanthropic work, and for artistic and scientific activity, until the end of his prime ministership in 1935. McCreery, *Order of Canada*, 51–56. After this, apart from the award of lower-level British honours during World War II and the Korean War, Canada reverted to its former opposition to imperial honours, and remained effectively without an official honours system until the 1960s.
31 NAA: A6661, 78, letter to H. W. Forster from [unreadable signature], General Manager of the Australian Natives Association Ltd, 28 April 1925.
32 'A.N.A. Federal Council', *Argus* (Melbourne), 30 April 1926, 8.
33 New South Wales, Legislative Assembly, *Parliamentary Debates*, 25 September 1923 (George Cann).

kinds (among them military ranks, university degrees, and clergy titles), and speeches in support from Nationalist member Hyman Goldstein and Labor member Mark Gosling, the motion was passed by 39 votes to 24.[34]

As Labor was not then in power—the Nationalist Government was led by Sir George Fuller, himself a KCMG (Knight Commander of the Order of St Michael and St George)—the motion had required the support of the government's coalition partner, the Progressives (soon to be called the Country Party), as well as that of one independent member and two Nationalists. Their willingness to cross the floor on the issue underlines the extent of public outrage caused by the revelations in Britain. Indeed, in his speech Goldstein had adverted to the royal commission's findings, stating that the report 'contained some scathing remarks' and arguing that it demonstrated the need for 'the greatest care' in making recommendations for honours. If that were lacking, he continued, 'the sooner we do away with the principle of recommending Australian citizens for honors at the hands of the King the better it will be for democracy'. Going further, he implied that 'mysterious influences' had been at work in some awards made in New South Wales in the past, leading to unworthy individuals being nominated, and argued that:

> in view of the strong suspicion that surrounds the whole business it would be advisable to pass a motion of this kind and to safeguard ourselves against any further cause for scandal.

Had previous recommendations been unimpeachable, he asserted, he would have opposed the motion, but as he did not believe they had been, he supported it.[35]

The following year the issue was taken up in the South Australian parliament. Labor Attorney-General William Denny introduced a bill to end the granting of titles to South Australians except where a resolution to recommend a particular person was passed by both the Legislative Assembly and the Legislative Council.[36] Speaking to the bill, he stated that the granting of titles was 'no longer regarded as a reward for merit, or

---

34 New South Wales, Legislative Assembly, *Parliamentary Debates*, 25 September 1923 (George Cann, Hyman Goldstein, and Mark Gosling). Although not apparently proposed or carried in the Legislative Council, the resolution was accordingly laid before the King, as the speaker of the house reported almost a year later. New South Wales, Legislative Assembly, *Parliamentary Debates*, 1 July 1924.
35 New South Wales, Legislative Assembly, *Parliamentary Debates*, 25 September 1923 (Hyman Goldstein).
36 South Australia, Legislative Assembly, *Parliamentary Debates*, 24 July 1924, 26 August 1924, and 4 September 1924.

distinction, or real public service'. He canvassed the discreditable history of titles in the United Kingdom, including the recent disclosures; Canada's decision to resolve against them; the motion adopted in New South Wales; and the preponderance of wealthy men among those honoured, concluding that the bill would ensure 'that our democratic institution can no longer be sullied by methods [that] merely aggrandise wealth, and gives a false outlook on what constitutes real public work and effort'. Although himself 'utterly opposed' to titles, the bill sought not to abolish them entirely but 'to provide that they shall be sparingly and fittingly awarded'.[37]

Attacking the legislation, the leader of the Opposition, Sir Henry Barwell, focused first upon the question of whether the sovereign's prerogative regarding honours could be limited in such a way. Soon, however, he turned to the issue of empire loyalty. The bill was 'anti-Imperialistic in design', falling in 'the same category' as

> the abolition of State Governors, the doing away with the observance of Empire Day, and the cutting out of our school history books all reference to those glorious deeds of arms on sea and land which have made England respected among the nations of the world, and helped to build up our Empire to what it is to-day.[38]

Perhaps anticipating this line of assault, Denny had in his own address asserted that it was 'merely puerile to say that the Bill emanates from a party which is not anxious about the Imperial connection', and that throughout his political life he had 'been an enthusiastic advocate for the maintenance of the bond of Empire between Great Britain and Australia'.[39] Finally, Barwell took issue with the whole premise of the bill. There had been no public demand for it, he said, and no suggestion that the process of recommendations had been abused in South Australia. He questioned what he considered the socialist premise that 'differences and distinctions' between people were in themselves an evil, and Denny's integrity in proposing the measure, given that he himself held the title 'Honorable'.[40] Meanwhile, Labor member Henry Kneebone expressed his support for the bill, his 'only complaint' being that it did 'not go quite far enough'. He wished not only to abolish titles entirely, but to 'make it

---

37   South Australia, Legislative Assembly, *Parliamentary Debates*, 4 September 1924 (William Denny).
38   South Australia, Legislative Assembly, *Parliamentary Debates*, 17 September 1924 (Sir Henry Barwell).
39   South Australia, Legislative Assembly, *Parliamentary Debates*, 4 September 1924 (William Denny).
40   South Australia, Legislative Assembly, *Parliamentary Debates*, 17 September 1924 (Sir Henry Barwell).

retrospective to the landing of Captain Cook'. Among his reasons was what he perceived to be the democratic nature of Australian society. 'Even if honors were properly distributed,' he asserted, 'it would perpetuate and encourage in the community a class distinction' that could not be tolerated in a 'young country' with 'a democratic constitution.'[41] Passed by the Legislative Assembly, the bill was defeated in the Legislative Council.[42]

A year later, the matter was debated in the federal House of Representatives. Charles McGrath, the Labor member for Ballarat, moved that conferring titles was 'contrary to the sentiments of the citizens of Australia', and that a resolution to that effect should be conveyed to the King. Noting that Labor held power in five States, and that two of those governments had passed resolutions against titles, McGrath suggested the other three would soon follow suit. In a comparison that would become familiar, he pointed to Canada and South Africa, both of which had decided to stop conferring titles, asserting that '[t]heir attitude is easily understood'. There had been sufficient corruption that titles were no longer honours at all, he said, and Australians did not want such corruption in their political life.[43] On this occasion the debate was adjourned before the motion could be voted on.[44] McGrath tried again in 1926 and in 1927, at which time the motion came to a vote and was defeated. Responding to the motion in 1926, Nationalist Prime Minister Stanley Bruce declared that McGrath's arguments provided a case against the misuse of titles, but not against their conferral per se.[45]

Some support was voiced in the press for these legislative attempts to discontinue the use of titular honours in Australia. Melbourne's *Age* approved of McGrath's motion in 1926, commenting that:

> If certain Governments and citizens combine in the absurd incongruity of perpetuating titles in this democratic country, they must not be surprised if the Australian people begin to express themselves frankly, even brutally.

---

41   South Australia, Legislative Assembly, *Parliamentary Debates*, 17 September 1924 (Henry Kneebone).

42   South Australia, Legislative Assembly, *Parliamentary Debates*, 25 September 1924; South Australia, Legislative Council, *Parliamentary Debates*, 2 October 1924.

43   Commonwealth of Australia, House of Representatives, *Parliamentary Debates*, 9 July 1925 (Charles McGrath).

44   Commonwealth of Australia, House of Representatives, *Parliamentary Debates*, 13 August 1925.

45   Commonwealth of Australia, House of Representatives, *Parliamentary Debates*, 29 July 1926 (Charles McGrath, Stanley Bruce); Commonwealth of Australia, House of Representatives, *Parliamentary Debates*, 13 October 1927.

The only people who supported the continuation of the system, the paper claimed, were 'those groups of tuft hunters that infest every community', and it hoped that soon 'all Australian Parliaments will petition [against titles] in unison'.[46] On the other hand, the *Sydney Morning Herald*, writing of Cann's 1923 motion, held that poor choices of recipients and misuse of the system not were reasons to abolish it altogether, and that there was an 'inverted snobbery' in the stance of those who purported to despise titles. The paper doubted that conferring titles went against the sentiments of the people of New South Wales, who might 'not set inordinate store' in them, but who were 'pleased' when a deserving member of the community received recognition.[47] Just how close did Australia come to following the example of Canada and South Africa and banning imperial honours and titles in the 1920s? Although largely failed, these were serious attempts to abolish the system in Australia, and as the example of New South Wales in particular demonstrates, there was sufficient support among the nation's politicians, fuelled by the revelations from Britain, that success was not impossible. It is not too much to say that in these years Australia came closer to banning the imperial honours system than would be the case for another half century.

Honours and the ALP

By this time, as discussed in the previous chapter, the Australian Labor Party (ALP) had begun to take a policy stance against British honours. Ending recommendations for imperial honours had been part of the party's federal platform since as early as 1918.[48] Over the following years, similar resolutions were occasionally passed at ALP conferences. In 1921, for example, the interstate conference carried a resolution calling for '[c]omplete Australian self-government'; among several aspects, it included that 'no further Imperial honours … be granted in any circumstances to Australian citizens'.[49] Reports in May 1930 stated that the federal conference had agreed to a motion '[t]hat the bestowal of all Imperial honours should be

---

46   *Age* (Melbourne), 30 July 1926, 8.
47   'Titles', *Sydney Morning Herald*, 29 September 1923, 14.
48   Review of Australian Honours and Awards, *A Matter of Honour: The Report of the Review of Australian Honours and Awards* (Canberra: Australian Government Publishing Service, 1995), 13; Ernest Alexander Lyall, 'Government Patronage in Australia: The Exercise of the Patronage Prerogative by Commonwealth and New South Wales Governments in the Period 1927–1969' (Master's thesis, The Australian National University, 1969), 194.
49   'A.L.P. Congress', *Sydney Morning Herald*, 17 October 1921, 9.

abolished through Parliamentary action'.[50] Opposition to British honours and titles was a product of the dominant interpretation within the party of its ideals of democracy and egalitarianism, which titular awards were seen to compromise, and of its nationalist orientation, according to which imperial distinctions were viewed as likely to inhibit the independence of Australian politicians in any instance of conflict between British Government objectives and Australian interests.

Labor governments, therefore, generally refused to participate in the imperial honours system. Among the copies of lists of recommendations from the State governors now held in the National Archives of Australia are numerous despatches informing the governor-general that no nominations would be forthcoming from a particular State.[51] Likewise, James Scullin's federal Labor Government declined to make any recommendations during its tenure.[52] In 1930, in response to a suggestion that aviator Charles Kingsford Smith should receive an honour, the Returned Sailors' and Soldiers' Imperial League of Australia (RSSILA) in New South Wales was told that 'the general policy of the Government is not to make recommendations', and that an exception would not be made for Kingsford Smith.[53] Unfortunately for Kingsford Smith, Labor was also in power in New South Wales. The RSSILA State executive was thus no more successful in seeking to have him knighted through the State list, with the premier, Jack Lang, refusing to make the recommendation because it was contrary to Labor policy. Moreover, Lang was reported to have said, since Kingsford Smith's achievements were international in nature, it would be more appropriate that he be honoured by the federal government.[54] Kingsford Smith did eventually get his knighthood, through the nomination of Joseph Lyons's United Australia Party Government, in June 1932.[55]

This anti-honours stance was by no means consistent across the country, however. Titles were generally viewed with greater hostility than were other awards, and Labor administrations sometimes took a more lenient

50   'Federal A.L.P.', *Sydney Morning Herald*, 31 May 1930, 15.
51   See NAA: A2924; NAA: A2925.
52   NAA: A2924, 1931/2, letter to Sir Isaac A. Isaacs, Governor-General, from J. A. Scullin, Prime Minister, 11 March 1931.
53   NAA: A1606, A22/1, letter to W. J. Stagg, State Secretary, Returned Sailors' and Soldiers' Imperial League of Australia, from J. E. Fenton, Acting Prime Minister, 25 November 1930.
54   'No Knighthood for Kingsford Smith', *Canberra Times*, 10 January 1931, 1.
55   NAA: A2924, 1932/6.

stance towards non-titular honours than titular ones. Ahead of a visit by the Duke of Gloucester in 1934, Queensland's deputy premier, Percy Pease, stated that the Labor Government would 'not express itself against' the award of honours that did not confer titles, and that it was likely that such distinctions would go to 'one or two leading citizens, and those most closely connected with' the arranging of the tour. This, said Pease, was the same approach as had been adopted for previous royal visits.[56] Hereditary distinctions, on the other hand, were the subject of still fiercer disapproval. In 1920 New South Wales Labor premier John Storey cancelled a recommendation made by his predecessor, William Holman, that Sir George Fuller be made a baronet, on the grounds that Australian attitudes were opposed to hereditary honours. While permitting Holman's other nominations—which included knighthoods—to proceed, in a departure from the usual standards of confidentiality he also revealed the names of individuals who had been recommended. Explaining his action, he said he had done so to make sure it would be known, if the distinctions were granted, that his government was not responsible for them.[57]

On rare occasions, too, Labor governments did nominate for titular honours. The New Year honours list in January 1925, for example, featured the businessman Alfred Ashbolt, agent-general for Tasmania in London from 1919 to 1924, who had been recommended by Joseph Lyons's Labor ministry in Tasmania.[58] 'That Tasmania should get a knighthood', crowed the Hobart *Mercury*, when it had a Labor Government, 'is a feather in our cap calculated to turn some of the Mainland sisters green with envy of Cinderella'.[59] Similarly, in 1932 the list included two knighthoods recommended by the Labor Government in South Australia. Walter Young, the managing director of Elder, Smith and Co. Ltd, who had been financial adviser to the government, was appointed KBE (Knight Commander of the Order of the British Empire), and William Goodman, the chief engineer and general manager of the Municipal Tramways Trust for 25 years, was created knight bachelor. Premier Lionel Hill was quoted in Adelaide's *Advertiser* explaining that '[p]olitics do not enter into the question of recognising distinguished public services', and that while his

---

56 'Labour Ban on Titles', *Courier-Mail* (Brisbane), 31 October 1934, 14.
57 'No Hereditary Honours', *Sydney Morning Herald*, 28 April 1920, 11; 'Honour List', *Sydney Morning Herald*, 30 April 1920, 8; 'In the Mother State', *Register* (Adelaide), 30 April 1920, 8.
58 NAA: A2925, 1925/2; NAA: A2925, 1925/4.
59 'The New Year Honours', *Mercury* (Hobart), 2 January 1925, 4.

government disapproved of 'the indiscriminate awarding of honors', they were nevertheless 'the only method available when it desires to show its appreciation of outstanding national work'.[60]

Outside Labor ranks, criticisms of the party's policy were frequent. Conservative politicians and commentators valued imperial honours and asserted that there was nothing wrong with awards given to recognise merit. Responding to McGrath's motion in the House of Representatives in 1926, for example, Bruce thought it good to be able to recognise public service in all fields of endeavour, and believed that most Australians would agree.[61] Likewise, honours were for the *Sydney Morning Herald* 'Royal recognition … for public service', and not at all 'undemocratic', since they conferred 'no special privileges' that would set recipients apart from their fellow citizens.[62] Supporters of British honours sometimes also put forth the old argument that the system was a way of binding the empire together, and a means of increasing loyalty to both monarch and empire. In the words of South Australian Liberal Thomas Pascoe in 1925, honours were

> one of the things that bring this great Commonwealth of nations in closer touch with the Sovereign, and help to keep the dominions loyal to the Empire and to the throne itself.[63]

Another common criticism of the ALP's stance was that the opinion of Labor parliamentarians, however sincerely held, should not be imposed upon everyone, no matter their own political persuasion. As one observer put it, Labor members' personal opposition to imperial honours was 'no reason why they should act like the foxes in the fable who cut off their tails and sought to dock others in a similar manner'. Australia was a member of the British empire, flying 'the British flag', and the residents of one State should not be excluded from 'the privileges enjoyed by other subjects of the King'.[64] As this last remark suggests, dismay at Labor prohibitions on honours was also provoked by the observation that a particular State— or in the case of federal Labor governments, Commonwealth politicians and civil servants—was missing out on rewards available elsewhere in the country. The *Brisbane Courier* asserted in 1933, for example,

---

60   'Knighthoods for Two South Australians', *Advertiser* (Adelaide), 1 January 1932, 7.
61   Commonwealth of Australia, House of Representatives, *Parliamentary Debates*, 29 July 1926 (Stanley Bruce).
62   'Birthday Honours', *Sydney Morning Herald*, 24 June 1936, 14.
63   South Australia, Legislative Council, *Parliamentary Debates*, 29 July 1925 (Thomas Pascoe).
64   NAA: A6661, 78, 'Choking the Fountain of Honor', unattributed press cutting, 4 June 1925.

that Queensland Labor's anti-honours stance was 'a mistake, especially where Australians in other States are being remembered for services not greater than those rendered by persons in Queensland'.[65] Finally, Labor politicians' use of the title 'Honourable', and their willingness to accept privy councillorships, with the attendant title of 'Right Honourable', drew the ire of critics. It was 'a case of political hypocrisy', suggested one letter writer in the Adelaide *Advertiser* in 1925.[66]

The case of David Gordon, 1925

Labor opposition to honours also added a new dimension to the old arguments over States' rights. The case of David Gordon provides a good example. Gordon, the leader of the Liberal Party in the South Australian Legislative Council and a former federal member of parliament, was knighted in the New Year list for 1925. Reports that the State's Labor Government was displeased by the honour quickly began to appear around the country. The day the knighthood was announced, the *Advertiser* quoted the South Australian attorney-general, William Denny, stating that for the federal government to nominate a citizen of South Australia for an imperial honour when the State government had itself refused to make recommendations—and, indeed, passed a bill against making them without the approval of both houses—raised a 'far-reaching constitutional question'. Before the announcement of Gordon's knighthood, Denny said, the federal government had notified the South Australian Government that it would not allow itself to be limited in its ability to confer honours on South Australians. His reply had been that if recommendations were made by the federal government, the State government might pass a resolution 'disapproving of a particular nomination'. The problem, as he saw it, was that the federal government 'intend to ignore the rights of the State Government in such matters, although it is claimed that South Australia is a sovereign State'. Denny also suggested that if a person held an honour 'obviously disapproved of by the majority of the people of the State', he or she 'must realise that he [or she] is placed in a very invidious position'.[67] The latter point evidently did not concern Gordon, who accepted the knighthood.

65 'New Year Honours', *Brisbane Courier*, 2 January 1933, 8.
66 'Anti-Humbug', letter to the editor, *Advertiser* (Adelaide), 3 January 1925, 11.
67 'The Conferring of Honors', *Advertiser* (Adelaide), 1 January 1925, 7.

Nor did it convince the *Advertiser*, which took the view that 'general satisfaction' would be the public reaction to Gordon's knighthood.[68] In an editorial, the paper stated that the knighthood was 'a well-merited recognition of distinguished service … both to the Commonwealth and the State'. It was 'to be regretted', the writer opined, that Denny 'should take the ungracious course of entering a protest, on alleged constitutional grounds'. Somewhat caustically, the paper pointed out that the bill to which Denny referred had been rejected by the upper house, and that ALP policy could not restrict the sovereign's honours prerogative or the federal government's ability to recommend Australians.[69] The federal government was likewise unconcerned. As the *Sydney Morning Herald* put it a few days later, federal ministers were 'not perturbed' that Labor in South Australia had 'taken exception to' the recommendation. A federal minister was quoted stating that where the federal government had chosen to nominate 'a distinguished citizen of the Commonwealth' who had 'rendered such service as to merit recognition', it was 'merely impertinence for exception to be taken by a State Ministry'.[70] British official opinion was also reported to be that the Commonwealth Government could recommend any Australian for an honour, regardless of their place of residence, and that '[i]t would be extraordinary' if a State government could veto a recommendation.[71]

Nevertheless, the issue lingered. Denny responded to the comments of the Colonial Office, asserting that while the State government and the federal government each had the right to make recommendations, and no right to veto those of the other, his objection concerned

> [the] propriety of the Commonwealth Government in making a recommendation that was turned down by the State Government, and in the face of a Bill which passed the House of Assembly by an overwhelming majority with the object of preventing such appointments in the future.

He asserted that the State government was '[s]urely … the best judge of which of its citizens, if any, should receive distinction', and he questioned what services Gordon had given to deserve the honour, having been a member of the Commonwealth Parliament for only a short time. Denny's

---

68 'New Year Honors', *Advertiser* (Adelaide), 1 January 1925, 7.
69 'Sir David Gordon', *Advertiser* (Adelaide), 1 January 1925, 6.
70 'Honours', *Sydney Morning Herald*, 6 January 1925, 8.
71 'South Australian Knighthood', *Sunday Times* (Perth), 4 January 1925, 1.

suggestion was that this had been 'a purely party recommendation', made to reward Gordon's efforts as leader of the opposition in the State's Legislative Council, where he had helped ensure bills passed in the House of Assembly were rejected; he suggested that the State parliament should start recommending members of the federal opposition for such honours.[72] On the other hand, the *Advertiser* suggested that Denny's and the government's opposition to Gordon being knighted had itself been motivated by party politics, Gordon being the leader of the Liberal Party in the Legislative Council; no complaint, the paper pointed out, was made about the fact that Archibald Strong, the Jury professor of English language and literature at the University of Adelaide, had also recently been knighted.[73]

David Gordon's elevation to the knightage was not to be the last time the ALP's stance on imperial honours led to friction between the States and the federal government. As was clear in that case, a State Labor government could be thwarted in its desire not to bestow awards on its residents by a conservative federal ministry, or vice versa. In 1936, Western Australia's Labor premier, Philip Collier, was reported to have expressed 'surprise' that the recent New Year list had included three Western Australian appointments to the Order of the British Empire. He argued that since the end of World War I it had been the custom for the federal government to consult with State governments when making nominations, stating his strong disapproval that this had not been done, and arguing that it was the State government that was best able to judge the services of its residents. Recommendations should not be made by the federal government in 'secrecy', he asserted.[74] In this case, the honours in question were not titular. Rather, three women—Emily Abel, Catherine Elliott, and Bessie Hubbard—had been appointed MBE (Members of the Order of the British Empire).[75] Although a relatively minor matter among the constellation of irritations that were to cause tension between State and federal governments over the coming decades, honours were

---

72 'A Party Recommendation', *Register* (Adelaide), 5 January 1925, 10.

73 'The Granting of Titles', *Advertiser* (Adelaide), 27 July 1925, 8.

74 'New Year Honours', *West Australian* (Perth), 4 January 1936, 14.

75 'New Year Honours', *Argus* (Melbourne), 6 January 1936, 8. Each of the three had been engaged in charitable or social welfare work: Abel was honoured as secretary of the State division of the Red Cross, Elliott for her work in infant and maternal welfare, and Hubbard for her services to social welfare. Australian Government, Department of the Prime Minister and Cabinet, 'Australian Honours Search Facility', *It's an Honour*, Department of the Prime Minister and Cabinet, accessed 13 June 2021, honours.pmc.gov.au/honours/awards/1087458; honours.pmc.gov.au/honours/awards/1085136; honours.pmc.gov.au/honours/awards/1084339.

always a possible source of friction. The hardening of Labor opposition to British awards, combined with the continued support for those awards by non-Labor governments, and the nature of the country's federal system, ensured it.

'A tribute to the women of Australia'

The honours granted to these three Western Australian women elicited a protest over the respective powers of the State and federal governments, but in England during the interwar years it was the lack of female recipients that provoked dismay.[76] Women's poor treatment in honours lists was a grievance of the Women's Freedom League, and their complaints on the subject in Britain were regularly reported in Australian newspapers. In 1924 the league wrote to Stanley Baldwin, the prime minister, objecting to the exclusion of women from the New Year list. Women's services should be recognised equally with men's, the letter argued.[77] Reports in 1930 revealed that the league had written again to the prime minister, then Ramsay MacDonald, expressing disappointment that Amy Johnson had received only 'so inadequate and inappropriate' a reward as a CBE (Commander of the Order of the British Empire) for her solo flight that year from England to Australia. A CBE might be appropriate for 'the secretary of the Northumberland Miners' Association or the honorary technical adviser to an area gas supply committee of the Board of Trade', but the organisation declared it far too lowly an award for such a feat. Honours lists did not include enough women, in the group's opinion, and did not recognise the extent of women's services to the nation.[78] Four years later the league was reported to have protested the omission of women from the higher levels of the Order of the British Empire. '[E]ven for a lifetime's political or public services', the league was quoted as saying, women were 'fobbed off' with OBEs and MBEs (respectively, officers and members of the order), while men were given 'peerages, Privy Councillorships, baronetcies, and knighthoods'.[79]

---

76 On feminist critiques of women's treatment in the honours system in Britain, see also Harper, *Servants of the Empire*, 81–82.

77 'Women an [sic] Honours', *Register* (Adelaide), 5 January 1924, 10.

78 '"Unsuitable Honor"', *News* (Adelaide), 4 June 1930, 1; 'Amy's Honor', *Evening News* (Sydney), 4 June 1930, 9.

79 'Honours for Women', *Argus* (Melbourne), 3 January 1934, 7.

Published two days after the New Year list had been announced, this report attracted some editorial comment in Australia, not all of it supportive. More information would be required to determine whether or not women had been treated fairly in the list, asserted the *Argus*. Perhaps there had been no woman deserving appointment to the order's upper levels this time. In any case, the writer argued, women had received such high honours in the past, and a whole new order with provision for women's inclusion had been created as a recognition of their war service. Women may receive fewer honours than men, but they had fewer opportunities to perform public services, and the honours system was not always just to men either. At least it should be a comfort that those women who had been honoured had been truly deserving of the distinctions they had received. Complete equality between men and women in all arenas of life, the writer concluded, would take time, if it was even to be desired, and after all, '[n]o victory worth having is easily won'.[80] On the other hand, 'Hestia' in Hobart's *Mercury* 'sympathise[d] heartily' with the Women's Freedom League. As well as the case of Amy Johnson, she declared, there were

> other works for the welfare of humanity, long years spent in self-denying humanitarian work … which, in comparison with some deeds and contributions of men for which high titles are given, are as a glorious star to a penny dip.[81]

Across the continent in Perth, 'Ixia'—the pen name of author, artist, and botanist Emily Pelloe—responded to the protest in the 'Woman's Interests' section of the *West Australian*.[82] Having noted several Australian women who had been appointed to the order, Pelloe suggested that the women in England 'clamouring for woman's advancement' did not realise 'how great an honour is the despised O.B.E. or M.B.E. awarded for actual individual merit', the implicit contrast being with the courtesy titles accorded the wives and children of peers and knights, or perhaps some of the less well deserved of the accolades bestowed upon men. Nevertheless, while true worth did not require honours, and she could not 'wish for a multiplicity of Dames in the Commonwealth', more numerous conferrals of the title, where merited, 'would be welcomed as evidence of royal appreciation for the part Australian women undoubtedly play in building up and

---

80   'Women's Rights—and Wrongs', *Argus* (Melbourne), 4 January 1934, 6.
81   'Hestia', 'A Woman to Women', *Mercury* (Hobart), 10 January 1934, 3.
82   Noël Stewart, 'Pelloe, Emily Harriet (1877–1941)', *Australian Dictionary of Biography*, accessed 5 October 2016, adb.anu.edu.au/biography/pelloe-emily-harriet-8012/text13963.

strengthening the British Empire'.[83] Meanwhile, in the same paper, 'Philos' suggested that since women were generally 'fonder of ornamentation than men', the whole arena of honours might be abandoned to them.[84]

Yet however it may have seemed to commentators at the time, with the benefit of hindsight the decades of the 1920s and 1930s appear something of a high point of women's participation in the honours system in Australia. In these first years after women's admission to the system in their own right, a reconceptualisation of what constituted service to the state began to take place. Besides the forms of service traditionally rewarded with honours—those in the armed forces, government and the public and foreign services, industry, science, and the arts—a new and different type of activity was coming to be seen as service that deserved official honour. Grounded in the motherly ideals of nurturance and morality that animated the maternalist model of citizenship then being developed by feminist women in Australia and elsewhere, this newly acknowledged kind of service was gendered feminine. Through the concept of 'maternal citizenship', as Marilyn Lake has argued, feminists could 'reconceptualize' women's service in the world as being 'not to an individual master/husband, but to the abstract entity of the state'.[85] That the Australian state reciprocated by approving this reimagining of women's role is suggested by the patterns evident in the conferral of honours on women in these decades.

Indeed, at times in these first years after the creation of the Order of the British Empire, women were appointed to it—at least, to the three non-titular levels—in proportions rarely to be equalled in later years.[86] Women represented 27 per cent of appointments to the fourth grade of

---

83 'Ixia', 'Honours for Women', *West Australian* (Perth), 5 January 1934, 6.

84 'Philos', 'From China to Peru', *West Australian* (Perth), 5 January 1934, 16.

85 Marilyn Lake, 'A Revolution in the Family: The Challenge and Contradictions of Maternal Citizenship in Australia', in *Mothers of a New World: Maternalist Politics and the Origins of Welfare States*, eds Seth Koven and Sonya Michel (New York and London: Routledge, 1993), 388. doi.org/ 10.4324/9781315021164-12. Joan Eveline has similarly noted that white feminist women in the first half of the twentieth century cast motherhood 'as a service to the state'. Joan Eveline, 'Feminism, Racism and Citizenship', in *Women as Australian Citizens: Underlying Histories*, eds Patricia Crawford and Philippa Maddern (Melbourne: Melbourne University Press, 2001), 158.

86 The statistics in this section were prepared using data from the Australian Government's online honours database, as it stood in 2011, and may not be comprehensive (see Author's Note). For further discussion of women's place in the honours system in Australia see Karen Fox, '"Housewives' Leader Awarded MBE": Women, Leadership and Honours in Australia', in *Seizing the Initiative: Australian Women Leaders in Politics, Workplaces and Communities*, eds Rosemary Francis, Patricia Grimshaw, and Ann Standish (Melbourne: eScholarship Research Centre, University of Melbourne, 2012), 171–84.

the order (OBE) in the five-year period from 1920 to 1924, 38.5 per cent between 1925 and 1929, 34.4 per cent from 1930 to 1934, and 18.1 per cent between 1935 and 1939 (see Table 1). In the order's third grade (CBE), representation of women was more uneven, reaching 25 per cent in the years from 1930 to 1934, but entirely lacking between 1920 and 1929, while in the fifth grade (MBE), near parity was achieved in the period from 1930 to 1934, with women gaining 46.2 per cent of awards. Although the figures are inconsistent, fluctuating between relatively high and distinctly low levels of inclusion, what is most startling is that these peaks were to be the pinnacle of women's inclusion in the honours system in Australia in the twentieth century, at least in numerical terms (see Table 2). Comparing women's share of honours bearing titles to that of men is more difficult, since the total numbers are too small to be statistically significant (see Table 3). Nevertheless, it is worth noting that in the five-year period from 1920 to 1924 one of the three grand crosses (GBE) conferred in Australia was received by a woman (Mary Hughes, the wife of Prime Minister Billy Hughes), while between 1925 and 1929 the only one of these distinctions—the highest within the Order of the British Empire—awarded in Australia went to a woman (the opera singer Nellie Melba).

Ever alert for the human interest factor in honours announcements, the press sometimes remarked upon women's new visibility in the biannual lists. Australian women would be 'delighted' with the representation of women in the latest group of recipients, thought Brisbane's *Telegraph* in 1934, noting that such levels of inclusion were 'becoming more and more inevitable with the advance of woman in all fields of public activity'.[87] The following year the *Sydney Morning Herald* declared that more Australian women had been included in the King's Birthday list than in any previous list, demonstrating their increasing participation 'in the affairs of the world'.[88] Similarly, Enid Lyons, then the wife of the prime minister, regarded her appointment as GBE (Dame Grand Cross of the Order of the British Empire) in 1937 not as an acknowledgement of personal effort or achievement, but as a broader recognition of women's work and place in the community. 'I can only regard this,' she was quoted as saying, 'as a tribute to the women of Australia.'[89]

---

87 'Honoured by the King', *Telegraph* (Brisbane), 4 June 1934, 10.
88 'Australian Women Honoured', *Sydney Morning Herald*, 6 June 1935, 12.
89 'Dame Enid Lyons', *West Australian* (Perth), 13 May 1937, 18; 'Tribute to Womanhood', *Sydney Morning Herald*, 11 May 1937, 4.

Table 1: Awards of the MBE, OBE, and CBE to Australians, 1915–1994

Period	CBE Male	CBE Female	CBE % Female	OBE Male	OBE Female	OBE % Female	MBE Male	MBE Female	MBE % Female
1915–1919	52	15	22.4	182	29	13.7	124	8	6.1
1920–1924	34	0	0.0	73	27	27.0	44	19	30.2
1925–1929	30	0	0.0	8	5	38.5	7	1	12.5
1930–1934	21	7	25.0	21	11	34.4	14	12	46.2
1935–1939	52	2	3.7	113	25	18.1	132	73	35.6
1940–1944	86	0	0.0	189	14	6.9	224	36	13.8
1945–1949	79	4	4.8	244	22	8.3	364	46	11.2
1950–1954	95	4	4.0	239	38	13.7	315	126	28.6
1955–1959	179	5	2.7	312	59	15.9	413	168	28.9
1960–1964	189	10	5.0	360	60	14.3	465	220	32.1
1965–1969	199	10	4.8	464	58	11.1	672	240	26.3
1970–1974	157	14	8.2	433	60	12.2	722	255	26.1
1975–1979	167	17	9.2	475	100	17.4	857	285	25.0
1980–1984	87	5	5.4	246	43	14.9	465	129	21.7
1985–1989	20	1	4.8	55	5	8.3	101	20	16.5
1990–1994	0	0	0.0	0	0	0.0	0	0	0.0

Note: CBE, OBE, and MBE indicate Commander, Officer, and Member of the Order of the British Empire, respectively. No awards were made in the 1990–1994 period, partly because agreement had been reached by late 1992 that no further nominations would be made for imperial awards (see Chapter 8).

Source: Author's summary, prepared using the Australian Government's online honours database, as it stood in 2011 (percentage figures given to one decimal place).

Table 2: Awards of the AC, AO, and AM to Australians, 1975–1999

Period	AC			AO			AM		
	Male	Female	% Female	Male	Female	% Female	Male	Female	% Female
1975–1979	34	1	2.9	162	5	3.0	458	92	16.7
1980–1984	25	2	7.4	216	8	3.6	643	96	13.0
1985–1989	73	5	6.4	347	45	11.5	1,031	185	15.2
1990–1994	61	10	14.1	312	60	16.1	982	223	18.5
1995–1999	27	6	18.2	208	38	15.4	779	215	21.6

Note: AC, AO, and AM indicate Companion, Officer, and Member of the Order of Australia, respectively.

Source: Author's summary, prepared using the Australian Government's online honours database, as it stood in 2011 (percentage figures given to one decimal place).

Table 3: Awards of the GBE, KBE, and DBE to Australians, 1915–1994

	KBE	DBE		GBE		
Period	Male	Female	% Female	Male	Female	% Female
1915–1919[90]	11	2	15.4	0	1	100.0
1920–1924	16	1	5.9	2	1	33.3
1925–1929	9	1	10.0	0	1	100.0
1930–1934	3	0	0.0	1	0	0.0
1935–1939[91]	14	4	22.2	0	1	100.0
1940–1944	6	0	0.0	1	0	0.0
1945–1949	2	1	33.3	0	0	n/a
1950–1954	25	2	7.4	0	1	100.0
1955–1959	34	2	5.6	0	0	n/a
1960–1964	21	6	22.2	0	0	n/a
1965–1969	27	8	22.9	0	0	n/a
1970–1974	25	8	24.2	0	0	n/a
1975–1979	34	16	32.0	0	0	n/a
1980–1984	17	9	34.6	0	0	n/a
1985–1989	1	1	50.0	0	0	n/a
1990–1994	0	0	n/a	0	0	n/a

Note: KBE, DBE, and GBE indicate Knight Commander, Dame Commander, and Knight/ Dame Grand Cross of the Order of the British Empire, respectively. No awards were made in the 1990–1994 period, partly because agreement had been reached by late 1992 that no further nominations would be made for imperial awards (see Chapter 8).

Source: Author's summary, prepared using the Australian Government's online honours database, as it stood in 2011 (percentage figures given to one decimal place).

Who gets what

If in Australia the numbers of women receiving honours during these years might have seemed the march of progress—perhaps not as swift as might be desired, but nonetheless moving in the right direction—not all criticism of the make-up of the lists was silenced. As well as continuing critiques of the use of imperial honours generally, and especially titles, the system drew expressions of dissatisfaction for a range of other reasons. One perennial criticism, which would continue to be heard in years

90   The figures for this period have been updated to include a GBE to Florence Reid.
91   The figures for this period (and those for 1955–1959) have been corrected, as the Australian Government's online honours database incorrectly displays Enid Lyons receiving a GBE in 1957; she in fact received it in 1937. *Supplement to the London Gazette*, no. 34396, 11 May 1937, 3095.

to come, and which is discussed further in the next chapter, related to political awards and patronage. Moving his resolution in the federal House of Representatives in 1926, McGrath had made reference to knighthoods in Australia as 'the result of political patronage', while a 1934 article in the Launceston *Examiner* suggested that honours ought to be 'reserved as acknowledgements of outstanding work in fields far removed from politics'.[92] A related, and equally familiar, concern was that those who most deserved awards missed out, while influential and wealthy individuals regularly received distinctions. While supportive of the idea of honours, the *Canberra Times* stated in 1934 that there were 'far too many examples in our midst of men who have deserved well of Australia and who have done great things for the British Commonwealth, who have fallen in the race for honours'. At the same time, the paper asserted, 'there ha[d] been undue favouritism of the less deserving, of political supporters and of the wealthy class'.[93]

And, of course, members of particular occupational groupings sometimes alleged that their profession was being overlooked. In 1936, for example, a correspondent to the *Sydney Morning Herald* using the pseudonym 'Teacher' complained that '[f]or some time past I have been struck by the official lack of recognition of the teachers' work'. There were many deserving teachers, the writer claimed, and their omission from honours lists was 'symptomatic' of a broader lack of appreciation for 'intellectual and cultural interests'.[94] The arts, indeed, was an area often considered ill-treated in honours lists. After Kate Baker—the great campaigner for Joseph Furphy's writings—was appointed OBE in 1937, one of the congratulatory letters she received noted that the award must be especially 'gratifying' since 'Australian literature ... is a branch that so seldom receives the recognition it deserves'.[95]

Some of these laments of ill-treatment were probably well founded. Although the retention of the Order of the British Empire after World War I had opened new space for a wider range of activities to be recognised,

---

92   Commonwealth of Australia, House of Representatives, *Parliamentary Debates*, 29 July 1926 (Charles McGrath); 'Bestowal of Honours', *Examiner* (Launceston), 23 March 1934, 6.
93   'Honours', *Canberra Times*, 4 January 1934, 2.
94   'Teacher', letter to the editor, *Sydney Morning Herald*, 4 January 1936, 10.
95   National Library of Australia, Canberra: MS2022, Papers of Kate Baker, 1893–1946, Box 1, Folder 8, letter to Kate Baker from Helen and Daisy Fowler, 11 May 1937, 618; John Barnes, 'Baker, Catherine (Kate) (1861–1953)', *Australian Dictionary of Biography*, accessed 12 September 2017, adb.anu.edu.au/biography/baker-catherine-kate-5104/text8527.

the figures suggest that earlier patterns persisted.[96] Knighthoods conferred upon men, particularly within the Order of St Michael and St George, still tended to cluster in fields of endeavour such as politics, public service, and the law, with a smattering also of businessmen, medical and university men, and philanthropists. For men, the lower grades of the Order of the British Empire were used most often to reward services during World War I or military veterans, public servants, local government service, and services to social welfare. Awards to women show a somewhat different pattern. Of the nine women who received damehoods between 1920 and 1939, two were rewarded for their wartime services, two were eminent in the arts, and the remaining five had given either community or public services. Lower-level awards to women tended to be concentrated either in community service, nursing, and teaching—occupations traditionally gendered feminine, and thus acceptable fields in which women could work and excel—or in areas historically attracting honours, such as public service and the professions, where the women in question stood out as exceptions to the rule in largely male-dominated fields.

Yet there were also signs of a broadening of the reach of the system. Besides the incorporation of women in relatively large numbers, two notable developments are evident. First, according to the citations given in the government database 'It's an Honour', a significant number of men were appointed to the lower grades of the Order of the British Empire for social welfare activities, a field also common in awards made to women, but for which few men in Australia had been honoured in the past. Second, for the first time in Australia, men and women began to be honoured— albeit in very small numbers—for their achievements in the arts. Thus, if the statistics largely reveal expected patterns, it is nonetheless the case that the distribution of honours in Australia had undergone significant change since the end of the war, and new departures suggested that old patterns might be beginning to shift.

Moreover, whatever complaints in the press might seem to suggest, it appears the majority of potential recipients were grateful to have their efforts recognised, and happy to accept a proffered distinction. Files in the National Archives of Australia include numerous letters from nominees expressing surprise and delight at the news they were to be

---

96   Research by Tobias Harper also demonstrates the resurgence of old patterns in the conferral of awards during the interwar years, in part as a result of a deliberate effort in Britain to reduce the numbers of honours bestowed. See Harper, *Servants of the Empire*, 71–80.

recommended.[97] Some also expressed their loyalty and allegiance to the monarch from whom the award ostensibly came, either unconscious of or rejecting the arguments of critics who charged that the monarch was unaware of most of those who received honours, as it was really politicians who distributed them. Journalist and charitable worker Zara Aronson, for example, wrote in 1935 after being offered an OBE that:

> in serving My King and my Country I have only given in 50 years what I consider is a very small emblem of loyalty and service to an Empire which in its magnitude of Imperialism stands pre-eminent.[98]

Only a small minority declined. Their reasons were varied, and as often personal as ideological, at least as far as can be ascertained by the explanations they sent in reply to the offer, or which have survived in other sources. Novelist Miles Franklin, for example, refused an OBE in disgust, considering it an insult when compared to the DBE conferred upon poet Mary Gilmore; charity worker Ruby Board declined an MBE on the grounds that it was not a high enough honour to fit her position as president of the National Council of Women in New South Wales; and poet Bernard O'Dowd refused a knighthood likely because of his radicalism and association with the Labor Party.[99] Others gave no explanation, simply asking to be allowed to decline the award, or stating that their reasons were personal.

97   See NAA: A2924; NAA: A2925.

98   NAA: A2924, 1936/4, letter to J. S. Lyons, Prime Minister of Australia, from Zara Baar Aronson, 25 June 1935; Martha Rutledge, 'Aronson, Zara (1864–1944)', *Australian Dictionary of Biography*, accessed 12 September 2017, adb.anu.edu.au/biography/aronson-zara-5059/text8411.

99   Paul Brunton, ed., *The Diaries of Miles Franklin* (Sydney: Allen and Unwin in association with the State Library of New South Wales, 2004), 67–73; NAA: A2924, 1937/11, letter to Captain L. S. Bracegirdle, Military and Official Secretary to the Governor [General] from [L. A.] Robb, Official Secretary [to the Governor of New South Wales], 10 June 1937; Jill Roe, *Stella Miles Franklin: A Biography* (Sydney: Fourth Estate, 2008), 373; Andrée Wright, 'Board, Ruby Willmet (1880–1963)', *Australian Dictionary of Biography*, accessed 12 September 2017, adb.anu.edu.au/biography/board-ruby-willmet-5276/text8895; Chris Wallace-Crabbe, 'O'Dowd, Bernard Patrick (1866–1953)', *Australian Dictionary of Biography*, accessed 12 September 2017, adb.anu.edu.au/biography/odowd-bernard-patrick-7881/text13701.

Conclusion

No sooner had the British honours system opened to women and embarked on a process of democratisation than it was engulfed in scandal. Revelations over the selling of honours in Britain provoked resolutions against their continuance in most of the parliaments of the old dominions, successful in Canada and South Africa, but at most temporarily so in Australia. Yet the scandal was surprisingly short-lived, quickly left behind once the royal commission had reported and new structures had been established to prevent the recurrence of such corruption. By the 1930s, the honours system appeared secure once more in Britain, and, despite Labor opposition, its future seemed almost as assured in Australia. Women were receiving awards in increasing numbers, and in 1936 gained entry to another honour when the Royal Victorian Order was opened to female participation. The ideal of the maternal citizen had provided a route for their labours as wives, mothers, and community workers to be more easily conceptualised as service to the state, and thus for women's public activity on behalf of mothers, children, and housewives to come within the ambit of the honours system. Thanks to the large size of the Order of the British Empire, and the broad range of grades contained within it, many more Australians—both women and men—were able to receive awards, and for a widening range of achievements and service, than in the past. Most offers of honours were accepted with gratitude, and often with expressions of loyalty to the monarch. Thus, by the end of the decade, it might have been assumed that the honours system was in the process of transitioning into a democratic and inclusive system suitable for a modern democracy. The taint of scandal would never quite disappear, however, and accusations of honours-selling would be heard again in the years to come. Nor would these early moves to encompass women's contributions to their communities easily translate to full gender equality, with the interwar years soon a largely forgotten high point of women's inclusion. However it might have developed, the peacetime trajectory of the honours system was about to be interrupted once more, as the outbreak of a second global conflict returned it to a war footing.

5

In war and peace, 1939–1967

A degree of calm and certainty may have seemed to come to the honours system during the 1930s, but it was another picture in the wider world. Many Australians had suffered greatly during the Depression that followed the 1929 Wall Street crash, and over the following decade the world grew ever nearer to war, until in 1939 Australia found itself once more embroiled in global conflict. Australians learned their nation was again at war on the evening of 3 September, when Prime Minister Robert Menzies announced the commencement of hostilities in a radio broadcast to the country. Over the months and years that followed, nearly a million Australian men and women served in the war, in theatres in North Africa, Europe, South-East Asia, and the Pacific, and tens of thousands were killed in action, wounded, or taken prisoner. War tested positions about honours that had become well established over the preceding decades, especially the hostility of the Australian Labor Party (ALP) to imperial awards, and to titles in particular. The Order of the British Empire renewed its function as a means of rewarding war services, most obviously after the ALP, led by John Curtin, came to power in 1941. Partly setting aside Labor's traditional opposition to British honours, Curtin was willing to nominate servicemen and women for awards, but—apart from one surprise exception—avoided recommending civilians. In the immediate postwar years, Ben Chifley's Labor Government also made use of British distinctions, but took a sterner position, refusing to make any non-operational awards to either military personnel or civilians.

In a pattern becoming familiar to Australians, the election of Menzies's second government in 1949 brought a change of practice. But if war had tested this well-established stasis around honours, so too did a range of events and pressures during the years of peace and prosperity that followed. Often characterised as years of conformity and stagnation, the 1950s were in many ways an era of lively cultural and political debate.[1] During his long period of office as prime minister, Menzies embraced the imperial honours system, and, with quotas for Australia increasing, the biannual lists grew ever longer. Across the country, the pattern of Labor hostility to British awards and Liberal enthusiasm for them became generally entrenched. There were, however, significant exceptions, as Labor premiers interpreted their party's platform in varying ways, and party members were not always averse to receiving distinctions. The tensions in Labor's position were highlighted by a minor controversy during the visit of Queen Elizabeth in 1954, an event more usually recalled by historians as remarkably politically harmonious. Yet the Liberal Party's position of support for imperial awards did not go unchallenged either. Accusations of political patronage were not a new phenomenon, but suspicion around the conferral of titles and other distinctions upon political supporters cast a shadow over the system, perhaps influenced in the 1960s by a fading of respect for monarchy and the institutions of government, and a new mood of satiric challenge to both authority and the link to Britain. Surveying these developments, this chapter also takes the opportunity provided by a relatively stable period in the history of honours in Australia to consider some of the perennial issues of that history—besides the use of awards as instruments of patronage, it also returns to the recurring question of who received what, and explores the attitudes of those who were offered an honour in this era.

The ALP and war: A time for exceptions?

In September 1939, Robert Menzies was relatively new to the prime ministership. Having risen to the leadership of the United Australia Party (UAP) after the death in office of Prime Minister Joseph Lyons, he led a minority government, for Country Party leader Sir Earle Page had withdrawn his party from coalition in response to Menzies's election as UAP leader. Menzies led the nation through the crisis until August 1941,

---

1   See John Murphy, *Imagining the Fifties: Private Sentiment and Political Culture in Menzies' Australia* (Sydney: UNSW Press, 2000).

from March 1940 at the head of a new UAP–Country Party coalition government, formed after successful negotiations with the Country Party's new leader, Archie Cameron. Following the federal election of September 1940, however, the UAP–Country Party coalition held the same number of seats as the ALP, and depended for its survival on the votes of two independent members of parliament. Unable to form an all-party national government with Labor leader John Curtin, and with the war situation deteriorating, Menzies's position became increasingly precarious. At last, at an emergency Cabinet meeting on 29 August 1941, he resigned the prime ministership, to be replaced by the new Country Party leader Arthur Fadden. Barely more than a month later, after the two independents changed allegiance, Fadden's administration was defeated and Curtin formed a government. He remained as prime minister almost for the duration of the war, until his death on 5 July 1945. For eight days Francis Forde held the position, but it was Ben Chifley, sworn in as prime minister on 13 July, who announced the arrival of peace, when he informed the country on 15 August that the war with Japan had ended.

As prime minister during the first two years of the war, Menzies had limited opportunity to make use of the honours system, either to recognise Australians' contributions to the war effort or to reward any other kind of services. The first standard list for the war ought to have appeared at New Year 1940, but rather than the usual array of awards, it was reported that King George VI had decided to acknowledge 'the valour and untiring energy, zeal, and devotion of the fighting men' through a list of military awards.[2] June's birthday list was postponed until July, and when it did appear, it too included only military awards, since it was considered 'inappropriate' at that point in the war to honour anyone not in the services.[3] Thus it was not until the preparation of the New Year list for 1941 that Menzies—or, for that matter, any State government inclined to give out honours—was able to make the usual range of appointments. Billy Hughes, then attorney-general and minister for the navy, headed the Commonwealth list published in January 1941, being appointed a Companion of Honour. High Court justice Owen Dixon received

---

2 Tobias Harper, *From Servants of the Empire to Everyday Heroes: The British Honours System in the Twentieth Century* (Oxford: Oxford University Press, 2020), 108. doi.org/10.1093/oso/9780198841180.001.0001; 'Naval Heroes', *Sydney Morning Herald*, 2 January 1940, 8; *Supplement to the London Gazette*, no. 34763, 1 January 1940, 1–5.
3 The National Archives [United Kingdom], T 305/7, Note by R. U. E. K., 25 June 1940, Half-Yearly Honours List (Civil), New Year, Birthday 1940, cited in Harper, *Servants of the Empire*, 108; *Supplement to the London Gazette*, no. 34893, 11 July 1940, 4243–69.

a KCMG (Knight Commander of the Order of St Michael and St George), while Harold Clapp, the general manager of the Aircraft Construction Branch of the federal Department of Supply and Development, and Geoffrey Syme, the managing editor of Melbourne's *Age* newspaper, gained KBEs (Knight Commander of the Order of the British Empire). Five other men were created knights bachelor, while a large number of men and women received non-titular awards of various kinds, both civil and military.[4] Another batch of distinctions was distributed in June, with the federal list this time topped by a KCMG for the former speaker of the House of Representatives, Colonel George Bell.[5]

By the time the next list was issued at the beginning of 1942, the ALP was in power at the federal level, and Curtin had decided against making nominations for any civil honours or medals.[6] In a partial concession to the special circumstance of being at war, however, military awards were made throughout the rest of the conflict, both operational and non-operational (that is, covering both services rendered in action against the enemy or in theatres designated as operational, and those given in other contexts). War had in any case complicated the situation. Besides the usual processes for recommending awards, King George VI had delegated authority to the commanders of the military forces to make immediate awards of some decorations to recognise gallantry in action, and Australians serving in the British forces were permitted to receive awards in British lists. Curtin's decision to permit military but not civilian awards thus avoided a situation in which only some Australian servicemen and women were able to receive honours. It also, however, created a puzzling inconsistency, for individuals working for the war effort in a civilian capacity, no matter how devotedly, were excluded from any recognition from the federal government. While non-Labor governments held power in Victoria and South Australia, this was not likely to offset the absence of Commonwealth recommendations to acknowledge war service, especially as the other States were led by Labor governments. Yet another inconsistency was that, despite ALP opposition to titles, several military knighthoods were conferred upon Australia's military leaders.[7]

---

4 'The Commonwealth List', *Sydney Morning Herald*, 1 January 1941, 5.
5 'Six Knighthoods in Honours List', *Sydney Morning Herald*, 12 June 1941, 7.
6 National Archives of Australia (hereafter NAA): A1209, 1959/206 PART 1, memorandum to Secretary, Department of Commerce, from Secretary [of the Prime Minister's Department], 29 May 1942.
7 John Hetherington, 'Will Fighting Men Now Be Knighted?' *Herald* (Melbourne), 1 March 1950, 4.

Widespread surprise was therefore expressed when newspapers announced in June 1943 that Frederick Shedden, the secretary of the Department of Defence, had been knighted. Shedden had played an influential role in Australia's war effort, including in the War Cabinet, and he had already been appointed a Companion of the Order of St Michael and St George (CMG) in 1941, while Menzies was prime minister. After Curtin took office as both prime minister and minister for defence, Shedden had become his main adviser, described by Curtin as '[my] right and left hand and head too'.[8] In other circumstances, his knighthood might have seemed not only unexceptional, but highly appropriate. But Shedden was also a civilian, and his honour thus seemed to conflict with the Labor Government's stated policy. More than that, the award was a knighthood. Press reports soon appeared quoting W. M. O'Neill, the New South Wales State president of the Australian Railways Union, warning that Curtin would face questions and criticisms at the upcoming party conference. Knighthoods were unnecessary, O'Neill said, 'in these days, when people are talking of a new social order and a more equitable system of society in general'.[9] Curtin had 'made a mistake', according to the secretary of the Labor Council of New South Wales, Legislative Council member Bob King, who was quoted explaining that the ALP objected to honours, seeing them as 'idle titles for people to play with'.[10] Refusing to comment, Curtin was quoted saying only that the knighthood fell into 'the same category as every other that his Majesty the King gives'.[11] Later that year, he offended a second time when he appointed the Duke of Gloucester, one of the King's younger brothers, as governor-general.[12] At the party's federal conference in December, future ALP governments were 'reminded' of two points of Labor policy: no more imperial honours should be given to Australians, and only Australians should be appointed to the role of governor-general.[13]

---

8   David Horner, 'Shedden, Sir Frederick Geoffrey (1893–1971)', *Australian Dictionary of Biography*, accessed 30 October 2017, adb.anu.edu.au/biography/shedden-sir-frederick-geoffrey-11670/text20853.
9   'Trouble About Knighthood', *Sydney Morning Herald*, 3 June 1943, 6; 'Knighthood Criticised', *Sun* (Sydney), 2 June 1943, 2; 'Labour Opposition to Birthday Honours', *Canberra Times*, 3 June 1943, 2.
10   'Trouble About Knighthood', *Sydney Morning Herald*, 3 June 1943, 6.
11   'Mr. Curtin Silent on Knighthood', *Sydney Morning Herald*, 4 June 1943, 6.
12   'Debate Expected at A.L.P. Conference', *Sydney Morning Herald*, 17 November 1943, 6; 'Claim by President of Victorian A.L.P.', *Sydney Morning Herald*, 18 November 1943, 6; Chris Cunneen, 'Gloucester, First Duke of (1900–1974)', *Australian Dictionary of Biography*, accessed 20 February 2017, adb.anu.edu.au/biography/gloucester-first-duke-of-10313/text18251.
13   'Governor-Generals of Future', *Argus* (Melbourne), 18 December 1943, 4; 'Honours and Governors-General', *Sydney Morning Herald*, 18 December 1943, 8.

After Chifley took office as prime minister, and following the end of the war, the federal government retreated further from the conferring of honours. A Cabinet decision of November 1945 determined that henceforth only operational awards would be recommended, and that the highest would be the companionship of the Order of the Bath (CB); in other words, both civilians and those servicemen and women whose military service was deemed non-operational would miss out, and no distinctions conferring knighthood or damehood would be bestowed.[14] While some minor exceptions were permitted, this new policy once again created potentially invidious distinctions, especially as it was not always easy to determine whether an individual's service had been in an operational or non-operational context, and because it extended also to foreign awards, which potential recipients needed government permission to accept.[15] It was not uncommon for allied nations to seek to bestow their own honours upon Australians who had made special contributions to the war effort, but Cabinet's decision sometimes precluded this. General John Northcott, the chief of the general staff from September 1942 until the end of the war, was irritated to find himself barred from accepting an honour from the United States in 1946, protesting unsuccessfully to Chifley against the ruling that his services had been non-operational.[16] Among others to miss out was (Sir) Fred White, the most significant figure in the development of radar in Australia, whose proposed award from the United States was vetoed along with decorations for fellow scientists (Sir) Mark Oliphant, Aubrey Burstall, and Neville Whiffen.[17] On the other hand, Norman Sparnon, a Japanese language specialist who had served in the Australian military forces, including with the British Commonwealth Occupation Force in Tokyo, until mid-1946, and had then become a civilian interpreter at the headquarters of the supreme commander for the Allied Powers, was given the Bronze Star by the United States in 1948.[18]

---

14 NAA: A5954, 1524/3, memorandum to the Hon. J. A. Beasley, M. P., Minister for Defence, from Secretary to Cabinet, 26 November 1945.

15 On the extension of the policy to foreign awards, see, for example, NAA: A5954, 1524/3, memorandum to Secretary, Department of External Affairs, from F. G. Shedden, Secretary [of the Department of Defence], 12 April 1946.

16 NAA: A5954, 1524/3, letter to Lieutenant-General J. Northcott, Governor of New South Wales, from J. B. Chifley, 18 October 1946; NAA: A5954, 1524/3, letter to Chifley from J. Northcott, 31 October 1946; NAA: A5954, 1524/3, letter to [Fred at Government House, Sydney], from J. Northcott, 31 October 1946; NAA: A5954, 1524/3, letter to Lieutenant-General J. Northcott, Governor of New South Wales, from J. B. Chifley, 3 December 1946.

17 Stewart Cockburn and David Ellyard, *Oliphant: The Life and Times of Sir Mark Oliphant* (Adelaide: Stewart Cockburn and David Ellyard in association with Axiom Books, 1981), 197–98.

18 Alison Broinowski, 'Sparnon, Norman James (1913–1995)', *Australian Dictionary of Biography*, accessed 3 September 2020, adb.anu.edu.au/biography/sparnon-norman-james-21619/text31832.

The denial of awards to military personnel, if not also to civilians who had contributed to the war effort, drew criticism in the press. Responding to Chifley's announcement that there would be no New Year honours list for 1946, due to Cabinet's decision, Melbourne's *Argus* editorialised against the refusal to confer honours on servicemen and women. 'Australian troops of all services are held in the highest respect by friend and foe', the paper stated, yet the government had chosen, 'now that the danger is past, to deny recognition'.[19] In Brisbane, the *Courier-Mail* also disapproved. Noting that the recent British list had been 'the longest in living memory', the writer suggested that the failure of both the federal and Queensland governments to make nominations 'makes us look a small-minded, ungrateful people'. 'Splendid Australians', he or she stated, were thus 'denied some simple honour … by politicians who are most generous when it comes to giving themselves gold railway passes and helping each other to public sinecures when they retire or are retired'.[20] Army officers, too, were reportedly unhappy.[21] General Thomas Blamey, while stressing that he was not concerned for himself, denounced the decision not to award honours higher than the CB, seeing it as 'tantamount to saying: "Nothing for the generals"', and arguing the change in practice after 1943 had resulted in 'unfair treatment'.[22] The *Sydney Morning Herald*, at least, agreed with him. It was 'within the rights of a Commander-in-Chief, and indeed his duty … to put forward for recognition his senior subordinates', the paper stated, 'and he may well be astonished at the churlish attitude of a Government which during the war was only too glad to lean heavily on its Service chiefs'.[23]

Prime Minister Menzies

The first federal election after the war was held on 28 September 1946. Returned to power, albeit with a smaller majority, Chifley's government continued to restrict honours recommendations to military operational awards. In November 1947, when the president of the Australian Literature Society, D. H. Rankin, wrote to Chifley hoping that poet

19   'Honours Dishonour', *Argus* (Melbourne), 4 January 1946, 1.
20   'No Honours For Service', *Courier-Mail* (Brisbane), 2 January 1946, 2.
21   'Army Men Expected New Year Honours', *Morning Bulletin* (Rockhampton), 4 January 1946, 5.
22   'Blamey Hits At Government Over Honours', *Sydney Morning Herald*, 2 February 1946, 1; 'Labour Switch on War Honours Criticised', *Canberra Times*, 5 February 1946, 1.
23   '"Nothing for the Generals"', *Sydney Morning Herald*, 5 February 1946, 2.

Bernard O'Dowd might receive some recognition of his contributions to literature, he was informed that it would be impossible, given the government's decisions only to recommend operational awards, and not to nominate civilians.[24] Yet Chifley's opposition to honours was not total. Perhaps inspired by a postwar report that Canada was considering establishing its own national decorations, late in 1949 a federal ministerial committee proposed the creation of a uniquely Australian award to replace British honours.[25] The government approved the idea, and a Cabinet subcommittee was formed to consider it.[26] Reporting in October, the three committee members—Arthur Calwell, Nick McKenna, and John Armstrong—noted that Australia was 'fast developing a national consciousness', and suggested that it might acknowledge 'outstanding services to the nation' through 'a purely Australian award'. They proposed a relatively small, single-class honour recognising 'meritorious service to Australia' in a wide range of fields, to be given by the King, and to rank among British knighthoods on the Commonwealth table of precedence; it would confer the prefix 'Honourable' upon recipients. Britain already having an Order of Merit and Brazil an Order of the Southern Cross, they had initially leaned toward the 'Order of the Golden Wattle', or something similar, but their final report recommended that the decoration be called the 'Order of the Southern Cross'.[27]

The committee suggested establishing the new honour at Australia's jubilee celebrations in 1951, but Cabinet deferred the matter for later discussion, and after Labor was removed from power at the December election the scheme was not revived.[28] Under Menzies, as the new Liberal prime minister, attention turned back to the use of British honours,

---

24   NAA: A463, 1959/3382, letter to the prime minister from D. H. Rankin, 18 November 1947; NAA: A463, 1959/3382, letter to D. H. Rankin, president of the Australian Literature Society, from F. Strahan, secretary [of the Prime Minister's Department], 19 November 1947.
25   'Canada to Award Own Decorations', *Argus* (Melbourne), 4 January 1946, 16; Review of Australian Honours and Awards, *A Matter of Honour: The Report of the Review of Australian Honours and Awards* (Canberra: Australian Government Publishing Service, 1995), 13.
26   *A Matter of Honour*, 13.
27   NAA: A462, 829/112, 'Commonwealth Jubilee Celebrations: Recognition of Meritorious Service to Australia', 21 October 1949, submission for Cabinet, Agenda No. 1609B; NAA: A462, 829/112, memorandum to Rt. Hon. J. B. Chifley, M. P., Prime Minister, from A. S. Brown, Secretary to Cabinet, 25 October 1949; NAA: A462, 829/112, 'Commonwealth Jubilee Celebrations: Recognition of Meritorious Service to Australia', no date.
28   NAA: A462, 829/112, 'Commonwealth Jubilee Celebrations: Recognition of Meritorious Service to Australia', 21 October 1949 submission for Cabinet, Agenda No. 1609B; NAA: A462, 829/112, memorandum to Rt. Hon. J. B. Chifley, M. P., Prime Minister, from A. S. Brown, Secretary to Cabinet, 25 October 1949; *A Matter of Honour*, 13.

although the idea of an Order of the Southern Cross was occasionally raised again by others over the following years.[29] One question that immediately faced Menzies was whether or not his government should attempt to redress the lack of honours granted during Chifley's prime ministership. Writing in the Melbourne *Herald*, war correspondent John Hetherington claimed that 'many people' had seen the denial of knighthoods to those who had led the forces during the war as an injustice, which the new government might now correct.[30] The *Sydney Morning Herald* too hoped that Menzies would make amends. Commenting approvingly on the birthday list for 1950, in which New South Wales governor and former Chief of the General Staff John Northcott had been appointed KCMG, and on Blamey's promotion to field marshal, the paper noted that there were yet 'other famous war leaders whom the churlish attitude of the Chifley regime [had] deprived of due recognition'. 'It may be hoped,' the paper concluded, 'that this injustice will not be allowed to go unremedied much longer.'[31]

And indeed Menzies did seek to make up for the past. He commented on the difficulty of his task as he put together his recommendations for the birthday list in 1950, noting the small number of awards available to Australia, and remarking that it appeared 'to have been overlooked … that for eight years there have been [almost] no recommendations for Honours … from the Commonwealth of Australia'. 'Now that I have come into office', he wrote, 'I find myself appalled by the volume of what might properly be called arrears', particularly in the military division, but also to acknowledge '[t]he enormous civilian war efforts of the country'. He felt himself in a bind: either he 'must write off the efforts of the last eight years and deal merely with current effort, or endeavour for the next few years to pick up some of the arrears, in which case current effort will remain unrecognised'.[32] Responding to the announcement of the New Year list in January 1951, the *Sydney Morning Herald* noted 'nine new knighthoods', and remarked that this 'larger than usual' number had

---

29 See NAA: A462, 829/112. For example, the *Courier-Mail* (Brisbane) and the National Council of Women. 'Australian Honour Award Suggested', *West Australian* (Perth), 2 July 1953, 14; 'No Wonder Labor Party Questions Matter', *Worker* (Brisbane), 11 January 1954, 4; 'Women Support Order of Southern Cross', *Courier-Mail* (Brisbane), 2 January 1954, 3.
30 John Hetherington, 'Will Fighting Men Now Be Knighted?' *Herald* (Melbourne), 1 March 1950, 4.
31 'The Commonwealth Honours List', *Sydney Morning Herald*, 8 June 1950, 2.
32 NAA: A2924, 1950/1, letter to W. J. McKell, Governor-General, from R. G. Menzies, prime minister, 13 March 1950.

'enabled belated recognition ... of claims that during the Labour regime were ignored because of a narrow-minded party ban on honours'.[33] There was no avalanche of delayed honours, however, and in later years it would be recalled by the public servants advising Malcolm Fraser, another new Liberal prime minister entering office after a period of Labor government, that Menzies had concluded that such arrears could not be made up. Each government must follow its own policy, and the population take its chances as to whether honours were available at the point when any particular individual rendered services marking them as deserving of one.[34]

Menzies did, however, make assiduous use of the honours system. An ardent anglophile and avid monarchist, he supported the continued use of British honours, just as he upheld the maintenance of other traditional ties to Britain. Loyalty to the sovereign was, in Menzies's view, a vital virtue, and indeed, his own devotion to the monarchy has become a central facet in how he is remembered. His declaration during the Queen's 1963 visit that 'I did but see her passing by, and yet I love her till I die' is frequently quoted as an example of the excesses of this passion, but his attachment to the monarchy was much more than sentimental; he considered it a key element in Australia's constitutional stability and success.[35] British honours, for Menzies, were likely thus not merely a token of achievement or a source of personal pleasure to the recipient, but part of a symbolic landscape that both expressed Australia's character as a British nation and cemented its place within that British world. When he was appointed a knight of the Order of the Thistle (KT)—an extremely rare honour of which he is thus far the only Australian recipient—in 1963, he was 'delighted'.[36] Being aware of the 'political element' frequently found in local nominations for knighthoods he had said in the past that he felt it 'improper' for a sitting prime minister to accept one. Such considerations did not apply in this case, for the honour was in the personal gift of the sovereign, and neither Menzies nor his Cabinet had known of it before the Queen informed Menzies she wished to confer it upon him. Freed of any such concerns, Menzies was able to fully rejoice in his new dignity.[37] Given his own affection both for honours and for the monarchy, as well as the past practices of non-Labor

---

33 'Australians Honoured By the King', *Sydney Morning Herald*, 2 January 1951, 2.
34 NAA: A1209, 1976/2235 PART 1, 'Honours and Awards', memorandum, Department of the Prime Minister and Cabinet, no date.
35 A. W. Martin, *Robert Menzies: A Life*, volume 2, *1944–1978* (Melbourne: Melbourne University Press, 1999), 454–55, quote on 455.
36 Martin, *Robert Menzies*, vol. 2, 456.
37 Martin, *Robert Menzies*, vol. 2, 456.

governments, it is thus not surprising that during his prime ministership imperial honours were fully embraced. Other non-Labor State governments would also make vigorous use of the system.

State Labor governments, meanwhile, generally continued to pursue the party's now equally traditional policy of spurning imperial honours, and particularly knighthoods. Having changed the phrasing of its stance on imperial honours in its federal platform in 1921 and 1930, in 1955 the ALP altered the wording again, to state '[n]o knighthoods or like honours to Australian citizens'.[38] By now a standard aspect of Australia's political landscape, this pattern of Labor rejection of British honours and Liberal support for them nonetheless continued to draw both criticism and controversy. Queensland's *Courier-Mail* seems to have felt the unfairness of its State being left out particularly strongly, regularly protesting Labor's stand. In June 1950, for example, the paper noted that there had been no honours list for Queensland because the State's government 'takes the view that no man should thus be signalled [sic] out for distinction or recognition'. 'Such a view', argued the editorialist, was 'mistaken', since distinctions did not 'elevate' individuals, but accorded 'proper recognition' to those who had 'already elevated themselves'. It was 'not a symptom of sturdy democracy' to withhold recognition from those of 'outstanding ability', but 'part of a destructive process of tearing-down that egalitarians throughout the world have practiced at different times'. '[O]utstanding' people were necessary, the writer concluded, and '[t]here is no future for a community which reveres mediocrity'.[39]

Labor's stance against British honours was never uniform, however. The wording of the party's platform left some room for interpretation, and some Labor administrations chose to make recommendations for awards below the level of knighthood, while upholding the prohibition against those that carried titles. From 1954, for instance, the New South Wales Labor Government of Joe Cahill began submitting nominations for honours under the level of knighthood, the highest award recommended being the CMG.[40] Others made exceptions to the ban on titles as well. In 1942, Queensland premier William Forgan Smith reportedly recommended the State's chief justice, William Webb, for knighthood,

---

38 Ernest Alexander Lyall, 'Government Patronage in Australia: The Exercise of the Patronage Prerogative by Commonwealth and New South Wales Governments in the Period 1927–1969' (Master's thesis, The Australian National University, 1969), 194.
39 'Men or Mice', *Courier-Mail* (Brisbane), 10 June 1950, 1.
40 Lyall, 'Government Patronage in Australia', 194–95.

later explaining that he thought 'our Chief Justice should not rank lower in precedence than the Chief Justice of any other State'.[41] Occasionally, too, ALP members accepted honours, including those that carried titles. Retiring senator Dorothy Tangney accepted appointment as a Dame Commander of the Order of the British Empire (DBE) in 1968. Quoted in the *Sydney Morning Herald* observing that 'I suppose I'll be criticised, but I'm pretty used to that by now', she admitted to having found it hard to decide whether or not to accept, but she thought honours were not 'simply handouts for the Liberals', and hoped to make that point by her decision. She also saw the honour as 'not so much a tribute to me as a tribute to the Labor movement, and particularly to the women in the Labor movement throughout Australia', and perhaps felt it should be accepted as such.[42] Tasmanian Labor premier Robert Cosgrove, meanwhile, not only recommended his wife, Gertrude, for a DBE (conferred in 1947), and several knighthoods, but also accepted knighthood himself in 1959.[43]

But Labor members' acceptance of honours could provoke criticism, especially in the case of knighthood. One particular controversy came in 1951, when McKell, as governor-general, accepted appointment as a Knight Grand Cross of the Order of St Michael and St George (GCMG). As he was a former Labor premier of New South Wales, his decision was not welcomed by many in the Labor movement. ALP leader Herbert Evatt declined to make public comment, but others were not so circumspect.[44] One member of the federal executive, parliamentarian J. F. Walsh, was reported to have said that McKell 'had gone against the traditions of the Labour Party', while the combative iconoclast Eddie Ward insinuated in a question in the House of Representatives that the honour was 'repayment' for granting Menzies a double dissolution earlier that year.[45] McKell himself, on the other hand, 'never had any doubt that his knighthood was appropriate'.[46]

---

41   'Queensland Has Only Nine Knights', *Courier-Mail* (Brisbane), 10 June 1953, 2.
42   'New Dame Says Honour is "Tribute to Labor"', *Sydney Morning Herald*, 8 June 1968, 6, newspaper cuttings on the Australian honours system, National Library of Australia, Canberra (hereafter NLA cuttings).
43   'Labour Premier Sponsored Titles', *Courier-Mail* (Brisbane), 3 January 1947, 3; W. A. Townsley, 'Cosgrove, Dame Gertrude Ann (1882–1962)', *Australian Dictionary of Biography*, accessed 21 November 2017, adb.anu.edu.au/biography/cosgrove-dame-gertrude-ann-10015/text17389; NAA: A2924, 1953/6, letter from Robert Cosgrove, premier, to the Governor of Tasmania, 17 February 1953; NAA: A2924, 1954/2, letter from premier to Governor of Tasmania, 8 March 1954.
44   'Labor Hit at Mr. McKell', *Mail* (Adelaide), 10 November 1951, 48; Christopher Cunneen, *William John McKell: Boilermaker, Premier, Governor-General* (Sydney: UNSW Press, 2000), 210.
45   '"Against A.L.P. Traditions"', *Sunday Herald* (Sydney), 11 November 1951, 3; Cunneen, *William John McKell*, 210; 'Question on G.-G.'s Knighthood', *Sydney Morning Herald*, 14 November 1951, 2.
46   Cunneen, *William John McKell*, 210.

The 1954 royal tour

This difference of opinion over imperial honours between the Labor and non-Labor parties provoked a brief but bitter controversy during one of the most highly anticipated events of the 1950s: the royal tour of 1954. That year Queen Elizabeth II and her husband, Prince Philip, Duke of Edinburgh, visited the country for the first time, in a two-month extravaganza during which around three-quarters of the population turned out to see the couple.[47] As often during such tours, the Queen made a number of appointments to the Royal Victorian Order in connection with her visit. The governor-general, Sir William Slim, was appointed GCVO (Knight Grand Cross) and the State governors KCVO (Knight Commander), while a range of lesser awards went to some of those involved in organising or running the tour.[48] For the most part, the tour was a moment of political harmony, with both Labor and non-Labor parties welcoming the royal couple and displaying firm support for the monarchy.[49] The peace was shattered in early March, however, after it was reported that John Cain, the Victorian Labor premier, had blocked decorations for royal tour staff in his State. Would-be recipients were to receive instead 'autographed portraits of the Queen and the Duke'.[50] In explanation, Cain cited Labor's 'long-standing' policy against imperial honours.[51] The *Argus* published a list of people who had missed out on honours as a result, including the State director of the tour, Jack Jungwirth, and Alexander Duncan, the chief police commissioner.[52]

Bolte, the leader of the Liberal Party in Victoria, castigated Cain's action as 'stupid and ridiculous'.[53] Refusing the awards, he asserted, had brought the 'highly successful' tour 'down to a parsimonious and petty level'.[54] Not only had Cain's decision 'prevented the Queen from showing her

---

47   Jane Holley Connors, 'The Glittering Thread: The 1954 Royal Tour of Australia' (PhD thesis, University of Technology, Sydney, 1996), 2; Peter Spearritt, 'Royal Progress: The Queen and Her Australian Subjects', *Australian Cultural History*, no. 5 (1986): 88.

48   NAA: A5954, 42/1, 'Honours Conferred by Her Majesty During the Royal Tour of Australia 1954'.

49   Jane Connors, 'The 1954 Royal Tour of Australia', *Australian Historical Studies* 25, no. 100 (1993): 373. doi.org/10.1080/10314619308595919.

50   'Mr Cain's Refusal of Honours', *Cairns Post*, 11 March 1954, 1.

51   'Refusal of Honours', *Sydney Morning Herald*, 11 March 1954, 5.

52   'Row on Honors Looming', *Argus* (Melbourne), 11 March 1954, press cutting in NAA: A5954, 42/1.

53   '"No" to Honors Stupid—Bolte', *Argus* (Melbourne), 3 April 1954, 5.

54   'Premier "Petty" on Honors, Says Mr. Bolte', *Age* (Melbourne), 10 March 1954, 3.

pleasure in her own way', it had barred potential recipients 'from wearing with pride a personal memento of their services to [her]'.[55] Labor's policy, he thought, could not have been intended to apply in the context of a reigning sovereign's visit.[56] The leader of the Country Party in Victoria, Jack McDonald, also criticised Cain's stance. He had long thought the ALP's honours policy 'mean and paltry', it was reported, and he considered that '[t]he good services of Royal Tour officials should have been recognised', particularly as the Queen had wanted that.[57] Some senior army officers were reported to be irritated because two fellow officers had missed out on awards, and the Returned Sailors', Soldiers', and Airmen's Imperial League of Australia protested as well, with State president N. D. Wilson reported to have said that '[t]o stand between Her Majesty and the one it is desired to honor was not democratic, it was dictatorial'.[58]

Among the wider community opinion was split, though the *Argus* claimed that a 'surge of public opinion against' Cain's move was evident in the correspondence it had received.[59] Letters to the editor published in the paper reveal several common themes. Some argued that Cain could hold any view he liked of honours, but he ought not to force that view on other people. '[I]f I were recommended for an honor,' wrote Miss P. Henderson, 'I would be sadly disappointed if you refused it on my behalf without even giving me the chance to speak'.[60] Another view was that the royal visit was a special event, into which politics should not intrude. M. J. K. Twaites felt that awards were 'the Queen's way of saying a personal "thank you"', and that politics should have been put aside, while another correspondent, although acknowledging that the decision had been an issue of party policy rather than of personal spite, thought that 'surely on this unique occasion, this non-political occasion, Caucus influence could have been laid aside'.[61] Others took the line that the refusal was ungracious, or insulted the Queen. 'If Mrs. Cain entertains a guest in her

---

55 'Cain to Give Reason for Honours Ban', *Sydney Morning Herald*, 10 March 1954, 6.
56 'No Review on Awards, Cain Says', *Herald* (Melbourne), 11 March 1954, 2.
57 'No Review on Awards, Cain Says', *Herald* (Melbourne), 11 March 1954, 2.
58 'Mr Cain's Refusal of Honours', *Cairns Post*, 11 March 1954, 1; 'Army Angry at Honors Rejection', *Herald* (Melbourne), 10 March 1954, 1; 'Labor Divided on Honors Question', *Age* (Melbourne), 11 March 1954, 3.
59 'The Premier Still Says "No" on Honors', *Argus* (Melbourne) 13 March 1954, 4; 'What Do You Think About the Honors?' *Argus* (Melbourne), 10 March 1954, 2.
60 P. Henderson, letter to the editor, *Argus* (Melbourne), 11 March 1954, 2.
61 M. J. K. Twaites, letter to the editor, *Argus* (Melbourne), 12 March 1954, 4; R. Herbert, letter to the editor, *Argus* (Melbourne) 13 March 1954, 4.

home,' asked A. D. Mims, 'and that guest presents her with some small suitable gift, does Mr. Cain rob them both of their pleasure in that gift by churlishly forbidding it?'[62]

Some correspondents, however, supported Cain's action. One reason given was that those who had organised the tour were well paid, and were not deserving of special honours. 'The satisfaction of a job well done should be enough reward', stated one.[63] Tour organisers were also said to be undeserving of honours because there had been errors in the planning. Pointing out that most people could not attend the official events and had had to 'stand for hours' merely 'to catch a glimpse of our Royal visitors', one letter writer asked what the tour organisers had 'done to deserve any honors?'[64] Others felt it was not fair to single out certain people for reward. In the opinion of Mrs Myrtle Canning it was 'quite wrong' to give awards to 'a few people', when '[c]redit and thanks were due to thousands'.[65]

Much more unanimous was editorial comment, which was largely negative. In Melbourne, the *Argus* considered that although Cain warranted credit for having handled the visit 'well and handsomely', it was the 'right' of potential recipients to make the decision on accepting or refusing awards, while the *Herald* deemed honours—or at least these ones, which were in the Queen's personal gift—'tokens of a Sovereign's thanks' that 'should be accepted as graciously as they are bestowed'.[66] The *Sydney Morning Herald* argued that, regardless of whether one supported honours or not, the Queen's desire 'should have been the only guide'.[67] The *West Australian* too held that Cain had displayed 'a distinct lack of courtesy' to the Queen.[68] A number of editorials also pointed out that the Victorian Government had taken a harder line than other Labor administrations. Other ALP leaders, snapped the *Sydney Morning Herald*, had not been 'so self-righteous'.[69] Vince Gair's government in Queensland was reported to have 'no objection', and Western Australia's Albert Hawke stated that if the Queen decided to bestow awards upon tour officials his

---

62   A. D. Mims, letter to the editor, *Argus* (Melbourne), 12 March 1954, 4.
63   L. Anstey, letter to the editor, *Argus* (Melbourne), 12 March 1954, 4.
64   W. Haines, letter to the editor, *Argus* (Melbourne) 13 March 1954, 4.
65   Myrtle Canning, letter to the editor, *Argus* (Melbourne), 12 March 1954, 4.
66   'Due Honors', *Argus* (Melbourne), 11 March 1954, 2; 'No Awards to Victorians', *Herald* (Melbourne), 9 March 1954, 4.
67   'A Fatuous Ban by Mr. Cain', *Sydney Morning Herald*, 11 March 1954, 2.
68   'Royal Honours', *West Australian* (Perth), 12 March 1954, 2.
69   'A Fatuous Ban by Mr. Cain', *Sydney Morning Herald*, 11 March 1954, 2.

government 'would not "step in the way"'.[70] In fact, there was reported to be disagreement within the Victorian ALP, too. While some members of the party held that its policy must be followed in all situations, others saw the royal visit as a special case. According to the *Age*, the division in opinion was generational: older party members were inclined to think that Cain 'might have stretched a point', since the Queen herself wished to confer the honours, while younger people 'were not particularly concerned whether the Royal tour organisers received any awards'.[71] Cain himself was unmoved by all the fuss. 'We have made our decision,' he said, 'and we will abide by it.'[72]

Honours and patronage

In a review of Australia's honours system in 1995, the committee conducting the process would remark that 'strong sentiments against British awards' had emerged during the 1960s, and suggest that these views were 'probably fuelled by the perceived overuse of the system for political reasons during the 1950s and 1960s'. By way of illustration, the report noted that, excepting Larry Anthony and Harold Holt, who both died in office, all of Menzies's first Cabinet 'ended up with at least a knighthood or were appointed Privy Counsellors'.[73] Whether or not opinion against imperial honours and titles was indeed more intense or widespread in these years than in earlier periods, these comments are significant. Patronage relationships and political uses of honours had long been a feature of the system—although almost certainly never to the extent that its more vocal detractors claimed—but such uses and abuses perhaps became the target of greater scrutiny and more assertive criticism during these decades. In postwar Britain, criticism rose over the 'administrative and quantitative domination' of the civil service in honours lists, and the possibility that a civil servant might gain an honour 'for simply doing

---

70 'No Objection to Decorations', *Morning Bulletin* (Rockhampton), 16 March 1954, 1; '"No Objection" to Queen's Honours', *Canberra Times*, 18 March 1954, 7; 'WA Will Accept Honors', *Argus* (Melbourne) 17 March 1954, 1.
71 'Labor Divided on Honors Question', *Age* (Melbourne), 11 March 1954, 3.
72 'Cain Adamant on Honors', *Argus* (Melbourne), 12 March 1954, 5.
73 *A Matter of Honour*, 13. This statement appears to overlook George McLeay, who also died in office without receiving an honour, as Lyall notes. Lyall, 'Government Patronage in Australia', 216. It should also be noted that Holt was appointed a Companion of Honour, as were a number of other prime ministers.

their job without distinction'.[74] In Australia, newspaper and magazine commentary sometimes dissected the occupational and political make-up of lists, pointing out the numbers of Liberal and Country Party politicians to receive awards, and the system—along with loyalty to the monarchy and other attitudes and behaviours perceived as outdated, subservient, or not sufficiently independent or Australian—was sometimes subjected to ridicule.

Some of this criticism simply continued longstanding labour opposition to the honours system. In 1954, for example, an article in Brisbane's *Worker* suggested that '[t]oo often honours are awarded to men whose only claim to service appears to be a close affinity with a Tory political party'. Many labourers did more to benefit the country 'than the nebulous contribution [made] by some Tory knights', the writer argued, asking whether it was 'any wonder' the Labor movement treated the system 'with such scepticism'.[75] Other commentary was more considered journalistic examination. Under the headline 'Is The Honours List Worth Preserving?', F. B. Morony wrote in the *West Australian* in 1967 that it had 'become the fashion … for senior Federal civil servants and some waning politicians to get knighthoods almost as fringe benefits'. Gently sceptical about the 'implication of a dual standard' implicit in weighing the contributions of 'a housewife who has given many years of voluntary service to the community' and 'a middle-grade functionary who is doing the job for which he is paid', Morony nevertheless thought the system 'hurt nobody'.[76] Less sure of this was Western Australian Labor leader Albert Hawke, who observed in 1953 that 'it was a "grave and undeserved reflection"' upon everyone who was not a politician that, since the Liberal Government had come to power in the State in 1947, a mere two out of eight knighthoods conferred had been granted to non-politicians. Rather than ending the system altogether, however, he advocated giving the right to make recommendations to an independent committee made up of the chief justice and two Supreme Court judges.[77] Federal Labor senator Bill Ashley was harsher still, reportedly claiming in 1958 that '[t]he high office of the Queen had been demeaned' through Menzies's '"scandalous abuse"'

---

74 Tobias Harper, 'Voluntary Service and State Honours in Twentieth-Century Britain', *Historical Journal* 58, no. 2 (2015): 652. doi.org/10.1017/S0018246X1400048X.

75 'No Wonder Labor Party Questions Matter', *Worker* (Brisbane), 11 January 1954, 4.

76 F. B. Morony, 'Is the Honours List Worth Preserving?' *West Australian* (Perth), 22 June 1967, 4, NLA cuttings.

77 'Hawke Sees A "Reflection" In Knighthoods', *West Australian* (Perth), 30 January 1953, 2.

of imperial honours'. Ashley commented on the number of knighthoods being given for political services, and stated that '[t]he Monarchy was being belittled by the obvious use of imperial honours as a means to confer party patronage'. Going further, he was quoted suggesting that an investigation would 'reveal a scandal similar to the Lloyd George sale of honours in Britain'.[78]

But was there indeed, as so many at times suspected, such political use of honours? Were awards indeed used as tools of political patronage? The question is a difficult one to answer, in part because, in the absence of clear evidence that any given appointment was a reward for political support or an act of political patronage, it is never possible to be certain that any individual award was the result of such manoeuvrings. As one student of government patronage put it:

> When we come to the vital question of assessing why a particular individual was awarded or denied a particular favour ... we are reduced substantially to conjecture on the basis of known affiliations, general political considerations and the assumed predispositions of the 'patron'.[79]

The matter is complicated further still by the fact that there was—and remains—a wide discrepancy in different individuals' knowledge and awareness of the honours system. While some organisations and groups (including civil service and professional organisations) were aware of the system and knew how to navigate the process of bringing an individual to the notice of the prime minister or premier, others were no doubt unaware they even had such a right. Some occupational groups were also privileged in more concrete ways. Not only did the permanent heads of government departments know the system well, but nominations were actively sought from them. At least by the time of Menzies's administration, letters were sent to each permanent head and to others in similar roles in the public service and government bodies before each list was prepared, asking for any nominations they might wish to make. This practice inevitably brought the names of many more public servants before the prime minister than could the occasional nomination from professional organisations and private individuals, and was thus likely a significant factor in the relatively high proportion of awards conferred upon public servants.

---

78   'Ashley Criticises Honours List', *Canberra Times*, 3 January 1958, 6.
79   Lyall, 'Government Patronage in Australia', 4.

Such caveats aside, the numbers of politicians to receive knighthoods, and the direction of their political sympathies, may be considered suggestive of a political patronage function for the system. Certainly these patterns could give rise to suspicion, or bring the system into disrepute, as the examples above suggest. Ernest Lyall considered the question in some detail in a Master's thesis completed in 1969, examining the use of the patronage prerogative by the federal and New South Wales governments over the previous 40 years. Hampered by the brief nature of award citations, and the fact that a recipient's political or parliamentary services were not always mentioned in citations, he was nevertheless able to discern a number of recipients with 'clear political affiliations', be that as a member of parliament or through some other affiliation with a political party.[80] Each of the presidents of the federal Liberal Party to that point, for example, had received honours.[81] The attitude of the ALP to the system, however, complicated the analysis. While he found that 'the greatest share of' titular honours had gone to 'the segments of society most sympathetic to non-Labor views', Lyall concluded that such a distribution was inevitable, given Labor's disavowal of the system as well as '[t]he implicit social differentiation on which the structure of awards is based'.[82] Moreover, Labor's refusal to make use of the system had left the field open for the non-Labor parties to draw loyalty not only from recipients, but from anyone hoping to receive an award, in any field of endeavour.[83]

Despite being unable to draw firm conclusions about the extent of political use of the system in Australia, Lyall nonetheless saw the danger of such abuse, both to the system itself, as a means of rewarding service to the community, and to effective governance. If it was to be retained and 'awards … to be made for genuine services to the community or the State', he suggested, 'there seems no valid reason why the choice should be made at the political level'.[84] Others, less circumspect, have been more certain that honours were sometimes used inappropriately for political or financial gain. One well-known allegation was made by David Hickie in his 1985 book *The Prince and the Premier*. Hickie alleged that New South Wales premier Sir Robert Askin had sold knighthoods to businessmen for

---

80 Lyall, 'Government Patronage in Australia', 210–20, quote on 210.
81 Lyall, 'Government Patronage in Australia', 218.
82 Lyall, 'Government Patronage in Australia', 207.
83 Lyall, 'Government Patronage in Australia', 203, 262.
84 Lyall, 'Government Patronage in Australia', 293.

between $20,000 and $60,000.[85] Similar claims would later be made about Queensland's premier Joh Bjelke-Petersen (see Chapter 7). True or not, such suspicions—an inevitable result of the power of nomination lying in the hands of political leaders—did nothing to enhance community opinion of the system, and a great deal to tarnish it.

Who gets what

Whatever the real extent of political patronage or corruption, it is important to acknowledge that it was possible for anybody to nominate someone for an award, either by writing directly to the prime minister or premier, or by communicating their suggestion via another member of parliament. Files on individual honours held in the National Archives of Australia reveal that this did occur, certainly by the time of Menzies's prime ministership, if not earlier in the century. Beulah Bolton, for example, was recommended three times before being appointed MBE (Member of the Order of the British Empire) in 1962. The secretary of the Victoria League in New South Wales and the honorary secretary of its national committee, she had been nominated in 1958 by the chair of the league in London, Sir Cuthbert Ackroyd; in 1960 by its chair in New South Wales, Mrs H. B. (Jean) Farncomb; and for a second time in 1961 by Ackroyd.[86] Elsa Chauvel, the wife and collaborator of film director Charles Chauvel—who had died without recognition—was appointed OBE (Officer of the Order of the British Empire) in 1964, having been nominated in 1960 by H. C. McIntyre, former managing director for the South Pacific at Universal Pictures, and in 1963 by Winifred Browne, a grazier and promoter of Australian wool who had contributed funding for several Chauvel films.[87] And Thistle Stead, a biologist, teacher, and conservationist who was a past president of the Wild Life Preservation Society of Australia, and its then current honorary secretary, was nominated unsuccessfully by the society through the minister for air, Leslie Bury, in 1962; she would later be appointed a Member of the Order of Australia (AM).[88]

---

85   David Hickie, *The Prince and the Premier* (Sydney and London: Angus and Robertson, 1985), 83–84.

86   NAA: A463, 1960/6311, 'Miss Beulah Bolton—Honours'.

87   NAA: A463, 1965/2317, 'Late Charles Chauvel and Mrs Chauvel—Honours'. On Browne's connections with the Chauvels, see Catherine Kevin, *Dispossession and the Making of Jedda: Hollywood in Ngunnawal Country* (London: Anthem, 2020), 23–28.

88   NAA: A463, 1962/3342, 'Mrs Thistle Y Stead—Honours'; Joan Webb, 'Stead, Thistle Yolette (1902–1990)', *Australian Dictionary of Biography*, accessed 6 December 2017, adb.anu.edu.au/biography/stead-thistle-yolette-15520/text26732.

Notwithstanding the possibility of such nominations from the community, however, there is no doubt that some occupational groups received proportionally many more awards than others. One reason for this, as indicated above, was likely that certain organisations and professions knew more about the system, and were more adept at engaging with it. As well, the fact that the power of recommendation lay in the hands of the prime minister or premier not only made it more likely that politicians or political supporters would receive honours, but it also meant an individual leader's personal interests and sympathies could potentially influence the make-up of the lists.[89] Some awards, too, had become essentially—or actually—automatic. From 1958 it became customary to confer knighthood upon justices of the High Court at the time of their appointment.[90] Permanent heads in the public service, too, could generally expect to receive awards in due course, with those who ranked highest being granted titles, while governors and governors-general might look for a knighthood in the Order of St Michael and St George, and possibly, if a royal visit took place during their tenure, also one in the Royal Victorian Order.[91]

Over the years of Menzies's prime ministership, at least 374 awards conferring knighthood were announced on either the federal or State honours lists, or occasionally as extra appointments outside those occasions.[92] Among the recipients were at least 45 current or former politicians, including premiers, ministers, and members; 36 judges at various levels; 8 governors-general, governors, or designates to those positions; 18 ambassadors, high commissioners, or agents-general in London, or their deputies; and 16 lord mayors or mayors. These awards constituted almost a third of knighthoods bestowed during this period, by any measure a significant proportion of distinctions conferred. Much of the remaining two-thirds of the total went to public servants or individuals who had served on government bodies, or—as it was often phrased in the brief citations—for services to medicine; to education or in university roles; to industry, commerce, or a specified sector of the economy, such as 'the sheep breeding industry', mining, or 'the aircraft

---

89   Lyall, 'Government Patronage in Australia', 203.
90   Lyall, 'Government Patronage in Australia', 208.
91   Lyall, 'Government Patronage in Australia', 208.
92   This number, and the figures that follow, are drawn from the Australian Government's online database of honours as it stood in 2011 (see Author's Note). Included in this number are awards made outside of the usual biannual lists, but not awards in the Royal Victorian Order, which were not given on the recommendation of the prime minister or premier, but were in the Queen's personal gift. It does, however, include Menzies's KT.

industry'; or military services, including both civil division awards for activities such as supporting returned servicemen and women, and military division awards. Each of these areas of activity—along with some difficult-to-categorise awards recognising similar services—was by this time a familiar feature of the country's honours lists. Only a small percentage of awards (around 10 per cent) seem to have been conferred for work in other fields of endeavour, as is discussed further below. While it is not always easy to determine the precise reasons for an individual award, and thus to categorise it appropriately in such a schema, it is clear that the ranks of Australia's knights were heavily concentrated in certain occupational groups.

Examining appointments to the highest levels of the system in these years reveals another, far more startling, pattern. Alongside the 374 knighthoods conferred between June 1950 (the first list of Menzies's prime ministership) and January 1966 (the last), one finds 12 damehoods, a mere 3 per cent of the total number of titles awarded.[93] Clearly, the complaint that women's services were not rewarded with higher-level honours had fallen on entirely deaf ears. Many lists during these years did not include a single woman at the upper two grades of the Order of the British Empire, and women remained ineligible for the honour of knight bachelor, by far the most frequently awarded title for men, as well as for the Order of St Michael and St George (until 1965) and the Order of the Bath. The awards themselves were split between honours given for services in traditionally male fields that mirrored those predominant among the knights, and those given for labour in traditionally female areas of activity. Three of the 12 could broadly be categorised as political services, with two going to serving politicians and one to May Couchman, a political activist in the conservative Australian Women's National League—by the time of her award the women's section of the Liberal Party of Australia— who had a great influence on Menzies.[94] Another two were the wives of prominent politicians: Menzies's wife Pattie, and Annie Mills McEwen, the wife of the deputy prime minister, John McEwen. The remaining seven included four awards for 'social welfare' or 'charitable' work, one for

93   Note that 13 damehoods appear in the Australian government's online honours database across this period; one of these, however, is a GBE (Dame Grand Cross of the Order of the British Empire) conferred on Enid Lyons that is mistakenly dated to 1957; it was in fact bestowed in 1937 (see Chapter 4).
94   On Couchman, see Judith Smart, 'Couchman, Dame Elizabeth May (1876–1982)', *Australian Dictionary of Biography*, accessed 19 July 2019, adb.anu.edu.au/biography/couchman-dame-elizabeth-may-ramsay-12359/text22205.

'service to nursing in Victoria', one for 'service to country women', and one for 'service to the performing arts'. Each of these represented an area of activity traditionally dominated by women, or which had long been open to women's success.

Even more disturbing for any feminist readers scrutinising the biannual lists must have been that the numbers of women included had fallen at the lower levels of the system, where in past decades women had received a larger share of awards. While women had made up more than a third of appointments to the fourth grade of the Order of the British Empire (OBE) in the five-year periods from 1925 to 1929 and 1930 to 1934, for example, that proportion never rose above 16 per cent in the five-year periods between 1950 and 1969. Likewise, while the proportion of women in the order's third grade (CBE) had reached as high as 25 per cent in the past (between 1930 and 1934), it remained at 5 per cent or less in the five-year periods between 1950 and 1969 (see Table 1 in Chapter 4). Women's workforce participation may have been increasing, and opportunities for women to pursue their ambitions in diverse fields much greater than in centuries past, but there remained many obstacles to their full participation in Australian society. One of the most significant for the history of the honours system was the 'marriage bar' in the public service, which prevented women from retaining their employment when they married, effectively closing off one of the most common avenues to distinction. Only after Menzies's retirement would this barrier to women's equal participation be removed in the federal public service, and thereafter in the States too.

Yet while in many respects the mid-twentieth century was a time of relative conservatism in the honours system, with a smaller percentage of awards going to women than in the 1920s and 1930s, and lists dominated by politics, public service, business, and the (male-dominated) professions, there were also some new departures. One was that awards related to sport were increasingly conferred at the highest levels. After the announcement of the Coronation honours list in 1953, newspapers proclaimed that the young Queen had 'saluted the new Elizabethan age with honors for those who represent its adventure, achievement, and spirit'. Particular mention was made of the knighthood conferred upon Gordon Richards, described as 'England's champion jockey', and Jack Hobbs, who had been a 'hero of world cricket'. Both were claimed to be firsts: the first jockey and the first 'cricketing professional' to be knighted.[95] This commentary, however, missed the fact that Australia had already gained its first cricketing knight four years previously, in the person of Don Bradman.[96] During Menzies's second prime ministership there were five knighthoods conferred upon men involved in securing and organising the 1956 Olympic Games in Melbourne, as well as one relating to the 1962 Commonwealth Games in Perth, and three that referenced horse racing in their citations. Another sign of change was that, as far as can be ascertained for the first time, an honour was conferred upon an Indigenous Australian. Doug Nicholls—who would later become the first Aboriginal person to be knighted and the first Indigenous State governor—received an MBE in 1957; he would be elevated to OBE in 1968, the same year Aboriginal boxer Lionel Rose was appointed MBE.

More broadly, the citations for knighthoods conferred during these decades suggest a greater variety of services was being rewarded with titles than in the past. Not only did medical men, educationists, and business leaders make up a greater proportion of titular awards than previously, but there were also religious leaders (including Frank Rolland, the moderator-general of the Australian Presbyterian church, in 1958; James Duhig, the Catholic archbishop of Queensland, in 1959; and Reginald Halse, the Anglican archbishop of Brisbane, in 1962), newspaper editors (such as Harold Campbell in 1957 and Frank Packer in 1959), and an architect (Arthur Stephenson in 1954). Rolland's knighthood was particularly noteworthy, as it was said to be 'the first conferred on an Australian minister of religion'.[97] Several men were also knighted for their services to the arts, including the theatre (Frank Tait in 1956), music (Eugene Goossens in 1955), and art (among others, Hans Heysen in 1959). These were not entirely new developments—artists Lionel Lindsay (1941) and

---

95   See, for example, 'Honors Hail Dawn of New Era', *Argus* (Melbourne), 1 June 1953, 1.

96   A former jockey and a former tennis player had also been knighted in the past in Australia: Colin Stephen, in his younger years '[a] noted amateur rider' who won a number of victories, was knighted in 1935 while chair of the Australian Jockey Club, and Norman Brookes, a champion tennis player and former president of the Lawn Tennis Association of Victoria, was knighted in 1939. Martha Rutledge, 'Stephen, Sir Colin Campbell (1872–1937)', *Australian Dictionary of Biography*, accessed 3 November 2020, adb.anu.edu.au/biography/stephen-sir-colin-campbell-1285/text15099; W. H. Frederick, 'Brookes, Sir Norman Everard (1877–1968)', *Australian Dictionary of Biography*, accessed 11 June 2021, adb.anu.edu.au/biography/brookes-sir-norman-everard-5373/text9091.

97   B. R. Keith, 'Rolland, Sir Francis William (Frank) (1878–1965)', *Australian Dictionary of Biography*, accessed 19 July 2019, adb.anu.edu.au/biography/rolland-sir-francis-william-frank-8261/text14469.

Arthur Streeton (1937) had both been knighted in the preceding decades, for instance—but they suggest a gradual opening up of the system to a wider variety of fields of endeavour.

Over the years many complaints have been expressed about the occupational balance of honours lists. At times, objections have focused narrowly upon certain occupations or fields of activity. In June 1950 a correspondent to the Perth *Daily News* wondered why 'none of our outstanding scientists and doctors and only one of the noble women of the nursing profession' had featured in the latest list. 'Does anyone do more for humanity than these unassuming, tireless workers,' she asked, 'and does anyone deserve honour more?'[98] The same month in the *Sydney Morning Herald* a letter commented upon the 'extremely small numerical representation' of clergy, with the writer arguing that they too deserved honours, and not merely rewards in the next world.[99] Another letter in June 1953 asked why the country's 'leading pastoralists, some of whom produce the finest wools, wheat, and stock in the world', did not receive more awards, while the following year a correspondent suggested that teachers were 'a glaring omission'.[100]

Other critical assessments, however, took a broader view, often taking aim especially at the proportion of honours conferred on politicians, public servants, and other professionals, who were perceived to be well remunerated already, and not in need of further reward. The political scientist Don Aitkin, in 1968, found 'the whole business' somehow 'ineffably dreary', with 'the sword fall[ing] on to the shoulders of the same old occupational groups' each time. Only four knighthoods among more than 200 conferred in the final eight years of Menzies's prime ministership, he lamented, had gone to figures associated with literature, art, and culture. In his view, it was 'time for … a new Honours system which gives credit where it might otherwise be overlooked'. Rather than awards for 'parliamentarians, public servants, company directors, [and] academics'—all of whom had 'achieved success already'—he advocated 'knight[ing] the unsung and the underpaid'. Perhaps with tongue in cheek, he added that 'a couple' might be 'given out at random, for services to Australia, which we would all be eligible for, just by living here'.[101] Four

98 Mrs. S., letter to the editor, *Daily News* (Perth), 19 June 1950, 6.
99 A. O. Robson, letter to the editor, *Sydney Morning Herald*, 13 June 1950, 2.
100 F. A. Lindsay, letter to the editor, *Sydney Morning Herald*, 4 June 1953, 2; John Kelso Hunter, letter to the editor, *Sydney Morning Herald*, 15 June 1954, 2.
101 Don Aitkin, 'Between the Lines', *Canberra Times*, 16 October 1968, 2.

years later, in the *National Times*, he again discussed the lists produced during the last eight years of Menzies's time as prime minister. Of those receiving a title for the first time, he said, 48 out of 216 had been company directors, 37 public servants, 30 members of parliament, 25 academics, 22 other professionals, 16 judges, 12 military figures, and 8 graziers (18 he classified as miscellaneous). It was time for the system to be abolished, in his view, and he was not persuaded by 'the argument that the MBEs are a useful way of rewarding people who give years of unselfish community service'. Not only did he not believe 'the great volume of community work would stop tomorrow if the honours system did', but there were far more deserving people than there were awards available, and 'if hardworking people are doing all this yakka for the chance of an MBE when they are 70 then they show surprisingly little wit'. If honours were to be retained, on the other hand, they should be 'destuffify[ed]', and 'opened ... to all who had achieved fame through their own efforts, especially where they had given real service to the community or done things for Australia's image abroad'.[102] The call for awards to recognise those perceived as truly serving the community (particularly in a voluntary role), rather than merely doing their jobs well, was and remains a staple of commentary on the honours system, as we shall see.

Offers, acceptances, and refusals

A different insight into public opinion comes from the reactions of those offered honours. Throughout the period of this study, potential recipients were informed of the award intended to be bestowed on them, and asked, confidentially, whether they wished to accept or decline. This process of 'sounding', as it was termed, was intended to avoid the embarrassment of announcing an honour, only to have the recipient publicly refuse it. Those who did decline were asked to keep both the offer and their response strictly to themselves, a directive that appears generally to have been followed. It is possible, however, to gain a sense of the numbers of people who refused awards, and of their reasons for doing so, from the files of 'sounding' documents held in the National Archives of Australia (NAA). Although these communications were written in a formal manner to officials administering the system, rather than privately to friends and

---

102 Don Aitkin, 'Now, if I were King, There'd be a Different Honours List', *National Times*, 10–15 January 1972, 12, NLA cuttings.

family, they nonetheless provide some idea of the varied reactions of individuals to the offer of an honour during these years, and of the range of reasons for which one might be repulsed.

Rejections were, however, rare. The files consulted for this research show that for most lists only one or two individuals, if any, chose to refuse the award they were offered. Many of the replies to 'sounding' letters held in the NAA, therefore, are only short telegrams indicating willingness to receive the award, in the requested form of 'gratefully accept' (those refusing were asked to write 'beg to decline'). Some recipients chose to follow this official response with a more personal letter, expressing their delight, and often asking that their gratitude be conveyed to the sovereign, or to the governor-general. One person in 1959, for example, wrote that '[a]ny service rendered by me has given me much pleasure over the years but it has been most exciting to be singled out for recognition'.[103] Another, in 1953, stated that he was 'deeply moved & appreciative', and asked that his 'humble & grateful acknowledgment' be communicated to the governor-general.[104] Rabbi Jacob Danglow, the rabbi of the St Kilda Hebrew Congregation and the Jewish chaplain to the army since 1942, asked that the King be informed of his 'humble and profound appreciation' at being granted an OBE in the June 1950 list. In the context of the recently revealed horrors of the Nazi Holocaust, he wrote that both he and his congregation 'deeply appreciated' the award, and he felt

> sure that Australian Jewry, as a whole, are equally gratified by this
> further manifestation of that broad vision and benign toleration
> which have always shed so much lustre upon the Throne and
> Person of our beloved Sovereign.[105]

As discussed in relation to an earlier period in Chapter 4, such letters of thanks sometimes expressed sentiments of loyalty to the monarch as well as personal pleasure. In 1959, one woman expressed her gratitude for the OBE she had received, writing that she accepted it 'with a strong sense of humility, & gratitude for this great Kindness shown to the women of Queensland through me'. Her letter concluded with a declaration of 'my most loving loyalty to Her Majesty, and … my wish to serve her and our

---

103 NAA: A2924, 1959/2, letter to the Governor-General from Lillian Mitchell, 15 June 1959.
104 NAA: A2924, 1953/4, letter to M. L. Tyrrell, official secretary, from Thomas G. Carter, 6 June 1953.
105 NAA: A2924, 1950/1, letter to M. L. Tyrrell, official secretary and comptroller to the Governor-General, from J. Danglow, 8 June 1950.

country'.[106] John Jensen, created knight bachelor in 1950, similarly asked that the governor-general 'place before His Gracious Majesty my humble duty and my deep sense of gratitude for this signal mark of the Royal favour, of which at all times I shall endeavour to be worthy'.[107]

Those who did decline were asked to follow their telegram with a letter explaining their reasons. Not all did so, and some wrote only that their reasons were personal. But those who did choose to explain presented a variety of reasons, both personal and political. Writer Vance Palmer, for instance, refused an OBE in 1952, stating that although 'deeply sensible of the Honour' he wished to refuse because 'those who work in my particular field—that of the Arts—are traditionally critical of such distinctions, and to be singled out would prove embarrassing to me'.[108] Bertha, Lady Leitch, who had practised medicine before marrying the businessman Sir Walter Leitch, and who was a long-term member of the board of the Women's Hospital in Melbourne, declined the same award in 1953 on the grounds that 'I do not feel that I have done anything to deserve an Honour being bestowed upon me'. 'I admit that I have always tried to be a good citizen and as helpful as possible for the welfare of others,' she wrote, 'but hundreds of others have done the same—and none of use [sic] are looking for awards.'[109] Public servant Fred Whitlam, the father of later prime minister Gough, declined an ISO (Companion of the Imperial Service Order) in 1951 because 'such service as I have been able to render to His Majesty and my country has been rendered willingly and with full loyalty, and the service itself has been entire satisfaction'. He wished it to 'continue to be unattended by external marks of distinction'.[110] Mining engineer and businessman Lindesay Clark refused a CBE (Commander of the Order of the British Empire) in 1958 on the grounds that he was 'engaged in negotiations of great difficulty & importance' in relation to his companies, and '[a]ny personal distinction bestowed on me would be a hindrance', while (Sir) Marcus Oliphant— who would accept a knighthood in 1959—declined an initial offer in

---

106 NAA: A2924, 1959/5, letter to the official secretary from Kathleen A. Mylne, 26 May 1959.
107 NAA: A2924, 1950/1, letter to the official secretary to the Governor-General from J. K. Jensen, 20 July 1950.
108 NAA: A2924, 1952/9, letter to Sir Arthur Fadden, acting prime minister, from [William Slim?], 5 June 1952.
109 NAA: A2924, 1953/4, letter to Sir Arthur Fadden, acting prime minister, from W. J. Slim, 19 May 1953. On Lady Leitch, see D. T. Merrett, 'Leitch, Emily Bertha (1873–1957)', *Australian Dictionary of Biography*, accessed 25 March 2021, adb.anu.edu.au/biography/leitch-emily-bertha-7754/text12383.
110 NAA: A2924, 1951/5, letter to R. G. Menzies, prime minister, from M. L. Tyrrell, 28 May 1951.

1954 because he was 'a comparative newcomer to Australia', working in a newly created university (The Australian National University) and a newly founded organisation (the Australian Academy of Science), and:

> [i]f I were to accept an honour which carried a title, at this critical stage in the early history of these bodies, I might well lose the confidence of colleagues who have striven devotedly for many years in causes to which I am a comparative newcomer.[111]

Antarctic scientist Phillip Law and theatre director Hugh Hunt, meanwhile, both refused OBEs in 1959 on the grounds that the awards were not high enough to uphold the prestige of the organisations they served. Honours, in Law's view, were 'offered in recognition not so much of the man but of the work and accomplishments of the organization of which he is the head', and in his view an OBE 'does not do justice to the work of the ANARE [Australian National Antarctic Research Expedition]'. In any case, he did not want to receive an honour ahead of those whom he had led.[112] Hunt, similarly, was concerned because the only previous awards of the OBE to people involved with theatre in Australia had been to two women who performed for charity, and he worried that others involved in the Elizabethan Theatre Trust, which he headed, might think it was seen as comparable to amateur theatre.[113] In both cases the governor-general, Sir William Slim, was inclined to agree, commenting privately on Hunt's case that there was 'rather a habit of offering Honours in too low a category to distinguished persons in the artistic and cultural world and for that matter, in other spheres'.[114] Two men would refuse the Queen's Silver Jubilee medal in 1977—an award that was not 'sounded', presumably because of the sheer number of people receiving it—because they opposed Australia's continuing connection to the monarchy. Left-wing Labor member of the New South Wales Parliament George Petersen reportedly described himself as 'a socialist', and 'said he could see no

---

111 NAA: A2924, 1958/14, letter to M. L. Tyrrell, official secretary to the Governor-General, from G. Lindesay Clark, 19 May 1958; NAA: A2924, 1954/11, letter to the official secretary to the Governor-General from M. L. Oliphant, 14 May 1954.
112 NAA: A2924, 1959/5, letter to the official secretary to the Governor-General, [M. L.] Tyrrell, from Phillip Law, 23 May 1959.
113 NAA: A2924, 1959/5, letter to Field Marshall Sir William Slim, Governor-General, from Peter [Carington?], high commissioner for the United Kingdom in Canberra, 26 May 1959.
114 NAA: A2924, 1959/5, unsent letter to Lord Carrington from [Sir William Slim], 2 June 1959.

reason to celebrate 25 years of rule "by the most overpaid Civil Servant in the world"', while author and journalist Craig McGregor was reported to have 'said that as a republican he would not be accepting'.[115]

Conclusion

The 1950s have often been seen by Australian historians as a staid period of conformity and cultural stagnation, albeit this characterisation of the decade has been challenged in recent years.[116] In some respects, the history of the honours system during this period bears out such a portrayal. These were years of relative stability for the system, with even the controversies—be they over Labor policy towards honours or the ratio of awards going to politicians and public servants—having an air of the routine. During the long years of Menzies's prime ministership, many hundreds of Australians were honoured, and most of them received the offered distinctions gratefully. While some declined, their reasons were as varied as the services for which the awards were given. Yet at the same time, just as World War II had tested the Labor Party's opposition to British honours, both Labor and Liberal positions on the system were tried during the decades that followed. From the outcry over John Cain's decision to deny distinctions to royal tour officials in 1954 to expressions of scepticism over Liberal governments' bestowal of awards upon political supporters, both parties found their stances challenged. By the later part of the 1960s, an air of change had come over the country, and its ties to Britain and the British monarchy were being questioned afresh by a younger generation. Menzies's heartfelt declaration of love for Queen Elizabeth during her 1963 tour, often quoted as an example of his Anglophilism and monarchism, drew forth cringes and scorn in equal measure, so greatly had the nation's mood shifted since 1954. In this changing atmosphere, in 1966 Menzies handed the prime ministership to Harold Holt, who held the office only for a short time before disappearing, presumed drowned, in the surf at Cheviot Beach in Victoria. The honours system, as always, was no exception to the currents of national opinion, and the years to come were years of upheaval, both for the honours system and for the wider nation.

---

115 'Two Refuse Jubilee Medal', *Sydney Morning Herald*, 2 August 1977, 1.
116 For example, in Murphy, *Imagining the Fifties*.

6

It's time, 1967–1975

Despite extensive sea and air searches after his disappearance while swimming in December 1967, Prime Minister Harold Holt's body was never recovered, and his loss—in the midst of the Cold War—provoked dramatic speculation and a range of conspiracy theories. On a practical level, it meant a new prime minister must be chosen. Deputy prime minister and Country Party leader John McEwen refused to serve under the Liberal Party's chosen successor to Holt, William McMahon, and soon crisis enveloped the party. Emerging as the somewhat unlikely victor in the ensuing leadership contest, the New Zealand-born former Royal Australian Air Force pilot and long-term senator John Grey Gorton became prime minister on 10 January 1968. He took office at a key moment for the future of the honours system. Australia in the late 1960s was experiencing a phenomenon termed 'new nationalism'. This newly assertive mood of Australian identity was at least partly a response to Britain's decision to seek entry to the European Economic Community, and the wave of national soul-searching that had followed as Australians decried Britain's abandonment of her antipodean kin. Writers, artists, politicians, and thinkers around the country sought to delineate and encourage a bolder, prouder, more vibrant, and more self-consciously Australian identity for the nation. At the same time, these years were a period of counter-cultural questioning of hierarchy and tradition, with diverse social movements pressing for change, particularly in gender and race relations, and a new suspicion of nationalism and patriotic ritual.

This chapter considers what happened to the honours system in this charged atmosphere. It had been more than half a century since the creation of a uniquely Australian honour had first been proposed, by the newspaper editor William Sowden, but that moment had not been propitious, and he had likely intended it only as a complement to British honours, not as a replacement. The mood of new nationalism in the late 1960s created much more favourable ground, and the possibility of bipartisan support for the institution of an Australian award. Had Gorton not lost the prime ministership a little more than three years after taking office, it might have been his version of a national order that today recognises the services and achievements of Australians. In the event, it was to be Gough Whitlam who created an Australian honour, as part of a wider attempt to transform Australian civic symbols to reflect the reality of Australia's independence and distinct identity.

The establishment of the new Order of Australia was, predictably, another moment of controversy for the honours system. Added to the longstanding divide over the use of imperial awards and titles was now a split over the value and meaning of the new distinction. For some an overdue statement of independence and national maturity, the Order of Australia was for others a sign of the loss of national heritage and a portent of further loss to come. On a more practical level, it was also another chapter in the long running tussle for authority between the States and the federal government. Having arrived in such a fiery birth, did the Order of Australia bring revolution also to the hoary question of who received awards, and in what fields? The chapter concludes by considering this question, asking whether there is any evidence that the first list of awardees for the new distinction appeared any different from the old. In a rapidly changing cultural landscape in which—as historian Michelle Arrow has shown—both politics and wider society were being transformed by the rise of social movements such as second-wave feminism and gay and lesbian liberation, and by the assertion that the personal was political, was the honours system also being remodelled?[1]

Gorton and honours

A new atmosphere of nationalist self-assertion was appearing in the Australia of the 1960s. As the British empire declined, and with it the appeal of both Britishness and empire as bases for 'myths of identity and belonging',

---

1   Michelle Arrow, *The Seventies: The Personal, the Political, and the Making of Modern Australia* (Sydney: NewSouth, 2019).

writers and thinkers began to raise questions about national consciousness, and to seek a fresh sense of nationhood suited to this new context.[2] As Stuart Ward has put it, this 'new nationalism' was one 'stripped of its British underpinnings—a self-conscious striving for a more self-sufficient, self-sustaining idea of the people, in place of the "old" nationalism with its entanglements in wider networks of British belonging'.[3] Operating both at the level of rhetoric and as 'a legitimate rationale for legislative action', the new nationalism was a shared phenomenon across the former British dominions of Australia, New Zealand, and Canada.[4] To the commentator Donald Horne in 1968, as Ward has noted, Gorton's prime ministerial style seemed to represent something new, in embodying precisely this kind of new nationalist spirit.[5] He must have seemed to the Liberal Party the man for the time. Described by Ian Hancock as '[a] determined non-conformist and a passionate Australian nationalist' who 'wanted to turn thinking in the party, and in the nation, in a more independent direction', Gorton was willing to take up the question of honours reform.[6] But for his loss of power he might have become the leader now associated with creating a new system of national honours.

At least initially, the possibility of altering Australia's honours system does not appear to have been on Gorton's radar. In May 1969 he answered yet another question from Labor leader Gough Whitlam about honours. Asked if he had thought about creating a national system of honours 'in anticipation of Australia's bi-centenary' (presumably a reference to the upcoming Captain James Cook bicentenary in 1970), as Canada had done in 1967 for its centenary of confederation, his answer was brief: he had not.[7] A year later, however, in May 1970, Gorton was mulling over the idea, and asked that it be developed for his government to discuss. He was given a proposal 'along the lines of the Canadian system', but it

2   Stuart Ward, 'The "New Nationalism" in Australia, Canada and New Zealand: Civic Culture in the Wake of the British World', in *Britishness Abroad: Transnational Movements and Imperial Cultures*, eds Kate Darian-Smith, Patricia Grimshaw, and Stuart Macintyre (Carlton: Melbourne University Publishing, 2007), 237.

3   Ward, 'The "New Nationalism"', 232. On this new nationalism, see also James Curran and Stuart Ward, *The Unknown Nation: Australia After Empire* (Melbourne: Melbourne University Press, 2010).

4   Ward, 'The "New Nationalism"', 242.

5   Ward, 'The "New Nationalism"', 232.

6   Ian Hancock, 'About John Gorton', *Australia's Prime Ministers*, National Archives of Australia, accessed 14 June 2021, www.naa.gov.au/explore-collection/australias-prime-ministers/john-gorton; 'Contributors', *Australia's Prime Ministers*, National Archives of Australia, accessed 30 October 2017, primeministers.naa.gov.au/about/contributor.aspx (site discontinued).

7   Commonwealth of Australia, House of Representatives, *Parliamentary Debates*, 29 May 1969 (Gough Whitlam and John Gorton).

was to come to nothing after he lost the prime ministership to McMahon in March 1971.[8] Perhaps Labor were unaware of the proposal, for the previous month Bill Hayden, then a member of the opposition front bench, had launched a stinging attack on the existing system in parliament. Describing the New Year honours list as 'an event ... somewhat analogous to an annual pantomime' and the system itself as an 'alien' one belonging to Britain, he suggested that those most deserving of recognition had been relegated to the lower levels of the list, while the highest awards had gone to individuals who had enriched themselves, or who were supporters of the government. The system should be abolished, he argued, and replaced by an Australian one, in which honours would be given for 'real merit' and 'contributions to mankind'.[9]

Regardless, Gorton's fall ended the possibility of a system of Australian honours being established with bipartisan support. McMahon, an ineffectual leader whom Gorton despised, appears to have been uninterested in creating national honours. His use of the British system, moreover, was unwise at best, although the extent of his folly would not be revealed until much later. Attempts to obtain life peerages for the Victorian premier, Sir Henry Bolte, and the high commissioner to London, Sir Alexander Downer, despite his personal reservations—efforts thwarted by British ministers perhaps more alert to the political dangers—were revealed when the National Archives opened diary notes of Sir Paul Hasluck in 2003.[10] Such excesses, to the extent they were known or suspected, could have done little for the system's reputation. In March 1972, perhaps in response to McMahon's honours picks, Labor member Jim Cope told the House of a (possibly fictional) rubbish truck worker who had complained bitterly to him about the way knighthoods were awarded. Adverting to the number of Liberal and Country Party politicians who had received titles under Coalition governments, Cope asserted that bestowing knighthoods was 'in many instances ... used as a political expedient', as well as being

---

8   Review of Australian Honours and Awards, *A Matter of Honour: The Report of the Review of Australian Honours and Awards* (Canberra: Australian Government Publishing Service, 1995), 14; Malcolm Hazell, 'The Australian Honours System: An Overview', in *Honouring Commonwealth Citizens: Proceedings of the First Conference on Commonwealth Honours and Awards*, ed. Michael Jackson (Toronto: The Honours and Awards Secretariat, Ontario Ministry of Citizenship and Immigration, 2007), 38.

9   Commonwealth of Australia, House of Representatives, *Parliamentary Debates*, 18 February 1971 (Bill Hayden).

10   See 'The Gong Show: Bitter Rivalries for Rewards', *Sydney Morning Herald*, 4 June 2005 [online]; Brendan Nicholson, 'Sir Henry's Push for Baron Bolte', *Age* (Melbourne), 10 August 2003 [online]; Anne Twomey, 'Dishonourable Honours', *Sydney Morning Herald*, 7 June 2014 [online].

'a method of creating class distinction' that ought to be discontinued.[11] Labor, of course, had opposed the use of imperial honours, and especially titles, for decades. But for the first time in decades, they were about to get the chance to do something about it.

It's time: Honours and the Whitlam revolution

Elected on the stirring cry of 'It's Time'—his campaign slogan—in December 1972, Gough Whitlam came into office with a whirl of activity. He was the first Labor prime minister since 1949, and he intended to waste no time in implementing the party's program. Until a full Cabinet was elected, he and his deputy prime minister, Lance Barnard, were sworn in to all 27 ministerial portfolios. Among the rapid decisions made by this first Whitlam ministry was the cancellation of recommendations for imperial honours. On the government's third day in office, moves were made to end the use of British honours; Whitlam would also decline to send to the Queen a list of recommendations prepared by McMahon before the election.[12] British awards were not entirely swept away, however. For one, they remained in use in Papua New Guinea, then an Australian territory. The government of Michael Somare had asked that its citizens might still be nominated for imperial honours, and received assent from Canberra. Until PNG became independent, therefore, the Australian prime minister endorsed nominations for British honours to be bestowed upon PNG citizens.[13] More significantly, the States retained the right to recommend for British honours independently of the Commonwealth Government. When it was reported in late 1974 that at the same time as seeking approval for a new suite of Australian honours—under one plan to be administered nationally from Canberra—Whitlam intended to ask the Queen to 'veto' nominations for imperial honours from the States, at least one of the non-Labor premiers responded with strong opposition.[14] Western Australia's Sir Charles Court was reported to have said that his

---

11 Commonwealth of Australia, House of Representatives, *Parliamentary Debates*, 1 March 1972 (James Cope).
12 Gough Whitlam, *The Whitlam Government 1972–1975* (Melbourne: Viking, 1985), 19, 141.
13 Whitlam, *The Whitlam Government*, 99.
14 Chris Anderson, 'PM to Ask Queen for Ban on State Honours', *Sun-Herald* (Sydney), 1 December 1974, 3.

government would inform its British counterpart that it strenuously objected, as well as that he thought 'most people' would rather have 'an honour from the Queen'.[15]

Writing about the matter to Sir Martin Charteris, the Queen's private secretary, Sir John Kerr, the governor-general from 1974, noted that '[t]he central question' was likely to be whether or not the Queen would 'be willing to indicate that' she desired any new Australian system of honours to be 'the only system'.[16] In an earlier letter, however, Charteris had already expressed hesitation about this idea. Charteris expressed the view that replacing British awards with 'an Australian Order' would be 'the best solution', if that were 'accepted throughout Australia', and stated his certainty that the Queen would 'give her full support' to such a proposal. But he foresaw a 'dilemma', given the existing arrangement whereby she bestowed 'United Kingdom Honours to certain States on the advice of the Foreign and Commonwealth Secretary'—according to the recommendation of State premiers, communicated by the State governors—as well as according to recommendations from the federal Australian Government.[17] Whatever Whitlam's early hopes, by February 1975 the governor-general was reporting to the Palace that the prime minister was 'reconciled' to the non-Labor States continuing to nominate for imperial honours, and to the idea that the new system would exist in parallel with the old, at least at first.[18]

Yet it was not only the non-Labor premiers who were angered by attempts to restrict their honours prerogative. In June 1971 the Australian Labor Party's (ALP) federal conference had decided that 'no titles should be conferred but appropriate recognition … given to persons who have rendered exceptional service to the community or to mankind', a resolution the party's federal executive interpreted in December as proscribing the use of all British awards, including non-titular ones.[19] According to Whitlam's

---

15 'PM Wants Royal Veto on Honours', *West Australian* (Perth), 2 December 1974, 1, newspaper cuttings on the Australian honours system, National Library of Australia, Canberra (hereafter NLA cuttings).

16 National Archives of Australia (hereafter NAA): AA1984/609, PART 1, letter to Sir Martin Charteris, private secretary to the Queen, from John R. Kerr, 10 December 1974.

17 NAA: AA1984/609, PART 1, letter to the Governor-General of Australia from Martin Charteris, 4 December 1974.

18 NAA: AA1984/609, PART 1, letter to Sir Martin Charteris, private secretary to the Queen, from John R. Kerr, 4 February 1975.

19 *A Matter of Honour*, 14; Whitlam, *The Whitlam Government*, 140; Allan Barnes, 'No British Royal Honors for Australians, Says ALP; Our Own Awards Instead', *Age* (Melbourne), 17 December 1971, 3, NLA cuttings.

own later account, South Australian Labor premier Don Dunstan was 'so riled by [this] curtailment of his prerogatives' he planned to establish an Order of South Australia.[20] Whether because, as Whitlam suggested, Dunstan discovered that only prime ministers could request the issue of royal warrants establishing awards, or for other reasons, the plan did not then progress.[21] It is possible the real reason was that Dunstan shelved his ideas for a South Australian honour when it became clear that Whitlam's federal government proposed to create a system of Australian honours to replace the British one, meaning that, after all, there would still be a way to honour meritorious service by Australians.

In creating a system of Australian honours, Whitlam was drawn to the Canadian model, which had interested him since its inception in 1967.[22] Accordingly, Australian officials visited Canada in 1974 and 1975, and were assisted in developing an Australian system by Carl Lochnan, the secretary of the Order of Canada, and other civil servants.[23] By this time considerable momentum and a degree of bipartisanship existed for the creation of uniquely Australian honours. Gorton had investigated the possibility, and Billy Snedden, McMahon's successor as Liberal leader, had made it known that he too approved the idea.[24] Public support also appeared to be growing. A February 1973 poll, which asked respondents if they would prefer to continue using imperial honours, to replace them with Australian awards, or to abolish all honours, found that the level of support for Australian honours had increased since the question was last asked in 1968. Forty-nine per cent now favoured home-grown awards, compared to 43 per cent in 1968, while 23 per cent preferred British (down from 24 per cent in 1968), and 17 per cent wanted to see all honours abolished (24 per cent had felt this way in 1968). No option was given to combine British and Australian systems. There was, however, a clear political difference, with 57 per cent of ALP voters preferring Australian awards, compared to 43 per cent of those who voted Liberal and Country Party. Respondents who favoured British awards, the

---

20   Whitlam, *The Whitlam Government*, 140.
21   Whitlam, *The Whitlam Government*, 140.
22   *A Matter of Honour*, 14; Whitlam, *The Whitlam Government*, 141; Hazell, 'The Australian Honours System', 39.
23   Hazell, 'The Australian Honours System', 39; Whitlam, *The Whitlam Government*, 141; Library and Archives Canada, Lochnan papers, R5769 10-5, kindly provided by Christopher McCreery.
24   Gavin Souter, 'For Services to Australia …', *Sydney Morning Herald*, 29 December 1973, 10, NLA cuttings.

Canberra Times reported, '[felt] strongly towards Britain and the Queen', while the '[m]ost common arguments for Australian awards were, "more appropriate" and "let's be separate"'.[25]

Despite the example of the Canadian system to draw from, it took some time to design the new national system. The delay occasioned in finalising the design and instituting the new system was too much for the progressive Dunstan in South Australia, whose ability to act quickly rivalled Whitlam's. In December 1974 it was reported that while he wanted to 'co-operate with' the federal government in creating a new system of Australian honours, in the face of continual delays his Cabinet had begun considering the establishment of State honours instead. A scheme for a three-level 'Company of Merit' was said to have been produced, but it lacked support both within Cabinet, and from the wider Labor caucus. As would the federal plan, this idea drew some ridicule. South Australian literary critic and editor Max Harris was quoted calling for an 'Order of the Hairy-nosed Wombat' and an 'Order of the Dingo', but also more seriously remarking that a new generation was 'no longer fooled or impressed by the snobbish, corrupt and anti-democratic honours system', and that Dunstan ought to be informed that 'we can live without the whole load of codswallop'.[26] It is now a matter of historical record that no such State award was ever developed, but the scheme is significant for the possibility it represented. Unlike Canada, where provincial awards have become an established and esteemed part of the honours system, no separate State awards have ever developed in Australia, and apart from this instance in South Australia, they have never seemed likely.

If Dunstan was a source of pressure on Whitlam, so too was the Tasmanian Labor Government. As Kerr informed the Palace, both States wished for a rapid introduction of a new Australian system of honours, partly because if the federal government were to lose power without creating such a system, they would be unable to bestow British awards, given the federal ALP's determination on the matter.[27] Neither had long to wait. In early 1975, the Queen signed the letters patent for the new suite of Australian honours. By this time, such a move away from imperial honours on the part of one of the former dominions must have seemed natural and inevitable in

---

25 'New Honours Favoured By Most', *Canberra Times*, 5 March 1973, 7. Eleven per cent were undecided, as 9 per cent had been in 1968.
26 'State Honours Scheme Meets Opposition', *Canberra Times*, 9 December 1974, 2.
27 NAA: AA1984/609, PART 1, letter to Sir Martin Charteris, private secretary to the Queen, from John R. Kerr, 4 February 1975.

Britain. Canada, after all, had abandoned imperial honours—apart from a brief revival in the 1930s—in 1919, and had created its own awards several years previously, and New Zealand would shortly announce the creation of its first national award, the Queen's Service Order and Medal.

Kerr announced the creation of the new system on 17 February. Later that day he spoke about the new awards on radio and television, outlining their structure, purpose, and criteria. Observing that the move was 'a logical development' from the change in the Queen's style and titles that had occurred in 1973—when she became Queen of Australia—he explained that the honours would be conferred in her name, and with her approval, and that they would be 'available to all Australians'.[28] The central component of the system was to be an Order of Australia, with three levels: Companion, Officer, and Member (AC, AO, and AM, respectively). Like its Canadian counterpart, it would be without titles, and it was to be accompanied by several bravery decorations, which would be called the Cross of Valour, the Star of Courage, the Bravery Medal, and the Commendation for Brave Conduct. A long-service decoration, the National Medal, was also to be instituted, to be given to 'members of uniformed services, including the armed forces, police, fire brigades and ambulance services'.[29]

New selection processes were also planned. Appointments to the Order of Australia's civil division would be recommended 'by a Council representative of national and state interests' to the governor-general, while the minister for defence would nominate for those in the military division and bravery decorations would be put forward by a new Decorations Advisory Committee. Nominations for the National Medal would be made to the governor-general by 'the respective chiefs of the Australian and State forces'. An office within that of the governor-general would 'administer all aspects of the new ... system'.[30] Criteria for the new awards differentiated the three grades of the Order of Australia in terms of the significance, scope, and responsibility of the services rendered by recipients.

---

28 NAA: M4799, 1/2, 'Text of an Address Given by His Excellency the Governor-General of Australia, the Honourable Sir John Kerr, K.C.M.G., K.St.J, Q.C., on Radio and Television', 17 February 1975.
29 NAA: M4799, 1/2, 'Text of an Address Given by His Excellency the Governor-General of Australia, the Honourable Sir John Kerr, K.C.M.G., K.St.J, Q.C., on Radio and Television', 17 February 1975; Whitlam, *The Whitlam Government*, 141–42.
30 NAA: M4799, 1/2, 'Text of an Address Given by His Excellency the Governor-General of Australia, the Honourable Sir John Kerr, K.C.M.G., K.St.J, Q.C., on Radio and Television', 17 February 1975; Whitlam, *The Whitlam Government*, 142.

The AC, which would be limited to no more than 20 appointments per year, was for 'eminent achievement and merit of the highest degree in service to Australia or to humanity at large'; the AO—up to 50 awards per year—for 'distinguished service of a high degree to Australia or to humanity at large'; and the AM—limited to 125 per year—for 'service in a particular locality or field of activity or to a particular group'. In the military division, the AC recognised 'eminent service in duties of great responsibility', the AO 'distinguished service in responsible positions', and the AM 'exceptional service or performance of duty'.[31] For the bravery decorations, the distinctions emphasised the level of gallantry and degree of danger: the Cross of Valour was 'for acts of the most conspicuous courage in circumstances of extreme peril'; the Star of Courage rewarded 'acts of conspicuous courage in circumstances of great peril'; the Bravery Medal acknowledged 'acts of bravery in hazardous circumstances'; and the Commendation for Brave Conduct was to be given 'for other acts of bravery which are considered worthy of recognition'. The key criterion for the National Medal was 'diligent service for not less than 15 years'.[32]

The Order of Australia was given very high precedence, as was necessary if its highest grade was ever to rival knighthood in prestige. The precedence of the order was explained a few months later by Sir Garfield Barwick, Chief Justice of the High Court and the chair of the order's council, in a letter to the editor published in major newspapers around the country. At the beginning of the council's first meeting, Barwick said, its members had learned that the Queen had decided upon the place in the order of precedence to be occupied by the order's various grades. Companions would rank above Companions of Honour and knights commander of all other orders; officers would be placed above companions/commanders of all other orders and just below knights bachelor; and members would fall between companions/commanders and members of all other orders. Barwick also announced several decisions the council had taken. First, recipients of British honours were not to receive Australian awards unless they had in the interim rendered further service of an appropriate standard. Second, the council would not consider self-nominations. Third, members of the council would not themselves make any nominations. And finally, he laid out the process by which awards would be made. Nominators

---

31   Hazell, 'The Australian Honours System', 40.
32   NAA: M4799, 1/2, 'Text of an Address Given by His Excellency the Governor-General of Australia, the Honourable Sir John Kerr, K.C.M.G., K.St.J, Q.C., on Radio and Television', 17 February 1975.

should clearly describe the services of the nominee, and suggest the names of referees who could substantiate those achievements. There would then be a process of checking, before the council considered the nominations and made recommendations to the governor-general for the twice-yearly lists, subject to the numerical limits in the letters patent establishing the order.[33]

Reactions to the Order of Australia in a time of 'new nationalism'

How was this new system of Australian honours received, in an era of so-called 'new nationalism'? Despite the new mood, it was not an entirely propitious time for creating new national symbols. Such a task would probably always have been liable to produce division, given the extent to which Australia's history and political culture was entangled with British institutional models and cultural forms. But in a moment of counter-cultural questioning of tradition and authority, and the growth of a certain scepticism towards nationalism and patriotism, it was even more complicated, with attempts—as was the case with efforts to find a new national anthem—sometimes seeming ridiculous rather than dignified, half-baked echoes of an earlier time.[34] Symptomatic of the confusion and uncertainty over national identity and national symbols, reactions to the new honours were mixed. State governments, predictably, split along party lines. The Labor governments of South Australia and Tasmania announced that they would make use of the new awards, and Dunstan stated that his government no longer intended to pursue the idea of a State honours system.[35] Each of the four non-Labor States, on the other hand, immediately dismissed the new Order. Victoria's Liberal premier, Rupert 'Dick' Hamer, said that his State would not be accepting the system, remarking that there had been no consultation from Canberra, and that anyway his government favoured British awards.[36] 'I can't see the necessity for the new system,' he

---

33 Garfield Barwick, letter to the editor, *Canberra Times*, 30 May 1975, 14. The letter also appeared in various formats in the *Australian*, 30 May 1975, 8; the *West Australian* (Perth), 2 June 1975, 7; the *Herald* (Melbourne), 29 May 1975, 3; and likely elsewhere: see NLA cuttings.
34 Curran and Ward, *Unknown Nation*. For further discussion of the complexities of Australia's honorific landscape during this period, see also Karen Fox and Samuel Furphy, 'The Politics of National Recognition: Honouring Australians in a Post-Imperial World', *Australian Journal of Politics and History* 63, no. 1 (2017): 93–111. doi.org/10.1111/ajph.12317.
35 'Non-Labor Premiers Reject Honours Plan', *Sydney Morning Herald*, 18 February 1975, 13.
36 Michelle Grattan, 'First New Honors in June', *Age* (Melbourne), 18 February 1975, 1.

stated, 'as there is nothing wrong with our present system'.[37] In New South Wales, premier Tom Lewis asserted that '[u]nder no circumstances' would the new awards be adopted in his State, and Western Australia's premier, Sir Charles Court, stated that his government would continue sending its own lists to the Palace.[38] Joh Bjelke-Petersen, the National Country Party premier of Queensland, declared that '[w]e stand by the present ... system and will continue to use it'.[39] Other countries envied the British system of honours, he said, and the Order of Australia would not come 'within a cooee' of them.[40]

At the federal level, a spokesman for the opposition leader, Snedden, said merely that the federal opposition would consider the new awards at a joint party meeting.[41] The governor-general, however, reported to the Queen that Snedden had told him privately that he 'favour[ed] ... an Order of Australia to replace, for Australian purposes, the Order of the British Empire', though he thought it ought to include knighthood, and—or so Kerr had 'reason to believe'—he wished awards within the other imperial orders to be retained. Somewhat hopefully, Kerr suggested that the States might eventually come to take Snedden's view, and he expressed his own opinion that the creation of the new order was 'a very good thing'.[42] The Palace itself responded supportively. Replying to Kerr, Bill Heseltine, the Queen's assistant private secretary (and an Australian), noted that it 'seem[ed] a sensible way of proceeding ... if the Australian States begin to use the Order of Australia in place of the Order of the British Empire'.[43] At the same time, the Queen was 'pleased', during the process of creating the new system, that Whitlam had assented to her continuing to make appointments to the lower grades of the Royal Victorian Order, an honour in her own personal gift that was often conferred during royal tours.[44]

---

37 '"States Wrong to Ignore New Honors List"', *Australian*, 19 February 1975, 3, NLA cuttings.

38 'New System of Federal Honours', *Canberra Times*, 18 February 1975, 1; 'Non-Labor Premiers Reject Honours Plan', *Sydney Morning Herald*, 18 February 1975, 13.

39 '"States Wrong to Ignore New Honors List"', *Australian*, 19 February 1975, 3, NLA cuttings.

40 'Non-Labor Premiers Reject Honours Plan', *Sydney Morning Herald*, 18 February 1975, 13.

41 'New System of Federal Honours', *Canberra Times*, 18 February 1975, 1.

42 NAA: AA1984/609, PART 1, letter to Sir Martin Charteris, private secretary to the Queen, from [John Kerr], 19 February 1975.

43 NAA: AA1984/609, PART 1, letter to the Governor-General of Australia from Bill Heseltine, 25 February 1975.

44 NAA: AA1984/609, PART 1, letter to the Governor-General of Australia from Martin Charteris, 10 February 1975.

The differences of opinion between State and federal governments can, of course, be seen as simply political, an example of the paralysing tendency of political parties to reject any idea put forward by their opponents, regardless of any merits it might have. They were also, as Curran and Ward have pointed out, as much a matter of the wider constitutional issue of States' rights as one of national identity or independence, one battle in the escalating war between the premiers and the prime minister, as he sought to centralise power in the federal capital, and they to defend their positions as the heads of sovereign territories.[45] As Kerr put it in a report to the Palace, Whitlam was engaged 'in a running battle with the Premiers' of the non-Labor States, and, while Snedden would face 'similar problems' if he became prime minister, Whitlam's 'vigorous challenges to the States' and '[h]is manner of handling' the premiers had 'exacerbated the problem'.[46] Hobart's *Mercury* recognised these aspects of the clash, describing the stand-off over honours as 'politically puerile', and observing that '[s]urely the States and the Commonwealth could be expected to work out a mutually acceptable system of national honours'. 'But,' the paper continued, 'the concept of the Commonwealth and the States working together evaporated with Labor centralism and the non-Labor States taking issue with both real and imagined intrusions into State rights.'[47] The *West Australian* felt similarly, but was more certain where the blame lay. Whitlam had not 'taken the trouble to canvass the views of the people, the States and other political parties', with the result that he had further damaged federal–State government relations, potentially politicised the honours system, and given the country a 'patchwork' system of honours and new awards that 'might not even survive a change of government in Canberra'.[48] A more immediate concern exercised the governor-general. When, despite their opposition to the new honours, all States except Western Australia nominated a representative for the Order of Australia's council—reportedly to prevent the possibility of his nominating Labor figures—Kerr told the Palace the four non-Labor States seemed 'to have come to an agreement amongst themselves' to select public servants 'with

---

45   Curran and Ward, *Unknown Nation*, 217.
46   NAA: AA1984/609, PART 1, letter to Sir Martin Charteris, private secretary to the Queen, from [John Kerr], 19 February 1975.
47   NAA: A3211, 1975/1182 PART 1, press cutting, 'At War Again', *Mercury* (Hobart), 19 February 1975.
48   NAA: A3211, 1975/1182 PART 1, press cutting, 'New Honours', *West Australian* (Perth), 19 February 1975.

a kind of watching brief', and he feared the chosen representatives might break the confidentiality of the council's deliberations by reporting its work to their respective premiers.[49]

Nevertheless, the dispute was also—and perhaps especially for media commentators and other members of the intelligentsia for whom the day-to-day political battles and constitutional implications were less immediate—part of an ongoing debate over identity. As noted above, and as Ward and others have discussed, in the wake of Britain's first bid to enter the European Economic Community in 1961, and its successful second attempt to do so in 1973, a 'new nationalism' had arisen in Australia, as politicians, artists, and thinkers sought to redefine the nation in more independent terms, and to establish for it a new and confident national identity suitable for a country no longer tethered to its British heritage. From the mid-1960s, as Curran and Ward have put it, Australians were 'confronted with the task of remaking their nation in the wake of empire', for Britishness could no longer provide a credible material, sentimental, or symbolic base for their self-image.[50] Official efforts to address this identity dislocation had included policy moves such as increased funding for the arts, in the hope that a uniquely Australian identity might develop from such initiatives.[51] For some, these were welcome developments, a sign that the country was finally ready to mature, to let go of the British apron strings, as the common metaphor went, and to come into its own as a nation. For others, the emphasis on developing a new Australian national identity was no more than a hurtful discarding of ties of heritage and loyalty that had sustained the nation and its people since its beginning. At the same time, as this history of honours demonstrates, there had long existed a strand of anti-imperial sentiment in some sectors of the community, and a perceived tension between the country's British

49   NAA: AA1984/609, PART 1, letter to Sir Martin Charteris, private secretary to the Queen, from John R. Kerr, 23 April 1975; NAA: AA1984/609, PART 1, press cutting, John O'Hara, 'NSW Still Objects to New Honours', *Sydney Morning Herald*, 11 April 1975; NAA: AA1984/609, PART 1, press cutting, Ian Frykberg, 'Names Sought for Honours', *Sydney Morning Herald*, 12 April 1975; NAA: AA1984/609, PART 1, press cutting, John O'Hara, 'Half of Honours Selectors There for Ride', *Sydney Morning Herald*, 16 April 1975. Western Australia, having initially refused to nominate a representative, then attempted to do so, only to find that in the interim Kerr had nominated Sir David Brand, a former Liberal premier of the State. NAA: AA1984/609, PART 1, letter to Sir Martin Charteris, private secretary to the Queen, from John R. Kerr, 23 April 1975.
50   Curran and Ward, *Unknown Nation*, 5.
51   See, for example, the comments of Peter Howson, Australia's first minister for the arts, quoted in Stuart Ward, '"Culture up to our Arseholes": Projecting Post-Imperial Australia', *Australian Journal of Politics and History* 51, no. 1 (2005): 64. doi.org/10.1111/j.1467-8497.2005.00360.x.

roots and its independent national existence were hardly new. Calls for distinctively Australian national symbols were also not novel. What was taking place in the 1960s was in this sense an intensification of the nation's identity dilemma, rather than an entirely new development.

Honours became another site in these identity wars. For Whitlam, creating Australian honours was part of a broader set of moves his government was making to bring the country's symbols into line with its changing relationship with Britain. Among those reforms were amendments to the Queen's style and titles to remove references to the United Kingdom and to the monarch's role as Defender of the Faith, and to describe her as the Queen of Australia; altering the way in which foreign ambassadors were nominated and their credentials accepted, and Australian ambassadors appointed; and adopting a new national anthem in place of 'God Save the Queen'.[52] As he put it in 1973, the changes his government had initiated stemmed from his determination to 'put our relationship [with Britain] on a more mature and contemporary basis and to reflect the development of a more independent Australian identity in the world'.[53] In a later account of his government, he recalled having been 'intent on placing Australia's relations with both Britain and the monarch on a contemporary basis, reflecting the realities and the aspirations of the Australian people'.[54] This was not, as he saw it, a move towards an Australian republic. Asserting that he was not 'anti-Pom', in 1974 he sought to reassure observers that the relationship between Australia and Britain remained strong, and in his later account he insisted that neither he nor his government were—then— republican.[55] Not only the name of the new honour, but also its design, reflected this concern for symbolism. Again Canada provided a model, with those involved in the order's creation viewing that country's insignia as 'a useful standard', and inclining toward 'something from nature' for the design—although preferring 'a floral rather than animal motif', and avoiding an Indigenous Australian one.[56]

---

52 Whitlam, *The Whitlam Government*, 131, 136–37, 145–46.
53 Whitlam, *The Whitlam Government*, 130–31.
54 Whitlam, *The Whitlam Government*, 130.
55 Russell Schneider, 'Local Titles Likely to Replace British Honors', *Australian*, 23 December 1974, 1, NLA cuttings; Whitlam, *The Whitlam Government*, 130.
56 NAA: A3211, 1975/1182 PART 1, letter to Stuart Devlin from K. McDonald, official secretary, 2 June 1975.

Public and media reactions to the new awards were ambivalent, but almost all recognised this aspect of national identity creation in their establishment. Some praised it, some bemoaned it, and some were undecided. In Melbourne, the *Herald* thought the order 'sensible and dignified', and 'a good deal more realistic ... than membership of an order of an empire which no longer exists', while the *Age* saw the new system as 'a step in the direction of national identity', though noting that it was 'more a healthy extension of tradition than a break with it' for the honours were 'to be approved by the Queen, [and] ... grafted on to the existing ... system'.[57] Another advantage, in the opinion of the *Age*, was the 'fresh chance' provided by the new awards 'to end the shoddy cult of political pay-off which so often supplanted real merit and distinction'.[58] Also writing in the *Age*, and despite his general scepticism about the whole concept of honours, columnist Claude Forell suggested that the Order of Australia was 'less inherently absurd' than continuing to appoint people to an order 'of a non-existent empire' or other 'overseas orders of chivalry'.[59] South Australia's *Advertiser*, while sympathetic to the fact that some may mourn the loss of traditional honours and links to Britain, considered there was 'no reason' why the new order could not be as successful as Canada's. Not only would it allow achievement and service to be recognised, it would

> do so in a form which at the same time embraces a national identity and abandons the relationship with ancient orders of chivalry whose significance has inevitably lessened with the passage of time.[60]

And in Hobart, the *Mercury* held that although Whitlam ('and several of his colleagues') had 'some peculiar ideas about a new nationalism for Australia', some of which 'smack[ed] more of banana republic xenophobia than of what should be expected of a responsible middle power', that did not mean 'all the moves to give Australia a new identity should be condemned out of hand by the non-Labor States mainly for reasons of

---

57 'Order of Australia Fits Our Identity', *Herald* (Melbourne), 18 February 1975, 4, NLA cuttings; 'Australia's Own Honors', *Age* (Melbourne), 18 February 1975, 7.
58 'Australia's Own Honors', *Age* (Melbourne), 18 February 1975, 7.
59 Claude Forell, 'New Honors and Old Pretensions', *Age* (Melbourne), 20 February 1975, 8, NLA cuttings.
60 NAA: A3211, 1975/1182 PART 1, press cutting, 'Australian Honors', *Advertiser* (Adelaide), 19 February 1975.

hidebound principle'. Just as Canada had, the paper asserted, Australia 'has progressed to a point in world status and prestige where she could be expected to have her own awards for service and bravery'.[61]

Even-handedly, or perhaps just confusedly, the *Sydney Morning Herald* declared there was 'not the slightest reason why Australia, as a sovereign independent commonwealth', could not have its own order, but avowed at the same time that the 'average Australian' might not appreciate 'the pretence' that British honours were not being diminished.[62] In its 'Candid Comment' column, R. T. Foster—the man behind the 'Onlooker' persona—foresaw dangers in the dual system that had, by default, been created. Not only would there be a proliferation of honoured people, but he anticipated 'jealousy' between the holders of the rival decorations and wondered what would be the fate of the new awards when its creators received 'the Order of the Boot' from voters.[63] The *Australian* too seemed reluctant to commit. Although positive about the assertion inherent in the new system that Australia had 'come of age as a nation', the paper forecast that the order would be 'labelled … the Ocker Award', and, at least for a time, 'feel a bit second-rate'.[64]

There were also more negative responses. Brisbane's *Courier-Mail* thought the Whitlam Government was 'behaving like Bazza McKenzie', seeking 'to proclaim its Australianism to the point of chauvinism', while others made '[s]nide references to Gough's Gongs and the Order of the Wombat'.[65] Such mockery was not—or at least not entirely—mere opposition for the sake of it. It tapped into the broader feeling of scepticism about the creation of new national symbols identified by Curran and Ward. In the irreverent 1970s, such symbols of nationalism as anthems and awards seemed to belong to an older era of jingoistic nationalism that was now perceived as humorous, if not dangerous, and it appeared difficult, if not impossible, to establish new symbols that carried appropriate meaning

---

61 NAA: A3211, 1975/1182 PART 1, press cutting, 'At War Again', *Mercury* (Hobart), 19 February 1975.

62 'E and OE', *Sydney Morning Herald*, 19 February 1975, 6.

63 'Onlooker', 'Candid Comment', *Sun-Herald* (Sydney), 23 February 1975, 42.

64 'Why We Need Our Own Honors', *Australian*, 19 February 1975, 8.

65 'What Papers Think About New Honours', *West Australian* (Perth), 21 February 1975, 5, NLA cuttings; Jane Brumfield, 'To the Top with Honors', *Australian*, 18 February 1980, 7, NLA cuttings; 'Gough's Gongs!' *Sun* (Sydney), 12 February 1975, 3, NLA cuttings; 'Gough's Gong', *Sun* (Sydney), 21 November 1974, 3, NLA cuttings. Barry McKenzie was a character invented by the comedian Barry Humphries to parody uncouth Australian behaviour overseas.

and dignity.[66] In the *Sydney Morning Herald* in late 1973, Gavin Souter had tried to reassure readers that the proposals Whitlam was receiving from the public servants tasked with preparing the new system had no such problem. Referencing the long tradition of mockery of local titles, he echoed the famous phrase that Daniel Deniehy had used to decry the idea of an Australian peerage more than a century ago, but this time in an effort to deflect any scepticism that the new honours might be just such an object of ridicule: 'it is understood that there is nothing of a bunyip aristocracy about them'. The department, he said, had 'looked closely at' other systems, especially that of Canada.[67]

Satire and mockery were also a common reaction to newly created honours, as demonstrated by the example of the establishment of the Order of the British Empire in 1917 (see Chapter 3). To some extent, then, satire about newly created Australian awards can be understood as a symptom of their very newness. Age and a sense of tradition—actual or invented—are part of what gives honours their weight and value. Before one can fully appreciate being elevated into the ranks of an illustrious company, there must be an illustrious company to join. Yet there was perhaps an extra edge to the mockery of newly created awards in the former settler dominions, which themselves were often viewed as young nations without a lengthy sense of tradition and history—appreciation of the long human history of the Australian continent being still to develop widely—and in an era of increased scepticism of both hierarchy and patriotic ritual. Jokes about local awards have also been heard across the Tasman, for instance. In the mid-1990s, when New Zealand undertook a review of its honours system and created the New Zealand Order of Merit, the country's minister for justice, Doug Graham, supported the continued use of titles in the new order, on the grounds that '[d]espite the rather quaint, even obsolete terminology, the fact is it is a form of tradition in a young country rather light on tradition'. 'I doubt,' he said, 'whether the Order of the Kakapo has the same impact as Knight Commander of the Most Distinguished Order of St Michael and St George.'[68] There seemed in such comments to be an air of embarrassment, a tone of uncertainty over whether Australia

---

66   Curran and Ward, *Unknown Nation*.
67   Gavin Souter, 'For Services to Australia ...', *Sydney Morning Herald*, 29 December 1973, 10, NLA cuttings.
68   '"Sirs" Go Way of Swords and Armour', *New Zealand Herald* (Auckland), 1 June 2003 [online]. On these comments, see also Mandy Wong, 'Royal Honours System', *Te Ara—The Encyclopedia of New Zealand*, accessed 14 May 2021, teara.govt.nz/en/royal-honours-system/print. A kakapo is a flightless native New Zealand parrot.

and New Zealand could produce the kind of solemn national symbols required for honours (notwithstanding that neither garters nor baths are especially dignified items from which to create high honours).

Reactions were not entirely focused on the issue of nationalism, however. In the *Australian Women's Weekly*, Ross Campbell reflected on the habit of dividing products into categories, such as 'economy, superior, and premium', and wondered if those who were appointed to the new order's third class would 'feel they are just regarded as utility citizens?'[69] This, of course, was hardly a new issue: British honours had long been divided into grades, and while the Order of Canada had been designed as a single-class award in order to avoid such insidious distinctions, this had soon been recognised to be too restrictive and been replaced by the more familiar multi-level version.[70] Meanwhile in the *Age*, shortly before the first list was announced, Tim Colebatch suggested that non-Labor politicians who wished to retain British honours were more concerned to preserve their ability to bestow titles upon each other than to maintain 'imperial links'. Examining editions of *Who's Who in Australia*, Colebatch had found that '[a]t least one in six' Australian knights and dames were current or former Liberal or Country Party politicians. Since recommendations for the new honours were to be made by a council, rather than by premiers or the prime minister, and since members of the public were being actively invited to nominate people, Colebatch hoped that 'purely political' honours would become a thing of the past.[71] As were media commentators, the wider public was divided. According to a Gallup poll, 44 per cent preferred the new Australian awards, and 44 per cent plumped for British ones (the remaining 12 per cent chose neither, or did not know). A political divide was clear: while 59 per cent of Labor voters expressed support for the new system, only 32 per cent of Liberal and Country Party voters did so. But approval of the Order of Australia did not necessarily translate to a desire to see the end of imperial honours, even among Labor supporters, with 65 per cent overall, and 56 per cent of Labor voters, wanting them retained.[72]

---

69   Ross Campbell, 'Better Than Super', *Australian Women's Weekly*, 26 March 1975, 57.
70   See Christopher McCreery, *The Order of Canada: Its Origins, History, and Development* (Toronto: University of Toronto Press, 2005), especially 117, 124–6, 152–4. doi.org/10.3138/9781442627963.
71   Tim Colebatch, 'Knights of the Right Parties', *Age* (Melbourne), 6 May 1975, 9, NLA cuttings.
72   'Keep UK Honors, Say 65%', *Herald* (Melbourne), 22 March 1975, 2, NLA cuttings. The proportion of Liberal and Country Party voters wishing British honours to remain was 74 per cent.

Diversity and inclusivity: Change or continuity?

As it was in the rest of the world, the early 1970s in Australia was a period of great social and cultural change. A new paradigm of politics was emerging focused on diversity and inclusivity, as a range of movements sought equality for various marginalised groups. With the gradual dismantling of the White Australia immigration policy from the end of World War II, and the development of a policy of multiculturalism, Australia's population was becoming increasingly ethnically diverse.[73] At the same time, there were intensifying protests from Indigenous Australians, and more assertive calls from Indigenous activists for land rights, the cessation of discrimination, and self-determination. Government policy began to respond to these calls, as has come to be epitomised for many in the iconic photograph of Whitlam pouring a handful of red sand into the hand of Vincent Lingiari, in symbolic acknowledgement of Aboriginal land rights, which his government was starting to move to accept. As in many other Western countries, too, a so-called second wave of feminism had arisen in the late 1960s, and women's liberation groups were soon forming in Australia. Challenging gender roles and family structures, these new, more radical feminist groups sought sweeping social and cultural changes. Governments in Australia, including Whitlam's, were beginning to bring feminist voices into their programs and bureaucracies, with Whitlam creating the office of women's adviser, and appointing Elizabeth Reid to the role. As Michelle Arrow has argued, Australian society and politics were being transformed by the feminist assertion that the personal was political, and individuals' personal experiences and identities were being deployed as a new basis for political action.[74]

Many of these changes had begun in the decade before Whitlam took office as prime minister, but he and his supporters had embraced them, feeling—in the words of his 1972 campaign slogan—that it was time for change. For many of those who felt this way, the creation of a new national system of honours was a step in that direction, away from an old-fashioned, hierarchical, anachronistically named set of awards bestowed by a sovereign who was, to some, a foreigner. But if it was in this way a response to, or a part of, the 'new nationalism' of the era, what of those other movements for change? Was the Order of Australia different

---

73   On the end of the White Australia policy, see Gwenda Tavan, *The Long Slow Death of White Australia* (Melbourne: Scribe, 2005).
74   See Arrow, *The Seventies*.

from its predecessors in terms of the ethnic diversity of its recipients, the proportion of women receiving awards, or the class status of those appointed to it? In other words, did the social and cultural change of the 1960s and 1970s flow through into the honours system to transform it as Australian society was being transformed? Was the optimism of the 'It's Time' campaign, and the symbolism of a new national award, carried through into a new era in honours practice?

The first awards for the new Order of Australia were announced in June 1975, just a few months after its establishment. Containing 110 names, the list included eight people appointed as companions, 13 officers, and 89 members, fewer in each case than the maximum number of appointments that could be made each year.[75] In this first batch of awards, there was an awareness of the importance for the order that the nominations be of suitably distinguished figures, 'whose selection will guarantee [its] quality and character'.[76] Some effort also appears to have been made to cover a range of fields of endeavour. In his periodical report to the Queen, Kerr indicated that he thought there had 'been a fine response' from nominees, despite four refusals of the AO.[77] At the highest level, the arts were well represented, with two of the eight ACs (those for author Patrick White and opera singer Joan Sutherland) conferred for achievements in this field, while historian Manning Clark was recognised for his work in 'Australian literature and history', and public servant Herbert Cole 'Nugget' Coombs for 'public services' and services to 'the arts and government'. While the prominence given to the arts in these awards is striking, it is difficult to draw firm conclusions about a change in the direction of honours from one list, and particularly from an initial list such as this, for which such prominent cultural figures were perhaps natural—even obvious—choices.

Moreover, if such generous recognition of the arts was something of a new departure, there was also a hefty serving of traditional awards. Besides the honour for Coombs, a public servant, one companionship went to a businessman (Sir Lindesay Clark, for services to the mining industry); one to a politician (Eric Reece, the former Tasmanian Labor premier);

---

75 '110 Get Order of Australia', *Canberra Times*, 14 June 1975, 1.
76 NAA: AA1984/609, PART 1, letter to Sir Martin Charteris, private secretary to the Queen, from John R. Kerr, 23 April 1975; NAA: AA1984/609, PART 1, letter to Sir Martin Charteris, private secretary to the Queen, from John R. Kerr, 4 February 1975.
77 NAA: AA1984/609, PART 1, letter to Sir Martin Charteris, private secretary to the Queen, from [John Kerr], 11 June 1975. The four refusals came from the poet Judith Wright, the journalist Tom Fitzgerald, the painter Sidney Nolan, and Jerry Price, the chair of the Commonwealth Scientific and Industrial Research Organization.

and two were appointments to the military division (Lieutenant-General Frank Hassett, the chief of the army general staff, and Admiral Sir Victor Smith, the chair of the chiefs of staff committee).[78] There was, nevertheless, something of Whitlam's broader vision for Australia here, and a definite flavour of 'new nationalism'. Clark, of course, was well known for his writings on the history of Australia, and was just beginning to assume the role of the prophet of Australian identity and nationalism that he would later seem to embody, while Coombs, through his role in supporting the arts, had contributed much to the push for a new and vibrant Australian literary and artistic voice.

A range of professions were honoured at the officer level, though with an unusual emphasis on science, research, and education. Four of the 13 AOs— half of those awarded in the civil division—went to individuals involved in these fields: Geoffrey Badger was the vice-chancellor of the University of Adelaide, where he had also been a professor of organic chemistry; Antarctic scientist Phillip Law was a former director of the Antarctic division at the Department of External Affairs and the vice-president of the Victoria Institute of Colleges; Byron Kakulas was a medical researcher specialising in muscular diseases and neuropathology; and Geoffrey Blainey was a professor of history at the University of Melbourne and the chair of the literature board of the Australia Council. The other AOs bestowed in the civil division encompassed two for community service or social welfare work (David Scott, the director of the Brotherhood of St Laurence, and Giacomo 'Jim' Bayutti, 'a confidante of' Whitlam who worked to assist migrants); one for 'transportation and public service' (Allan George Gibbs); and one for 'management and international relations' (Allan George Moyes).[79] Five men were appointed AO in the military division: Rear Admiral Geoffrey Gladstone, Major-General Stuart Graham, Air Vice-Marshall Geoffrey Newstead, Major-General Cedric 'Sandy' Pearson, and Major-General Alan Stretton, who had been director-general of the Natural Disasters Organisation and had headed the emergency operation during Cyclone Tracy in Darwin the previous year.[80] It might also be noted that four of the 13 were named Geoffrey, surely an anomaly demonstrating that not all statistics are meaningful.

---

78 'First List of Australian Order', *Canberra Times*, 14 June 1975, 9; '110 Get Order of Australia', *Canberra Times*, 14 June 1975, 1.
79 'Multicultural Pioneer', *Sydney Morning Herald*, 6 February 1991, 4; 'First List of Australian Order', *Canberra Times*, 14 June 1975, 9; '110 Get Order of Australia', *Canberra Times*, 14 June 1975, 1.
80 'First List of Australian Order', *Canberra Times*, 14 June 1975, 9; '110 Get Order of Australia', *Canberra Times*, 14 June 1975, 1.

A great deal of variety is evident among the names appointed to the third level of the order, the membership. Besides the 36 individuals who became members of the military division, the awards recognised activities as diverse as soil conservation (Sam Clayton, the first director of the New South Wales Soil Conservation Service); 'amateur sport' (David Henry McKenzie); aviation (Sergeant Ralph John Naughton); and 'photography and the study of nature' (Athel D'Ombrain, an optical dispenser who became a naturalist and photographer). Easily the largest clusters of awards in the civil division appointments were those for community service or services to social welfare, of which there were 19, and those for services to local government, of which there were eight.[81] These are both significant proportions: 36 per cent and 15 per cent respectively. After these fields of endeavour, the next most commonly recognised were the arts, industry and commerce, conservation and the environment, and education, with stray awards for other types of activity (such as two for trade union activity, one for sport, and one for journalism).[82] In this sense, the list both followed tradition—both community service and service to local government were traditionally common categories in honours lists, particularly at the lower levels—and departed from it, as in the extent of recognition given to individuals active in the arts and in environmental causes. It is notable that, unlike in almost all lists of British honours, excepting those during the two world wars, the military AMs outnumbered the next biggest category, making military service seem the most highly awarded at this level on this list. It is possible, however, that this is a reflection of the order's new existence, which meant that both divisions of the order were, as it were, empty, and needing to be filled, and it was not necessarily a pattern to be expected in the future.

In a context of intense movements for social and political change, which Whitlam's own 'It's Time' campaign had appealed to, it might have been expected that this first list of awards in the new order would look different in terms of demographics, too. But how far was any such hope borne out? At the upper levels of the new order, the answer must be: not especially. Only one of the eight people appointed as companions of the order was a woman. Joan Sutherland, as an internationally renowned opera singer

81   'First List of Australian Order', *Canberra Times*, 14 June 1975, 9; '110 Get Order of Australia', *Canberra Times*, 14 June 1975, 1. Another two were conferred for services to women's welfare, and to Aboriginal welfare, respectively.
82   'First List of Australian Order', *Canberra Times*, 14 June 1975, 9; 110 Get Order of Australia', *Canberra Times*, 14 June 1975, 1.

who was widely popular and unlikely to be a controversial choice, was in many ways an obvious inclusion. No women, however, were included among the 13 individuals who were made officers.[83] The proportion was more respectable, if hardly groundbreaking, among the third tier, with 20 women made members of the order, six of those in the military division. This represents a total proportion of around 22 per cent of members, and 17 per cent of military division memberships. It is much more difficult, as always, to ascertain the ethnic breakdown of the list. While there are a couple of names that appear recognisably non-Anglo-Australian, any attempt at statistics is largely guesswork, and any assertion made on the basis of names alone is even more flawed than in the case of gender, potentially concealing long residence (even generations long) in Australia and missing recent migrants, particularly those who had anglicised their names. It is notable, however, that there is only one recognisably non-European name in the list: Jusaf John Khan, an appointment on the military list. Other signs, though, did suggest that there was at least some desire to recognise individuals connected with these new social movements. Irene Greenwood, a radio broadcaster and feminist, was made AM for her services to women's welfare. Keith Langford-Smith, who was a non-Indigenous missionary at Roper River and then Kellyville in New South Wales, was appointed AM for services to Aboriginal welfare. And, as mentioned above, Jim Bayutti was appointed AM for his services to the migrant community. These awards did suggest an openness to recognising the efforts of those who were working for social inclusion, equality, and rights in these diverse areas.

Was this any better than the record under Gorton or McMahon, or on recent State honours lists? Or indeed, than the lists issued under Menzies, Holt, or any other earlier leader? It has to be said that, purely on the numbers, it was not. Looking at all appointments to the Order of the British Empire, both federal and State, in the years 1965 to 1969, women had made up 4.8 per cent of CBEs (commanders), 11.1 per cent of OBEs (officers), and 26.3 per cent of MBEs (members), the latter proportion particularly notable for being higher than the 22 per cent of AMs granted to women in that first Order of Australia list. In the following five-year period, from 1970 to 1974, the difference is similar, with women receiving 8.2 per cent of CBEs, 12.2 per cent of OBEs, and 26.1 per cent

---

83   One, however, had been nominated: the poet Judith Wright, who had declined. NAA: AA1984/609, PART 1, letter to Sir Martin Charteris, private secretary to the Queen, from [John Kerr], 11 June 1975.

of MBEs. At the level of titles, women had gained 22.9 per cent of awards between 1965 and 1969, and 24.2 per cent of them from 1970 to 1974 (see tables provided in Chapter 4). These figures, however, may simply reflect the difficulty in getting enough names for the first list for the Order of Australia, and perhaps also being in a hurry, factors which might have frustrated any efforts to ensure a more evenly gender balanced list.

Nor did the new order's first list compare especially well to recent lists of British awards in relation to ethnic diversity. Numbers of awards to Indigenous Australians had been slowly increasing after the first identifiable award (an MBE to pastor and activist Doug Nicholls) in the 1950s. Several Indigenous Australians had been honoured in the late 1960s and early 1970s. On the New Year list for 1968, Methodist minister Lazarus Lamilami and activist Margaret (Lilardia) Tucker were appointed MBE, and medical assistant Phillip Roberts received a British Empire Medal (BEM), while Nicholls was promoted to OBE and boxer Lionel Rose made MBE in June.[84] Community leaders Nandjiwarra Amagula and Teddy Plummer were granted respectively an MBE and a BEM at New Year 1970, while that June MBEs were conferred on poet Kath Walker (later known as Oodgeroo Noonuccal), community worker Annie Rankine, and the chair of the South Australian Aboriginal Lands Trust, Timothy Hughes, and BEMs on guide and interpreter Tommy Dodd and tracker Nyibayarri, known as Jack Bohemia or Newbu.[85] Among those appointed MBE in 1971 were community leader Gladys Elphick, artist Yirawala, land rights activist Roy Marika, and former army officer Reg Saunders, by then a liaison officer in the Office of Aboriginal

84 '3 Territorians in Queen's New Year's Honors', *Northern Territory News* (Darwin), 1 January 1968, 3, NLA cuttings; Keith Cole, 'Lamilami, Lazarus (1913–1977)', *Australian Dictionary of Biography*, accessed 14 July 2017, adb.anu.edu.au/biography/lamilami-lazarus-10778/text19113. These and other awards mentioned in this section may be found at Australian Government, Department of the Prime Minister and Cabinet, 'Australian Honours Search Facility', *It's an Honour*, Department of the Prime Minister and Cabinet, accessed throughout this project, honours.pmc.gov.au/honours/search (see Author's Note).

85 'These Are Leaders—Giese', *Northern Territory News* (Darwin), 2 January 1972, 3, NLA cuttings; 'Works For Her People', *Advertiser* (Adelaide), 13 June 1970, 4, NLA cuttings; 'Jack Traps a Medal', *Herald* (Melbourne), 13 June 1970, 2, NLA cuttings; W. H. Edwards, 'Dodd, Tommy (1890–1975)', *Australian Dictionary of Biography*, accessed 14 July 2017, adb.anu.edu.au/biography/dodd-tommy-10027/text17677; Judith Raftery, 'Rankine, Annie Isabel (1917–1972)', *Australian Dictionary of Biography*, accessed 14 July 2017, adb.anu.edu.au/biography/rankine-annie-isabel-11488/text20487; Robert Hall, 'Hughes, Timothy (1919–1976)', *Australian Dictionary of Biography*, accessed 14 July 2017, adb.anu.edu.au/biography/hughes-timothy-10567/text18767.

Affairs.[86] In 1972, Nyamal lawman Peter Coppin received a BEM for 'services to the Aboriginal community' on the New Year list, and didjeridu player George Winunguj was appointed MBE for his 'services to the community and the performing arts' on the birthday list.[87] Australia had also gained its first Aboriginal knight in 1972: Nicholls, whose name appeared on the federal list at Queen's Birthday that year. While most other names on the lists remained—insofar as names are any guide— largely Anglo-Celtic, it is worth noting that the same Commonwealth list that announced Nicholls's knighthood also contained the names of William Lee, who for 25 years had 'assisted Chinese migrants to adapt to the Australian way of life' and who was appointed MBE for 'services to the community'; Giacomo Natoli, awarded the BEM for 'services to the Italian community'; and Elda Vaccari, who received the same honour for her 'services to migrants'.[88]

It was not the case, however, that recent lists of imperial awards had been shining beacons of diversity, or had gone uncriticised. During the late 1960s and early 1970s several articles had appeared in the media critiquing the system, a common target being the occupational balance of awards. As discussed in the previous chapter, in October 1968 Don Aitkin had perceived the system as stale and rigid, citing among other aspects the occupational balance of the lists.[89] A little more than three years later he returned to the issue, and argued for the abolition of the whole system, or, if that was too much to swallow, at least its alteration.[90] There had been other signs of discontent in recent years, too. Unhappy with the low-level awards often given to community workers and those in the arts (two occupations where women were more likely to figure), two women in 1972 planned to send back their awards, announced that June. Rose Skinner, an art gallery owner from Perth, was quoted saying that her MBE

86   'Awards for 10 Territorians', *Northern Territory News* (Darwin), 12 June 1971, 1, NLA cuttings; E. M. Fisher, 'Elphick, Gladys (1904–1988)', *Australian Dictionary of Biography*, accessed 14 July 2017, adb.anu.edu.au/biography/elphick-gladys-12460/text22411.

87   Jolly Read and Peter Coppin, *Kangkushot: The Life of Nyamal Lawman Peter Coppin* (Canberra: Aboriginal Studies Press, 1999), 163; 'The 1972 Queen's Birthday Honours List', *Canberra Times*, 3 June 1972, 8; 'Five Territorians Honored—Including George Winunguj', *Northern Territory News* (Darwin), 3 June 1972, 3, NLA cuttings.

88   'The 1972 Queen's Birthday Honours List', *Canberra Times*, 3 June 1972, 8; 'Five Territorians Honored—Including George Winunguj', *Northern Territory News* (Darwin), 3 June 1972, 3, NLA cuttings.

89   Don Aitkin, 'Between the Lines', *Canberra Times*, 16 October 1968, 2.

90   Don Aitkin, 'Now, If I Were King, There'd Be a Different Honours List', *National Times*, 10–15 January 1972, 12, NLA cuttings.

was 'an insult to Western Australia'. She had accepted it, she said, while in hospital, in the belief that she was being offered an OBE (still a grade lower than the CBE she thought her efforts in support of artists deserved), and she now wished to reject it.[91] It was then reported that Mary Logus, described as an 'elderly Red Cross worker', had said that she would not accept her BEM either. Quoted terming it 'an insult and a slap in the face' to volunteers, she compared it to the MBEs received by the Beatles, declaring that '[a]ny voluntary worker should be equal at least to a prize fighter, the Beatles or what have you'. 'I am not speaking for myself,' she said, 'but on behalf of all voluntary workers.'[92] Skinner, meanwhile, was reported to have changed her mind. She had been 'overcome with the feeling that the honor was an insult to the art medium', she said, but had decided to accept it after reflecting that 'any small recognition might help the plight of the artist'.[93]

Nor were awards, in and of themselves, always welcome or acceptable. Adding names to a list, even in an admirable attempt to increase diversity, could in some cases ignore underlying or larger issues, or cause hurt and offence. In the New Year list for 1972, Indigenous community leader Jacob Oberdoo had rejected a BEM, reportedly informing the Department of Prime Minister and Cabinet that, as 'a law carrier', he could not 'do business with or accept favours from law carriers in bad standing'. Asserting the supremacy of Indigenous law, Oberdoo challenged white Australians' lack of knowledge and respect for it, and the usurpation and exploitation of his people's land.[94] In another news report, he was quoted stating that Aboriginal people had neither land nor money, and 'haven't had much help from any government'. 'They don't need medals,' he said.[95] How the sounding process had failed so signally that the award was announced without his approval—and the same year as Logus received the BEM despite having, as she claimed, refused it—is not easy to determine.

---

91   'Gallery Owner Plans to Return Her MBE', *Canberra Times*, 3 June 1972, 9.

92   '"I'll Send Back BEM"', *Herald* (Melbourne), 3 June 1972, 1, NLA cuttings. A miscommunication of some kind appeared to have occurred, for she said that she had declined the award when sounded, and that her declining had been acknowledged; she would have 'considered' an MBE. '"I'll Send Back BEM"', *Herald* (Melbourne), 3 June 1972, 1, NLA cuttings.

93   '"I'll Send Back BEM"', *Herald* (Melbourne), 3 June 1972, 1, NLA cuttings.

94   'Aboriginal Rejects Honour', *West Australian* (Perth), 15 January 1972, 1, 4, NLA cuttings; John Bucknall, 'Oberdoo, Jacob (Minyjun) (1920–1989)', *Australian Dictionary of Biography*, accessed 13 July 2017, adb.anu.edu.au/biography/oberdoo-jacob-minyjun-15386/text26593.

95   'Aborigine Rejects Empire Medal', *Canberra Times*, 20 January 1972, 15.

In Oberdoo's case at least, it may simply have been a consequence of the time required for the post to reach recipients in remote places and return to Canberra.

Conclusion

By the time Harold Holt was lost in the surf at Cheviot Beach in 1967, many previously accepted fundamentals of Australian life had already begun to disappear. A new mood of assertive nationalism had begun to arise, with far-reaching consequences for the honours system as for so many other aspects of national existence. In the wake of Britain's decision to seek entry to the European Economic Community, Australia entered a new and unsettling era, in which civic symbols such as honours played an important role as prisms through which identity and the future of the nation could be debated. Coming to power on a platform of change in 1972, Whitlam brought his reforming energy to the honours system as to so much else. The establishment of the Order of Australia brought mixed reactions, emblematic of the broader political and generational divides produced by this uncertain period. To some a second-rate newcomer, lacking the gravitas and tradition of imperial awards and symbolising the loss of a valued British heritage, it was greeted by others as an exciting step towards national maturity and independence. Yet perhaps even more importantly, it was also a theatre in the ongoing war over States' rights, to which the election of Whitlam had given a new intensity. In the coming years, the battle over States' rights would continue to shape the honours system in ways distinct from the trajectory taken in other former British dominions and colonies. Birthed in such fire, the Order of Australia needed to make a strong start to its life to win acceptance, and the first list of awards included a number of prominent figures whose inclusion might aid that goal. In some ways quite distinctive, the list was yet by no means a dramatic shift in the pattern of awards. How the order would have developed under Whitlam and Labor must remain a matter of speculation, for its very existence would soon be threatened.

7

A system divided, 1975–1990

The Order of Australia had been only one brushstroke in the new vision of the nation Gough Whitlam had sought to create as prime minister, and it was only one of many initiatives in jeopardy as that vision crashed down unfinished on 11 November 1975. Following Whitlam's dismissal by Governor-General Sir John Kerr, Liberal leader Malcolm Fraser took office as caretaker prime minister. Despite Whitlam's exhortations to voters to 'maintain the rage', in December 1975 Fraser and his Liberal and National Party colleagues won the ensuing election with a large swing. Honours were never likely to be a major election issue, but given the longstanding differences of opinion over the system between the Labor and non-Labor parties, the switch of government spelled probable change. By the time of the election, while one list of appointments to the Order of Australia had been announced, no awards had been presented, excepting a companionship for the governor-general, as the chancellor and principal companion. It was thus particularly vulnerable, for it must have been easier to disestablish such a newly created order, whose first recipients were still awaiting their investitures, than one that had been in existence for several years and gained a measure of community acceptance. Australia's own national honour had barely begun its life, and already its survival was uncertain.

Within the context of the new nationalism of the 1970s, however, Fraser's approach to national symbols would be more complicated than simply reversing Whitlam's reforms. His moves to return to traditional forms in the nation's ceremonial life might have been intended to reassure more conservative constituents who felt unsettled by changes in the country's relationship with Britain and general orientation in the world, but he chose not to revert entirely to a pre-Whitlam ceremonial landscape. While such attempts to have it both ways could appear confused, and drew some ridicule, they reflected the reality that the nation was deeply divided over issues of identity, heritage, and future pathways. As the nation's British identity dissolved in the wake of Britain's decision to seek entry to the European Economic Community, migration shifted its demographic make-up, and the country's leaders increasingly looked in new directions, particularly towards Asia, Australians found themselves attempting to construct a new national image in a period of deep suspicion about the very idea of nationalism. The honours system, as a component in the nation's symbolic repertoire, was a central part of that tussle.

The struggle continued after the election of Labor's Bob Hawke as prime minister in 1983, despite the rise of a more confident—even somewhat brash—Australian nationalism as the nation approached its Bicentennial celebrations of 1988. In part, the stalemate was due to the country's constitutional arrangements, which enshrined the sovereignty of the States and encouraged a dual system of honours, as well as to the party divide that had become entrenched in honours policy. At the same time, in a political and cultural landscape being transformed by social movements such as those seeking women's liberation and Indigenous rights, there were hints of a greater scrutiny of the system's ability to encompass diversity. Critical attention was also drawn to the imperial system by the ways in which the government of Queensland premier Joh Bjelke-Petersen chose to use it. Changing times may have been slowly draining support for British honours, but the honorific decisions of the Bjelke-Petersen administration were quickly discrediting them.

Rolling back the changes ... sort of

Fraser's new government moved quickly to restore federal recommendations for imperial honours. But the Order of Australia—the continued existence of which had indeed reportedly been in doubt—was granted a reprieve.[1] Two key objections to the Australian order had

---

1   According to Barney Murray in the *Australian*, Fraser had been considering abolishing the Order of Australia, but was attracted by the possibility of adding knighthood to it instead. Barney Murray, 'How a New Knighthood Evolved', *Australian*, 12 June 1976, 9, newspaper cuttings on the Australian honours system, National Library of Australia, Canberra (hereafter NLA cuttings).

threatened its survival: its three grades were considered insufficient for recognising the range of achievements and services deserving reward, and decisions on appointments to it had been placed out of government control. Nevertheless, Cabinet's decision on 14 January 1976 was not only to reintroduce British honours, but to award them in parallel with those in the Order of Australia. Ministers recognised that this decision would necessitate settling on 'criteria to ensure that awards under the two systems were appropriate and compatible'.[2] Such plurality was a feature of the Fraser Government's approach to ceremonial matters. A few days after Cabinet made its decision on honours, a press release announced that, as well as combining Australian and imperial awards, the government would use the titles 'Commonwealth of Australia' and 'Commonwealth Government' for internal use but 'Australia' and 'Australian Government' in external relations, and event organisers would be able to choose from four national songs, except on vice-regal occasions, when 'God Save the Queen' was to be reinstated.[3] As the *Age* noted in some confusion, Australians thus found themselves with 'two systems of honors, ... four national anthems and four official titles for the national Government'.[4]

In February officials from Government House and the departments of Administrative Services and Prime Minister and Cabinet met to discuss the decision to bring back British honours alongside Australian ones. A discussion paper by Steve Wenger at Administrative Services laid out the major issues—how to reintroduce imperial honours most effectively, and how to manage both the relationship between British and Australian awards, and the potential impact of the return of British honours on local ones. Several ways of proceeding were identified. At one end, the prime minister might make recommendations for British awards while leaving the Order of Australia to operate independently, or nominate people for both the Order of Australia and British awards, using imperial honours only where there was no Australian equivalent. Another possibility was to amend the Order of Australia's constitution, either to give an allocation of awards to the prime minister, or to add knighthood to it, with a right for the prime minister to sidestep the council in recommending awards; in that case, only lower-level imperial honours might be needed. A far

---

2   National Archives of Australia (hereafter NAA): A1209, 1976/2235 PART 1, Cabinet minute, Decision No. 57, 14 January 1976.
3   NAA: A4204, 1985/404, 'Honours, Musical Salutes and the Title "Commonwealth"', press release from the prime minister, 21 January 1976.
4   'Honors and Diversity', *Age* (Melbourne), 26 January 1976, 9.

more dramatic possibility was to abolish the council for the Order of Australia, and to transform it into a five-grade honour, a path that Wenger noted might remove any need to revive imperial awards, for 'two of the objections to the Order of Australia, viz. that it fails to provide awards carrying a title and that its awards are not within the control of the Prime Minister', would thus be eliminated.[5]

Wenger recognised the potential for harm to be done to the fledgling Australian order. But with four States having refused to abandon British honours for Australian ones, returning imperial awards at a federal level would only add one more British list to those already appearing. It would be worse, he suggested, to politicise the Order of Australia, for then 'any advantage ... it has over British awards would be lost'. Concluding that there was 'no ideal answer' to the challenge of operating a 'dual system', he suggested that the best approach would be to retain the Order of Australia as it was—'apart from rectifying certain deficiencies which have become manifest through experience'—while the prime minister made 'a limited and very select number of nominations' for imperial awards.[6]

A report on the best way to implement Cabinet's decision made three main proposals: civil British awards other than the Order of the British Empire should be revived; appointments to the Order of Australia should go on; and a knighthood and a medal should be added to the Order of Australia. Explaining the advice to dispense with the Order of the British Empire, the authors stated that its 'continued use ... is not recommended because of its anachronistic name'. It was also, they suggested, less necessary now that an Australian order existed. Of the Order of Australia, they observed that it had 'become apparent that there are insufficient available levels'.[7] Both the order's chancellor, Governor-General Sir John Kerr, and the chair of its council, Chief Justice Sir Garfield Barwick, were understood to support the idea of adding an upper level of knighthood and a lower-level medal, and the Public Service Board had contended that relying on the order alone had reduced the number of awards available to

---

5 NAA: A4204, 1985/404, 'Honours and Awards', discussion paper, S. Wenger, Honours Branch, Department of Administrative Services, 8 February 1976.
6 NAA: A4204, 1985/404, 'Honours and Awards', discussion paper, S. Wenger, Honours Branch, Department of Administrative Services, 8 February 1976.
7 NAA: A1209, 1976/2235 PART 2, 'Honours and Awards—Report of Officers'. The report was authored by A. W. McCasker and Wenger from Administrative Services; David Smith, the official secretary to the governor-general; and A. G. Kerr, assistant secretary at the constitutional and legal affairs branch in Prime Minister and Cabinet.

public servants, especially 'in the middle and lower levels of the Service'.[8] Defence authorities had also objected to the order on the grounds that it did 'not provide knighthoods for Chiefs of Staff', and had 'inadequate provision for awards at the lower level'. The proposed additions would produce a five-level honour, which 'would be in conformity with most British Orders and enable a much wider range of service to be recognised'. There was, however, an obvious difficulty. While adding knighthood would 'enhanc[e] the prestige of the Order', it would be necessary to consider carefully 'the situation of those persons who have already been appointed Companions … in the belief that that was and would continue to be the ultimate award in the Order'.[9]

Addressing the prime minister's role, the report recommended that he submit names for the Order of Australia to its council, while also inviting nominations for British honours to be sent to himself. A series of recommendations then addressed military decorations, bravery awards, and long-service medals, advocating that British awards not be revived for these categories, except in the case of wartime bravery, where the possibility of using imperial awards was left open. Once again, a key factor was the ability of the government to decide who received honours. The authors observed that since it was, in effect, the minister for defence who determined distinguished service awards to the forces,

> one of the reservations about civil awards in the Order of Australia viz that the Commonwealth Government has no control over who does or who does not get an award, is absent.

Finally, the report addressed matters of process. It would be necessary to ensure that people did not receive awards in both systems, for example, and both British and Australian awards should be announced at the same time, on Australia Day rather than New Year's Day.[10]

Near the end of February Fraser requested a report on the situation, instructing that while it was 'intended' that Australian and British awards 'should proceed together … if there are any problems in achieving this, the

---

8   NAA: A1209, 1976/2235 PART 2, 'Honours and Awards—Report of Officers'; NAA: A1209, 1976/2235 PART 1, letter to J. L. Menadue, secretary, Department of the Prime Minister and Cabinet, from A. S. Cooley, chairman, Public Service Board, 23 January 1976.
9   NAA: A1209, 1976/2235 PART 2, 'Honours and Awards—Report of Officers'.
10   NAA: A1209, 1976/2235 PART 2, 'Honours and Awards—Report of Officers'.

British system is to be re-instituted forthwith'.[11] The Order of Australia was not out of the woods yet, it seemed. One public servant, commenting on the various proposals raised for the prime minister's consideration, had remarked that establishing knighthood within it 'might be the key to preserving [it] as our principal honour'. Recipients and governments that disliked knighthoods, after all, 'need not receive or make awards at this level'.[12] Politically necessary it may have been, but it was also extremely tricky. Any way it was done, it seemed to create difficulties. In a way, it was the same issue that had faced the designers of the Order of the British Empire 60 years earlier: how to ensure that eminent people who would not accept a title could still be honoured? But it was further complicated by the short but significant incarnation of the order as a three-class, non-titular one. What would happen to existing companions? And how would the change be received by people who had accepted the honour on the basis that it did not confer any titles?

Administrative Services proposed to alter the grade of companion so that recipients chose 'either to be a Knight Companion ... or ... a Companion'—in other words, whether or not to use the title 'Sir'. (Women, presumably, would have had the option of being Dame Companions.) Such an approach could be retrospective, covering those already appointed companions. While the unusual nature of the suggestion was recognised, it avoided the difficulties inherent in creating a separate knighthood ranked above or below the companionship:

> If the knighthood goes below A.C. [Companion of the Order of Australia] people meriting the highest award but desiring a title cannot be provided for. If a knighthood goes immediately above A.C. the reverse applies. If it goes much higher than A.C. its quota would presumably be very small and its availability would be limited.[13]

Prime Minister and Cabinet too preferred a knighthood 'comparable' to the grade of companion.[14]

---

11   NAA: A1209, 1976/2235 PART 2, letter to secretary from Malcolm Fraser, 25 February 1976. The resulting report can be found at NAA: A1209, 1976/2235 PART 2, 'Changes to the Australian Honours System', memorandum to the prime minister from P. J. Lawler, secretary, 27 February 1976.
12   NAA: A1209, 1976/2235 PART 1, 'Honours and Awards', unsigned memorandum, no date.
13   NAA: A1209, 1976/2235 PART 2, 'Changes to the Australian Honours System', memorandum to the prime minister from P. J. Lawler, secretary, 27 February 1976.
14   NAA: A1209, 1976/2235 PART 2, memorandum to the prime minister from J. L. Menadue, secretary, Department of the Prime Minister and Cabinet, 26 February 1976.

But optional knighthood also had its problems, as the framers of the Order of the British Empire had discovered in 1916. For one, the Palace was not receptive. 'All of us here see considerable difficulties', wrote Sir Martin Charteris, the Queen's private secretary, to Geoffrey Yeend, a deputy secretary at Prime Minister and Cabinet. Charteris offered a different solution. A class of knighthood could be introduced with around the same high precedence as the companion, the companion dropped further down the order of precedence, and people already appointed companions be given the chance to move up to become knights or dames. For the British, an important consideration was commensurability between the two systems. As Charteris put it:

> If, as we hope, Mr. Fraser intends to make use of the traditional British Orders, we must try to ensure that the two systems … do not get too far out of kilter.[15]

Disapproval from the Palace was moot, however, for Fraser did not like the idea. He agreed with the recommendation to create a lower award, but stressed that a very high upper-level one—with only one or two conferrals a year—must be added as well. Dealing with the other points, he stated that the government should not officially make nominations to the Order of Australia, and emphasised that he wanted the whole range of British honours available, including the Order of the British Empire.[16] The additions were announced by the governor-general at the end of May. At the top of the order was inserted a high-level knighthood or damehood, placed above the GCMG (Knight or Dame Grand Cross of the Order of St Michael and St George) in the order of precedence and known as Knight or Dame of the Order of Australia (AK/AD). At the bottom was a new lower grade, named the Medal of the Order of Australia (OAM). The AK/AD was to 'be a rare award, for extraordinary and pre-eminent achievement and merit'; no more than two appointments would be made per year. Another change revealed at the same time was that the 'civil' division would become a 'general' division, meaning that awards within it could be given to those in the defence forces, 'for services … not necessarily military in character'.[17]

---

15   NAA: A1209, 1976/2235 PART 2, letter to Geoffrey Yeend from Martin Charteris, 8 March 1976.
16   NAA: A1209, 1976/2235 PART 2, memorandum to A. W. McCasker from A. R. Palmer, 7 March 1976. Fraser was willing, however, to countenance ceasing to use the British Empire Medal.
17   NAA: A1209, 1976/2235 PART 3, press release, David I. Smith, official secretary to the governor-general, 31 May 1976.

The nation reacts

Grafting a medal on to the country's national order was relatively uncontroversial. Adding titles to it was not. Over the next two months, four people who had been appointed to the Order of Australia the previous year resigned in protest. Educator Jean Blackburn and Brotherhood of St Laurence director David Scott had been created officers (AO), while public servant H. C. 'Nugget' Coombs and author Patrick White had been made companions (AC).[18] Having declined knighthood more than once, Coombs stated that he had 'long been opposed to the granting of honours which carry with them titles which differentiate the recipient from other members of the community', and that he had only 'felt able to accept [the AC] … because the order did not confer such titles at any of its levels'.[19] Although Scott had held the distinction for only a little over a year, he had already threatened to return it once before. In that case, he had been protesting Australia's stance on East Timor.[20] This time, he was quoted saying that he felt the order should not include 'titles of distinction'.[21] White, meanwhile, told the press that the honour had been created as a 'democratic' one, and that knighthoods were 'really quite contrary to the original concept'; besides, he added, he had 'no respect' for the order's head, Sir John Kerr.[22]

Coombs's comments drew some ridicule when they were reported in the press. Did he then, asked one letter to the *Sydney Morning Herald*, plan 'to join the band of ordinary people as plain Mr?'[23] 'Nothing is more heart-warming than a well-publicised stand on egalitarian principle', wrote another correspondent, but Coombs's action was 'puzzling'. How had he accepted the honour at all, if he objected to differentiating people from the wider community? And if the difficulty was titles themselves, how did he 'endure' being Dr Coombs?[24] However, it appears that many Australians

---

18 'Dr Coombs Resigns From Order of Australia', *Sydney Morning Herald*, 11 June 1976, 1; 'Another Protest at Titles', *Canberra Times*, 23 June 1976, 8; 'Resigned Order', *Canberra Times*, 30 June 1976, 13; 'Honour Returned', *Canberra Times*, 7 July 1976, 8; Review of Australian Honours and Awards, *A Matter of Honour: The Report of the Review of Australian Honours and Awards* (Canberra: Australian Government Publishing Service, 1995), 20.
19 'Coombs Rejects Honour as Protest', *Canberra Times*, 11 June 1976, 1; Tim Rowse, *Nugget Coombs: A Reforming Life* (Cambridge: University of Cambridge Press, 2002), 360.
20 'Patience, You O of A's, the Medals are Coming', *Australian*, 12 December 1975, 11, NLA cuttings.
21 'Another Protest at Titles', *Canberra Times*, 23 June 1976, 8.
22 'No Knights for Patrick White', *Sydney Morning Herald*, 23 June 1976, 24.
23 A. Burns, letter to the editor, *Sydney Morning Herald*, 14 June 1976, 6.
24 A. W. Sparkes, letter to the editor, *Sydney Morning Herald*, 18 June 1976, 6.

drew a distinction between such titles as 'Doctor' and 'Reverend', which tended to be perceived as appropriately earned, and that of 'Sir', which carried the whiff of a despised aristocratic order. At least one opponent of Fraser's creation of an Australian knighthood turned to that overworked phrase of Daniel Deniehy's, which had hovered mockingly over the idea of titled Australians since he first uttered it in 1853. Fraser was attempting, suggested Barrie Unsworth, the assistant secretary of the New South Wales Labour Council, to establish 'a "bunyip aristocracy"'.[25]

Restoring British honours also provoked some criticism, largely on the grounds that it was a retrograde step, out of line with the country's developing identity as a mature and independent nation. In South Australia Labor premier Don Dunstan repudiated any possibility of reviving them in his State, arguing that Britain's empire was 'finished' and it was 'inappropriate' to appoint people to 'the order of the non-existent British Empire'.[26] Writer and social critic Donald Horne, in the past several years one of the loudest voices advocating a vigorous new Australian nationalism, argued that imperial honours were 'immutably linked with branch office definitions of Australia'. He imagined an 'ideal republic' where—'as a reminder of our common humanity'—no titles would be used, not even 'Mr', 'Mrs', and 'Miss', and condemned the continuation of knighthoods as 'display[ing], at the best, a shabby, provincial elitism and, at the worst, assert[ing] … that the british empire [sic] still exists'.[27] A cartoon by Ron Tandberg showed Fraser as a king dubbing a man a knight, while an onlooker remarked that 'next we'll be back to pounds, shillings and pence'.[28] One person responded by returning his own British honour. Ian Bisset wrote to Fraser, Kerr, and the Queen in January 1977, relinquishing the OBE (Officer of the Order of the British Empire) he had received in 1968. In his letter to Fraser he explained that '[c]hanged circumstances' had 'compelled me to take this action'. While his major reason was Kerr's dismissal of Whitlam—which he described as 'completely anachronistic' in a world without the British empire, for Australia had 'reached maturity' and ought to be 'free of any limiting links with its country of origin'—the return of imperial honours had played a part too. He expressed support for a system of honours

---

25   'Committee "Sought Honours Changes"', *Canberra Times*, 2 June 1976, 12.
26   'Era of "Take Your Pick" Pomp and Pageantry', *Age* (Melbourne), 26 January 1976, 9.
27   Donald Horne, 'Eureka Flags Wave Amid the Titles', *Nation Review*, 18–24 June 1976, 875, NLA cuttings.
28   Cartoon by Tandberg, *Age* (Melbourne), 22 January 1976, 1.

that acknowledged those who contributed to the community, but was 'convinced that it should be an appropriate Australian system'. 'In the absence of such a system and as a mark of protest', he wrote, he had returned his OBE.[29]

Others, however, were pleased with Fraser's changes. Western Australian premier Sir Charles Court told Fraser that he and his colleagues were 'delighted' that recommendations for British honours would be resumed— at the same time pointedly noting that Western Australia had never ceased using them, 'in spite of efforts by your predecessor' to abolish this State right.[30] Sir Eric Willis, the recently installed Liberal premier of New South Wales, wrote that while his State had eschewed the Order of Australia during Whitlam's prime ministership, his government was now prepared to consider participating, since Fraser had decided to retain it alongside imperial awards.[31] And Lance Milne, a chartered accountant from Adelaide, wrote to express 'great pleasure' at the reinstatement of imperial awards. Using both British and Australian awards, in his view, was 'the right way to approach the whole matter of recognition', for '[t]he sudden switch to Australian Honours created much resentment and confusion and destroyed a great deal of the value of the Order of Australia'.[32]

Such differences of opinion were symptomatic of wider confusion and disagreement in the matter of national identity, as discussed in the previous chapter. Buoyed by an exuberant mood of new nationalism, some politicians and commentators sought to throw off such symbols of the country's British past as imperial honours and knighthoods. Titular awards had always seemed to some to conflict with the nation's cherished egalitarian ideals, and there was a growing sense that it was anachronistic to receive awards in an order named for a defunct empire, and from a monarch who resided in another country. For others, these winds of change were disorienting, and the breaking of ties to a place that had for so long been 'Home' was a cause for mourning. To many who regretted the reshaping of relations between Britain and Australia, the changes might have been inevitable, but they were also too rapid, and there seemed a disconcerting rush to abandon a heritage that, in their view, had built Australia into the successful and democratic

---

29   NAA: A1209, 1976/2235 PART 3, letter to the prime minister from Ian J. W. Bisset, 6 January 1977.
30   NAA: A1209, 1976/2235 PART 1, teleprinter message to J. M. Fraser from Charles Court, 22 January 1976.
31   NAA: A1209, 1976/2235 PART 1, letter to J. M. Fraser from Eric Willis, 30 January 1976.
32   NAA: A1209, 1976/2235 PART 1, letter to J. M. Fraser from K. L. Milne, 3 February 1976.

nation it was. Polls reflected this division in public opinion, although support for the Order of Australia appeared to be growing. A Gallup poll of February 1976 found that 50 per cent of respondents preferred Australian honours, and only 39 per cent British honours, compared to 44 per cent each in March 1975. The demographic differences revealed by the poll hinted at the ongoing tug-of-war over the nation's identity, with the vote in favour of Australian honours noticeably higher among younger people than older.[33]

Change and change again

As commentators had predicted when Whitlam established Australian awards in the teeth of opposition from non-Labor State premiers and many in the federal opposition, honours had become something of a political football, if they had not been already. With British awards used by Liberal–National Country Party governments, and Labor administrations using only Australian ones, it could have come as no surprise that after Labor won the 1983 federal election the new prime minister, the former union leader Bob Hawke, once again ended federal recommendations for imperial honours, as Labor had indicated it would do during the campaign.[34] Initially, however, although making no nominations for the titular grade of the Order of Australia, Hawke's government also did not abolish it. Whether as a result of a government directive, in accordance with the administration's known wishes, or purely by coincidence, the council for the order would nevertheless make no appointments at this level in the following lists, although one knighthood in the order was announced on the June list immediately after the election.[35]

33 'More Favour Aust. Honours', *Courier-Mail* (Brisbane), 16 March 1976, 11, NLA cuttings. It was also observed that more men than women preferred the new national awards. A second question asked for views on the dual system; it found that 44 per cent of respondents supported maintaining both imperial and Australian honours, and 49 per cent disapproved.
34 'Queen's Honours to Stop', *Canberra Times*, 12 April 1983, 3; 'Hawke Rejects Granting of Imperial Honors', *Australian*, 12 April 1983, 3, NLA cuttings.
35 Since Hawke had said in April that the list for the upcoming Queen's Birthday announcement had been prepared by the previous government, this AK may perhaps have been recommended by the previous administration. 'Queen's Honours to Stop', *Canberra Times*, 12 April 1983, 3.

By 1986, having won a second election, Hawke felt able to officially remove the level of knight or dame from the Order of Australia.[36] At the same time, his government introduced new defence force awards to reward gallantry and exceptional service during wartime, and for non-operational service, bringing to an end the use of British awards such as the Distinguished Service Order, which had remained available for use in wartime under Whitlam's changes. The Victoria Cross would be retained as the country's highest gallantry award, due to its historic significance, but it would be rendered Australian through the issue of Australian letters patent.[37] In the same year, the Australian and British governments both enacted an *Australia Act*, among other things bringing to an end the ability of the British parliament to legislate for Australia, removing the necessity for it to approve certain State legislation, and terminating appeals to the Privy Council.[38] As Anne Twomey has written, these acts abolished the last constitutional links between Australia and the United Kingdom.[39] Although they did not themselves contain any provisions about honours, they did have implications for the system. Under the changed constitutional arrangements, British awards conferred on State lists were no longer to be recommended officially to the Queen by a minister of the British Government, but by the premier of the relevant State.[40]

Australians by this stage could have been forgiven for being entirely sick of the back-and-forth battle over titles and honours being waged by successive federal and State governments. Few, it seemed, could muster the energy to care enough to write an editorial or letter to the editor on this latest manoeuvre. An exception was the *Sydney Morning Herald*, which suggested the government was 'doing some curious things' in its desire 'to create a nationalist mood ... appropriate to its vision splendid of the Bicentennial' of European settlement in Australia, coming in 1988.

---

36 Stanley Martin, 'Perspectives on the Honours of Australia', in *Honouring Commonwealth Citizens: Proceedings of the First Conference on Commonwealth Honours and Awards*, ed. Michael Jackson (Toronto: The Honours and Awards Secretariat, Ontario Ministry of Citizenship and Immigration, 2007), 56–57.
37 'New Awards in Australian Honours System', *Canberra Times*, 27 January 1986, 1. Uniquely Australian awards were also introduced to replace decorations for the police, the fire services, the public service, and Antarctic exploration. The Northern Territory and the Australian Capital Territory were also granted representation on the council of the Order of Australia, and non-government representation on the council rose from three persons to seven.
38 A. D. Watts, 'The Australia Act 1986', *International and Comparative Law Quarterly* 36, no. 1 (1987): 136–38. doi.org/10.1093/iclqaj/36.1.132.
39 Anne Twomey, *The Australia Acts 1986: Australia's Statutes of Independence* (Sydney: Federation, 2010).
40 Watts, 'The Australia Act', 138–39; Twomey, *Australia Acts*, 355. On the implications of these constitutional changes for honours practices, see also Twomey, *Australia Acts*, especially 154–56.

Scrapping titles, the paper observed, was merely 'an open invitation' to a future Liberal–National Government to restore them, as well as being likely to encourage State governments that supported the use of titles to prefer the imperial system to the Australian one. Nor could the *Herald* see a good reason to exchange highly respected and well-known military honours for new decorations, particularly when both old and new were given 'in the name of the Queen of Australia'. What irked the editorialist most of all, however, was the 'force-fed patriotism' of these actions. With neither public pressure to jettison the AK/AD, nor popular displeasure at the maintenance of British gallantry awards, he or she accused the government of stubbornly attempting 'to create an aura of nationalism', no matter how 'contrived or artificial', in time for the Bicentenary.[41] Some years later, Anglican bishop and scholar Tom Frame would characterise the abolition of the AK/AD as 'an action flavoured by vindictiveness'. Not only had it supplied a means to reward the further achievements and service of companions who went on to higher and greater things, by conferring a courtesy title on the wives of knights it had acknowledged their part in their husband's success; the husbands of dames, he suggested, should be similarly recognised. 'The days of a bunyip aristocracy buying knighthoods are over', he concluded, and bringing the title back 'would prove to Australians that they can take something from the past, something that had merit, and refashion it into something useful and proudly Australian'.[42] It would not be the last time such arguments in favour of titles would be heard. Advocates for titles may have resembled a voice crying out in the wilderness in the 1990s, but the issue of titles had life in it yet, and it would provide one of the more surprising twists in the story of honours in Australia in coming years.

Despite the *Sydney Morning Herald*'s scepticism of enforced nationalism, historians have since seen the 'remembered' 1980s as an era of 'a newly confident Australian nationalism'.[43] A range of events, from the victory of *Australia II* in the 1983 America's Cup and the resulting euphoric national celebration, to the enormous success of the film *Crocodile Dundee* in 1986, demonstrate the increasingly assertive and lively nationalism of the era. The Bicentennial celebrations struck a chord of national pride

---

41 'Definitely Beyond the Call of Duty', *Sydney Morning Herald*, 30 January 1986, 10.
42 Tom Frame, 'Time for Knights Once More to Venture Forth', *Canberra Times*, 22 October 1990, 9.
43 Frank Bongiorno, *The Eighties: The Decade that Transformed Australia* (Melbourne: Black Inc., 2015), xii, quoting (in part) Graeme Turner, *Making It National: Nationalism and Australian Popular Culture* (Sydney: Allen and Unwin, 1994), 3–4, quote on 4.

in many Australians, notwithstanding the highly visible protests of those who felt left out of the nation (especially Indigenous Australians), the crass commercialism, and the sneers of some cultural commentators.[44] Hawke was—as his exuberant performance after the America's Cup victory showed—a master of recognising and taking advantage of this national fervour, and along with the often rash entrepreneurship of the period, it is perhaps the rise of such confident nationalism the decade is best remembered for.

In such a context, it is perhaps not surprising that support for the Order of Australia appeared to have grown in the community, while that for British honours had declined. Even in 1979, a *Sydney Morning Herald* survey had showed only 5 per cent of respondents preferring imperial honours alone, while more than three-quarters supported the use of Australian honours, either alone or in combination with British awards.[45] Yet as this survey demonstrated, neither had support for British honours entirely evaporated, particularly as part of a dual system. An unnamed spokesperson for the honours secretariat in the Department of Administrative Services told the *Australian* in 1980 that British honours retained an appeal for those who continued to think of Australia within the context of the wider Commonwealth of Nations. These, he said, were people who had possibly 'fought in a world war', and who 'remember[ed] the strong ties with Britain which are no longer as bonding as they used to be'.[46] Nevertheless, even Fraser had reportedly been considering a gradual move away from British awards by the end of his prime ministership. In 1980, when Queensland's imperial honours list was half its usual size, the *Courier-Mail* reported that although Premier Joh Bjelke-Petersen had not given a reason for the reduction, 'senior government sources' had said that Fraser wished for 'less emphasis on Imperial awards'.[47]

---

44 On this sense of pride among Australians as they marked the Bicentenary in their various ways, see Frank Bongiorno, 'Inaugural Professorial Lecture—Is Australian History Still Possible? Australia and the Global Eighties', *ANU Historical Journal II*, no. 1 (2019): 207–8. doi.org/10.22459/ANUHJII.2019.15.

45 'Strong Backing for Aust Honours System', *Sydney Morning Herald*, 26 December 1979, 2. Support for Australian honours alone and for the dual system of British and Australian honours was almost even, at 39 per cent and 38 per cent respectively. As usual, a political and demographic divide remained, with Labor voters more likely to support Australian honours, and Liberal and National Country Party voters either British and Australian honours together or British honours alone, and the strongest support for British honours by themselves to be found among older people.

46 Jane Brumfield, 'To the Top with Honors', *Australian*, 18 February 1980, 7, NLA cuttings.

47 Peter Morley, 'Honors Slashed by Half', *Courier-Mail* (Brisbane), 1 October 1980, 1, NLA cuttings.

National versus imperial

During the years of Fraser's and Hawke's prime ministerships, the honours system, like other national symbols such as the anthem, was caught up in a struggle over ideas of nation and national identity. James Curran and Stuart Ward have argued that from the 1960s, as Australia's British identity broke down, with Britain entering the European Economic Community and the relationship between Australia and Britain shifting irrevocably, Australians faced the difficult task of constructing a new national image, in an era when nationalism was often looked upon with suspicion as a force that was potentially threatening to world peace. Older British symbols could not continue to be drawn on as they had been, but, as Curran and Ward show, it was no easy task to create new national symbols and markers of identity to take their place.[48] John Rickard has suggested that 'the Australian temperament was uneasy with nationalist gestures', and observed that '[t]he complexity of the relationship with Britain meant that any assertion of Australian identity ran the risk of being interpreted as a rejection of the British heritage'.[49] Yet, as argued above, this was for the honours system an intensification of an existing dilemma rather than a new predicament. Arguments against imperial honours and titular awards, and calls for distinctively Australian ones, had a very long history. What was new was the overt tug-of-war between two existing systems, one national and one imperial. In such a climate, the gradual process of shifting from older British symbols and creating new Australian ones in their place was a site of political drama and manoeuvring during the 1970s and 1980s, as can be seen in the example of the honours system. Awards, like other symbols such as the national anthem, were in this period a site of this identity drama, caught between the necessity of acknowledging Australia's independent status as a nation, and the continued existence of ties to Britain, both in terms of residual constitutional links, and in terms of the emotional and sentimental attachments of many, especially older, Australians.[50]

---

48   James Curran and Stuart Ward, *The Unknown Nation: Australia After Empire* (Melbourne: Melbourne University Press, 2010).

49   John Rickard, *Australia: A Cultural History*, 3rd ed. (Melbourne: Monash University Publishing, 2017), 207.

50   For a further discussion of this, in relation to both the official honours system and the Australian of the Year award, see Karen Fox and Samuel Furphy, 'The Politics of National Recognition: Honouring Australians in a Post-Imperial World', *Australian Journal of Politics and History* 63, no. 1 (2017): 93–111. doi.org/10.1111/ajph.12317.

Such duality about honours and the national identity was obvious every January and June, particularly in January with British awards continuing to be announced on New Year's Day and Australian ones on Australia Day. Reflecting the different priorities of the two major political groupings, non-Labor State governments generally continued to use British honours (although also having representation on the council for the Order of Australia and thus participating at least on a minimal level in the Australian system as well), while Labor State governments usually eschewed British honours and resolutely supported the Order of Australia. As in the past, however, the divide was not as stark as might have been expected. In New South Wales, the Labor Government of Neville Wran chose to make recommendations for imperial honours below knighthood for the New Year list in 1977, with Wran explaining that the decision was in conformity with the practice of previous Labor governments in his State. He added that he would end the use of British honours when it became clear that the public no longer found them attractive.[51] Going further—as the governor-general, Kerr, explained in a report to the Palace—Wran also recommended Joan Sutherland for a damehood within the Order of Australia, on the rationale that she would have received this honour had it existed at the time she was appointed a companion in 1975. Kerr found it 'all a little puzzling', and wondered if the Australian Labor Party (ALP) were 'coming to realise how popular the two Honours systems really are and … how popular all aspects of our monarchical system remain'.[52] Such flexibility of choice, for Labor ministries at least, would not last long, however. In 1979 the party's national conference decided on a policy of abolishing British awards for Australians, departing from its more flexible past platform, which had banned titles but supported suitable recognition for services to the community and to humanity, thus leaving room for a Labor ministry to decide to nominate individuals for non-titular, lower-level imperial honours. An amendment ensuring that Labor administrations would also not bestow knighthoods in the Order of Australia was also accepted by the conference.[53]

---

51 'Wran Defends Nominations for Honours', *Sydney Morning Herald*, 1 January 1977, 3.

52 NAA: AA1984/609, PART 5, letter to Sir Martin Charteris, private secretary to the Queen, from John [Kerr], 11 November 1976. Intriguingly, Sutherland was instead appointed DBE (Dame Commander of the Order of the British Empire), in the 1979 New Year honours.

53 'No British Titles by Labor', *Sydney Morning Herald*, 17 July 1979, 2.

Not only governments but also potential recipients divided on the question of which set of honours the country should use. Whether because it was still relatively new, or due to its politically divisive birth, the Order of Australia had not yet gained universal approval as a desirable reward. To some it seemed 'second prize, not quite having the cachet of something from the Old Country'.[54] Others—among them supporters of the republican cause—found a national award far more acceptable than an imperial one. Author Kylie Tennant had twice refused the OBE, but accepted appointment as AO on the 1980 Australia Day list.[55] For the 'fiercely republican' and '[o]utrageously pugnacious' writer Xavier Herbert, however, even the Order of Australia was too closely linked to the monarchy.[56] In 1984 he declined the AO as being 'still an Imperial award' emanating from the Queen of England, 'even if she were also the Queen of Australia'.[57]

Unsurprisingly, the dual system of honours also did nothing to resolve the longstanding friction over whose right it was to make nominations, of whom, and for what services. Almost since the moment of Federation, as discussed in earlier chapters, tensions had periodically arisen between federal and State governments over honours. This situation was largely due to the creation of a federal system that emphasised the sovereignty of the States, leaving State governments considerable powers over anything not explicitly surrendered to Commonwealth control. The operation of a dual system of awards, with the two sides of politics favouring different awards, only added further potential for disagreement. One instance of such discord took place in January 1977, after the announcement of the New Year list of awards. A South Australian agriculturalist, Robert Herriot, had been appointed OBE on the Commonwealth list, and acting premier Des Corcoran wrote to the prime minister to complain, and to seek a change in federal policy. In Corcoran's view, Herriot's career had been largely as a State employee, and the federal government had appropriated a State responsibility by putting his name forward, as well as embarrassing the State's Labor administration, which did not use British honours.

---

54   Sally Loane, 'Australian Honors Stand Alone at Last', *Age* (Melbourne), 29 May 1991, 2, NLA cuttings.
55   Kylie Tennant, *The Missing Heir: The Autobiography of Kylie Tennant* (Melbourne: Macmillan, 1986), 165.
56   Russell McDougall, 'Herbert, Albert Francis Xavier (1901–1984)', *Australian Dictionary of Biography*, accessed 24 July 2017, adb.anu.edu.au/biography/herbert-albert-francis-xavier-12623/text22741.
57   'Xavier Herbert Knocks Back a Royal Honour', *Sydney Morning Herald*, 9 June 1984, 5.

Several other awards involving local government service also struck him as questionable.[58] Unmoved, Fraser responded merely that prime ministers had long nominated people for honours, and these particular recommendations had been 'justified and [the] awards fully deserved'. He saw 'no reason' for any change in practice.[59] Premier Don Dunstan, back in the saddle some weeks later, was not willing to let the matter drop. Reminding Fraser that it had been usual for the federal government to avoid nominating State public servants, and vice versa, he asserted that previous ministries in Canberra would not have nominated Herriot, and sought a return to a past practice he described as 'not nominating people who have served Governments other than our own'.[60] No reconsideration was forthcoming. Fraser's brief reply said only that the comments had been noted, and he had nothing to add to his previous letter.[61]

Equity, diversity, and inclusion

The late 1970s and 1980s were not merely a time of shifts in Australians' conception of their place in the world, but also years of transformation in other, perhaps even more profound, ways. How far did the biennial lists of new awards—British or Australian—reflect the social and cultural movements and changes sweeping Australia, from women's liberation and second-wave feminism, to intensifying Indigenous activism and the rise of multiculturalism? Gender inequity, in particular, had long been a target of feminist critics of the honours system, and such criticism seems only to have increased during the 1970s and 1980s. By the end of the period, it was almost a staple of commentary on honours announcements. In 1987 David Smith, the secretary of the council of the Order of Australia, wrote to various newspapers observing that '[o]nce again, publication of the [honours] list has been followed by a spate of complaints—not enough women, not enough migrants, scientists, industrialists, engineers, farmers ... '. His response was simple: 'If our honours lists fail to include all the achievers in our community it is because the community has failed to nominate them'.[62] Not everyone was impressed with this stance. Writing to the *Canberra Times*, J. D. Stanhope—presumably the future Australian

58 NAA: A1209, 1976/2235 PART 3, letter to J. M. Fraser from Des Corcoran, 6 January 1977.
59 NAA: A1209, 1976/2235 PART 3, letter to D. A. Dunstan from Malcolm Fraser, 7 March 1977.
60 NAA: A1209, 1976/2235 PART 3, letter to J. M. Fraser from Don Dunstan, 22 March 1977.
61 NAA: A1209, 1976/2235 PART 3, letter to D. A. Dunstan from J. M. Fraser, 26 April 1977.
62 'Reply to Medals Complaints', *Canberra Times*, 23 June 1987, 3.

Capital Territory chief minister—labelled it 'defensive' and argued that that whatever the situation regarding the other groups, there were certainly too few women receiving honours. If a shortage of nominations was the problem, he asked, had the government or the order's council made any effort to solve it? Instead of 'blaming the community', the government and the council 'should at least mount an advertising campaign … or, heaven forbid, take some other affirmative action'.[63]

The following year Stanhope used the occasion of International Women's Day to invite 'reflect[ion]' on the Order of Australia's performance in relation to gender equity. Assessing the proportion of women included in the most recent Australia Day awards as 'paltry', he suggested that if the order's council 'persists in delivering its insults to the women of Australia … it may be just as well to abolish it altogether'.[64] Smith defended the order in a letter to the *Canberra Times*, noting that—as he had already informed Stanhope—the council had in recent years recommended women for around 25 per cent of awards, while only 20 per cent of the nominations it had received had been of women.[65] Stanhope, however, was not to be convinced that the council was blameless, arguing that something further needed to be done, such as a publicity drive to increase nominations of women.[66]

An examination of the numbers of awards going to women would certainly not have lifted the spirits of feminist critics of the system. As I have suggested elsewhere—and unlike the picture on the other side of the Tasman in New Zealand—there is relatively little evidence to suggest that the emergence of women's liberation and the second wave of the feminist movement had any significant impact on the numbers of women receiving awards, possibly due to some reluctance among left-wing women in Australia to accept imperial honours.[67] Between 1975

---

63   J. D. Stanhope, letter to the editor, *Canberra Times*, 6 July 1987, 2.
64   J. D. Stanhope, letter to the editor, *Canberra Times*, 14 March 1988, 2.
65   David I. Smith, letter to the editor, *Canberra Times*, 26 March 1988, 2.
66   J. D. Stanhope, letter to the editor, *Canberra Times*, 10 April 1988, 2. A further reply from David Smith dealt largely with a suggestion made by Stanhope that he had been unable to mount his own drive for increased nominations of women by Smith's reluctance to assist. David I. Smith, letter to the editor, *Canberra Times*, 18 April 1988, 2.
67   See Karen Fox, 'Dames in New Zealand: Gender, Representation and the Royal Honours System, 1917–2000' (Master's thesis, University of Canterbury, 2005), 70–78; Karen Fox, '"Housewives' Leader Awarded MBE": Women, Leadership and Honours in Australia', in *Seizing the Initiative: Australian Women Leaders in Politics, Workplaces and Communities*, eds Rosemary Francis, Patricia Grimshaw, and Ann Standish (Melbourne: eScholarship Research Centre, University of Melbourne, 2012), 176.

and 1989, while 310 men were knighted, only 28 women were granted the honour of damehood—only 8.3 per cent of the total number of titles conferred. At the third level of the Order of the British Empire, the CBE (commander), women remained below 10 per cent of awards in each of the five-year periods from 1975 to 1989, and indeed the proportion of awards going to women fell, from 9.2 per cent between 1975 and 1979, to 5.4 per cent between 1980 and 1984, and 4.8 per cent between 1985 and 1989 (see tables in Chapter 4). Even at the fifth level of the order, the MBE (member), women did not receive more than a quarter of awards made in each of these five-year periods. Perhaps most concerning and surprising, the trend of a fall in the proportion of awards going to women was repeated for both the OBE and the MBE. Yet the situation was no more promising in Australia's own order. A mere two women were appointed AD during its brief existence, and women consistently received less than 10 per cent of awards of the AC during the five-year periods from 1975 to 1989. At the lower levels of the order, women fared only marginally better: in the five-year period between 1975 and 1979, for example, they received 16.7 per cent of AMs (Members of the Order of Australia) awarded, a proportion that decreased to 13 per cent between 1980 and 1984, and 15.2 per cent between 1985 and 1989.

By the beginning of the 1990s, women's low rates of inclusion in the honours system were starting to receive serious attention from the federal government. In September 1990 Senator Margaret Reynolds— until that April the minister assisting the prime minister for the status of women—presented a report on women's position in relation to the Order of Australia. Finding that women were under-represented, the report suggested the inequity might be 'a factor of the number of nominations made, rather than the selection process', with '[o]nly a quarter of the nominations received' being for women.[68] Reynolds asserted that women's organisations had 'a unique responsibility to alert their members and encourage them' to improve the situation.[69] The following year the government announced that, as part of an ongoing Inquiry into Equal Opportunity and Equal Status for Australian Women, an investigation would be held 'into whether or not the ... system is fair to women'.[70]

---

68 Margaret Reynolds, *Women and the Order of Australia* (Canberra: September 1990), 1.
69 Reynolds, *Women and the Order of Australia*, introductory letter from Reynolds.
70 'Govt to Look at Honours and Equality', *Canberra Times*, 12 April 1991, 12; House of Representatives Standing Committee on Legal and Constitutional Affairs, *Half Way to Equal: Report of the Inquiry into Equal Opportunity and Equal Status for Women in Australia* (Canberra: Australian Government Publishing Service, 1992), 1.

In June, Attorney-General Michael Lavarch, the chair of the House of Representatives standing committee conducting the inquiry, was quoted describing honours as 'a mirror to our society' that was 'tarnished' by the under-representation of women, which was 'yet another example of how we underrate and undervalue the contribution women make to society'.[71] Titled *Half Way to Equal*, the final report issued in April 1992 included a section on recognition, in which one subsection dealt specifically with the Australian honours system.[72] Having found that 'only a little more than 24 per cent of all awards' made in the Order of Australia since 1975 had gone to women, the committee recommended a 'public awareness campaign' to increase knowledge of the order and 'encourage nominations'; that an investigation be carried out as to how to 'mak[e] the process more accessible to the public to ensure that the contribution of women, particularly in the voluntary sector, is recognised and nominations are made'; and that consideration be given to 'the order of precedence', and especially to the question of 'whether Long Service Awards should take precedence over Merit Awards'.[73] This last was a relatively radical recommendation that, predictably, appears to have sunk without trace.

Another potentially radical solution, which was raised during the discussion around the inquiry but does not appear in the final report, was quotas. This possibility, however, was rejected by significant figures connected with the system. Robin Rawson, the director of the honours secretariat, was quoted in the media agreeing that nominations of women needed to increase, but opposing 'enforced quotas'. It needed to be remembered, she said, that women had historically had fewer opportunities than men to rise to the level of achievement represented by the AC, the highest grade of the order.[74] Establishing quotas for women was also not an option in the view of the order's instigator, former prime minister Gough Whitlam. Speaking at a conference on 'Recognition for Women in Australia' held as part of the inquiry in July 1991, he was quoted explaining that '[y]ou don't want the position where women get honours because of a political decision'. 'I would think it insulting that people would think: "Oh, she only got it because she is a woman"', he stated, asserting that honours

---

71   Sue Neales, 'Tarnished Society Mirror in Need of Some Polish', *Australian Financial Review*, 1 June 1991, 63, NLA cuttings.
72   *Half Way to Equal*, 168–74.
73   *Half Way to Equal*, xxxv, 169, 177.
74   Sue Neales, 'Tarnished Society Mirror in Need of Some Polish', *Australian Financial Review*, 1 June 1991, 63, NLA cuttings.

should be awarded for an individual's 'qualities', without gender, race, geography, religion, or another such factor being a consideration.[75] In the committee's final report, Whitlam was quoted making similar comments to those of Rawson:

> It is an unfortunate fact that the qualifications which have to be borne in mind for the Order do mean that many women have not yet had the opportunity to meet those requirements in as great numbers as men …[76]

As the committee noted, however, not everyone found this kind of response convincing. 'Rather than accepting that women do not fit the current standards for awards,' the report noted, 'many submissions … suggested that perhaps the rules should be changed so that a broader range of values and activities should be recognised with equal merit.'[77] As with so many aspects of women's unequal participation in public life, views were sharply divided between those who advocated such interventionist methods of creating gender equity, and those who advocated a strategy of waiting and allowing the imbalance to resolve naturally, as women gained new opportunities to make their marks.

Although considerably more muted, issues of ethnic inequity in the system, or in Australian society more generally, also made their presence felt on occasion. In 1981 Nick Zervos, the assistant secretary of the Greek Orthodox Community of Melbourne and Victoria, asserted that the awards announced for Australia Day that year were skewed towards individuals of Anglo-Saxon descent. Although the government was 'pushing the concept of a multi-cultural society', he argued, it was 'consistently ignoring members of that society', while giving honours specifically for services to migrant communities, rather than to migrants in other fields of endeavour, implied a 'cultural straitjacket'.[78] Responding to the criticism in a press statement, Smith stated that Zervos was 'plainly wrong' and that if he felt there were other people who ought to be honoured, he should put their names forward.[79]

---

75   Kylie Davis, 'Whitlam Sees Insult in Honours Quotas', *Australian*, 26 July 1991, 3, NLA cuttings; *Half Way to Equal*, 5.
76   *Half Way to Equal*, 169–70.
77   *Half Way to Equal*, 171.
78   '"Honors List Bias to Anglo-Saxons"', *Mercury* (Hobart), 27 January 1981, 2, NLA cuttings.
79   'Top-Level Denial of Honors Bias', *Mercury* (Hobart), 29 January 1981, 2, NLA cuttings.

Several Indigenous Australian leaders, on the other hand, made use of the honours system as a vehicle for expressing their dissatisfaction with Australia's treatment of its Indigenous people more generally. The poet Jack Davis threatened in 1977 to return the BEM (British Empire Medal) he had been awarded the previous year, in protest against a proposed amendment to Western Australia's *Electoral Act*, which would have restricted the rights of illiterate voters, among them Indigenous Australians.[80] In 1987 fellow poet Oodgeroo Noonuccal (formerly Kath Walker) did send back her MBE, which she had received in 1970, as 'a protest against what the Bicentenary "celebrations" [stood] for'.[81] Assessing the position of migrant or non-Anglo-Celtic groups in the honours system is next to impossible, as data on ethnicity was not collected and names are an imperfect marker of ethnic identity, but such examples do suggest that at least some members of the community felt that official commitments to multiculturalism and Indigenous self-determination were not yet being reflected in the country's honours system.

Then, too, there continued the old criticisms that had always been voiced. In a scathing piece directed largely but not entirely at the imperial system, in June 1976 in Melbourne's *Age* Peter Cole-Adams dismissed the whole institution of honours as an 'odd anachronism'. Titles in particular drew his ire: they were 'totally at odds with the principle of egalitarianism which Australians are apt to proclaim'. Although he acknowledged that non-titular awards had a use, for they allowed recognition to be given to people who had done charitable or other such work, the problem was that 'the system is so appallingly arbitrary'. There were many more deserving people than received awards, he said, and he questioned the possibility of ever fairly or appropriately comparing the achievements of people in diverse fields so as to assign them to particular grades.[82] Another familiar critique focused upon the question of occupational balance— and with it, relatedly, class bias. In 1987 the federal government whip, Ben Humphreys, complained that honours were 'becoming something of a farce'. He was reported to have raised the issue of public servants and

---

80 'Black Leader: I'll Protest', *Age* (Melbourne), 11 November 1977, 4.
81 Oodgeroo Noonuccal, 'Why I Am Now Oodgeroo Noonuccal', *Age* (Melbourne), 30 December 1987, 11. For more on these, and other instances of Indigenous Australians' responses to the offer of an award, see Karen Fox, 'Ornamentalism, Empire and Race: Indigenous Leaders and Honours in Australia and New Zealand', *Journal of Imperial and Commonwealth History* 42, no. 3 (2014): 486–502. doi.org/10.1080/03086534.2014.895480.
82 Peter Cole-Adams, 'The Puzzles of the Honors System: Who, How and Why?' *Age* (Melbourne), 19 June 1976, 15, NLA cuttings.

politicians receiving awards at the Labor caucus meeting, arguing that as they were well rewarded already with good salary and superannuation packages, they did not deserve honours, except in cases where they had retired and then given voluntary service to the community. According to the *Sydney Morning Herald*, Humphreys's protest struck a chord with David Smith, who was quoted speaking disapprovingly of a public service committee 'specifically established to ensure that public servants received their fair share of honours'. It had, he stated, 'interfered with the proper functions of the council'.[83] A similar point arose during the inquiry into women's status and opportunity. 'A general criticism' of the system, according to the committee's final report, had been 'that awards tend to go to people who have already been recognised', with 'a heavy preponderance of people who have imperial honours amongst the ranks of recipients of ... the Order of Australia', and 'a feeling that awards are given for positions which the recipient occupied rather than personal achievement'. The National Women's Consultative Council, the committee stated, had observed that '[m]any men seem to obtain this recognition for service to government, public service and industry—often for doing a job for which they were well paid', while '[u]npaid or voluntary work ... [had] less apparent value'.[84]

Such criticisms, as we have seen, were not new, and nor were they surprising, given the continuation of established patterns in the conferral of awards. Glancing through the names of those who received the highest levels of awards, those bestowing the title of Sir or Dame in the imperial system and the AK/AD and AC in the Australian system, it is hard to escape the feeling that little had changed in patterns of award since the years of the second Menzies prime ministership. The creation of the Order of Australia was in this sense not transformative. While it was innovative in many ways, in its highest awards it too tended to perpetuate these older patterns of award. The 14 AKs and ADs awarded between January 1976 and June 1989 were three governors-general (John Kerr, Zelman Cowen, and Ninian Stephen), former prime minister Robert Menzies, premier of Western Australia Charles Court, governor of New South Wales Roden Cutler, politician Enid Lyons, High Court chief justice Garfield Barwick, medical researcher Macfarlane Burnet, professor of physiology and University of Melbourne chancellor Pansy Wright, Walter and Eliza Hall

83   Milton Cockburn, 'How Bureaucrats Gather Their Gongs', *Sydney Morning Herald*, 19 February 1987, 1.
84   *Half Way to Equal*, 169.

Institute of Medical Research president Colin Syme, businessman Gordon Jackson, author and historian (and wife of a former governor-general) Alexandra Hasluck, and Charles, Prince of Wales. Of the 143 awards of the AC made during the same period, at least 43 were bestowed either wholly or partially for political or public services, or for services to the Crown or government. Another 19 were for services to the law, 26 for services to business or industry (including industrial relations), and 29 for services to the community (again, in each case, either wholly or partially).[85] While such broad descriptions conceal as much as they reveal, it is fair to say that each of these categories was an area of activity commonly rewarded with honours under the British system. The extent to which existing patterns of awards continued is also evident in that only nine citations mentioned contributions to the arts (music, art, literature, and so on), a mere two citations mentioned conservation or the environment, and one AC was awarded for services to a sport (Donald Bradman, for cricket).

Moreover, there was also a degree of class hierarchy still inherent in the honours system in Australia, at least in relation to awards for public and military service in the imperial system. It is clear from material held in the National Archives of Australia that a person's position in an occupational hierarchy still played a part in determining the level of award made, at least in the late 1970s. A list produced in 1977 placed particular positions against particular grades of award, presumably as examples of the kinds of persons who might receive each category of honour. Governors-general might expect a GCMG and justices of the High Court a KBE (Knight Commander of the Order of the British Empire), while 'First Division officers' of the federal public service might receive knighthood at the level of knight bachelor or the non-titular CBE, and 'Second Division' officers could hope at best for an OBE. Those in the 'Third Division' and 'Fourth Division' were confined to the ISO (Companion of the Imperial Service Order), MBE, and BEM, depending on their level of seniority.[86] By this time, however, there was clearly a degree of unease about such formulaic and class-ridden scales. Responding to the list, Geoff Yeend, the deputy

---

85　These figures have been compiled using the citations given in the Australian Government's online honours database. Australian Government, Department of the Prime Minister and Cabinet, 'Australian Honours Search Facility', *It's an Honour*, Department of the Prime Minister and Cabinet, accessed 6 May 2021, honours.pmc.gov.au/honours/search. Note that these figures include honorary awards, and that one award has since been terminated.

86　NAA: A1209, 1976/2235 PART 3, 'Imperial Awards in the Commonwealth List', attached to letter to G. J. Yeend, deputy secretary, Department of the Prime Minister and Cabinet, from P. J. Lawler, 29 June 1977.

secretary of the Department of Prime Minister and Cabinet, cautioned against sending it to government ministers and public service heads, noting that '[s]ome of the descriptions might need another look if they were to go out'.[87] Whether similar questions of position, and the appropriateness of using occupational hierarchies as a proxy for award levels, occupied the council for the Order of Australia cannot be determined, as records remain unavailable. It seems likely, however, that such scales of award were a legacy of British practices, to which the new Australian order may not have been subject.

Corruption in the sunshine state

The worst examples of the operation of the honours system, which brought a spectre of the ill-repute that Lloyd George's honours-selling scandals had visited upon the British system in the 1920s, were found in Bjelke-Petersen's Queensland. Premier since 1968, Bjelke-Petersen was a larger-than-life figure in Australian politics. Described by the historian Geoffrey Bolton as '[a]n ungenerous fundamentalist, but financially shrewd', and by the political scientist Rae Wear as 'an authoritarian' with little tolerance for opposition, he was capable of both great courtesy and terrible rages.[88] He had become leader of the Country Party, and premier, in August 1968 after the death of Jack Pizzey, and would remain in power until December 1987. Many aspects of his time as premier were controversial, even notorious, and one of those aspects was his use of honours.

In their history of the Queensland parliament John Wanna and Tracey Arklay state that '[t]he conservative government had long favoured the awarding of knighthoods to its own senior members' but that 'the tradition ... was accelerated' after Bjelke-Petersen became premier.[89] Moreover, according to Wanna and Arklay, '[b]y the 1970s' there was 'a new dimension' to 'the government's practice of awarding knighthoods to its members' as 'local successful businessmen close to the Premier, and often with close associations with the National Party itself' were granted

---

87   NAA: A1209, 1976/2235 PART 3, letter to P. J. Lawler, secretary, Department of Administrative Services, from G. J. Yeend, deputy secretary, no date.

88   Geoffrey Bolton, *1942–1995: The Middle Way*, vol. 5 of *The Oxford History of Australia*, 2nd ed. (Melbourne: Oxford University Press, 1996), 224; Rae Wear, *Johannes Bjelke-Petersen: The Lord's Premier* (Brisbane: University of Queensland Press, 2002), xi, 87, 133–36.

89   John Wanna and Tracey Arklay, *The Ayes Have It: The History of the Queensland Parliament, 1957–1989* (Canberra: ANU E Press, 2010), 402. doi.org/10.22459/AH.07.2010.

titles.[90] This did not go unnoticed. An article in the *National Times* in 1986 investigated the continuing use of knighthoods in Queensland, noting that the upcoming Queen's Birthday list was 'sure to bring renewed accusations of political cronyism from the Labor Opposition', followed by 'retorts of "sour grapes"' from the government. After suggesting the State seemed to be receiving more knighthoods than it was technically entitled to, journalist Murray Hogarth noted that Bjelke-Petersen's own electorate, Barambah, also seemed to be 'disproportionate[ly]' favoured. He quoted Queensland Labor MLA Bob Gibbs alleging that it was 'commonly touted' that 'to get a knighthood you perform a major service for the National Party' or contribute 'nothing less than $120,000', and listed some of 'the brave defenders of the National Party … called to Bjelke-Petersen's round table'. Among them were Edward Lyons, a 'friend and mentor' of Bjelke-Petersen as well as a powerbroker within the National Party, who had been knighted in 1977; the National Party State president, Robert Sparkes (1979); party treasurer William Allen (1981); and former party trustee Frank Moore (1983). According to Hogarth, 'at least half' of the knighthoods included on the Queensland honours list since Bjelke-Petersen became premier had—or afterwards came to have—'links to the Government', including as party members, public servants, or members of the Liberal Party, the government's past partner in coalition.[91]

Hogarth also named several who had made significant donations to the National Party, such as Justin Hickey, a Sydney businessman who was knighted in 1979, before in 1980 being revealed as the source of a donation of $100,000 to the premier's preferred charity (a hospice at Kingaroy).[92] The allegation was also made in the federal Senate in September 1992: referring to a federal National Party council decision to seek the reintroduction of titles into the Order of Australia, Chris Schacht claimed that '[p]eople could get a knighthood for a $100,000 donation to the National Party or Bjelke-Petersen Fund'.[93] Wanna and Arklay are quite clear that 'sycophantic business leaders' were also able to 'purchase knighthoods' through 'mak[ing] significant donations to the National Party through its fundraising arm'. Hickey was, as they say, a 'celebrated

---

90   Wanna and Arklay, *Ayes Have It*, 403.
91   Murray Hogarth, 'It's Knighthoods Galore in the Realm of Sir Joh …', *National Times*, 6–12 June 1986, 4, NLA cuttings.
92   Murray Hogarth, 'It's Knighthoods Galore in the Realm of Sir Joh …', *National Times*, 6–12 June 1986, 4, NLA cuttings.
93   Commonwealth of Australia, Senate, *Parliamentary Debates*, 9 September 1992 (Chris Schacht).

case'. Some time later, in 1982, he was asked about his knighthood in an episode of the Australian Broadcasting Commission's television program *Four Corners*, and said that he had made a substantial donation to a hospice located in the premier's electorate; he was quite clear that he had done so before his honour was granted.[94] The most recent addition to the group at the time of the *National Times* article was the police commissioner, Terence Lewis, who, according to Evan Whitton, had 'relentlessly' pursued a knighthood.[95] Lewis was later dismissed and jailed for forgery, corruption, and perjury, as well as being stripped of his title.[96]

When Bjelke-Petersen himself was knighted at Queen's Birthday 1984, he told journalists he would not reveal who had written the laudatory citation, which described him as 'not only an inspiration and a guiding light' as premier, but 'a living embodiment of the spirit of self-sacrifice and service' who had in his career displayed 'integrity', 'dignity', and 'humility, the true mark of greatness'. Responding to the citation, the Labor Opposition leader, Keith Wright, 'suggested that whoever was responsible for the wording ... "deserves a knighthood for services to creative writing and comedy"'.[97] Bjelke-Petersen's title, and his use of honours more generally, even aroused comment in the British House of Commons, with Scottish Labour member Bryan Williams tabling a motion asserting that Bjelke-Petersen 'and his cronies' had 'discredited the honors system'.[98] Wanna and Arklay agree, suggesting that 'such abuses of state-nominated honours [as occurred under Bjelke-Petersen] merely helped discredit the imperial honours system'.[99]

Bjelke-Petersen also played a part in another honours scandal during the Fraser years, which erupted in June 1976 when the president of the Queensland Labor Party's central executive and senior vice-president of the federal ALP, Jack Egerton, accepted a knighthood. According to

---

94   Wanna and Arklay, *Ayes Have It*, 403; 'Farewell, Sir Joh, the Great Divider', *Sydney Morning Herald*, 25 April 2005 [online].

95   Murray Hogarth, 'It's Knighthoods Galore in the Realm of Sir Joh ...', *National Times*, 6–12 June 1986, 4, NLA cuttings; Wanna and Arklay, *Ayes Have It*, 567; Evan Whitton, *The Hillbilly Dictator: Australia's Police State*, revised ed. (Sydney: ABC Books, 1993), 104–7, quote on 105.

96   Wanna and Arklay, *Ayes Have It*, 607.

97   'Queensland Premier Knighted', *Canberra Times*, 16 June 1984, 1.

98   Hedley Thomas, 'Scottish MP Hits Joh Over Honors', *Courier-Mail* (Brisbane), 15 December 1989, 1, NLA cuttings. An earlier version of the motion had specifically condemned the knighthoods received by Bjelke-Petersen 'and his cronies', but it had been amended in order not to appear to criticise the Queen.

99   Wanna and Arklay, *Ayes Have It*, 403.

Johannah Bevis, Bjelke-Petersen's government had deliberately sought 'to manufacture problems within Labor ranks' by nominating Egerton.[100] At the least, however, Fraser must have been a willing accomplice, since Egerton's name appeared on the federal list. The governor-general, Kerr, noted this recommendation with surprise, remarking in correspondence with the Palace that a surprising aspect of that batch of recommendations was the inclusion of three current or former members of the Labor Party. Along with Egerton, Fraser nominated Lance Barnard, a former Labor Cabinet minister who was by then ambassador to Sweden, and the secretary of the Trades and Labour Council of New South Wales, John Ducker.[101] If his desire was discord, Bjelke-Petersen certainly got his wish. Many Labor figures reacted to Egerton's honour with shock and anger, and Egerton was removed from his positions in the movement and expelled from the party.[102] At the South Australian party convention, which passed a motion condemning his action, he was denounced for 'outraging principles', going 'above the workers', and abandoning those he was meant to represent.[103] Nicknamed 'Jumping Jack' and pilloried as a 'Labor Rat', Egerton himself thought his detractors 'a narrow vocal minority' and argued that the title was 'recognition of the work I have done within the trade union movement, and recognition of the whole trade-union movement'.[104] He asserted that he was 'not aware that I have broken any rules of the trade-union movement or the Labor Party', and observed that '[a]ll honours, imperial or otherwise, emanate from the same source'.[105] Despite persistent efforts, however, he was never permitted to rejoin the party he had once served.[106] Salt was later rubbed in Labor wounds by the fact that the person to confer the title on Egerton was none other than Kerr.[107] Nevertheless, according to Kerr himself, it had been commented that 'on balance', Fraser had 'lost from the recommendation'

---

100 Johannah Bevis, 'No More Labour for the Knight: An Overview of Sir Jack Egerton's Leadership', *Queensland Journal of Labour History*, no. 21 (2015): 5.

101 NAA: AA1984/609, PART 3, letter to Sir Martin Charteris, private secretary to the Queen, from John Kerr, 4 May 1976.

102 Bevis, 'No More Labour for the Knight', 5.

103 'Knight Called on to Quit Party Posts', *Canberra Times*, 14 June 1976, 3.

104 Bevis, 'No More Labour for the Knight', 5; 'Critics "Narrow" Says Egerton', *Sun-Herald* (Sydney), 13 June 1976, 3.

105 'Critics "Narrow" Says Egerton', *Sun-Herald* (Sydney), 13 June 1976, 3; NAA: AA1984/609, PART 4, press cutting, John Bragg, '"Gough is Not Loyal"', *Mail* (Brisbane), 20 June 1976.

106 Bevis, 'No More Labour for the Knight', 5.

107 Barry York, 'Knighthoods and Dames', 3 November 2015, Museum of Australian Democracy at Old Parliament House blog, accessed 14 June 2019, www.moadoph.gov.au/blog/knighthoods-and-dames/#.

of Egerton, for 'a very strong leader of moderate persuasion' had departed the labour movement, leading to 'the strengthening of the left in the ALP and ACTU [Australian Council of Trade Unions]'.[108]

Egerton himself was later reported to have declared 'that not all his fellow knights deserved the honour', and that '[i]t was common knowledge ... that knighthoods could be obtained for a fee', whether 'in the form of a political donation' or 'a bribe to a government official'. He went so far as to claim that 'the going rate' in the early 1980s 'was $60,000', and that he personally knew of someone who had paid $70,000 in the hope of obtaining a title.[109] Such bold claims, however, have been rare in Australia, and—given the clandestine nature of any such transactions—it seems nigh impossible to prove or disprove them. While such claims have been most often made regarding honours in Queensland, occasional claims of impropriety—undeserved awards or cronyism if not outright sale of honours—have also been made regarding other parts of the honours system. In 1991, for example, it was reported that the royal commission then investigating the WA Inc era in Western Australia had learned that Labor premier Brian Burke had telephoned the person in charge of arranging the State's nominations for the Order of Australia, Les Smith, in 1986, aiming to help the chair of the collapsed Rothwells merchant bank, Laurie Connell, achieve appointment to the order.[110] If there has occasionally been suspicion of such practices, however, this was never more so than in relation to the corrupt and cowboy-like Bjelke-Petersen era in Queensland.

Conclusion

The 1970s and 1980s were a confused time in Australian honours policy. Two discrete systems of award operated alongside each other, with State and federal governments able to pick and choose between them according to their political flavour. This confusion in large measure reflected the nation's own uncertainty about its identity, and its future, an uncertainty that, together with the approaching Bicentennial celebrations, provoked

108 NAA: AA1984/609, PART 4, letter to Sir Martin Charteris, Private Secretary to the Queen, from John R. Kerr, 22 June 1976.
109 Philip Derriman, 'Keating Works a Knight Shift: No New Sirs', *Sydney Morning Herald*, 6 October 1992, 1.
110 Deborah Light, 'A Call to the Golf Course and Laurie was on his Way to an AO', *Sydney Morning Herald*, 14 June 1991, 5.

a flurry of thought and reflection on the subject. Such a mix-and-match approach to the country's ceremonial life was never sustainable, however, and these years of operating a dual system merely provided time for a more durable solution to be formulated. By the end of 1989, imperial honours had fallen out of use around Australia. When Queensland's new Labor premier, Wayne Goss, withdrew the 1990 New Year list prepared by the previous administration, the *Australian* sought comment from Sir Robert Norman, whom it expected would be 'Australia's last knight'. Norman reportedly 'said that while he was proud to have been recognised and knighted by the Queen, it was time imperial honours gave way to a new order'. 'I believe it is all part of a process of growing up', he was quoted as saying, '[a]nd as a nation we can't feel like we are fully through with it until we sever the ties with the parent'.[111] Indeed, opposition to British honours was no longer a Labor preserve. Bipartisan support for concluding their use had been growing for some time. New South Wales Liberal premier Nick Greiner, for instance, had been reported stating in 1988 that the country 'had grown up enough to settle on one system of local honours'.[112] Sentiment and electoral politics seemed to be aligning against imperial honours, which were increasingly viewed as the preserve of elderly conservatives, not to mention being tarnished by their association with corruption under Bjelke-Petersen. Yet, particularly in the growing chorus of criticism around the place of women in the system, there were hints that the future would not be all smooth sailing, even after the resolution of the long tug-of-war over imperial and national awards.

---

111 Peter Morley, 'Macrossan, Kennedy Miss Out on Knighthoods', *Courier-Mail* (Brisbane), 5 December 1989, 1, NLA cuttings; Anne Jamieson and Jamie Walker, 'Knights Out in the New Dawn', *Australian*, 6 December 1989, 1–2, NLA cuttings.
112 'Row Over Greiner's Knight Shift', *Sydney Morning Herald*, 9 January 1988, 4.

8

Barbeque stopper, 1990–2015

It was the Queen herself who gave the final stimulus to end recommendations for British honours in Australia. A letter from Sir William Heseltine, her private secretary, in February 1990 informed the governor-general of Her Majesty's feeling that, since the most recent British honours list had not included nominations from any Australian Government, the time might be right for the country to consider employing only its own awards.[1] State governors received similar missives.[2] The Queen's wish was divulged by New South Wales premier Nick Greiner, who explained that she had 'indicated to me privately that it was unseemly to have a lottery depending on which party was in power'. 'She thought that was a ping-pong game', he said, and would rather see 'a commitment to the Order of Australia'.[3] Breaking with Liberal Party tradition, Greiner had promised to eschew imperial honours during the 1988 election campaign, despite some resistance from fellow Liberals and members of the National Party, and he had carried that commitment through after his victory at the polls.[4] The federal Liberal–

---

1   Review of Australian Honours and Awards, *A Matter of Honour: The Report of the Review of Australian Honours and Awards* (Canberra: Australian Government Publishing Service, 1995), 21; Malcolm Hazell, 'The Australian Honours System: An Overview', in *Honouring Commonwealth Citizens: Proceedings of the First Conference on Commonwealth Honours and Awards*, ed. Michael Jackson (Toronto: The Honours and Awards Secretariat, Ontario Ministry of Citizenship and Immigration, 2007), 41–42.
2   'British Awards Going Going Gong', *Canberra Times*, 18 February 1990, 6.
3   Luis M. Garcia, 'An End to Imperial Honours "Lottery"', *Sydney Morning Herald*, 15 February 1990, 3.
4   Luis M. Garcia, 'An End to Imperial Honours "Lottery"', *Sydney Morning Herald*, 15 February 1990, 3.

National opposition was willing to agree to the Queen's request, but intended also to consider reviving the level of knighthood/damehood in the Order of Australia.[5]

Although this initiative for abandoning British honours had come from the Queen, rather than arising out of any one political party's policy platform, it was some time before all States agreed. After seeking renewal of the Queen's request and consulting State premiers and opposition leaders, as well as the federal opposition leader, Labor Prime Minister Paul Keating was able to announce in October 1992 that no further nominations would be made for imperial awards, at either federal or State level. One only among his fellow party heads had refused to agree: Richard Court, the leader of the Liberals in Western Australia, and the son of that vigorous supporter of British honours, former Liberal premier Sir Charles Court.[6] Keating's well-known support for an Australian republic led to some suspicion that the move was a portent of things to come, but this was a notion the government was quick to hose down. Ending the use of British honours was not, insisted a spokesman, part of a drive to create a republic.[7]

The announcement that imperial honours were finally to be abolished seems to have attracted little attention, perhaps indicating that their appeal had faded significantly over the past decade. A tongue-in-cheek snap poll in the *Sydney Morning Herald* described the AO (Officer of the Order of Australia) as 'sound[ing] … like a movie classification' [Adults Only], and asked prominent individuals to nominate a more 'Australian' title to replace the familiar British 'Sir' and 'Dame'. Malcolm Turnbull—then an investment banker—responded seriously, suggesting that there was 'something wrong with anyone who wants a handle before or after their name', while broadcaster and social commentator Phillip Adams thought people might be termed 'Nugget' (in gold, silver, or bronze) in honour of public servant H. C. Coombs. Blanche d'Alpuget—biographer of former prime minister Bob Hawke—offered 'Kangaroo, Wombat and Bandicoot' for men and 'Brolga instead of Dame, Kookaburra instead of Lady, and

5   'It's Good Night to the Knights', *Canberra Times*, 1 June 1990, 3.
6   *A Matter of Honour*, 21–22; Jodie Brough, 'Another Tie to Britain is Severed', *Canberra Times*, 6 October 1992, 3; Philip Derriman, 'Keating Works a Knight Shift: No New Sirs', *Sydney Morning Herald*, 6 October 1992, 1.
7   Jodie Brough, 'Another Tie to Britain is Severed', *Canberra Times*, 6 October 1992, 3; Philip Derriman, 'Keating Works a Knight Shift: No New Sirs', *Sydney Morning Herald*, 6 October 1992, 1.

Wagtail for those nice young second wives of Kangaroos'.[8] Some, though, regretted the decision. One such was former minister of defence Sir James Killen, who professed himself 'puzzled as to why there's this anxiety to get rid of the past'. British honours had a history stretching 'back to the Norman Conquests', he said, while 'British authority' remained a key element of the country's legal and parliamentary systems.[9]

Yet notwithstanding such laments, with the abandonment of the dual system and strong bipartisan support for the ending of imperial honours, it might have seemed the Australian honours system had at last entered a halcyon phase, widely accepted and free of controversy. The events of the next 25 years would prove any such hope misplaced. First came a sweeping review of the system, considering processes and practices as well as the awards themselves. Although the most radical of the recommendations would not be acted upon, the review—and the responses of those surveyed through questionnaires and focus groups—revealed both a lack of awareness of the system among the public, and a degree of dissatisfaction with aspects of it. More significantly, a growing chorus of criticism attacked the lack of gender balance in the system, as the proportion of women remained stubbornly low. But most astonishing of all was Prime Minister Tony Abbott's revival of knighthoods and damehoods in 2014, and his subsequent choice to honour the Queen's husband, Prince Philip, with one of the newly resurrected titles. Never before had the honours system been quite so central to national political debate, or to the fortunes of a sitting prime minister. National honours, it seemed, were no more immune to controversy than had been the imperial system.

A Matter of Honour: The 1995 review

Signs of further honorific struggles ahead, indeed, emerged hard on the heels of the announcement that imperial honours would cease to be used. In early 1993 Keating's government announced that, if it were returned at the forthcoming election, the system would undergo a thorough review. Duly re-elected in March, his new ministry proceeded as promised, with a two-stage inquiry announced in May. First would come a review of awards relating to defence; after that would be a full inquiry into the system,

8   'Snap Poll', *Sydney Morning Herald*, 8 October 1992, 25.
9   'Keating's Newest Anti-Royal Move Disturbs Knight', *Canberra Times*, 7 October 1992, 5.

taking into account the findings of the first stage.[10] The Committee of Inquiry into Defence and Defence-related Awards reported in March the following year, having received more than 800 submissions and considered the issue of equity in the recognition of defence personnel and others in related activities. Of its 40 recommendations, the government accepted 39, including those to establish a Civilian Service Medal 1939–45 and an Australian Service Medal 1945–75. Questions relating to the relationship between the military and the general divisions of the Order of Australia, and to awards for 'overseas humanitarian service in hazardous circumstances', the committee suggested be referred to the full inquiry.[11]

Frank Walker, the minister for administrative services, announced the membership of a committee to conduct the second stage of the review in October 1994. Coming 20 years after Australian awards were established, the inquiry would respond to criticisms that the honours system was 'one for the elite groups in society', and that too few women, migrants, and less wealthy individuals were included among recipients.[12] Or, as Leonie Lamont and Adam Harvey put it in the *Sydney Morning Herald*, that the system 'was slanted in favour of well-heeled, well-educated Anglo-Saxon males in the professions and the Public Service'.[13] Eight people would sit on the committee, which would be chaired by Clare Petre, a senior officer at the New South Wales Community Services Commission and board member of the Administrative Review Council. It would seek to establish 'what services, achievements and contributions' the Australian community wished to see honoured, and whether the system reached the 'standards of fairness, equity and access' the nation expected.[14] For 'the first time', Walker said, Australians would be able to have 'a say' in the shape of the country's honours system.[15]

Senator Rod Kemp, the shadow minister for administrative services, acknowledged that the review would enable 'any problems relating to fairness and access' to be tackled, as well as offering a chance 'to build

---

10   *A Matter of Honour*, xiv–xvi.
11   *A Matter of Honour*, xvi.
12   *A Matter of Honour*, xvi-xvii, quote on xvii; Minister for Administrative Services, 'Review of Honours and Awards', media statement, 14 October 1994, accessed 31 July 2017, available via parlinfo.aph.gov.au/parlInfo/search/search.w3p.
13   Leonie Lamont and Adam Harvey, 'Two Officers Ask: Is the System Fair?' *Sydney Morning Herald*, 26 January 1995, 8.
14   Minister for Administrative Services, 'Review of Honours and Awards', media statement, 14 October 1994, accessed 31 July 2017, available via parlinfo.aph.gov.au/parlInfo/search/search.w3p.
15   *A Matter of Honour*, xvii.

community awareness', but 'warned' that it must not be used to 'advance the ALP's [Australian Labor Party] republican agenda'.[16] Kemp's view, as he explained in the Senate the following week, was that the inadequate representation of 'women, migrants and the less affluent' could be blamed at least partly on 'the lacklustre effort' of Labor ministers to ensure that Australians understood their honours system. Awards announced in the Australian system, Kemp stated, generally attracted little controversy, and the fact that nominations could be made by any person or organisation meant that the appointment process for the Order of Australia was 'totally democratic and as egalitarian as most members in the community would want'. He again raised the spectre that the review might be used to advance the republican cause, expressing concern that Walker had stated that the country 'need[ed] "a modern system that Australians own"', and had spoken of his desire to see the awards given by a president, rather than by the governor-general. Moreover, while 'finetuning' the system might be defensible, it would be the behaviour of a 'banana republic' to alter it dramatically, when it had existed for such a short time.[17]

Whether or not Walker's reference to 'a modern system that Australians own' had indeed referenced a republican desire to remove the Queen's influence from the nation's awards, he did look hopefully to an Australian republic on the horizon, and he did see in that coming republic an imperative for change in the country's honours system. Discussing the review's progress in the House of Representatives in June 1995, he stated that Australians were being asked 'whether the system is still relevant to a nation about to become a republic'. The core question was 'what sorts of contributions deserve recognition and who ... should be recognised and celebrated', but his vision for the future of honours was about something more too: it was about what the system represented. Asserting that '[o]verwhelmingly' the country desired a different system, Walker argued that what Australians wanted 'more than anything else' was 'a sense of ownership over it'. 'They do not want something remote, accessible only to insiders and elites, operating in a shroud of conservative

---

16   Rod Kemp, 'Review of Australian Honours and Awards', news release, 14 October 1994, accessed 31 July 2017, available via parlinfo.aph.gov.au/parlInfo/search/search.w3p.
17   Commonwealth of Australia, Senate, *Parliamentary Debates*, 19 October 1994 (Rod Kemp). Kemp also criticised the make-up of the committee, including its apparent lack of expertise in the matter of honours; Walker, in turn, vigorously disputed these claims. Commonwealth of Australia, Senate, *Parliamentary Debates*, 19 October 1994 (Rod Kemp); Commonwealth of Australia, House of Representatives, *Parliamentary Debates*, 20 October 1994 (Frank Walker).

mystique', he said, and they disliked 'excessive hierarchy'. What they did want was 'something uniquely Australian that operates like Australians operate—openly and fairly'.[18]

Whether the majority of Australians would have agreed with this statement, they probably would have accepted that the community wished 'to see ordinary people ... recognised for doing things the community values— that is, working not for reward or prestige but voluntarily to keep together the fabric of our society'. Walker's republican vision was perhaps most evident in his closing claim that the inquiry would advise 'how to put a truly national stamp' on the institution, and his accompanying call for the leader of the opposition to 'put away his ancient views of society ... get up to date, reject his adherence to the imperial system of old, and come up with a truly Australian system'.[19] It was a bold vision, in many ways, for a system of honours that would avoid the pitfalls of elitism and patronage that always threatened, and which would at last be free of controversy and scandal. In its certainty that a republic was just around the corner, it also appears from the vantage point of the twenty-first century, after the failure of the 1999 referendum, too confident, too willing to assume unanimity of dreams for the country's future. Yet even if such unanimity had existed, determining how to implement such a vision was a tall order for the review committee.

The breadth of the task was reflected in the committee's terms of reference. Its overarching task was 'to advise ... what steps need to be taken to ensure that the [honours] system serves the needs of Australian society into the next century'. More specifically, it was to gauge 'community awareness' of the system; ascertain 'the range and types of achievements' that Australians believed deserved honours; assess 'the appropriateness' of the existing system, and of the areas of endeavour which it recognised; consider whether it met 'community standards of access, equity, fairness and social justice', and determine 'any barriers to recognition'; investigate whether any new awards were needed, or any alterations to present ones; explore the issue of precedence, and the question of what kinds of activities received (or should receive) which levels of award; look at the

---

18 Commonwealth of Australia, House of Representatives, *Parliamentary Debates*, 21 June 1995 (Frank Walker).
19 Commonwealth of Australia, House of Representatives, *Parliamentary Debates*, 21 June 1995 (Frank Walker).

processes by which nominations were made and considered; and 'make appropriate recommendations'.[20] Such a comprehensive brief raised the possibility of a complete overhaul of the system.

When the committee presented its report in November 1995, it was a large and detailed document, coming in at more than 400 pages, including over 100 pages of appendices. After reviewing the existing system and its history, the committee outlined the research and public consultation it had undertaken. An initial survey by the market research company AGB-McNair had revealed that many people knew little about the country's honours system, with less than half of the respondents able to name the Order of Australia, and more than half unaware that it was possible for them to make nominations. Perhaps unsurprisingly, 'bravery' and 'community service' were deemed most worthy of recognition, while 'long service' and 'political and public service' were each considered unworthy by almost a quarter of participants.[21] Focus group research then sought to delve more deeply into attitudes towards, and knowledge of, the system.[22] The results affirmed that members of the public lacked familiarity with it, and were unsure about its processes. They also showed 'resistance towards' the conferral of honours upon people perceived 'to be "just doing their job"', such as public servants or members of the legal profession, and a desire to see rewarded instead '[a]cts of heroism, community service and medical/scientific achievement'. The research suggested to the committee that honours were viewed 'mainly as the preserve of organisations and powerful or well-connected individuals', and it showed a desire on the part of the community for awards to go more often to '"ordinary Australians" and "quiet achievers"', as well as for a greater emphasis on 'community service and the environment'.[23]

The committee had also surveyed the Order of Australia Association, learning the opinions of recipients towards their honours, and examined awards and nominations within the order over the preceding five years.[24] Among their findings was that while the success rate for nominations of people born overseas was relatively high, the number of nominations was low, and that both the quantity of nominations of women and their representation at the upper levels of the order were 'concern[s]'. Observing

---

20 *A Matter of Honour*, xiv.
21 *A Matter of Honour*, 94–96, quotes on 96.
22 *A Matter of Honour*, 99.
23 *A Matter of Honour*, 101.
24 *A Matter of Honour*, 114–52.

a 'perception that class, status or wealth play[ed] some role in the allocation of awards and the determination of award level', the committee thought this view would continue 'as long as the current concentration of higher awards in affluent areas and high status occupations continues'.[25] Finally, the committee undertook a process of public consultation, seeking submissions, holding public meetings, and meeting interested parties.[26] A wide range of issues were pressed by respondents during this process, including a need for better publicising the system, a desire to see more emphasis placed on voluntary work over paid, and 'broader access ... and a fairer distribution of awards at all levels', as well as matters relating to specific awards, suggestions for the revival of British honours or the creation of new distinctions, and a range of other matters.[27]

Having outlined its research and findings, the committee then dealt with the structure and administration of the honours system, and the issue of accessibility, making a total of 67 recommendations.[28] Among the most intriguing was that a group award be created within the Order of Australia, which would allow for the recognition of 'collective effort'; such a distinction 'would have particular value for Aboriginal and Torres Strait Islander communities', for whom 'the group is of prime importance'.[29] Redrafting of the criteria for awards in the order was also suggested, in order to focus more upon the extent to which the service being recognised went 'above and beyond' what might usually be expected in a specific area of activity, rather than whether it was performed at a local, national, or global level.[30] Several recommendations dealt with the question of publicity, suggesting a range of strategies for increasing public awareness and knowledge of the system. The development of materials for school children and new citizens, as well as in translation, was urged, as well as the creation of an information kit about the Order of Australia.[31] In order to redress inequities, the committee recommended both 'raising awareness of ... imbalances' among those responsible for administering the system or selecting recipients, and 'changes to award processes', as well as 'improved data collection and management'; the possibility of quotas was rejected.[32]

---

25 *A Matter of Honour*, 152.
26 *A Matter of Honour*, 153.
27 *A Matter of Honour*, 155–73, quote on 163.
28 *A Matter of Honour*, xxii–xxxv.
29 *A Matter of Honour*, xxiii, 194–96, quotes on xxiii and 194.
30 *A Matter of Honour*, xxiii.
31 *A Matter of Honour*, xxvii–xxviii.
32 *A Matter of Honour*, xxix, 263–64, quotes on xxix and 264.

Whether the changes would have been implemented and Walker's bold vision realised—if indeed the committee's proposals were enough to accomplish that vision—would never be tested, for the government lost office in March 1996, and the incoming administration of Liberal leader John Howard was not likely to be sympathetic to it. Detailing which of the recommendations his government had accepted in the House of Representatives in October 1997, Howard stated that full assent had been given to 35, while four had been partly accepted, 21 rejected, and seven left to the prerogative of Government House. Four other resolutions 'unconnected with the report' had also been made. Among those dismissed were that the Order of Australia should revert to having three levels only (companion, officer, and member); that the military and general divisions should be combined; that eligibility criteria for the order's grades should be rewritten 'to be clearer and more inclusive'; and that a group award should be created. Nor was the government keen to create all of the suggested new awards, discarding proposals for a Conspicuous Service Order for defence services, a 'community based merit award, outside the Order of Australia', and a Voluntary Service Medal for long-term community work. Unsurprisingly, the committee's recommendation that the prime minister request the Queen to no longer make awards in her personal gift was also rejected, and, probably wisely, the government also refused to insist that 'the nomination and assessment process for awards in the Order of Australia address the nominee's commitment to Australian community values'.[33]

Other recommendations turned down included those for the restructuring of the council for the Order of Australia—the intent of which was partly to insist upon a more equal gender balance and greater diversity in that body—and to expect the honours secretariat to play a more active role in seeking nominations from under-represented groups, as well as that the Queen's Birthday honours list be abandoned in favour of announcing all awards in the Order of Australia on 26 January and all defence awards on Anzac Day. Those that did meet with approval tended to be those that represented less far-reaching change—'finetuning', to use Kemp's word, rather than transforming the system. Among them were proposals for the development of a publicity strategy, to make the system part of the civics curricula, and for the extension and enhancement of various

---

33 Commonwealth of Australia, House of Representatives, *Parliamentary Debates*, 29 October 1997 (John Howard).

defence and other service medals. The committee's emphases on raising the participation of previously under-represented groups, increasing the transparency of the awards process, and better reflecting community values in the types of work being honoured were to be followed largely through the government's agreement to proposals for improving publicity and producing more detailed citations when awards were conferred.[34] If it was a shame that the committee's hard work and thoughtful recommendations were not given more support, however, the government's lukewarm response may also have avoided some potential hazards, particularly in the idea that nominees should display a commitment to Australian values, a deeply complicated and slippery concept that could have consumed much effort for little gain.

Holding up half the sky: Women and honours

A significant strand in the review committee's consideration of access to the honours system was the issue of women's lack of representation. This under-representation was not new, and nor, as we have seen throughout this book, was it a novel concern. According to the 1995 review, women were 'under-represented as both nominators and nominees' for the Order of Australia, making up less than a quarter of nominators, and receiving only slightly over a quarter of nominations.[35] As we saw in the previous chapter, one common response to complaints about the lack of gender balance in awards in recent years had been that while women received fewer nominations, when they were nominated they had a higher chance of success; thus, the solution was for greater numbers of women to be nominated. The review committee poured some cold water over this idea, observing that while nominations for women were more successful than those for men at the lowest level of the order—the OAM (Medal of the Order of Australia)—it was not so at any of the other grades. In their view, the likely explanation was that community service, in which field women predominated, tended to be recognised at this level. According to their figures, 36 per cent of OAMs went to women, but only 15 per cent

---

34   Commonwealth of Australia, House of Representatives, *Parliamentary Debates*, 29 October 1997 (John Howard).
35   *A Matter of Honour*, 250.

of the highest grade, the AC (Companion of the Order of Australia).[36] Agreeing with 'many submissions writers', the committee felt that 'these outcomes show women are not receiving appropriate recognition … for their contribution to society', and suggested that 'the primary reason' was '[t]he lack of relevance of the system to women'.[37]

Various factors contributed to women's low levels of inclusion, in the committee's view. One was that women were less conversant with the system than men, and 'less likely to see the Order of Australia as a mechanism for community acknowledgement of the sorts of contributions they make to society'. Another was a lack of access to professional or business networks that could offer guidance on making use of the system. The fact that information aimed especially at women had not been produced was also deemed 'a significant factor', while a number of submissions had also observed a lack of female representation on the council for the Order of Australia. More consequential, however, was the way that the criteria for awards were framed. Those for the upper grades emphasised 'the sphere in which contributions are made'—whether local, national, or global—and were 'interpreted as relating to contributions in the professional, research and business fields', where men generally predominated.[38] Other areas of activity, in the committee's view, were equally important, but were being overshadowed. In their assessment, the Order of Australia 'appear[ed] to contain an institutionalised bias' that led to community service at a local level being undervalued compared to contributions in professional arenas, 'regardless of how pre-eminent or outstanding the local contribution is'.[39] These observations underlay the recommendations to enhance publicity for the Order of Australia, increase female representation on its council, and rewrite the criteria for its various grades. The latter two proposals not being adopted, it is not possible to ascertain whether or not they would have improved women's position in the biannual distribution of awards. What is beyond doubt, however, is that the issue has only grown in prominence in the years since.

Indeed, by the early twenty-first century, the issue of gender inequity had become perhaps the strongest strand of criticism of the Australian honours system, and of the Order of Australia in particular. A campaign to address

---

36 *A Matter of Honour*, 250–51.
37 *A Matter of Honour*, 251.
38 *A Matter of Honour*, 252.
39 *A Matter of Honour*, 253.

the situation was initiated in 2011 by Carol Schwartz, the founding chair of the Women's Leadership Institute Australia and herself a member of the order, supported by Our Community, a group supporting not-for-profit organisations. In February that year Schwartz launched *Advancing Women: Women & the Order of Australia*, a guide to the nomination process intended to boost the inclusion of women in the order, which was sent to all members of parliament, mayors, and shire presidents.[40] Explaining that they desired to 'challenge and change women's role in society', Schwartz and the group managing director of Our Community, Denis Moriarty, sought to increase women's inclusion in the Order of Australia as part of a larger effort to seek 'systems changes' and 'to empower women at all levels to take their place in all parts of Australian society'.[41] Honours, the guide observed, embodied that which the community considered 'deserving of recognition' or 'honourable'; there was 'no reason why women should not make up half the honours lists'.[42] Readers were encouraged to nominate a woman—or indeed, someone from another under-represented group, such as those from non-English-speaking backgrounds—and led through the process of preparing a nomination, including identifying potential recipients, gathering material, writing convincingly, and arranging referees.[43]

The next year, in an opinion piece in the Melbourne *Age* following the announcement of the Australia Day list, Schwartz suggested that, if the list embodied 'the qualities Australia admires and the fields that Australians look up to', it also showed 'that Australians think the things men do are twice as worthy as the things that women do'. Finding women once again honoured more frequently at the lower levels of the order than the upper, and constituting less than a third of the list overall, she was especially 'discourag[ed]' to observe that, rather than improving, women's share of recognition had begun shrinking. It seemed clear to Schwartz that women's inclusion in the system would not reach parity without some form of active intervention. Although she did not claim discrimination in the process of making awards, she suggested the problem was systemic. Fields of activity in which women predominated tended not to receive

40 *Advancing Women: Women and the Order of Australia* (Melbourne: Our Community and Women's Leadership Institute Australia, 2011); Women's Leadership Institute Australia and Our Community, 'New Campaign Launched to Boost the Number of Female Order of Australia Recipients: Business Leader Says Public Recognition of Women Remains Elusive', media release, 25 January 2011.
41 *Advancing Women*, 3.
42 *Advancing Women*, 7.
43 *Advancing Women*, 7, 10–15.

recognition—she cited teaching, nursing, and social work as examples—while women in more frequently recognised areas of activity still received fewer awards than men in those fields. Past award choices, she argued, created 'stereotypes' of the kinds of individuals who deserved to be nominated, and these were 'self-perpetuating'. What was needed was a 'widening [of] concepts' as to the kinds of activities that were worthy of recognition, and for women to become better at 'organising networks' to recognise each other. The problem would soon disappear, she concluded, if more people simply began nominating women.[44]

Schwartz and others continued to pursue the goal of gender parity in honours lists over the following years, and numerous critiques appeared in media coverage of those lists. In June 2012, enjoining readers 'to be proud of all our leaders, male and female', and 'to act with respect for their efforts and achievements … with a blind spot to their gender', Schwartz insisted that there was 'no reason why our Honours would not be split equally between men and women'.[45] A couple of years later, after the announcement of the 2014 Australia Day list, veteran feminist activist Anne Summers, who had been women's issues adviser for the governments of Bob Hawke and Paul Keating and who had been appointed AO in 1989, was quoted asserting that 'urgent intervention' and 'affirmative action' were necessary.[46] The chair of the Order of Australia's council, Air Chief Marshal Angus Houston, was reported to have stated that '[w]e need to encourage more nominations for deserving women' if 'a 50:50 split' was to be attained.[47] A few days later in an opinion piece in the *Age*, Schwartz expressed 'great disappointment' that the list had shown no improvement—while in Britain, for the first time, women had outnumbered men—and advocated a '50-50 target' for membership of the order's council, for the names put forward by nominating organisations, and for each honours list, as well as greater transparency in award criteria.[48]

---

44   Carol Schwartz, 'Too Little Honour for the World and Work of Women', *Age* (Melbourne), 8 February 2012 [online].

45   Carol Schwartz, 'Women Experts: A Shameful Decline', 25 June 2012, Women's Leadership Institute Australia, accessed 22 April 2014, www.wlia.com.au/story_page?sId=32&PHPSESSID=24b 4493b29f2e31d5d353aab64d4f78d (site discontinued, available at web.archive.org/web/20150318 115341/http://wlia.com.au/story_page?sId=32).

46   Jill Stark, 'Women Still Short-Changed in the Mystery-Box Honours List', *Sunday Age* (Melbourne), 26 January 2014 [online].

47   Jill Stark, 'Women Still Short-Changed in the Mystery-Box Honours List', *Sunday Age* (Melbourne), 26 January 2014 [online].

48   Carol Schwartz, 'Lots of Awards, But Too Few Women', *Age* (Melbourne), 1 February 2014 [online].

In June the Queen's Birthday list provoked further censure, with feminist and writer Clementine Ford questioning why women remained under-recognised, and what assumptions about the relationship between ideas of merit and gender underlay the imbalance. Like so many before her, she called upon the community to nominate more women in future.[49]

By the beginning of 2017 it was being reported that the system required reform, although also that the proportions of women nominees and recipients were higher than at any time in the past five years. Nevertheless, they remained firmly stuck at around a third. Summers thought such a rate of inclusion came 'pitifully short'. Worse, she contended that, with its reliance on nominations from the community, the system was 'cumbersome, onerous and ultimately biased'. It did not help, she suggested, that it did not allow for 'measuring BAME [Black, Asian, and minority ethnic] or disability or how many Aboriginal and Torres Strait Islanders' had received awards. If the country did not 'change radically the way we select honourees' it would not be able 'to maintain our pretensions towards equality', she concluded.[50] While the 'elderly white well-educated males' who dominated the list were undoubtedly worthy, wrote Vivienne Pearson in the *Sydney Morning Herald*, 'surely they deserve to be joined by others who make up our rich society'. Besides the gender disparity evident in the list, Pearson noted that names 'of Anglo-Celtic origin' seemed to predominate. She joined the chorus calling for Australians to use their power to nominate to remedy the problem; as well as women, she encouraged readers to nominate individuals of non-European backgrounds, younger people, those in same-sex relationships, immigrants, and refugees. To those who felt that the system was 'old fashioned and meaningless in this modern day', she replied that this could only be so 'if we allow it to remain unrepresentative of our communities'.[51]

Jenna Price, writing in the same paper a little later in the year, was less forgiving of the system's failings. Each new list, she stated, left her 'totally infuriated'. They were catalogues of 'white men getting yet another reward for the jobs they are already paid to do', she wrote, while the process for

---

49   Clementine Ford, 'Why Are So Few Women Awarded OAMs?' 9 June 2014, *Daily Life*, accessed 6 September 2014, www.dailylife.com.au/news-and-views/dl-opinion/why-are-so-few-women-awarded-oams-20140608-39qyj.html?rand=1402258561372.

50   Anne Summers, 'Our Honours System Doesn't Reflect Who We Are', *Sydney Morning Herald*, 6 January 2017 [online].

51   Vivienne Pearson, 'The Australia Day Honours List Still Has a Gender Problem. But You Can Help', *Sydney Morning Herald*, 26 January 2017 [online].

nominating someone was too demanding to make it easy to put other kinds of people forward. She found a ray of hope in the establishment of a group known as 'Honour A Woman', which was working to achieve gender parity in the system by supporting those seeking to make a nomination; the group aimed to achieve their goal by 2020.[52] When the next list, in June 2017, revealed no increase in women's rate of inclusion, but rather a slight decrease, Price argued that it was time to 'entirely recast' the Order of Australia's council, which itself did not include women in equal numbers.[53] As these examples suggest, a new note of frustration had by now begun to creep into calls for gender equity in honours. With the proportion of women seemingly stuck at around a third—a figure that had been achieved, at least at the lower levels of the system, as long ago as the 1920s and 1930s—and little evidence that the dramatic changes in women's statuses and life experiences since the 1960s were being reflected in the distribution of honours, some critics were no longer willing to adopt a strategy of waiting for the system to catch up to wider social currents. It is too early to tell whether the efforts of individuals and groups such as Price and Honour A Woman will produce lasting change, but it appears clear that the chorus of voices demanding gender parity is growing louder with each passing list. One indication they might be beginning to find success was provided by the June 2018 list, in which women outnumbered men in awards of the AC for the first time.[54]

2014: Return of the knighthood

Prominent as the question of gender equity in awards was becoming, it was not the most arresting controversy over the system in the second decade of the twenty-first century. Few would have guessed when the federal election of September 2013 delivered victory to the Liberal–National coalition led by Tony Abbott that the question of honours would become a defining feature of his government. Yet so it was. To the general surprise of almost the entire country—including most of his own

---

52   Jenna Price, 'Fill Out That Bloody Form and Nominate a Woman for an Australian Honour', *Sydney Morning Herald*, 18 April 2017 [online]. See also 'Honour A Woman', Facebook group, accessed 5 August 2021, www.facebook.com/Honourawoman/.
53   Jenna Price, 'Australian Honours: It's Time to Ditch the Men at the Top', *Sydney Morning Herald*, 12 June 2017 [online].
54   'More Women Than Men in Top Queen's Birthday Honours', *Guardian* (Australia), 11 June 2018 [online].

party colleagues—in March 2014 Abbott announced that the Queen had, at his request, amended the letters patent relating to the Order of Australia to re-establish the grade of knight or dame (AK/AD). Up to four of the new awards could be made in any one year, with the first two recipients to be the departing governor-general, Quentin Bryce, and her replacement, Peter Cosgrove. Asserting that it was 'fitting that the Queen's representative be so honoured', Abbott's statement declared that the titles would be conferred upon individuals who had 'accepted public office rather than sought it and who can never, by virtue of that office, ever entirely return to private life'.[55] Responding to questions following the announcement, he described the titles as 'an important grace note in our national life'. Charged with having apparently rejected the possibility of restoring titles the previous year, when discussing suggestions that he might follow New Zealand's example, he stated that what he had then dismissed was doing 'what New Zealand ha[d] done', and altering the companionship of the order to become a knighthood.[56]

What New Zealand had done, in fact, was to restore the titles of knight and dame to the upper two grades of the New Zealand Order of Merit, from which they had been removed by the Labour Government of Helen Clark in 2000. After taking office in November 2008, the country's National Party prime minister, John Key, had announced the following year that the top two levels of the order—which since 2000 had been known as principal companions and distinguished companions, and had not conferred titles upon recipients—would revert to being termed knights or dames grand companion, and knights or dames companion, each carrying the titles of 'Sir' and 'Dame'. Reactions within New Zealand had been mixed. The *Waikato Times* applauded the switch, remarking that the system established in 2000 had been 'a veritable alphabet soup of honours long in letters but short in standing'. Contesting the idea that it represented a return to the days of subservience to Britain, or was inconsistent with the nation's egalitarian spirit, the paper contended that New Zealand's 'growing cultural maturity and underlying egalitarian

55   Tony Abbott, 'Press Conference, Parliament House, Canberra', transcript, 25 March 2014, *PM Transcripts: Transcripts from the Prime Ministers of Australia*, Australian Government, Department of the Prime Minister and Cabinet, accessed 3 June 2019, pmtranscripts.pmc.gov.au/release/transcript-23367.
56   Tony Abbott, 'Press Conference, Parliament House, Canberra', transcript, 25 March 2014, *PM Transcripts: Transcripts from the Prime Ministers of Australia*, Australian Government, Department of the Prime Minister and Cabinet, accessed 3 June 2019, pmtranscripts.pmc.gov.au/release/transcript-23367; 'PM Tony Abbott Rules Out Reinstating Knights and Dames in Oz', *Sunday Telegraph* (Sydney), 22 December 2013 [online].

ethos … creates a better environment for titles', which were now earned through merit rather than rewards of time serving or birth.[57] Key's own argument was that the titles were 'a visible sign of celebrating success for a lifetime of service and achievement'.[58]

Certainly the decision was acceptable to many who had received the distinctions of principal or distinguished companion in the interim. Seventy-two (out of a total of 85) soon accepted an offer to be redesignated knights or dames.[59] But the move did not escape criticism. Describing herself as 'an English-born New Zealander', one correspondent to the Christchurch *Press* expressed concern that the government appeared to be 'hankering after a corrupt system … based on cronyism and privilege' and decried awards that '[set people] above their fellows'. '[A]s a modern democracy', she argued, the country ought to 'have grown beyond the need for such archaic and feudal recognition of service to country'.[60] Labour Party leader Phil Goff, meanwhile, was reported to have condemned the revival of titular distinctions as having 'brought back colonial airs and graces New Zealand had worked for decades to free itself of'.[61] Another, more complex, response has been to suggest that titles be retained, but made 'more Kiwi' by the adoption of Māori language equivalents or translations, such as 'Tā' in place of 'Sir', and 'Kahurangi' in place of 'Dame'.[62]

Resurrection of the titles of knight and dame in the Order of Australia had been advocated occasionally since their abolition by the Hawke Government in 1986. In 1990 it was reported that John Hewson, the leader of the Liberal Party and opposition leader, was considering bringing back Australian knighthoods, and in 1992 a motion to include knighthoods in the order was accepted by the National Party's federal council, though it rejected the possibility of reviving recommendations for British honours.[63] Beginning in 2006, the monarchist group Australians for Constitutional Monarchy (ACM) had conducted an energetic if ineffective campaign for

57   'Nothing Like a Dame, or a Sir', *Waikato Times* (Hamilton), 11 March 2009, 6.
58   Tracy Watkins, 'Arise New Zealand', *Dominion Post* (Wellington), 9 March 2009, 1.
59   Mandy Wong, 'Royal Honours System', *Te Ara—The Encyclopedia of New Zealand*, accessed 8 August 2017, www.TeAra.govt.nz/en/royal-honours-system/print.
60   Diana Bradley, letter to the editor, *Press* (Christchurch), 10 March 2009, 10.
61   'Nothing Like a Dame, or a Sir', *Waikato Times* (Hamilton), 11 March 2009, 6.
62   Dean Knight, 'New Zealand Order of Merit: Te Reo Appellations', 31 December 2010, *LAWS179 Elephants and the Law*, accessed 8 August 2017, www.laws179.co.nz/2010/12/new-zealand-order-of-merit-te-reo.html.
63   Tracey Aubin, 'Knighthoods on Hewson Agenda', *Australian*, 1 June 1990, 3, newspaper cuttings on the Australian honours system, National Library of Australia, Canberra; Michael Gordon, 'Bring Back Knights—Nats', *Sunday Age* (Melbourne), 6 September 1992, 7.

the restoration of the AK/AD. David Flint, ACM's national convenor, authored several posts on the subject for the group's website, arguing that Australia's highest achievers lacked the recognition on the world stage afforded by a knighthood or damehood, and that the AK/AD level of the order should be restored, either allowing recipients who objected to titles to refuse them, or without conferring the title or accolade.[64] Another to support the idea was columnist Rex Jory, who suggested in the Adelaide *Advertiser* in 2009 that there was 'surely … no harm in our leading citizens being recognised by being given a simple honorific in front of their names'. Noting the argument that titles were elitist, Jory asked, '[i]sn't that precisely the point?' 'Aren't Australia's leading citizens, people, who have made a unique contribution to society,' he continued, 'entitled to be instantly recognised?' Moreover, he pointed out, a range of other titles were accepted and used in Australian society, including in the army, academia, the church, and politics.[65]

Abbott, as many commentators were aware, had been ACM's inaugural executive director in the early 1990s, and perhaps this goes some way towards explaining a decision that many found inexplicable. His mentor, former prime minister John Howard, had during his time in office explicitly ruled out restoring either knighthoods or imperial honours in Australia. Quoted in 2002 saying that he considered 'imperial honours and imperial descriptions' to be 'something in the past for Australia', he gave it as his opinion that neither imperial honours nor titular awards 'suit[ed] the egalitarian Australia of which I am prime minister'.[66] Journalists delighted in noting that he had stated in his autobiography, *Lazarus Rising*, that although he had been encouraged to resuscitate knighthoods, he had chosen not to do so, believing that they were seen by 'many, even conservative Australians, [as] somewhat anachronistic'.[67]

---

64   See, for example, David Flint, 'Order of Australia: A Canadian View', 12 February 2006, *Australians for Constitutional Monarchy*, accessed 5 August 2021, norepublic.com.au/order-of-australia-a-canadian-view-2/; David Flint, 'Knights and Dames', 28 January 2008, *Australians for Constitutional Monarchy*, accessed 5 August 2021, norepublic.com.au/knights-and-dames-2/; David Flint, 'There is Nothing Like a Dame', 25 April 2007, *Australians for Constitutional Monarchy*, accessed 5 August 2021, norepublic. com.au/there-is-nothing-like-a-dame/. The accolade is the traditional touch on both shoulders with a sword that accompanies knighthood.

65   Rex Jory, 'Hypocrisy and a Lack of Political Courage Will Block a Return to Knighthoods', *Advertiser* (Adelaide), 31 August 2009, 18.

66   'PM Not Interested in Knighthood', *Age* (Melbourne), 12 April 2002 [online]. A decade later, however, Howard was appointed to the Order of Merit, an honour in the Queen's personal gift. 'John Howard Appointed to Order of Merit', *Sydney Morning Herald*, 1 January 2012 [online].

67   John Howard, *Lazarus Rising: A Personal and Political Autobiography*, revised ed. (Sydney: HarperCollins, 2011), 240.

A wave of criticism from across the political spectrum followed the announcement that the AK/AD was to be awarded once more. One target was Abbott's lack of consultation, even within his own party room.[68] Another line of critique, which had arisen when the award had first been established under the Fraser Government, focused upon the position in which other recipients were placed. Michael Shmith noted this change to their status, describing those who had been appointed companions as 'suddenly down a notch: second-class citizens', with officers, members, and medal-holders likewise downgraded.[69] For both media commentators and members of the public, however, it was the symbolism and meanings of Abbott's action that drew the most attention. Many saw the revival of knighthood as embodying a desire on Abbott's part to return to a more comfortable past, free of the uncertainties over identity, and the social and cultural upheaval that had transformed Australian life since the 1960s. This was the theme of one letter to the *Sydney Morning Herald*, which portrayed the move as part of a 'headlong race towards the Good Old Days', and, among other things, pondered if an 'Abbottian Calendar, in which 2014 becomes 1954' would be next.[70] Similar jokes were rife in newspapers and social media. Another letter 'look[ed] forward to the sight of Sir Peter Cosgrove greeting visitors in a suit of mail', while still another was eager 'to spend the new shilling and for the declaration of war on Germany'.[71] Labor's Mark Dreyfus, meanwhile, wondered if the country was 'rushing back to a reintroduction of slavery or some other institution from the 19th century'.[72]

Part of this association with the past was a perception that the titles were themselves outdated, relics of a bygone era that conjured images not only of medieval knights on horseback, but of a long-defunct British empire. By the beginning of the twenty-first century, if not before, the term 'imperial honours' was often applied not only to British awards, as it had been in the past, but also to knighthoods (and, by extension, damehoods) more generally. Counting out the possibility of reviving

---

68   See 'Abbott on Back Foot Over Knights and Dames', *Sydney Morning Herald*, 26 March 2014 [online].

69   Michael Shmith, 'Abbott Drags Us Back in Time to a Knights' Realm', *Sydney Morning Herald*, 27 March 2014 [online].

70   David Barrett, letter to the editor, *Sydney Morning Herald*, 27 March 2014 [online].

71   Don Wormald, letter to the editor, *Sydney Morning Herald*, 27 March 2014 [online]; Andrew Dillon, letter to the editor, *Sydney Morning Herald*, 27 March 2014 [online].

72   Stephanie Balogh and Pia Akerman, 'Good Knight to a Dame as Tony Abbott Revives Titles', *Australian*, 26 March 2014 [online].

either British honours or titular awards in 2002, Howard had used the phrase 'imperial honours and imperial descriptions', but many others were not so nuanced. By nature, knighthoods were for many observers imperial awards, redolent of and indistinguishable from the aristocracy that had been so much a part of empire, and equally unsuited to an independent and egalitarian Australia. Commentary on Abbott's revival of the AK/AD sometimes blurred the distinction in precisely this way. 'God Save the Queen', cried the front page of Brisbane's *Courier-Mail* the following morning, announcing that the '[i]mperial honours system' had been 'reintroduced'.[73] James Jeffrey, writing in the *Australian*, also referred to 'the restoration of imperial honours', while Chris Uhlmann, presenting the *AM* program on Australian Broadcasting Corporation (ABC) radio, described Abbott's action as 'restor[ing] a hybrid of the British honours system'.[74]

Such was also the association behind the many negative responses that suggested the titles were inherently aristocratic and thus unsuited to an egalitarian society—the selfsame arguments that had been made more than a century earlier, and with which this book began. Bringing back these titles, argued one correspondent in the *Australian*, 'show[ed] that the Abbott government is hell-bent on returning to a society with lords and ladies and all the petty social snobbery and class distinctions that are an inevitable concomitant'.[75] Former Western Australian Labor and then independent member of parliament Larry Graham wrote that Abbott had 'woke[n] up back in 18th century UK and re-introduced the class system here'; he lamented the weakening of what he considered one of Australia's 'great strengths', its avoidance of 'the pitfalls of entrenched class and privilege'. Like many others would do, he turned to Daniel Deniehy's famous phrase—'bunyip aristocracy'—to decry the move.[76] The *Sydney Morning Herald* did the same, with a front-page headline reading 'Welcome to Abbott's Bunyip Aristocracy'.[77] Although not himself using the phrase, Labor's Sam Dastyari seemed to be seeking to

---

73   'God Save the Queen', *Courier-Mail* (Brisbane), 26 March 2014, 1.

74   James Jeffrey, 'Knight and Dame', *Australian*, 26 March 2014 [online]; 'Bemusement in the UK Over Australian Plans to Reintroduce Knighthoods', *AM with Chris Uhlmann*, story reported by Mary Gearin, 26 March 2014, Australian Broadcasting Corporation, accessed 27 March 2014, www. abc.net.au/am/content/2014/s3971472.htm.

75   Barry Fox, letter to the editor, *Australian*, 27 March 2014 [online].

76   Larry Graham, 'Abbott is Seeking a World That Simply Doesn't Exist', *Canberra Times*, 26 March 2014 [online].

77   Tony Wright, 'Welcome to Abbott's Bunyip Aristocracy', *Sydney Morning Herald*, 26 March 2014 [online].

emulate Deniehy's scathing rhetoric in a mocking speech delivered in the Senate. 'What greater honour could the subjects of this land girt by sea aspire to', Dastyari asked, in a later edited version published in the *Sydney Morning Herald*, than to have their 'tasselled shoulders touched in accolade, kneeling before the court of a distant Queen'?[78] But Deniehy's phrase had come a long way since he first uttered it. As it had come to be used during the twentieth century, it was no longer a critique of hereditary title and privilege alone, but also of the non-hereditary titles attached to knighthood and damehood.

In a similar way, many people found the titles of 'Sir' and 'Dame' too evocative of monarchy, and critiqued them—and those who received them—on the grounds that they were incompatible with a future Australian republic. One correspondent to the *Australian*, for example, found Bryce's acceptance of the title of 'Dame' irreconcilable with her declared support for an Australian republic, describing it as 'an honour that reeks of the monarchy'.[79] Indeed, much of the debate that followed Abbott's announcement revolved around the issue of an Australian republic, with monarchist and republican advocates squaring off throughout the media. David Morris, the national director of the Australian Republican Movement, was quoted saying that reviving the titles was returning to 'a colonial frame of mind that we have outgrown as a nation', while Flint argued that reviving 'knighthoods and titles such as Queens Counsel' was 'appropriate while we remain a constitutional monarchy'.[80] Introducing a televised debate between Flint, as the monarchist voice, and former republic referendum political campaign director Greg Barns, as the republican one, the ABC's 7.30 host Sarah Ferguson stated that reviving the titles had '[brought] the Queen back into the centre of Australia's highest order', describing it as a step that had 'delighted monarchists and brought howls of dismay from Republicans'. The conversation that followed centred on the question of whether such titles were a suitable way

---

78   Sam Dastyari, 'Knighthoods Return: Welcome to the Game of Tones', *Sydney Morning Herald*, 26 March 2014 [online].

79   Ewan McLean, letter to the editor, *Australian*, 27 March 2014 [online].

80   Matthew Knott, 'Tony Abbott Reintroduces Knight and Dame Honours for Australians', *Sydney Morning Herald*, 25 March 2014 [online].

to recognise achievement and service, and part of the country's tradition, or merely silly and inappropriate in a modern, independent country no longer tied to Britain.[81]

Such was the passion aroused by this contest that relatively few acknowledged—or, perhaps, realised—that the AK/AD was an Australian award, within the country's own national honour, and as able to be awarded by any future president as the other grades of the Order of Australia, of which the Queen had been sovereign ever since its inception in 1975. One who did was Malcolm Turnbull, by this time a former leader of the Liberal Party but an emerging rival for the prime ministership, who had once led the country's republican movement. Observing that a number of republics had orders of knighthood, including France, Italy, Argentina, Peru, Guatemala, and Chile, he advised supporters of an Australian republic not to 'lose too much sleep over the Prime Minister's decision'.[82] Some commentators took his reference to Peru, Argentina, and Guatemala to be a concealed criticism, however, and it almost certainly was. In the *Sydney Morning Herald*, Lisa Cox suggested that he was 'gently mock[ing]' the decision.[83] Such a focus on the split between monarchists and republicans was probably inevitable, when Abbott himself was known to be a committed monarchist, and his main rival for the party leadership, Turnbull, a former leader of the republican movement. Whatever the legal or constitutional status of the revived titles, however, they carried with them too much baggage from the past to be evaluated simply as a mode of recognition for deserving individuals.

Yet it is important to remember that, as ever, community views were not unanimous, and there were those who supported the resurrection of titular honours. For one correspondent to the *Australian*, the issue was one of heritage. Praising Abbott's move, he stated that '[i]f we throw off the past, eventually we will be left with nothing'.[84] Another appeared

81   Sarah Ferguson, David Flint, and Greg Barns, '"Juvenile Baubles" or "Appropriate Recognition"—Knights and Dames Debated', transcript of debate on *7.30*, 25 March 2014, Australian Broadcasting Corporation, accessed 11 August 2017, www.abc.net.au/7.30/content/2014/s3971393.htm.

82   Malcolm Turnbull, 'Australian Knights and the Republic', 25 March 2014, *Malcolm Turnbull*, accessed 15 June 2021, www.malcolmturnbull.com.au/media/australian-knights-and-the-republic. He repeated the comparison in a speech at Parliament House. Lisa Cox, 'Australia Like Esteemed Republics Peru and Guatemala: Malcolm Turnbull Gently Mocks Reintroduction of Knights and Dames', *Sydney Morning Herald*, 27 March 2014 [online].

83   Lisa Cox, 'Australia Like Esteemed Republics Peru and Guatemala: Malcolm Turnbull Gently Mocks Reintroduction of Knights and Dames', *Sydney Morning Herald*, 27 March 2014 [online].

84   Paul Chandler, letter to the editor, *Australian*, 27 March 2014 [online].

to agree with Abbott's characterisation of the awards as a 'grace note' in society, writing that the return of titles was 'to be welcomed, as a way of bringing back a form of cultural etiquette that recognises long-term and committed service by our citizens'. For that writer too it was also a matter of being able to feel part of, and to be proud of, a past heritage. 'Not all aspects of Australia's monarchial [sic] history have to be dumbed down, or cringed at, in order for us to feel proud or patriotic', he wrote.[85] Moreover, while it may have appeared from much of the public discussion—in both old media and social media—that support for the move was rare, the dramas of Britain's Brexit vote in June 2016 and Donald Trump's election as United States president that November must make us wary of easy assumptions about community opinion. One indication that support was not as entirely absent as it might have appeared was an online poll on News. com.au asking whether bringing knighthoods and damehoods back was '[a] suitable honour for great Australians' or '[a]n imperial anachronism'. While such polls are problematic sources and cannot be taken at face value, not least because respondents are self-selected consumers of a particular media source, it is noteworthy that at the time of access, more than 40 per cent of a total of 7,541 respondents had plumped for the former.[86]

Conclusion

Whatever measure of acceptance the revived titles might have gained over time, however, one choice of recipient probably ended that possibility. Unlike the other levels of the order, the AK and AD would be conferred not on the recommendation of the council for the order, but at the prime minister's nomination, although the council's chair would be 'consulted'.[87] This arrangement in itself had led to some concern, but when it was announced on Australia Day 2015 that the prime minister's choice had fallen upon the monarch's consort, Prince Philip, Duke of

---

85   Peter Waterhouse, letter to the editor, *Sydney Morning Herald*, 27 March 2014 [online].

86   See Jennifer Rajca, 'Labor Slams Tony Abbott's Decision to Bring Back Knights and Dames', 26 March 2014, *News.com*, accessed 28 March 2014, www.news.com.au/news/national/labor-slams-tony-abbotts-decision-to-bring-back-knights-and-dames/news-story/4e85d23cd49dc691f751258bd 3a950c7.

87   Tony Abbott, 'Press Conference, Parliament House, Canberra', transcript, 25 March 2014, *PM Transcripts: Transcripts from the Prime Ministers of Australia*, Australian Government, Department of the Prime Minister and Cabinet, accessed 3 June 2019, pmtranscripts.pmc.gov.au/release/transcript-23367; Department of the Prime Minister and Cabinet, 'Reinstatement of Knights and Dames in the Order of Australia', factsheet, March 2014.

Edinburgh, concern became outrage. A key criticism was that the nation's highest honour, announced on the country's national day, had gone to a member of the British royal family, rather than to one of the many deserving Australians who might have been selected. Such was the view of Labor leader Bill Shorten, who was quoted saying that he saw it as 'anachronistic' to 'giv[e] our top award to a British royal', and wondering why 'someone who is Australian in character and activity' had not been picked.[88] National Party deputy leader Barnaby Joyce too expressed his 'preference ... that these awards go to Australians'.[89] Yet there were also voices of support. Scott Coleman saw it as 'only right' that someone who had 'devoted his life to the service of the Commonwealth and the people of Australia' should be recognised, while Kevin Andrews, the minister for defence, saw the prince's years of service as 'a phenomenal contribution' and suggested that 'we should just be generous about it'.[90]

Nevertheless, opposition to the award was sufficiently widespread that the media were soon asking whether Abbott's 'knightmare' could spell the end of his prime ministership.[91] Attempting to undo the damage, he stated that in the future all appointments to the Order of Australia, including the AK/AD, would be chosen by the order's council.[92] No further appointments were made, however. Having survived a leadership spill only a fortnight after the debacle of Prince Philip's award, in September Abbott was replaced as prime minister by Turnbull, and very soon after that, the AK/AD was dropped once more from the honours system. Announcing its removal from the order once again, Turnbull stated that Cabinet had agreed, and the Queen had approved the move. 'Knights and dames', he was quoted as saying, were 'titles that are really anachronistic ... they're

88   Rosie Lewis, 'Prince Philip Knighthood: Tony Abbott Defends Decision', *Australian*, 26 January 2015 [online].

89   Jared Owens, 'Prince Philip Knighthood: Awards "Should be Reserved for Australians"', *Australian*, 27 January 2015 [online].

90   Scott Coleman, 'Prince Philip is a Great Bloke Who Deserves This Knighthood', *Sydney Morning Herald*, 27 January 2015 [online]; Anna Henderson and Alexandra Kirk, 'Prince Philip "Extremely Deserving" of Australian Knighthood, Says Minister; PM Facing Continuing Backlash From Party Colleagues', 27 January 2015, *ABC News*, accessed 14 June 2021, www.abc.net.au/news/2015-01-27/abbott-facing-growing-backlash-over-prince-philip-knighthood/6047750?nw=0.

91   See, for example, Mark Kenny, 'Tony Abbott Foolish If He Ignores Leadership Rumblings in Wake of Knighthood Decision', *Canberra Times*, 28 January 2015 [online]; James Law and Charles Miranda, 'Tony Abbott's Knightmare Could Be Fatal If His Government Fails to Change Tack', *Courier-Mail* (Brisbane), 27 January 2015 [online].

92   Mark Kenny and James Massola, 'Tony Abbott Moves to Head Off Critics', *Sydney Morning Herald*, 3 February 2015 [online].

out of date, they're not appropriate in 2015 in Australia'.[93] In the ensuing analysis of Abbott's prime ministership, several writers agreed that the decision to bestow the resurrected title on Prince Philip was a significant factor in his downfall. For Wayne Errington and Peter Van Onselen it was 'the catalyst' for the unsuccessful spill motion against Abbott in February 2015; to Niki Savva it was 'the last straw' that brought on the motion.[94] Surely the honours system had never been so central to public debate, or so controversial, as at this moment, when the choice of one recipient had threatened the political future of a sitting prime minister.

---

93   Rosie Lewis, 'Knights and Dames Removed From Order of Australia by Malcolm Turnbull', *Australian*, 2 November 2015 [online].
94   Wayne Errington and Peter Van Onselen, *Battleground: Why the Liberal Party Shirtfronted Tony Abbott* (Melbourne: Melbourne University Press, 2015), 11, 128, quote on 11; Niki Savva, *The Road to Ruin: How Tony Abbott and Peta Credlin Destroyed Their Own Government* (Melbourne: Scribe, 2016), 147.

Epilogue

As an institution with profound implications for our understandings of merit, success, and honour—and one with a rich history of debate—the honours system continues to attract controversy and contestation today. As we enter the third decade of the twenty-first century, the scrutiny of the gender balance of honours lists discussed in the final chapter persists. Ahead of the announcement of the Queen's Birthday list in June 2020, journalist Tom McIlroy stated: 'we already know who the winners are. Men'. McIlroy highlighted differences in the gender ratio by State and territory, observing that statistics from Honour a Woman and the Workplace Gender Equality Agency showed that South Australia and Victoria had almost reached parity, while Western Australia trailed behind, with 'less than a third of honours … going to women'.[1] After the list was made public, the *Australian* took a more positive stance, headlining one article with the suggestion that the 'pendulum [was] swinging to women' in relation to awards. Reporting that 'the proportion of women [had] reached its highest level', the article's author, Ean Higgins, quoted the governor-general, David Hurley, stating that the representation of women could achieve parity 'in the next few years'.[2] In the online magazine *Crikey*, however, David Hardaker was less certain, reporting comments from Ruth McGowan, one of the founders of the Honour a Woman campaign, that the system itself was 'broken'. McGowan pointed to the significance of ongoing inequity, suggesting that '[w]hen you are recognised it gives you a level of gravitas that can't be bought', and that honours 'increase the opportunities for people in their career'.[3] Ahead of the

1   Tom McIlroy, 'Men Set to Dominate Queen's Birthday Honours, Again', *Australian Financial Review*, 5 June 2020 [online].
2   Ean Higgins, 'Honours Pendulum Swinging to Women', *Australian*, 7 June 2020 [online].
3   David Hardaker, 'Why Are Women Under-Represented in the Order of Australia Awards?' 23 July 2020, *Crikey*, accessed 10 June 2020, www.crikey.com.au/2020/07/23/why-are-women-under-represented-in-the-order-of-australia-awards/.

next list, in January 2021, Hurley agreed in an interview that critiques of the gender balance of honours were just, and noted that this was something he wanted to alter.[4]

The years 2020 and 2021 also saw controversies over individual awards. The conferral of the AM (Member of the Order of Australia) on the sex therapist Bettina Arndt in the Australia Day list in 2020 was criticised by a number of people, among them former Australian of the Year Rosie Batty and the attorney-general of Victoria, Jill Hennessy. The latter reportedly wrote to Hurley to request that Arndt's award—which, according to the citation, she had received partly for service 'to gender equity through advocacy for men'—be cancelled, as did Victorian State parliamentarian Tim Smith and senator Sarah Henderson.[5] In her letter, Henderson suggested that remarks that Arndt had made on Twitter regarding the murder of Hannah Clarke and her children in February, in which she had congratulated the police in Queensland for remaining open-minded, even to the chance that Clarke's estranged husband could 'have been "driven too far"', amounted to 'conduct which has brought disrepute on the Order' and thereby provided grounds for the termination of her award.[6] Hurley referred this correspondence to the council for the Order of Australia, along with some regarding the writer and radio host Mike Carlton, whose June 2020 award had also been criticised due to tweets he had made.[7] Some months later, Shane Stone, the chair of the council, announced that both would retain their awards, noting that 'recommendations for an award were not "an endorsement of the political, religious or social views of recipients"', and that honours were usually only revoked in cases involving 'criminal convictions, adverse court findings

4   Jacqueline Maley and Nigel Gladstone, 'Order of Australia Biased Against Women, Admits Governor-General', *Sydney Morning Herald*, 22 January 2021 [online].
5   Luke Henriques-Gomes, 'Rosie Batty "Dismayed" by Decision to Give Bettina Arndt an Australia Day Honour', *Guardian* (Australia), 27 January 2020 [online]; Luke Henriques-Gomes, 'Bettina Arndt's Order of Australia Honour Referred to Awards Council for Review', *Guardian* (Australia), 24 February 2020 [online]; Australian Government, Department of the Prime Minister and Cabinet, 'Australian Honours Search Facility', *It's an Honour*, Department of the Prime Minister and Cabinet, accessed 13 June 2021, honours.pmc.gov.au/honours/awards/2005258.
6   Letter from Sarah Henderson, Liberal Senator for Victoria, to Shane Stone, Chairman of the Council for the Order of Australia, 24 February 2020, accessed 15 October 2020, sarahhenderson. com.au/wp-content/uploads/2020/02/200224-Letter-Mr-Shane-Stone-AC-QC.pdf.
7   Paul Karp, 'Bettina Arndt and Mike Carlton Can Keep Their Orders of Australia, Council Decides', *Guardian* (Australia), 4 September 2020 [online]; Jenna Price, 'Who Should Pick Our Australia Day Honourees', *Canberra Times*, 4 September 2020 [online].

or misrepresentations about personal achievements'.[8] 'Unanimous community approval,' Stone was quoted explaining, 'is not a criteria for council to make a recommendation'.[9]

June's list drew further fire, with awards to several former politicians, particularly Tony Abbott, Bronwyn Bishop, Philip Ruddock, and Graham Richardson, attracting criticism.[10] And in January 2021 a wave of criticism greeted the news that tennis player Margaret Court was to be elevated to AC (Companion of the Order of Australia). The Victorian premier, Daniel Andrews, was among those to lambast Court's honour on the grounds that her position on LGBTQI+ rights made her an inappropriate person for the nation to honour. Andrews said:

> I don't believe that she has views that accord with the vast majority of people across our nation that see people, particularly from the LGBTQ community, as equal and deserving of dignity, respect and safety.

'I don't believe she shares those views,' he continued, 'and I don't believe she should be honoured because of that.'[11] Requests were made for the award to be reviewed, and several people—medical practitioner Clara Tuck Meng Soo, medical researcher Caroline de Costa, artist Peter Kingston, and journalist Kerry O'Brien—were reported to be returning their own awards in protest against Court's award.[12] In the *Sydney Morning Herald*, Clara Tuck Meng Soo stated that:

---

8   Luke Henriques-Gomes, 'Bettina Arndt's Order of Australia Honour Referred to Awards Council for Review', *Guardian* (Australia), 24 February 2020 [online]; Sharri Markson, 'PM Under Pressure to Review Honours System', *Daily Telegraph* (Sydney), 10 June 2020 [online]; Paul Karp, 'Bettina Arndt and Mike Carlton Can Keep Their Orders of Australia, Council Decides', *Guardian* (Australia), 4 September 2020 [online].
9   Paul Karp, 'Bettina Arndt and Mike Carlton Can Keep Their Orders of Australia, Council Decides', *Guardian* (Australia), 4 September 2020 [online].
10   Michael Koziol, '"It is a Secret Society": Does Our Honours System Need a Shake Up?' *Sydney Morning Herald*, 28 June 2020 [online]; Orietta Guerrera, '"Irrelevant and Out of Touch": Readers Respond to Queen's Birthday Honours List', *Sydney Morning Herald*, 12 June 2020 [online].
11   'Courting Controversy: Backlash Grows Over Margaret Court's Australia Day Gong', 23 January 2021, updated 25 January 2021, *New Daily*, accessed 14 June 2021, thenewdaily.com.au/news/national/2021/01/23/margaret-court-australia-day-backlash/.
12   Rashida Yosufzai, 'Council Asked to Review Margaret Court's Australia Day Honour as More Return Awards in "Disgust"', 28 January 2021, *SBS News*, accessed 14 June 2021, www.sbs.com.au/news/council-asked-to-review-margaret-court-s-australia-day-honour-as-more-return-awards-in-disgust.

> Someone elevated to the highest civilian honour in Australia should not only have reached the pinnacle of achievements in their field of endeavour … but should also be considered a role model by the rest of the Australian community.[13]

Such controversies raise significant and difficult questions regarding the place and purpose of official honours: are they bestowed for achievements in a particular field, or as recognition of a whole person? Should one's views on a given issue disqualify one for receiving an honour for work or achievements in another field of activity? And what actions, omissions, or opinions are sufficient to disqualify a person from an award? As ever, community opinion on these questions is not unanimous. Writing about the June 2020 list, at least one commentator expressed a willingness to see at least some controversial figures receive awards. In a piece in the *Sydney Morning Herald*, Xavier Symons reflected on his youthful indignation at the 2012 award of an AC to the philosopher Peter Singer, an honour he had protested at the time. Looking back, he felt that his earlier argument that 'someone as controversial as Singer' should not be 'raise[d] up … as a model of Australian excellence' was incorrect. Instead, considering the recent award made to Abbott, he now believed there was 'a clear danger in basing the criteria for an Order of Australia on a partisan view of politics and society', and that '[t]he way in which we celebrate achievement and service should reflect the plurality of reasonable worldviews that characterise our community'. Thus, he argued:

> We should be willing to accept the full implications of a commitment to liberal pluralism, even if we vehemently disagree with the politics and philosophy of those whom this might protect—or, in this case, honour.[14]

The COVID-19 pandemic also prompted some discussion of who really deserves rewards such as these. Writing in the *Sydney Morning Herald* in August 2020, Margaret Fitzherbert expressed her 'hope that along with all the other painful disruptions it's brought, COVID-19 also disrupts Australia's honours system'. She listed several 'inadequacies' of the system as she perceived them, including that 'most recipients are white, male and middle class', and that '[t]oo many people seem to get a medal simply for

---

13   Clara Tuck Meng Soo, 'Why I Handed Back My Order of Australia, and Why Margaret Court Should Be Stripped of Hers', *Sydney Morning Herald*, 24 January 2021 [online].
14   Xavier Symons, 'Tony Abbott's Views May Be Repellent to Many but that's No Reason Not to Honour Him', *Sydney Morning Herald*, 10 June 2020 [online].

doing their already well-paid jobs'. The 'brave and caring people ... on the front line with COVID-19', including medical staff, volunteers, and necessary workers, were providing 'a master class in what service to the community looks like'. Drawing parallels with the service medals received by military personnel and the police, Fitzherbert suggested 'a COVID-19 service medal for those at the front line'.[15] Yet these comments perhaps reveal more about which jobs are seen as most valuable to the community, given that many of these workers are also arguably doing their jobs, albeit well and in difficult and potentially dangerous conditions. At least one commentator even wondered if the institution in its current form was under threat. 'The unveiling of honours lists are rarely without controversy,' observed Orietta Guerrera in the *Sydney Morning Herald*, 'but are we seeing a groundswell for a reinvention of the awards systems?' She pointed to 'sharp criticism' of the awards to Abbott, Bishop, and other former politicians from readers, quoting a range of comments, including several critical of the conferral of awards on those perceived to have simply done their jobs. The paper's chief political correspondent, David Crowe, observed that 'the feedback made him "wonder why we don't invert the entire system"' and why 'volunteers doing huge work in their local communities' received only an OAM (Medal of the Order of Australia), while 'the well-connected and wealthy' received higher awards.[16] Yet as I have demonstrated, such criticisms are not new: heated debate over both individual recipients and broader patterns in the conferral of awards have taken place before.

Indeed, as this history has shown, several themes endure in understandings and debates about the honours system in Australia. These themes have persisted even while the system itself has changed in profound ways, from its expansion to include more groups of people and occupations to the inclusion of women, and from the creation of new national awards to the ending of the use of British awards. If it has generally existed quietly out of public attention (apart from the brief flurry of interest when each new list is announced), the Australian honours system, as a way for the nation, through its leaders, to recognise and acknowledge great service and

---

15   Margaret Fitzherbert, 'COVID-19 Community Spirit Reveals Honours System's Flaws', *Sydney Morning Herald*, 4 August 2020 [online].

16   Orietta Guerrera, '"Irrelevant and Out of Touch": Readers Respond to Queen's Birthday Honours List', *Sydney Morning Herald*, 12 June 2020 [online]; David Crowe, '"History will be Kind": Abbott Says Cuts Paved Way for COVID-19 Response', *Sydney Morning Herald*, 7 June 2020 [online]. See also the criticisms expressed in Michael Koziol, '"It is a Secret Society": Does Our Honours System Need a Shake Up?' *Sydney Morning Herald*, 28 June 2020 [online].

achievement, has also on occasion been a focus of intense debate. It has been the site of apathy and lack of knowledge, with many people unaware of the differences between the various grades, but also of great passion and contestation, as when Abbott brought back knighthoods and conferred one on Prince Philip. To many it may seem relatively unimportant when placed alongside weighty matters of economic or social policy that affect our lives in more obviously concrete ways, but as a symbolic means to recognise service and achievement it is a significant national institution, and an opportunity to celebrate and encourage that which we consider worthy. Its history shows that this imperative has always been present within it, negotiated alongside other imperatives and practicalities, such as the usefulness of the system for patronage purposes, or its entanglement with political and constitutional realities.

Over the past two centuries, Australia's honours system has changed along with wider social and cultural realities, and along with the country's constitutional and political arrangements and its own conception of itself and its place in the world. In his history of the British honours system, Tobias Harper suggested there was a 'fundamental tension at the heart of' that system, 'between hierarchy and merit and between new elites and old regimes'.[17] We might add as well, between service, as in the dedicated work of volunteers and perhaps even in one's job, and accomplishment, as in the world-beating achievements of sports stars. Such a tension—in the Australian system as in the British—is captured in awards to eminent medical researchers and similar figures, whose lives and work demonstrate both service to humanity and immense professional accomplishment based on their talents and abilities. Thus another fundamental question lies at the heart of the system: what is merit? Is it possible to agree on what is meritorious? Or, to return to the tension between hierarchy and merit, what is *most* meritorious, and therefore deserving of the highest awards?

The history of honours—both imperial and national—in Australia epitomises other tensions as well, particularly two longstanding tensions in Australian history. First, it has encapsulated the ongoing tug-of-war that has existed between the opposing values of egalitarianism and hierarchy, between abandoning the class structures of the Old World to create a new and more equal society, or reproducing those structures in

---

17   Tobias Harper, *From Servants of the Empire to Everyday Heroes: The British Honours System in the Twentieth Century* (Oxford: Oxford University Press, 2020), 26. doi.org/10.1093/oso/978019884 1180.001.0001.

this new setting. Honours have also acted as a flashpoint for a second, and related, tug-of-war in Australian history, between maintaining and valuing imperial links and the country's British character, and breaking away from that past as a fully independent nation with its own distinctive identity. Over the years, as the ongoing debates about honours demonstrate, the nation's two major political groupings developed sharply different visions of Australia's future in these two respects. In this way, then, the history of honours in Australia may be seen as a series of battles in an ongoing war for the nation's character.

There were few signs of any such future struggles in the early history of the British honours system in Australia. The system was small and highly exclusive during the first years of the Australasian colonies: it was centred on the aristocracy, linked to military service, and almost entirely male. As the number of awards bestowed on Australians increased dramatically, however, debate ignited over the appropriateness and use of titles of honour in democratic New World societies, where egalitarianism was already becoming a cherished ideal. From the beginning, honours held conflicting meanings. For some a valuable means of recognising individual merit and binding the empire together, they were for others inextricably—and unacceptably—linked to monarchy, aristocracy, and a hierarchical system of class privilege. With the coming of Federation in 1901, honours became a focus for struggles over prestige at another level as well, as the six powerful States sought to defend their prerogatives against the new federal government, while federal leaders attempted to assert the freshly created nation's prestige within the wider British empire, to which they still felt pride in belonging.

The outbreak of war in 1914 brought a permanent transformation to the system when the King announced the creation of the Order of the British Empire. Almost at the same moment, however, the entire institution was threatened with extinction in Australia by the revelations emerging about the selling of honours for political purposes by the Lloyd George Government in Britain. While unsuccessful, attempts to end the conferral of imperial honours or titles played into an emerging political divide, as the Australian Labor Party solidified its opposition to them, thus adding a new dimension to the clash between federal and State authorities over the right to nominate for honours and setting off a long contest between Labor and non-Labor forces. At the same time, the interwar decades were a high point of women's participation in the system, with women receiving awards in proportions that would not be reached again until the end of the century.

During the long years of Liberal Party Government after World War II, the honours system entered a period of relative stability, although Liberal use of awards did not go entirely unchallenged. By the late 1960s, however, a new air of scepticism about the value of monarchy, authority, and the British connection had arisen, shifting the scale once more towards those who valued egalitarianism above hierarchy, and national identity above imperial. The newly assertive mood of this era, in which writers, artists, politicians, and thinkers sought a bolder, more vibrant, and more self-consciously Australian identity, created more favourable ground for the creation of a uniquely Australian honour. It was that transformative whirlwind of a prime minister, Gough Whitlam, who brought the idea to fruition in the form of the Order of Australia, creating another flashpoint in the ongoing contest over honours through its attempts to enshrine egalitarianism over hierarchy by rejecting titular honours, and to assert the country's increasing distance from its British beginnings. In the context of increasingly virulent divisions over States' rights, the order also became a theatre in that ongoing war, to which the election of Whitlam had given a new intensity, and which had throughout the century shaped the history of the honours system in ways distinct to the trajectories taken in other former British dominions and colonies.

As the country's next prime minister, Liberal leader Malcolm Fraser attempted to satisfy a deeply divided population by reverting to more traditional forms in the nation's ceremonial life, while also retaining some aspects of the Whitlam-era symbolic landscape. Such efforts both to maintain the nation's British heritage and develop its independent identity could seem confused, but they were a reflection of just how divided the country was over issues of identity, heritage, and future pathways. Two different visions of the nation coexisted, one emphasising the country's British heritage and broadly accepting of hierarchical social structures, and the other valuing egalitarianism and national autonomy and distinctiveness. By the 1990s, however, bipartisan support for the cessation of British honours was emerging and they were finally abolished in 1992. Yet as both the final chapter and this epilogue have demonstrated, this decisive move did not mean the end of controversy for the honours system, or of the divisions over visions of the country's character and future. Nevertheless, by the time of Prime Minister Tony Abbott's revival of knighthoods and damehoods within the Order of Australia in 2014, it was evident that there had been a slow but steady—perhaps generational—change in ideas about the nation's identity and place in the world. The powerful reaction against the return of titles, and especially against Abbott's choice to confer one of the titles on Prince Philip the following year—not to mention the speed with which the titles were once more removed from the order by another Liberal prime minister, Malcolm Turnbull—revealed the extent to which one vision of the nation had triumphed. The triumph of this vision of Australia is not complete, but the swift ending of Abbott's initiative showed clearly its ascendency in the second decade of the twenty-first century.

The story of honours in Australia can be understood at three related levels. It is, firstly, an Australian story, shaped in distinctive ways by the nature of the country's federal system, which gives strong powers and responsibilities to its constituent States, and by the differences in the visions for the country's future of its major political parties. It is also a colonial or New World story, sharing much with the history of honours in other former parts of the British empire, and especially the former dominions. In this way, the history of honours in Australia is part of a larger phenomenon, that of decolonisation. As A. G. Hopkins suggested in 2008, there is a parallel to be found between the 'moment of decolonization' in former British colonies, where new national flags, anthems, and other symbols were created as part of the break with the empire, and the similar changes taking place in the dominions at around the same time. Hopkins considered these changes more than 'mere window dressing': in his view the formation of new civic emblems 'represented a fundamental and remarkably neglected transformation of the whole of the empire-Commonwealth', and were

> in some respects ... more profound than the achievement of formal independence was for the colonies because they involved the destruction of the core concept of Britishness, which had given unity and vitality to Greater Britain overseas, and the creation of new national identities.[18]

---

18 A. G. Hopkins, 'Rethinking Decolonization', *Past and Present* 200, no. 1 (2008): 211, 215. doi.org/10.1093/pastj/gtn015. A more precise term for this process may be 'de-dominionisation', for while Australia, Canada, and New Zealand are post-imperial nations, they are not postcolonial. Phillip Buckner, 'Introduction: Canada and the British Empire', in *Canada and the British Empire*, ed. Phillip Buckner (Oxford: Oxford University Press, 2008), 15. The term 'de-dominionisation' was coined by Jim Davidson in 1979. See Jim Davidson, 'De-Dominionisation Revisited', *Australian Journal of Politics and History* 51, no. 1 (2005): 108–13. doi.org/10.1111/j.1467-8497.2005.00364.x.

Australia's experience of honours shares resonances with New Zealand and Canada in particular, both in terms of the country's gradual disentangling from Britain and the growth of an independent national identity, and of the cherishing of values of egalitarianism and supposed classlessness as against the hierarchy of the Old World. For Harper, the abandonment of British honours across the former empire is, in a sense, a story of that system's failure:

> [a failure] to create a sense of imperial or national unity and … win the loyalty of its recipients and their communities to a higher ideal of service and deference to the nation and empire.[19]

Yet it might also be seen, from another perspective, as a successful transition, in which a British institution has been made national, as discussed below. Finally, the story of honours in Australia may be seen as part of a more global story, or at least a Western story, in which society has moved away from hierarchy towards an embrace of the values of equality, egalitarianism, and inclusivity.

Throughout this book, I have also concentrated on the theme of inclusion and diversity. In the aftermath of Abbott's short-lived restoration of knighthoods and damehoods, the most persistent controversy regarding the honours system has undoubtedly been the stubbornly unequal ratio of male and female awards. The Honour a Woman campaign, and the publicity around the gender inequity of the biennial announcements, appears to have had some impact, with women outnumbering men at the top of the list—the level of the AC—for the first time in 2018, and a slowly increasing proportion of awards overall going to women.[20] There is no doubt, however, that gender inequity has been one of the enduring themes of the history of honours, a feature of criticisms of the system since at least the 1890s. A century on, the proportions of awards going to women, and the split between the various levels, remains an issue. One reason for this, as many feminist critics have suggested, is likely inherent in the criteria for the awards, which tend to privilege internationally prominent work and achievement over local and community efforts, which have

---

19   Harper, *Servants of the Empire*, 248.

20   Heather Ford, Tamson Pietsch, and Kelly Tall have also observed the impact of the Honour a Woman campaign, noting that it 'has played an important role in increasing the number of women nominated and awarded', although also that 'there is still a way to go'. Heather Ford, Tamson Pietsch, and Kelly Tall, 'Producing Distinction: Wikipedia and the Order of Australia', 2021, University of Technology Sydney, accessed 12 June 2021, hfordsa.github.io/who-do-we-think-we-are.html.

traditionally been where many women have made their contributions to society. While this does not necessarily mean that women will continue to receive lower-level awards in greater numbers than higher-level ones—it should go without saying that women are equally capable of achieving on the international stage as are men—it has assuredly been a factor in these patterns of gender inequity in the past.

Apart from the issue of gender, one of the enduring criticisms of the honours system has been that such work—voluntary, unpaid, for one's community—has not received the same level of recognition as has dedicated service and achievement in other fields of activity that themselves are well remunerated and bring a level of prominence and prestige, be that in politics, the public service, business, or the professions. This has certainly been a persistent theme, and possibly also a growing critique, as society has changed and moved away from older modes of deference to positions of authority such as statesmen, judges, and professionals; certainly it was a key piece of feedback in the submissions to the review in 1995. According to Harper's assessment of the British system, what has happened has been that:

> [s]hifts in the moral economy of service culminated in a move towards the celebration of working- and middle-class voluntary service at the low levels of the system and professional eminence and visible wealth at the top.[21]

As an issue for the honours system, this critique has also been linked to gender inequity, for women have in the past had fewer opportunities, and have held correspondingly fewer of such positions as tended to attract high honours. Again, over time, the situation may change: as women enter more and more such roles, these patterns in the awarding of honours may eventually no longer cause gender inequity. It is, however, part of a larger question about inclusivity and diversity, not only in terms of demographic factors—for although it is not possible to confirm statistically, it seems almost certain that Indigenous Australians and non-Anglo-Celtic migrants have been under-represented in the conferral of awards—but also in terms of all the various ways that people live and work and contribute to their society. The *Australian Dictionary of Biography*, another institution that is dedicated to recognising the significant life, and which has also been plagued by problems of under-representation of women and non-Anglo-

---

21   Harper, *Servants of the Empire*, 251.

Celtic Australians, has always prided itself on attempting to include the representative life as well as the significant.[22] While difficult to arrange operationally, perhaps this points to a model for the honours system, which might allow those who are exemplary in other fields of occupation and activity than those traditionally honoured to receive recognition for their endeavours.

These issues matter not only because some worthy individuals may miss out, but because of the importance of recognition itself. Matters of recognition are not issues of fringe importance, but are central to the feminist project of women's equality, and to all movements for equal rights and inclusion. Honours—like statues, placenames, and other symbols of recognition—acknowledge achievements and contributions by making them visible, and thereby stake a claim for their significance in our history. Full participation in a society is not merely a matter of rights and freedoms, but of being able to see oneself as a welcomed part of that society. Being able to recognise oneself in the lists of recipients of honours is thus important. It can inspire us to achieve and to serve others, and it can provide role models, allowing us to imagine ourselves contributing to our societies in a range of ways. Just as the drive to interpret the personal as political in the 1970s was partly about recognition—having one's realities, challenges, and stories acknowledged—the importance of diversity and inclusion in honours is about being seen, having the nation recognise and value the range of ways its members contribute to our wellbeing as a community.[23]

Yet the difficulty of levels of award remains, and has been a persistent one for honours systems in the former British settler colonies of Australia, New Zealand, and Canada, all of which pride themselves on their egalitarian and classless ethos. These views have led some to feel uncomfortable about the very idea of dividing recipients of honours into grades: each is worthy, and how difficult to say that some are more worthy than others. In 1998, the *Sydney Morning Herald* suggested there was 'something inherently unAustralian in an honours list that differentiates the worth of various honours winners with titles of Companion, Officers, Members and Awardees of the Medal', a 'differentiation' that was 'based, essentially,

---

22   See 'Frequently Asked Questions', *Australian Dictionary of Biography*, accessed 15 October 2020, adb.anu.edu.au/faqs/.
23   On the personal as political, see Michelle Arrow, *The Seventies: The Personal, the Political, and the Making of Modern Australia* (Sydney: NewSouth, 2019).

on the class system gradations in Britain which remain the basis for its honours system', whereas the Australian system 'was set up, supposedly, to be classless'.[24] At the same time, there has always been a tension in that there remains a desire to raise up those whose services and achievements are seen to be *especially* deserving of recognition, and a concern that if an honours system had only one level of award, the standard would be so high that few awards would be given. These are almost intractable problems. As Harper has noted in the British context, even as class was 'formally' excluded from honours determinations, hierarchy remained. 'Merit had a rank', and judgements—often reflecting old patterns in the conferral of awards—were still made about which services and achievements were deserving of the highest honours.[25]

For the most part, Australians seem to have come to a general consensus that while titles are unacceptable, a range of grades is broadly acceptable. One reason for this stance may be that the particular titles used, coming out of the particular history that they do, carry a whiff of aristocracy that is deeply uncomfortable for many people who are not inherently discomforted by titles per se—if they are perceived to be earned (the lack of outcry over titles such as Doctor, Reverend, or Colonel being suggestive). The uproar around Abbott's restoration of knighthoods and damehoods indicates how wide this basic consensus appears to be: that an Australian system of honours is a good thing, that it is widely esteemed and valued, and that it should be egalitarian to the extent that no recipients are elevated above others by the conferral of titles, at least those that evoke Old World class associations. At the same time, as noted above, there is also a clear public belief that the most worthy recipients are those who generally receive the lowest honours: dedicated local volunteers who serve their communities without expecting reward.

Part of the furore around Abbott's revival of titles, of course, was about Australian identity in another way: that of the country as independent as well as egalitarian. While it must be evident to any cursory examination that the Order of Australia derives from the British model of honours, the fact that many saw the re-establishment of titles as the revival of imperial awards was deeply revealing. The discomfort, on another level, was not so much about the titles themselves as about their meanings in a context of an Australia that now felt—and was—fully independent from Britain.

---

24 'Australia Day Honours List?', *Sydney Morning Herald*, 26 January 1998, 16.
25 Harper, *Servants of the Empire*, 245.

The idea that something imperial had been revived then, was a large part of the uproar. It is also the source of one ongoing complaint about the honours system, which is that one of the two annual lists of awards is announced on Queen's Birthday. In 2003, for instance, an editorial in the *Sydney Morning Herald* questioned 'whether the Queen's birthday holiday is still an appropriate awards date for a mature multicultural Australia', and the following year the *Australian* argued that it was 'time to acknowledge that we are honouring the achievements of Australians for Australians and change the name of the mid-year awards'.[26] A similar argument appeared in a piece by John Warhurst in the *Canberra Times* in 2005. Warhurst supported the views of Senator Guy Barnett, who was seeking 'to "Australianise" our institutions and honours system', and argued that as an occasion for distributing the awards, 'the Queen's Birthday is now clearly inappropriate as it fails the basic test of being an occasion that enhances the distinctive Australian character of the awards'.[27] Again in 2006, the *Sydney Morning Herald* suggested that announcing awards on the Queen's Birthday holiday 'might have made sense when Australia's awards were imperial honours', and argued that all the honours ought now to be presented on Australia Day.[28]

Perhaps these kinds of issues have played a part in the elevation of the Australian of the Year award, announced on 26 January alongside the first of the two annual honours lists, to a status alongside or perhaps above the Order of Australia in the public mind. Having started uncertainly, and been caught up in many of the same issues and tensions as the honours system itself in the 1970s and 1980s, the Australian of the Year award has become a national event that attracts interest and support.[29] Indeed, a great part of the outrage over Abbott's award of the AK (Knight of the Order of Australia) to Prince Philip was that it was seen to overshadow the award of Australian of the Year to the domestic violence campaigner Rosie Batty. As a smaller-scale award, in the sense that it is given to a small number of individuals, and after State and territory finals, the

---

26   'Happy Birthday King George', *Sydney Morning Herald*, 10 June 2003, 10; 'No Name for Aussie Awards', *Australian*, 14 June 2004, 8.

27   John Warhurst, 'It's Time for the Next Evolutionary Step in Our Honours System', *Canberra Times*, 1 July 2005, 17.

28   'A Matter of Honour', *Sydney Morning Herald*, 12 June 2006, 12 [online].

29   For a comparison of the Order of Australia and the Australian of the Year award in the 1970s and 1980s, see Karen Fox and Samuel Furphy, 'The Politics of National Recognition: Honouring Australians in a Post-Imperial World', *Australian Journal of Politics and History* 63, no. 1 (2017): 93–111. doi.org/10.1111/ajph.12317.

Australian of the Year award perhaps attracts greater interest than does the long list of appointments to the Order of Australia. With its system that gives one person the year of their incumbency to campaign on an issue of their choice, it bestows a greater visibility on that individual than other recipients of honours have (including those who receive the associated senior, young, and local hero Australian of the Year awards). It has at times had a higher proportion of Indigenous recipients and women, and it has become a significant part of Australia's honorific landscape. It is not, however, a replacement for Australia's honours system, which allows for the recognising of larger numbers of people in a variety of fields across the country. The two systems seem to have reached an equilibrium and to complement each other.

Australia's honours system has been made national, undoubtedly, but it also carries and will continue to carry the country's British heritage. As Harper has pointed out in the case of the Order of Canada, from which Australia drew inspiration for its own order, the new national system 'did not revolutionize what it replaced': '[a] three-tier honour with the Queen at its head had been a staple of the British system'.[30] Unless the entire structure of the award system is changed, this will remain the case, even if Australia becomes a republic and replaces the Queen as the fount of honour with a president. Yet this need not be considered a matter for lament. Like the parliamentary system itself, the honours system is a British institution that has been made Australia's own. None of the ongoing debates and controversies around the system have really threatened it—perhaps the most serious was an internal threat, in that it was corruption through the selling of awards in Britain that brought the system closest to disestablishment in Australia. While it has occasionally been suggested that the time had come to do away with the whole thing, the majority of criticisms have been aimed more at ensuring that the system best reflects the things that Australians truly want to celebrate and recognise—the kinds of achievements and service they believe are most admirable, and which most reflect what Australians value.

At the same time, some of the most passionate arguments and controversies about honours have not really been about honours as means for recognising merit at all, or at least, not wholly or solely about honours. In settler societies such as Australia and New Zealand, from

---

30   Harper, *Servants of the Empire*, 154.

the nineteenth century to the twenty-first, many debates about titles and honours have been proxies for debates about much deeper issues of identity and constitutional arrangements. They have been about the country's British heritage and relationship with Britain, and the extent that should be maintained or disregarded; about the extent to which Australia should mirror or repudiate British models of society in terms of class; or about the ongoing connection to the monarchy and whether that should be retained or abandoned. Likewise, the arguments and criticisms about gender inequity in the system, or about other issues of diversity and inclusion, should not be seen as closed debates about the honours system. They too are lenses on to wider social and political issues, such as the extent to which Australian society, politics, and culture generally embrace and make room for diversity, or fail to do so, and the extent to which women and minorities feel there is room for them to flourish and be recognised as an integral and valuable part of the community. It is perhaps this proxy nature that makes arguments about honours so passionate, in the nineteenth as well as the twenty-first centuries. We are not really arguing merely over whether Bob or Mary deserves recognition, or at what level, but over our values: what matters to us, and whether we feel that we are an integral and valuable part of the community.

To end on an uplifting note, this is why the honours system is important. It is, at heart, the nation's opportunity to say that some things are worth celebrating—our love and concern for our neighbours, expressed in many and varied ways, be it through voluntary work or life-saving medical research, through dedication to our work and the community in the best traditions of public service, or through the creation of beautiful artworks to inspire and uplift. In an era of great negativity and difficulty, of economic tribulation and 'haters' on social media, of disposable celebrities whose physical forms are admired above their hearts, of self-aggrandising politics and a me-above-others pursuit of wealth and fame, this is surely a valuable thing. We should treasure it, and guard it, and make it our own, nominating and recognising those who inspire us and give us hope, wherever they are found.

Works cited

Manuscripts and archival collections

National Archives of Australia series

A2
A462
A463
A1209
A1606
A2922
A2923
A2924
A2925
A3211
A4204
A5954
A6661
A11804
A11812
A12378
AA1984/609
M4799

National Library of Australia

Newspaper cuttings on the Australian honours system
MS2022, Papers of Kate Baker, 1893–1946

Library and Archives Canada

R5769, Carl Lochnan papers

Official publications

Canada, House of Commons, *Debates*.

Commonwealth of Australia, House of Representatives, *Parliamentary Debates*.

Commonwealth of Australia, Senate, *Parliamentary Debates*.

Department of the Prime Minister and Cabinet. 'Reinstatement of Knights and Dames in the Order of Australia.' Factsheet. March 2014.

House of Representatives Standing Committee on Legal and Constitutional Affairs. *Half Way to Equal: Report of the Inquiry into Equal Opportunity and Equal Status for Women in Australia*. Canberra: Australian Government Publishing Service, 1992.

Legal and Constitutional Affairs References Committee, Australian Senate. *Nationhood, National Identity and Democracy* (Canberra: Senate Printing Unit, 2021).

New South Wales, Legislative Assembly, *Parliamentary Debates*.

Review of Australian Honours and Awards. *A Matter of Honour: The Report of the Review of Australian Honours and Awards*. Canberra: Australian Government Publishing Service, 1995.

South Australia, Legislative Assembly, *Parliamentary Debates*.

South Australia, Legislative Council, *Parliamentary Debates*.

Supplement to the London Gazette.

Newspapers and magazines

Advertiser (Adelaide)
Age (Melbourne)
Argus (Melbourne)
Australasian (Melbourne)
Australian
Australian Financial Review
Australian Women's Weekly
Australian Worker (Sydney)
Barrier Miner (Broken Hill)

Brisbane Courier

Bunbury Herald

Cairns Post

Canberra Times

Catholic Freeman's Journal (Sydney)

Clarence and Richmond Examiner (Grafton)

Clarence and Richmond Examiner and New England Advertiser (Grafton)

Courier-Mail (Brisbane)

Daily Herald (Adelaide)

Daily Mail (Brisbane)

Daily News (Perth)

Daily Telegraph (Launceston)

Daily Telegraph (Napier, New Zealand)

Daily Telegraph (Sydney)

Darling Downs Gazette (Toowoomba)

Dominion Post (Wellington, New Zealand)

Evening News (Sydney)

Examiner (Launceston)

Freeman's Journal (Sydney)

Goulburn Evening Penny Post

Guardian (Australia)

Herald (Melbourne)

Inquirer and Commercial News (Perth)

Kalgoorlie Miner

Mail (Adelaide)

Mail (Brisbane)

Manawatu Herald (Foxton, New Zealand)

Maryborough Chronicle, Wide Bay and Burnett Advertiser

Mercury (Hobart)

Morning Bulletin (Rockhampton)

National Times

New Zealand Herald (Auckland)

News (Adelaide)

North Queensland Register (Townsville)

Northern Miner (Charters Towers)

Northern Star (Lismore)

Northern Territory News (Darwin)

Otago Daily Times (Dunedin, New Zealand)

Otago Witness (Dunedin, New Zealand)

Press (Christchurch, New Zealand)

Register (Adelaide)

Sun (Sydney)

Sunday Age (Melbourne)

Sunday Herald (Sydney)

Sunday Telegraph (Sydney)

Sunday Times (Perth)

Sun-Herald (Sydney)

Sydney Morning Herald

Telegraph (Brisbane)

Truth (Melbourne)

Tuapeka Times (Lawrence, New Zealand)

Waikato Times (Hamilton, New Zealand)

Weekly Times (Melbourne)

Weekly Times (Victoria)

West Australian (Perth)

Western Mail (Perth)

Worker (Brisbane)

Books

Advancing Women: Women and the Order of Australia. Melbourne: Our Community and Women's Leadership Institute Australia, 2011.

Arrow, Michelle. *The Seventies: The Personal, the Political, and the Making of Modern Australia*. Sydney: NewSouth, 2019.

Bennett, J. M. *George Higinbotham: Third Chief Justice of Victoria 1886–1892*. Sydney: Federation, 2006.

Blakeley, Brian L. *The Colonial Office 1868–1892*. Durham: Duke University Press, 1972.

Bolton, Geoffrey. *1942–1995: The Middle Way*. Vol. 5 of *The Oxford History of Australia*, 2nd ed. Melbourne: Oxford University Press, 1996.

Bongiorno, Frank. *The Eighties: The Decade that Transformed Australia*. Melbourne: Black Inc., 2015.

Boulton, D'Arcy Jonathan Dacre. *The Knights of the Crown: The Monarchical Orders of Knighthood in Later Medieval Europe 1325–1520*. Woodbridge: Boydell, 1987.

Brunton, Paul, ed. *The Diaries of Miles Franklin*. Sydney: Allen and Unwin in association with the State Library of New South Wales, 2004.

Cannadine, David. *The Decline and Fall of the British Aristocracy*. New York: Vintage, 1999.

——. *Ornamentalism: How the British Saw Their Empire*. Oxford: Oxford University Press, 2001.

Clark, Samuel. *Distributing Status: The Evolution of State Honours in Western Europe*. Montreal and Kingston: McGill-Queen's University Press, 2016.

Cockburn, Stewart, and David Ellyard. *Oliphant: The Life and Times of Sir Mark Oliphant*. Adelaide: Stewart Cockburn and David Ellyard in association with Axiom Books, 1981.

Collins, Hugh E. L. *The Order of the Garter 1348–1461: Chivalry and Politics in Late Medieval England*. Oxford: Oxford University Press, 2000.

Cook, Andrew. *Cash for Honours: The Story of Maundy Gregory*. Stroud: History Press, 2008.

Cullen, Tom. *Maundy Gregory: Purveyor of Honours*. London: Bodley Head, 1974.

Cunneen, Christopher. *King's Men: Australia's Governors-General from Hopetoun to Isaacs*. Sydney: George Allen and Unwin, 1983.

——. *William John McKell: Boilermaker, Premier, Governor-General*. Sydney: UNSW Press, 2000.

Curran, James, and Stuart Ward. *The Unknown Nation: Australia After Empire*. Melbourne: Melbourne University Press, 2010.

Curthoys, Ann, and Jessie Mitchell. *Taking Liberty: Indigenous Rights and Settler Self-Government in Colonial Australia, 1830–1890*. Cambridge: Cambridge University Press, 2018. doi.org/10.1017/9781316027035.

de la Bere, Ivan. *The Queen's Orders of Chivalry*. London: Spring Books, 1964.

De-la-Noy, Michael. *The Honours System*. London: Allison and Busby, 1985.

de Serville, Paul. *Pounds and Pedigrees: The Upper Class in Victoria 1850–1880.* Melbourne: Oxford University Press, 1991.

Errington, Wayne, and Peter Van Onselen. *Battleground: Why the Liberal Party Shirtfronted Tony Abbott.* Melbourne: Melbourne University Press, 2015.

Galloway, Peter. *Companions of Honour.* Hinckley: Chancery Publications, 2002.

——. *Exalted, Eminent and Imperial: Honours of the British Raj.* London: Spink, 2014.

——. *The Most Illustrious Order: The Order of St Patrick and its Knights.* London: Unicorn, 1999.

——. *The Order of St Michael and St George.* [London]: Third Millennium for the Central Chancery of the Orders of Knighthood, 2000.

——. *The Order of the Bath.* Chichester: Phillimore, 2006.

——. *The Order of the British Empire.* [London]: Central Chancery of the Orders of Knighthood, 1996.

——. *The Order of the Thistle.* London: Spink, 2009.

Gisborne, William. *New Zealand Rulers and Statesmen: 1840 to 1885.* London: Sampson Low, Marston, Searle, & Rivington, 1886.

Glass, Margaret. *Tommy Bent: Bent by Name, Bent by Nature.* Melbourne: Melbourne University Press, 1993.

Harper, Tobias. *From Servants of the Empire to Everyday Heroes: The British Honours System in the Twentieth Century.* Oxford: Oxford University Press, 2020. doi.org/10.1093/oso/9780198841180.001.0001.

Hickie, David. *The Prince and the Premier.* Sydney and London: Angus and Robertson, 1985.

Hirst, John. *The Sentimental Nation: The Making of the Australian Commonwealth.* Melbourne: Oxford University Press, 2000.

——. *The Strange Birth of Colonial Democracy: New South Wales 1848–1884.* Sydney: Allen and Unwin, 1988.

Howard, John. *Lazarus Rising: A Personal and Political Autobiography*, revised ed. Sydney: HarperCollins, 2011.

Kevin, Catherine. *Dispossession and the Making of Jedda: Hollywood in Ngunnawal Country.* London: Anthem, 2020.

La Nauze, J. A. *Alfred Deakin: A Biography.* 2 vols. Melbourne: Melbourne University Press, 1965.

Macmillan, Harold. *The Past Masters: Politics and Politicians 1906–1939.* London: Macmillan, 1975.

Martin, A. W. *Robert Menzies: A Life,* vol. 2, *1944–1978.* Melbourne: Melbourne University Press, 1999.

Martin, Ged. *Bunyip Aristocracy: The New South Wales Constitution Debate of 1853 and Hereditary Institutions in the British Colonies.* Sydney: Croom Helm, 1986.

Martin, Stanley. *The Order of Merit: One Hundred Years of Matchless Honour.* London and New York: I. B. Tauris, 2007.

Matikkala, Antti. *The Orders of Knighthood and the Formation of the British Honours System, 1660–1760.* Woodbridge: Boydell, 2008.

Maton, Michael. *Australian Recipients of Imperial Honours and Awards: 1901–1989.* Sydney: M. Maton, 2002.

McCreery, Christopher. *The Order of Canada: Its Origins, History, and Development.* Toronto: University of Toronto Press, 2005. doi.org/10.3138/9781442627963.

McKenna, Mark. *The Captive Republic: A History of Republicanism in Australia 1788–1996.* Cambridge: Cambridge University Press, 1996.

Moore, Geraldine. *George Higinbotham and Eureka: The Struggle for Democracy in Colonial Victoria.* Melbourne: Australian Scholarly, 2018.

Murphy, John. *Imagining the Fifties: Private Sentiment and Political Culture in Menzies' Australia.* Sydney: UNSW Press, 2000.

Pamm, Anthony N. *Honours and Rewards in the British Empire and Commonwealth.* 2 vols. Aldershot: Scolar, 1995.

Patrick, Aaron. *Credlin & Co.: How the Abbott Government Destroyed Itself.* Melbourne: Black Inc., 2016.

Read, Jolly, and Peter Coppin. *Kangkushot: The Life of Nyamal Lawman Peter Coppin.* Canberra: Aboriginal Studies Press, 1999.

Rickard, John. *Australia: A Cultural History,* 3rd ed. Melbourne: Monash University Publishing, 2017.

Ridley, Jane. *Bertie: A Life of Edward VII.* London: Chatto and Windus, 2012.

Risk, James C. *The History of the Order of the Bath and its Insignia*. London: Spink and Son, 1972.

Roe, Jill. *Stella Miles Franklin: A Biography*. Sydney: Fourth Estate, 2008.

Rose, Kenneth. *King George V*. London: Weidenfeld and Nicolson, 1983.

Rosen, Andrew. *Rise Up, Women! The Militant Campaign of the Women's Social and Political Union 1903–1914*. London and Boston: Routledge and Kegan Paul, 1974.

Rowse, Tim. *Nugget Coombs: A Reforming Life*. Cambridge: University of Cambridge Press, 2002.

Russell, Penny. *A Wish of Distinction: Colonial Gentility and Femininity*. Melbourne: Melbourne University Press, 1994.

Savva, Niki. *The Road to Ruin: How Tony Abbott and Peta Credlin Destroyed Their Own Government*. Melbourne: Scribe, 2016.

Sowden, Will. J. *An Australian Native's Standpoint: Addresses*. London: Macmillan, 1912.

Tavan, Gwenda. *The Long Slow Death of White Australia*. Melbourne: Scribe, 2005.

Taylor, Alistair, ed. *The Australian Roll of Honour: National Honours and Awards 1975–1996*. Sydney: Roll of Honour, 1997.

Tennant, Kylie. *The Missing Heir: The Autobiography of Kylie Tennant*. Melbourne: Macmillan, 1986.

Tink, Andrew. *William Charles Wentworth: Australia's Greatest Native Son*. Sydney: Allen and Unwin, 2009.

Trigg, Stephanie. *Shame and Honor: A Vulgar History of the Order of the Garter*. Philadelphia: University of Pennsylvania Press, 2012. doi.org/10.9783/9780812206630.

Troy, Jakelin. *King Plates: A History of Aboriginal Gorgets*. Canberra: Aboriginal Studies Press, 1993.

Turner, Graeme. *Making It National: Nationalism and Australian Popular Culture*. Sydney: Allen and Unwin, 1994.

Twomey, Anne. *The Australia Acts 1986: Australia's Statutes of Independence*. Sydney: Federation, 2010.

Walker, John. *The Queen Has Been Pleased: The British Honours System at Work*. London: Martin Secker and Warburg, 1986.

Wanna, John, and Tracey Arklay. *The Ayes Have It: The History of the Queensland Parliament, 1957–1989*. Canberra: ANU E Press, 2010. doi.org/10.22459/AH.07.2010.

Wear, Rae. *Johannes Bjelke-Petersen: The Lord's Premier*. Brisbane: University of Queensland Press, 2002.

Whitlam, Gough. *The Whitlam Government 1972–1975*. Melbourne: Viking, 1985.

Whitton, Evan. *The Hillbilly Dictator: Australia's Police State*, revised ed. Sydney: ABC Books, 1993.

Journal articles and book chapters

Aldrich, Robert, and Cindy McCreery. 'European Royals and Their Colonial Realms: Honors and Decorations.' In *Realms of Royalty: New Directions in Researching Contemporary European Monarchies*, edited by Christina Jordan and Imke Polland, 63–88. Bielefeld: transcript Verlag, 2020. doi.org/10.14361/9783839445839-005.

Bailey, Christian. 'Honor Among Peers: A Comparative History of Honor Practices in Postwar Britain and West Germany.' *Journal of Modern History* 87, no. 4 (2015): 809–51. doi.org/10.1086/683600.

Barnes, John. 'Baker, Catherine (Kate) (1861–1953).' *Australian Dictionary of Biography*, accessed 12 September 2017, adb.anu.edu.au/biography/baker-catherine-kate-5104/text8527.

Bevis, Johannah. 'No More Labour for the Knight: An Overview of Sir Jack Egerton's Leadership.' *Queensland Journal of Labour History*, no. 21 (2015): 4–15.

Bongiorno, Frank. 'Inaugural Professorial Lecture—Is Australian History Still Possible? Australia and the Global Eighties.' *ANU Historical Journal II*, no. 1 (2019): 193–208. doi.org/10.22459/ANUHJII.2019.15.

Bridge, Carl. 'Sowden, Sir William John (1858–1943).' *Australian Dictionary of Biography*, accessed 6 September 2017, adb.anu.edu.au/biography/sowden-sir-william-john-8593/text15005.

Broinowski, Alison. 'Sparnon, Norman James (1913–1995).' *Australian Dictionary of Biography*, accessed 3 September 2020, adb.anu.edu.au/biography/sparnon-norman-james-21619/text31832.

Bucknall, John. 'Oberdoo, Jacob (Minyjun) (1920–1989).' *Australian Dictionary of Biography*, accessed 13 July 2017, adb.anu.edu.au/biography/oberdoo-jacob-minyjun-15386/text26593.

Buckner, Phillip. 'Introduction: Canada and the British Empire.' In *Canada and the British Empire*, edited by Phillip Buckner, 1–21. Oxford: Oxford University Press, 2008.

Cole, Keith. 'Lamilami, Lazarus (1913–1977).' *Australian Dictionary of Biography*, accessed 14 July 2017, adb.anu.edu.au/biography/lamilami-lazarus-10778/text19113.

Connolly, C. N. 'Class, Birthplace, Loyalty: Australian Attitudes to the Boer War.' *Historical Studies* 18, no. 71 (1978): 210–32. doi.org/10.1080/10314617 808595588.

———. 'The Origins of the Nominated Upper House in New South Wales.' *Historical Studies* 20, no. 78 (1982): 53–72. doi.org/10.1080/10314618208595671.

Connors, Jane. 'The 1954 Royal Tour of Australia.' *Australian Historical Studies* 25, no. 100 (1993): 371–82. doi.org/10.1080/10314619308595919.

Crowley, F. K. 'Forrest, Sir John (1847–1918).' *Australian Dictionary of Biography*, accessed 3 November 2015, adb.anu.edu.au/biography/forrest-sir-john-6211/text10677.

Cunneen, Chris. 'Gloucester, First Duke of (1900–1974).' *Australian Dictionary of Biography*, accessed 20 February 2017, adb.anu.edu.au/biography/gloucester-first-duke-of-10313/text18251.

Davidson, Jim. 'De-Dominionisation Revisited.' *Australian Journal of Politics and History* 51, no. 1 (2005): 108–13. doi.org/10.1111/j.1467-8497.2005.00364.x.

Edwards, W. H. 'Dodd, Tommy (1890–1975).' *Australian Dictionary of Biography*, accessed 14 July 2017, adb.anu.edu.au/biography/dodd-tommy-10027/text17677.

Eveline, Joan. 'Feminism, Racism and Citizenship.' In *Women as Australian Citizens: Underlying Histories*, edited by Patricia Crawford and Philippa Maddern, 141–77. Carlton South: Melbourne University Press, 2001.

Fisher, E. M. 'Elphick, Gladys (1904–1988).' *Australian Dictionary of Biography*, accessed 14 July 2017, adb.anu.edu.au/biography/elphick-gladys-12460/text22411.

Fox, Karen. 'Grand Dames and Gentle Helpmeets: Women and the Royal Honours System in New Zealand, 1917–2000.' *Women's History Review* 19, no. 3 (2010): 375–93. doi.org/10.1080/09612025.2010.489346.

———. '"Housewives' Leader Awarded MBE": Women, Leadership and Honours in Australia.' In *Seizing the Initiative: Australian Women Leaders in Politics, Workplaces and Communities*, edited by Rosemary Francis, Patricia Grimshaw, and Ann Standish, 171–84. Melbourne: eScholarship Research Centre, University of Melbourne, 2012.

———. 'An "Imperial Hangover"? Royal Honours in Australia, Canada and New Zealand 1917–2009.' *Britain and the World* 7, no. 1 (2014): 6–27. doi.org/10.3366/brw.2014.0118.

———. 'Ornamentalism, Empire and Race: Indigenous Leaders and Honours in Australia and New Zealand.' *Journal of Imperial and Commonwealth History* 42, no. 3 (2014): 486–502. doi.org/10.1080/03086534.2014.895480.

———. '"A Pernicious System of Caste and Privilege": Egalitarianism and Official Honours in Australia, New Zealand and Canada.' *History Australia* 10, no. 2 (2013): 202–26. doi.org/10.1080/14490854.2013.11668468.

Fox, Karen, and Samuel Furphy. 'The Politics of National Recognition: Honouring Australians in a Post-Imperial World.' *Australian Journal of Politics and History* 63, no. 1 (2017): 93–111. doi.org/10.1111/ajph.12317.

Frederick, W. H. 'Brookes, Sir Norman Everard (1877–1968).' *Australian Dictionary of Biography*, accessed 11 June 2021, adb.anu.edu.au/biography/brookes-sir-norman-everard-5373/text9091.

Grimshaw, Charles. 'Australian Nationalism and the Imperial Connection 1900–1914.' *Australian Journal of Politics and History* 3, no. 2 (1958): 161–82. doi.org/10.1111/j.1467-8497.1958.tb00380.x.

Hall, Robert. 'Hughes, Timothy (1919–1976).' *Australian Dictionary of Biography*, accessed 14 July 2017, adb.anu.edu.au/biography/hughes-timothy-10567/text18767.

Hanham, H. J. 'The Sale of Honours in Late Victorian England.' *Victorian Studies* 3, no. 3 (1960): 277–89.

Harper, Tobias. 'Harold Wilson's "Lavender List" Scandal and the Shifting Moral Economy of Honour.' *Twentieth Century British History* 31, no. 1 (2020): 79–100. doi.org/10.1093/tcbh/hwy048.

———. 'The Order of the British Empire after the British Empire.' *Canadian Journal of History* 52, no. 3 (2017): 509–32. doi.org/10.3138/cjh.ach.52.3.05.

——. 'Philanthropy and Honours in the British Empire.' *New Global Studies* 12, no. 2 (2018): 257–76. doi.org/10.1515/ngs-2018-0028.

——. 'Voluntary Service and State Honours in Twentieth-Century Britain.' *Historical Journal* 58, no. 2 (2017): 641–61. doi.org/10.1017/S0018246X 1400048X.

Hazell, Malcolm. 'The Australian Honours System: An Overview.' In *Honouring Commonwealth Citizens: Proceedings of the First Conference on Commonwealth Honours and Awards*, edited by Michael Jackson, 38–51. Toronto: The Honours and Awards Secretariat, Ontario Ministry of Citizenship and Immigration, 2007.

Hirst, John. 'Egalitarianism.' *Australian Cultural History*, no. 5 (1986): 12–31.

Hobsbawm, Eric. 'Introduction: Inventing Traditions.' In *The Invention of Tradition*, edited by Eric Hobsbawm and Terence Ranger, 1–14. Cambridge: Cambridge University Press, 1983. doi.org/10.1017/cbo9781107295636.001.

Hopkins, A. G. 'Rethinking Decolonization.' *Past and Present* 200, no. 1 (2008): 211–47. doi.org/10.1093/pastj/gtn015.

Horner, David. 'Shedden, Sir Frederick Geoffrey (1893–1971).' *Australian Dictionary of Biography*, accessed 30 October 2017, adb.anu.edu.au/biography/ shedden-sir-frederick-geoffrey-11670/text20853.

Inglis, Ian. 'The Politics of Stardust or the Politics of Cool: Popular Music and the British Honours System.' *International Review of the Aesthetics and Sociology of Music* 41, no. 1 (2010): 51–71.

Jenkins, T. A. 'The Funding of the Liberal Unionist Party and the Honours System.' *English Historical Review* 105, no. 417 (1990): 920–38. doi.org/ 10.1093/ehr/CV.CCCCXVII.920.

Keith, B. R. 'Rolland, Sir Francis William (Frank) (1878–1965).' *Australian Dictionary of Biography*, accessed 19 July 2019, adb.anu.edu.au/biography/ rolland-sir-francis-william-frank-8261/text14469.

Kingston, Beverley. 'The Lady and the Australian Girl: Some Thoughts on Nationalism and Class.' In *Australian Women: New Feminist Perspectives*, edited by Norma Grieve and Ailsa Burns, 27–41. Melbourne: Oxford University Press, 1986.

Kirk, Neville. 'The Conditions of Royal Rule: Australian and British Socialist and Labour Attitudes to the Monarchy, 1901–11.' *Social History* 30, no. 1 (2005): 64–88. doi.org/10.1080/0307102042000337297.

Knox, Bruce. 'Democracy, Aristocracy and Empire: The Provision of Colonial Honours, 1818–1870.' *Australian Historical Studies* 25, no. 99 (1992): 244–64. doi.org/10.1080/10314619208595909.

Lake, Marilyn. 'A Revolution in the Family: The Challenge and Contradictions of Maternal Citizenship in Australia.' In *Mothers of a New World: Maternalist Politics and the Origins of Welfare States*, edited by Seth Koven and Sonya Michel, 378–95. New York and London: Routledge, 1993. doi.org/10.4324/9781315021164-12.

Martin, Stanley. 'Perspectives on the Honours of Australia.' In *Honouring Commonwealth Citizens: Proceedings of the First Conference on Commonwealth Honours and Awards*, edited by Michael Jackson, 52–59. Toronto: The Honours and Awards Secretariat, Ontario Ministry of Citizenship and Immigration, 2007.

McDougall, Russell. 'Herbert, Albert Francis Xavier (1901–1984).' *Australian Dictionary of Biography*, accessed 24 July 2017, adb.anu.edu.au/biography/herbert-albert-francis-xavier-12623/text22741.

McGregor, Russell. 'The Necessity of Britishness: Ethno-Cultural Roots of Australian Nationalism.' *Nations and Nationalism* 12, no. 3 (2006): 493–511. doi.org/10.1111/j.1469-8129.2006.00250.x.

McLeod, John. 'The English Honours System in Princely India, 1925–1947.' *Journal of the Royal Asiatic Society*, 3rd ser., 4, no. 2 (1994): 237–49. doi.org/10.1017/S1356186300005460.

Meaney, Neville. 'Britishness and Australian Identity: The Problem of Nationalism in Australian History and Historiography.' *Australian Historical Studies* 32, no. 116 (2001): 76–90. doi.org/10.1080/10314610108596148.

Merrett, D. T. 'Leitch, Emily Bertha (1873–1957).' *Australian Dictionary of Biography*, accessed 25 March 2021, adb.anu.edu.au/biography/leitch-emily-bertha-7754/text12383.

Mincham, Hans. 'Stirling, Sir Edward Charles (Ted) (1848–1919).' *Australian Dictionary of Biography*, accessed 5 September 2017, adb.anu.edu.au/biography/stirling-sir-edward-charles-ted-939/text7675.

Nairn, Bede. 'Abbott, Sir Joseph Palmer (1842–1901).' *Australian Dictionary of Biography*, accessed 4 September 2017, adb.anu.edu.au/biography/abbott-sir-joseph-palmer-2858/text4069.

Oliver, Bobbie. '"A Wanton Deed of Blood and Rapine": Opposition to Australian Participation in the Boer War.' In *The Boer War: Army, Nation and Empire*, edited by Peter Dennis and Jeffrey Grey, 191–99. Canberra: Army History Unit, 2000.

Palsetia, Jesse S. '"Honourable Machinations": The Kamsetjee Jejeebhoy Baronetcy and the Indian Response to the Honours System in India.' *South Asia Research* 23, no. 1 (2003): 55–75. doi.org/10.1177/02627280030231003.

Phillips-Peddlesden, Bethany. '"A Stronger Man and a More Virile Character": Australian Prime Ministers, Embodied Manhood and Political Authority in the Early Twentieth Century.' *Australian Historical Studies* 48, no. 4 (2017): 502–18. doi.org/10.1080/1031461X.2017.1323932.

Playford, John. 'Playford, Thomas (1837–1915).' *Australian Dictionary of Biography*, accessed 22 August 2016, adb.anu.edu.au/biography/playford-thomas-8064/text14071.

Raftery, Judith. 'Rankine, Annie Isabel (1917–1972).' *Australian Dictionary of Biography*, accessed 14 July 2017, adb.anu.edu.au/biography/rankine-annie-isabel-11488/text20487.

Reynolds, Margaret. *Women and the Order of Australia*. Canberra: September 1990.

Russell, Penny. 'The Brash Colonial: Class and Comportment in Nineteenth-Century Australia.' *Transactions of the Royal Historical Society*, 6th ser., 12 (2002): 431–53. doi.org/10.1017/S008044010200018X.

Rutledge, Martha. 'Aronson, Zara (1864–1944).' *Australian Dictionary of Biography*, accessed 12 September 2017, adb.anu.edu.au/biography/aronson-zara-5059/text8411.

——. 'Buchanan, David (1823?–1890).' *Australian Dictionary of Biography*, accessed 24 February 2015, adb.anu.edu.au/biography/buchanan-david-3099.

——. 'Stephen, Sir Colin Campbell (1872–1937).' *Australian Dictionary of Biography*, accessed 3 November 2020, adb.anu.edu.au/biography/stephen-sir-colin-campbell-1285/text15099.

——. 'Ward, Hugh Joseph (1871–1941).' *Australian Dictionary of Biography*, accessed 13 May 2021, adb.anu.edu.au/biography/ward-hugh-joseph-8983/text15811.

Ryan, J. A. 'Wise, Bernhard Ringrose (1858–1916).' *Australian Dictionary of Biography*, accessed 23 March 2021, adb.anu.edu.au/biography/wise-bernhard-ringrose-9161/text16175.

Smart, Judith. 'Couchman, Dame Elizabeth May (1876–1982).' *Australian Dictionary of Biography*, accessed 19 July 2019, adb.anu.edu.au/biography/couchman-dame-elizabeth-may-ramsay-12359/text22205.

Southcott, R. V. 'Verco, Sir Joseph Cooke (1851–1933).' *Australian Dictionary of Biography*, accessed 5 September 2017, adb.anu.edu.au/biography/verco-sir-joseph-cooke-8914/text15663.

Spearritt, Peter. 'Royal Progress: The Queen and Her Australian Subjects.' *Australian Cultural History*, no. 5 (1986): 75–94.

Stevenson, Katie. 'The Unicorn, St Andrew and the Thistle: Was There an Order of Chivalry in Late Medieval Scotland?' *Scottish Historical Review* 83, no. 1 (2004): 3–22. doi.org/10.3366/shr.2004.83.1.3.

Stewart, Noël. 'Pelloe, Emily Harriet (1877–1941).' *Australian Dictionary of Biography*, accessed 5 October 2016, adb.anu.edu.au/biography/pelloe-emily-harriet-8012/text13963.

Stout, Robert. 'Titles for Colonists.' *Melbourne Review* 6, no. 23 (1881): 221–32.

Taylor, Antony, and Luke Trainor. 'Monarchism and Anti-Monarchism: Anglo–Australian Comparisons c. 1870–1901.' *Social History* 24, no. 2 (1999): 158–73. doi.org/10.1080/03071029908568060.

Townsley, W. A. 'Cosgrove, Dame Gertrude Anne (1882–1962).' *Australian Dictionary of Biography*, accessed 21 November 2017, adb.anu.edu.au/biography/cosgrove-dame-gertrude-ann-10015/text17389.

Waddington, Raymond B. 'Elizabeth I and the Order of the Garter.' *Sixteenth Century Journal* 24, no. 1 (1993): 97–113. doi.org/10.2307/2541800.

Wallace-Crabbe, Chris. 'O'Dowd, Bernard Patrick (1866–1953).' *Australian Dictionary of Biography*, accessed 12 September 2017, adb.anu.edu.au/biography/odowd-bernard-patrick-7881/text13701.

Ward, Stuart. '"Culture up to our Arseholes": Projecting Post-Imperial Australia.' *Australian Journal of Politics and History* 51, no. 1 (2005): 53–66. doi.org/10.1111/j.1467-8497.2005.00360.x.

——. 'The "New Nationalism" in Australia, Canada and New Zealand: Civic Culture in the Wake of the British World.' In *Britishness Abroad: Transnational Movements and Imperial Cultures*, edited by Kate Darian-Smith, Patricia Grimshaw, and Stuart Macintyre, 231–63. Carlton: Melbourne University Publishing, 2007.

Watts, A. D. 'The Australia Act 1986.' *International and Comparative Law Quarterly* 36, no. 1 (1987): 132–39. doi.org/10.1093/iclqaj/36.1.132.

Webb, Joan. 'Stead, Thistle Yolette (1902–1990).' *Australian Dictionary of Biography*, accessed 6 December 2017, adb.anu.edu.au/biography/stead-thistle-yolette-15520/text26732.

Wright, Andrée. 'Board, Ruby Willmet (1880–1963).' *Australian Dictionary of Biography*, accessed 12 September 2017, adb.anu.edu.au/biography/board-ruby-willmet-5276/text8895.

Theses and unpublished papers

Connors, Jane Holley. 'The Glittering Thread: The 1954 Royal Tour of Australia.' PhD thesis, University of Technology, Sydney, 1996.

Fox, Karen. 'Dames in New Zealand: Gender, Representation and the Royal Honours System, 1917–2000.' Master's thesis, University of Canterbury, 2005.

Lyall, Ernest Alexander. 'Government Patronage in Australia: The Exercise of the Patronage Prerogative by Commonwealth and New South Wales Governments in the Period 1927–1969.' Master's thesis, The Australian National University, 1969.

Satherley-Peacocke, Jonathon. 'Victoria's Gentlemen of Honour: Symbols, Rituals, and Conventions of Colonial Honours.' Master's thesis, Victoria University of Wellington, 1997.

Women's Leadership Institute Australia and Our Community. 'New Campaign Launched to Boost the Number of Female Order of Australia Recipients: Business Leader Says Public Recognition of Women Remains Elusive.' Media release. 25 January 2011.

Websites and online sources

Abbott, Tony. 'Press Conference, Parliament House, Canberra.' Transcript, 25 March 2014. *PM Transcripts: Transcripts from the Prime Ministers of Australia.* Australian Government, Department of the Prime Minister and Cabinet. Accessed 3 June 2019, pmtranscripts.pmc.gov.au/release/transcript-23367.

Australian Government, Department of the Prime Minister and Cabinet. 'Australian Honours Search Facility.' *It's an Honour*. Department of the Prime Minister and Cabinet. Accessed throughout the course of this project, honours.pmc.gov.au/honours/search.

'Bemusement in the UK Over Australian Plans to Reintroduce Knighthoods.' *AM with Chris Uhlmann*. Story reported by Mary Gearin. 26 March 2014. Australian Broadcasting Corporation. Accessed 27 March 2014, www.abc. net.au/am/content/2014/s3971472.htm.

Birkenhead Returned Services Association. 'The New Zealand Cross (1869).' Birkenhead Returned Services Association. Accessed 6 June 2019, www.birken headrsa.com/gallantry-bravery-awards/new-zealand-cross-1869/.

'Constitution of the Irish Free State (Saorstát Eireann) Act, 1922.' *Electronic Irish Statute Book*. Government of Ireland. Accessed 30 September 2016, www.irish statutebook.ie/eli/1922/act/1/enacted/en/print.html.

'The Constitution of the United States: A Transcription.' *America's Founding Documents*. U. S. National Archives and Records Administration. Accessed 3 August 2021, www.archives.gov/founding-docs/constitution-transcript.

'Contributors.' *Australia's Prime Ministers*. National Archives of Australia. Accessed 30 October 2017, primeministers.naa.gov.au/about/contributor.aspx (site discontinued).

'Courting Controversy: Backlash Grows Over Margaret Court's Australia Day Gong.' 23 January 2021. Updated 25 January 2021. *New Daily*. Accessed 14 June 2021, thenewdaily.com.au/news/national/2021/01/23/margaret-court-australia-day-backlash/.

Department of the Prime Minister and Cabinet/Te Tari o te Pirimia me te Komiti Matua. 'Overview of the New Zealand Royal Honours System.' Department of the Prime Minister and Cabinet/Te Tari o te Pirimia me te Komiti Matua. Accessed 17 August 2017, www.dpmc.govt.nz/our-programmes/new-zealand-royal-honours/new-zealand-royal-honours-system/overview-new-zealand-royal.

Ferguson, Sarah, David Flint, and Greg Barns. '"Juvenile Baubles" or "Appropriate Recognition"—Knights and Dames Debated.' Transcript of debate on *7.30*. 25 March 2014. Australian Broadcasting Corporation. Accessed 11 August 2017, www.abc.net.au/7.30/content/2014/s3971393.htm.

Flint, David. 'Knights and Dames.' 28 January 2008. *Australians for Constitutional Monarchy*. Accessed 5 August 2021, norepublic.com.au/knights-and-dames-2/.

———. 'Order of Australia: A Canadian View.' 12 February 2006. *Australians for Constitutional Monarchy*. Accessed 5 August 2021, norepublic.com.au/order-of-australia-a-canadian-view-2/.

———. 'There is Nothing Like a Dame.' 25 April 2007. *Australians for Constitutional Monarchy*. Accessed 5 August 2021, norepublic.com.au/there-is-nothing-like-a-dame/.

Ford, Clementine. 'Why Are So Few Women Awarded OAMs?' 9 June 2014. *Daily Life*. Accessed 6 September 2014, www.dailylife.com.au/news-and-views/dl-opinion/why-are-so-few-women-awarded-oams-20140608-39qyj.html?rand=1402258561372.

Ford, Heather, Tamson Pietsch, and Kelly Tall. 'Producing Distinction: Wikipedia and the Order of Australia.' 2021. University of Technology Sydney. Accessed 12 June 2021, hfordsa.github.io/who-do-we-think-we-are.html.

'Frequently Asked Questions.' *Australian Dictionary of Biography*. Accessed 15 October 2020, adb.anu.edu.au/faqs/.

Hancock, Ian. 'About John Gorton.' *Australia's Prime Ministers*. National Archives of Australia. Accessed 14 June 2021, www.naa.gov.au/explore-collection/australias-prime-ministers/john-gorton.

Hardaker, David. 'Why Are Women Under-Represented in the Order of Australia Awards?' 23 July 2020. *Crikey*. Accessed 10 June 2020, www.crikey.com.au/2020/07/23/why-are-women-under-represented-in-the-order-of-australia-awards/.

Henderson, Anna, and Alexandra Kirk. 'Prince Philip "Extremely Deserving" of Australian Knighthood, Says Minister; PM Facing Continuing Backlash From Party Colleagues.' 27 January 2015. *ABC News*. Accessed 14 June 2021, www.abc.net.au/news/2015-01-27/abbott-facing-growing-backlash-over-prince-philip-knighthood/6047750?nw=0.

Henderson, Sarah, Liberal Senator for Victoria, to Shane Stone, Chairman of the Council for the Order of Australia, 24 February 2020. Accessed 15 October 2020, sarahhenderson.com.au/wp-content/uploads/2020/02/200224-Letter-Mr-Shane-Stone-AC-QC.pdf.

'Honour A Woman.' Facebook group. Accessed 5 August 2021, www.facebook.com/Honourawoman/.

Kemp, Rod. 'Review of Australian Honours and Awards.' News release, 14 October 1994. Accessed 31 July 2017, parlinfo.aph.gov.au/.

Knight, Dean. 'New Zealand Order of Merit: Te Reo Appellations.' 31 December 2010. *LAWS179 Elephants and the Law*. Accessed 8 August 2017, www.laws179.co.nz/2010/12/new-zealand-order-of-merit-te-reo.html.

Minister for Administrative Services. 'Review of Honours and Awards.' Media statement, 14 October 1994. Accessed 31 July 2017, parlinfo.aph.gov.au/.

Ministry for Culture and Heritage. 'New Zealand Cross Created.' Updated 12 April 2017. *New Zealand History*. Ministry for Culture and Heritage. Accessed 4 September 2017, nzhistory.govt.nz/the-new-zealand-cross-is-instituted-by-order-in-council.

National Archives of Australia. 'Andrew Fisher: During Office.' *Australia's Prime Ministers*. National Archives of Australia. Accessed 3 September 2020, www.naa.gov.au/explore-collection/australias-prime-ministers/andrew-fisher/during-office#last-shilling.

National Foundation for Australian Women. *Faith, Hope, Charity: Australian Women and Imperial Honours: 1901–1989*. 2003. Accessed 27 November 2014, www.womenaustralia.info/exhib/honours/honours.html.

Official Record of the Debates of the Australasian Federal Convention (Third Session), Held at Parliament House, Melbourne, Victoria, Thursday, 20th January 1898. Accessed 17 April 2018, parlinfo.aph.gov.au/parlInfo/search/search.w3p.

Rajca, Jennifer. 'Labor Slams Tony Abbott's Decision to Bring Back Knights and Dames.' 26 March 2014. *News.com*. Accessed 28 March 2014, www.news.com.au/news/national/labor-slams-tony-abbotts-decision-to-bring-back-knights-and-dames/news-story/4e85d23cd49dc691f751258bd3a950c7.

The Royal Household. 'Companion of Honour.' *The Royal Family*. Accessed 13 October 2020, www.royal.uk/companion-honour.

———. 'Order of the Bath.' *Official Website of the British Monarchy*. Accessed 6 October 2014, www.royal.gov.uk/MonarchUK/Honours/OrderoftheBath.aspx (site discontinued).

———. 'Order of the Garter.' *Official Website of the British Monarchy*. Accessed 17 October 2014, www.royal.gov.uk/monarchUK/honours/Orderofthegarter/orderofthegarter.aspx (site discontinued).

———. 'Order of St Patrick.' *Official Website of the British Monarchy*. Accessed 6 October 2014, www.royal.gov.uk/MonarchUK/Honours/OrderofStPatrick.aspx (site discontinued).

——. 'Order of the Thistle.' *Official Website of the British Monarchy*. Accessed 15 October 2014, www.royal.gov.uk/MonarchUK/Honours/Orderofthe Thistle.aspx (site discontinued).

Schwartz, Carol. 'Women Experts: A Shameful Decline.' 25 June 2012. Women's Leadership Institute Australia. Accessed 22 April 2014, www.wlia.com.au/story_page?sId=32&PHPSESSID=24b4493b29f2e31d5d353aab64d4f78d (site discontinued, available at web.archive.org/web/20150318115341/http://wlia.com.au/story_page?sId=32).

Turnbull, Malcolm. 'Australian Knights and the Republic.' 25 March 2014. *Malcolm Turnbull*. Accessed 15 June 2021, www.malcolmturnbull.com.au/media/australian-knights-and-the-republic.

Wong, Mandy. 'Royal Honours System.' *Te Ara—The Encyclopedia of New Zealand*. Accessed 14 May 2021, teara.govt.nz/en/royal-honours-system/print.

York, Barry. 'Knighthoods and Dames.' 3 November 2015. Museum of Australian Democracy at Old Parliament House blog. Accessed 14 June 2019, www.moadoph.gov.au/blog/knighthoods-and-dames/#.

Yosufzai, Rashida. 'Council Asked to Review Margaret Court's Australia Day Honour as More Return Awards in "Disgust".' 28 January 2021. *SBS News*. Accessed 14 June 2021, www.sbs.com.au/news/council-asked-to-review-margaret-court-s-australia-day-honour-as-more-return-awards-in-disgust.

www.ingramcontent.com/pod-product-compliance
Lightning Source LLC
Chambersburg PA
CBHW040820280326
41926CB00093B/4604